Microsoft Press

Computer User's Dictionary

Microsoft Press

PUBLISHED BY
Microsoft Press
A Division of Microsoft Corporation
One Microsoft Way
Redmond, Washington 98052-6399

Library of Congress Cataloging-in-Publication Data
Microsoft Press Computer User's Dictionary / Microsoft Corporation.
p. cm.
ISBN 1-57231-862-7
1. Computers--Dictionaries. I. Microsoft Corporation.
QA76.15.M544 1998
004'.03--dc21 98-13998
CIP

Printed and bound in the United States of America.

1 2 3 4 5 6 7 8 9 MLML 3 2 1 0 9 8

Distributed in Canada by ITP Nelson, a division of Thomson Canada Limited.

A CIP catalogue record for this book is available from the British Library.

Microsoft Press books are available through booksellers and distributors worldwide. For further information about international editions, contact your local Microsoft Corporation office or contact Microsoft Press International directly at fax (425) 936-7329. Visit our Web site at mspress.microsoft.com.

Acquisitions Editor: Kim Fryer
Project Editors: Teri Kieffer, Maureen Williams Zimmerman
Manuscript Editor: Mary Renaud
Technical Editors: John Conrow, Mary DeJong, Jim Fuchs, Roslyn Lutsch, Robert Lyon, Dail Magee, Jr., Kurt Meyer, Gary Nelson, Jean Ross

Contents

Introduction

The *Microsoft Press Computer User's Dictionary* is designed to be a handy reference to the terms and abbreviations you'll encounter while using your personal computer. You'll find it handy when reading online help or computer manuals, using programs, browsing the Internet, reading advertisements for computer hardware and software, or thumbing through computer magazines.

The dictionary includes terms drawn from a variety of topics, such as these:

- The Internet and the World Wide Web, with subjects ranging from security to Web page construction to newsgroup slang
- Communications (e-mail, modems, and faxes)
- Network computing
- Information processing and data storage
- Computer graphics
- Hardware, including entries for popular computers and processors as well as descriptions of various boards, connectors, and peripherals

Because most computer users operate personal computers and desktop systems at home, at work, or both, the majority of the entries in this dictionary cover the terminology used in describing and working with these systems.

The definitions provided for these terms are clear, concise, and jargon-free. You'll also find traditional dictionary elements, such as parts of speech, spelling variants, and numbered lists for terms that have more than one definition.

Order of Presentation

Entries are alphabetized by letter. Spaces are ignored, as are characters such as hyphens and slashes; for example, *README* falls between *read error* and *read notification*, and *machine-independent* falls between *machine error* and *machine instruction*. Entries that consist of numbers or symbols (*80386*, for example, or @) are located at the beginning of the dictionary and are listed in ascending ASCII order.

Entries

Entries are of two types: main entries, which contain full definitions; and cross-references, which contain *See* references to the appropriate main entries. In many cases, the cross-reference is synonymous—that is, the cross-referenced term is a secondary or less common way of referring to the term that appears as the main entry, and the definition at the main entry can be substituted as a definition for the synonymous cross-reference:

sign off *vb.* *See* log off.

In other cases, the *See* reference directs you to a main entry that contains an explanation of the cross-referenced term:

required hyphen *n.* *See* hyphen.

Format

Information in each main entry is presented in a consistent format: entry name in boldface, spelling variants (if any), part of speech (as applicable), definition, acronym (if any), alternative names (if any), and cross-references (if any).

Main Entries

Entries that are acronyms or abbreviations or that are shortened forms of several words or a phrase show those words spelled out at the beginning of the definition. In those words, the letters that make up the acronym, abbreviation, or short form appear in boldface type.

When two main entries have the same spelling, the two terms are differentiated by adding a superscript numeral after each term. These entries are called homographs, and they are generally different parts of speech. For example, **e-mail**^{1} is a noun, and **e-mail**^{2} is a verb.

Spelling Variants

When a main entry can be spelled in two or more different ways, each spelling variant is provided after the main entry, following the word *or*. For example:

e-mail^{1} or **E-mail** or **email**

Parts of Speech

Nearly all entries are designated as one of the following four parts of speech, abbreviated as shown here:

n.	noun
vb.	verb
adj.	adjective
adv.	adverb

For entries that are prefixes, the designation *prefix* is used rather than one of the four parts of speech. Additionally, the part of speech is omitted in a small number of entries for which it is not appropriate (for instance, an acronym representing a more complex phrase that is not clearly described by one of the four parts of speech).

Definitions

Each of the more than 4,700 entries is written in clear, standard English. Many go beyond a simple definition to provide additional detail and to put the term in context for a typical computer user. When an entry has more than one sense or definition, the definitions are presented in a numbered list, to make it easier to distinguish the particular, sometimes subtle, variations in meaning.

Acronyms

Terms used in the computer field are often shortened to form acronyms. Sometimes an acronym is the more common way of referring to a concept or an object; in these cases, the dictionary lists the acronym as the main entry. In other cases, the acronym is not as commonly used as the words or phrase for which it stands; in these cases, the words or phrase constitute the main entry, and the acronym is provided after the definition, following the word *Acronym*.

Alternative Names

Some items or concepts in the computer field can be referred to by more than one name. This dictionary uses the generally preferred terminology as the main entry and lists alternative names after the definition and any acronyms, following the phrase *Also called*.

Cross-References

Cross-references are of three types: *See, See also*, and *Compare*. A *See* reference simply points to another entry that contains the relevant information. A *See also* reference points to one or more entries that contain additional information about a topic; this type of reference follows any acronyms or alternative names after the definition. A *Compare* reference points to an entry or entries that offer contrasting information; this type of reference follows any acronyms, alternative names, or *See also* references after the definition.

Future Printings

Every effort has been made to ensure the accuracy of this book. If you find an error, please let us know so that we can correct it in future printings and online updates. Address your letter to: Dictionary Editor, Microsoft Press, One Microsoft Way, Redmond, WA 98052-8302. Or you can send e-mail to mspcd@microsoft.com.

Further References

If you seek a definition that is not in this dictionary, you may wish to consult our larger and more comprehensive reference, the *Microsoft Press Computer Dictionary, Third Edition* (ISBN 1-57231-446-X), which contains more than 7,600 terms. The *Microsoft Press Computer Dictionary, Third Edition*, is available at most bookstores that carry computer books.

Online Updates

Quarterly updates and revisions will be made to our dictionaries on the Microsoft Press Web site. These updates are meant to supplement the content of our dictionaries and keep them up to date in a field that's rapidly evolving. To view the updates, simply point your Web browser to http://mspress.microsoft.com.mspress.products/1031.

Numbers & Symbols

$0.02 *See* my two cents.

& 1. The default character used to designate a character entity (special character) in an HTML or SGML document. *See also* HTML, SGML. **2.** In spreadsheet programs, an operator for inserting text into a formula specifying the relationship between cells.

***** *See* asterisk.

. *See* star-dot-star.

.. DOS and UNIX syntax for the parent directory. A single dot refers to the current directory.

/ 1. A character used to delimit parts of a directory path in UNIX and FTP or parts of an Internet address in Web browsers. **2.** A character used to flag switches or options that control the execution of a program invoked by a command-line interface. *See also* command-line interface.

// A notation used with a colon to separate the URL protocol (such as http or ftp) from the URL host machine name, as in http://www.yahoo.com. *See also* URL.

: A symbol used after the protocol name in a URL. *See also* URL.

<> 1. A pair of symbols used to set off a tag in an HTML document. *See also* HTML. **2.** In an Internet Relay Chat or a multi-user dungeon, a set of symbols used to designate some action or reaction, as in <chuckle>. *See also* emotag, IRC, MUD. **3.** A pair of symbols used to set off a return address in an e-mail header.

> 1. A symbol used in DOS and UNIX to direct the output resulting from some command into a file. **2.** A symbol commonly used in e-mail messages to designate text included from another message.

? *See* question mark.

@ The separator between account names and domain name in Internet e-mail addresses. When spoken, @ is read as "at."

**** *See* backslash.

100BaseT *n.* An Ethernet standard for baseband local area networks using twisted-pair cable carrying 100 Mbps. *Also called* Fast Ethernet. *See also* Ethernet (definition 1).

101-key keyboard *n.* A computer keyboard modeled after the enhanced keyboard; introduced by IBM for the IBM PC/AT. The 101-key keyboard and

#
A
B
C
D
E
F
G
H
I
J
K
L
M
N
O
P
Q
R
S
T
U
V
W
X
Y
Z

the enhanced keyboard are similar in the number and function of their keys; they may differ in the way the keys are laid out, the amount of tactile feedback expressed when a key is pressed, and the shape and feel of the keycaps. *See also* enhanced keyboard.

1024×768 *n.* A standard super VGA computer display having a resolution of 1,024 columns of pixels by 768 rows of pixels. *See also* SVGA.

10Base2 *n.* The Ethernet standard for baseband local area networks using a thin coaxial cable up to 200 meters long and carrying 10 Mbps in a bus topology. A network node is connected to the cable by a BNC connector on the adapter card. *Also called* Cheapernet, thin Ethernet, ThinNet, ThinWire. *See also* BNC connector, bus network, coaxial cable, Ethernet (definition 1).

10Base5 *n.* The Ethernet standard for baseband local area networks using a thick coaxial cable up to 500 meters long and carrying 10 Mbps in a bus topology. A network node is equipped with a transceiver that plugs into a 15-pin AUI (Attachment Unit Interface) connector on the adapter card and taps into the cable. *Also called* thick Ethernet, ThickNet, ThickWire. *See also* coaxial cable, Ethernet (definition 1).

10BaseF *n.* The Ethernet standard for baseband local area networks using fiber-optic cable carrying 10 Mbps in a star topology. All nodes are connected to a repeater or to a central concentrator. A node is equipped with a fiber-optic transceiver that plugs into an AUI (Attachment Unit Interface) connector on the adapter card and attaches to the cable with an ST or SMA fiber-optic connector. *See also* Ethernet (definition 1), fiber optics, star network.

10BaseT *n.* The Ethernet standard for baseband local area networks using twisted-pair cable carrying 10 Mbps in a star topology. All nodes are connected to a central hub known as a multiport repeater. *See also* Ethernet (definition 1), star network, twisted-pair cable.

1.2M *adj.* Short for 1.2-megabyte. Refers to the capacity for high-density 5.25-inch floppy disks.

14.4-Kbps modem *n.* A modem with a maximum data transfer rate of 14.4 kilobits per second.

1.44M *adj.* Short for 1.44-megabyte. Refers to the capacity for high-density 3.5-inch floppy disks.

16-bit *adj.* *See* 8-bit, 16-bit, 32-bit, 64-bit.

16-bit application *n.* An application written to run on a computer with a 16-bit architecture or operating system, such as MS-DOS or Windows 3.*x*.

16-bit color *n.* RGB color in which the level of each of the three primary colors in a pixel is represented. Typically the red and blue elements each take up 5 bits. Because the human eye is more sensitive to shades of green than to red and blue, the green element takes up 6 bits. A 16-bit color image can contain up to 2^{16} (65,356) colors.

16-bit machine *n.* A computer that works with data in groups of 16 bits at a time. A computer may be considered a 16-bit machine either because its microprocessor operates internally on 16-bit words or because its data bus can transfer 16 bits at a time. The IBM PC/AT and similar models based on the Intel 80286 microprocessor are 16-bit machines in terms of both the word size of the microprocessor and the size of the data bus. The Apple Macintosh Plus and Macintosh SE use a microprocessor with a 32-bit word length, but they have 16-bit data buses and are generally considered 16-bit machines.

16-bit operating system *n.* An operating system, now outdated, that can work with 16 bits, or 2 bytes, of information at one time. A 16-bit operating system, such as MS-DOS or Windows 3.*x*, reflects the functionality of a 16-bit processor because the software and the chip must work together so closely. The main advantage of a 16-bit operating system over its earlier 8-bit predecessors was its ability to address more memory and use a larger (16-bit) bus. The 16-bit operating system has since been eclipsed by 32-bit operating systems, such as the Mac OS, Windows NT, and Windows 95, and by 64-bit operating systems, such as some versions of UNIX. *See also* 32-bit operating system.

1NF *n.* Short for first normal form. *See* normal form.

2000 time problem *n. See* Year 2000 problem.

24-bit color *n.* RGB color in which the level of each of the three primary colors in a pixel is represented by 8 bits of information. A 24-bit color image can contain over 16 million different colors. Not all computer monitors support 24-bit color. Those that do not may use 8-bit color or 16-bit color. *Also called* true color. *See also* bit depth, pixel, RGB. *Compare* 16-bit color, 32-bit color.

286 *n. See* 80286.

287 *n. See* 80287.

28.8-Kbps modem *n.* A modem with a maximum data transfer rate of 28.8 kilobits per second.

2NF *n.* Short for second normal form. *See* normal form.

32-bit *adj. See* 8-bit, 16-bit, 32-bit, 64-bit.

32-bit application *n.* An application written to run on a computer with a 32-bit architecture or operating system, such as the Mac OS or Windows 95.

32-bit color *n.* RGB color that is similar to 24-bit color, with 8 additional bits used to allow for faster transfer of an image's color. *See also* bit depth. *Compare* 16-bit color, 24-bit color, RGB.

32-bit driver *n.* A software subsystem that controls either a hardware device (device driver) or another software subsystem. The 32-bit versions of this software take full advantage of the instruction sets of the 486 and Pentium processors for improved speed. *See also* driver, instruction set.

32-bit machine *n.* A computer that works with data in groups of 32 bits at a time. The Apple Macintosh II and higher models are 32-bit machines, in terms of both the word size of their microprocessors and the size of the data buses, as are computers based on the Intel 80386 and higher-level microprocessors.

#
A
B
C
D
E
F
G
H
I
J
K
L
M
N
O
P
Q
R
S
T
U
V
W
X
Y
Z

32-bit operating system *n.* An operating system in which 4 bytes, or 32 bits, can be processed at one time. Windows NT, Linux, and OS/2 are examples. *See also* instruction set, protected mode.
3.5-inch floppy disk *n. See* microfloppy disk.
360K *adj.* Short for 360-kilobyte. The capacity for standard 5.25-inch floppy disks.
386 *n. See* 80386.
387 *n. See* 80387.
3-D *adj.* **1.** Short for three-dimensional. Of, pertaining to, or being an object or image having or appearing to have all three spatial dimensions (height, width, and depth). **2.** Having the illusion of depth or varying distances, as in 3-D audio.
3-D audio *n.* Short for three-dimensional audio. Recorded as stereo sound, 3-D audio enables the listener to feel immersed in the sound and to determine its exact location (up, down, left, right, forward, or backward). This technology is commonly used in video games and virtual-reality systems, as well as in some Internet applications. *Also called* 3-D sound, binaural sound.
3-D graphic *n.* Any graphical image that depicts one or more objects in three dimensions—height, width, and depth. A 3-D graphic is rendered on a two-dimensional medium; the third dimension, depth, is indicated by means of perspective and by techniques such as shading or gradient use of color.
3-D metafile *n.* A device-independent file for storing a 3-D display. *See also* metafile.
3-D model *n. See* three-dimensional model.
3-D sound *n. See* 3-D audio.
3NF *n.* Short for third normal form. *See* normal form.
486 *n. See* i486DX.
4mm tape *n. See* digital audio tape.
4NF *n.* Short for fourth normal form. *See* normal form.
5.25-inch floppy disk *n. See* floppy disk.
56K *adj.* Having 56 kilobits per second available for traffic on a communications circuit. One voice channel can carry up to 64 Kbps (called a T0 carrier); 8 Kbps are used for signaling, leaving 56 Kbps available for traffic. *See also* T-carrier.
56-Kbps modem *n.* An asymmetric modem that operates over POTS (Plain Old Telephone Service) to deliver data downstream at 56 kilobits per second, with upstream speeds of 28.8 and 33.6 kilobits per second. In contrast to earlier, slower modems, which invoke a two-conversion transmission process, 56-Kbps modems achieve faster speeds by converting analog data to digital data only once, typically at the telephone company's switching office near the beginning of the transmission. Designed to improve download times for Internet users, 56-Kbps modems rely on a public phone network that allows for a single conversion and on the availability of a digital connection, such as ISDN or T1, at the ISP location that provides the actual connection to the Internet. *See also* ISDN, ISP, T1.

586 *n.* The unofficial name used by industry analysts and by the computer trade press to describe Intel's successor to the i486 microprocessor prior to its release. In the interest of using a name whose trademark could be more easily protected, however, Intel decided to name the microprocessor Pentium. *See also* Pentium.

5NF *n.* Short for fifth normal form. *See* normal form.

64-bit *adj. See* 8-bit, 16-bit, 32-bit, 64-bit.

64-bit machine *n.* A computer that works with data in groups of 64 bits at a time. A computer may be considered a 64-bit machine either because its CPU operates internally on 64-bit words or because its data bus can transfer 64 bits at a time. A 64-bit CPU thus has a word size of 64 bits, or 8 bytes; a 64-bit data bus has 64 data lines, so it ferries information through the system in sets of 64 bits at a time. Examples of 64-bit architecture include the Alpha AXP from Digital Equipment Corporation, the Ultra workstation from Sun Microsystems, Inc., and the PowerPC 620 from Motorola and IBM.

68000 *n.* The original microprocessor in the 680x0 family from Motorola, introduced in 1979 and used in the first Apple Macintosh computers as well as the Apple LaserWriter IISC and Hewlett-Packard's LaserJet printers. The 68000 has 32-bit internal registers but transfers data over a 16-bit data bus. The 68000 can address 16 megabytes of memory—16 times as much memory as does the Intel 8088 found in the IBM PC.

68020 *n.* A microprocessor in the 680x0 family from Motorola, introduced in 1984. This chip has 32-bit addressing and a 32-bit data bus and is available in speeds from 16 MHz to 33 MHz. The 68020 is found in the original Macintosh II and the LaserWriter IINT from Apple.

68030 *n.* A microprocessor in the 680x0 family from Motorola, introduced in 1987. This chip has 32-bit addressing and a 32-bit data bus and is available in speeds from 20 MHz to 50 MHz.

68040 *n.* A microprocessor in the 680x0 family from Motorola, introduced in 1990, with 32-bit addressing and a 32-bit data bus. The 68040 runs at 25 MHz and includes a built-in floating-point unit and memory management units.

68K *n. See* 68000.

80286 *n.* A 16-bit microprocessor from Intel, introduced in 1982 and included in the IBM PC/AT and compatible computers in 1984. The 80286 has 16-bit registers, transfers information over the data bus 16 bits at a time, and uses 24 bits to address memory locations. The 80286 operates in two modes: real mode, which is compatible with the 8086 and supports MS-DOS; and protected mode, which enables the CPU to access 16 megabytes of memory and protects the operating system from incorrect memory accesses by ill-behaved applications, which could crash a system in real mode. *Also called* 286. *See also* protected mode, real mode.

80287 *n.* A floating-point coprocessor from Intel for use with the 80286 family of microprocessors. Available in speeds from 6 MHz to 12 MHz, the 80287 offers expanded mathematical capabilities. Because the 80287 conforms to the 80286 memory management and protection schemes, it can be used in both the real and protected modes of the 80286. Also, if the computer manufacturer implements support for it in the motherboard design, the 80287 can be used in a system with an 80386 microprocessor. *See also* floating-point processor.

80386 *n.* A 32-bit microprocessor from Intel, introduced in 1985. The 80386 is a full 32-bit microprocessor; that is, it has 32-bit registers, it can transfer information over its data bus 32 bits at a time, and it can use 32 bits to address memory. Like the earlier 80286, the 80386 operates in two modes: real mode and protected mode. The latter allows the CPU to access 4 GB of memory directly, supports multitasking, and protects the operating system from crashing as a result of an incorrect memory access caused by an application program error. The 80386 also includes a virtual 8086 mode (also called virtual real mode), which emulates the 8086 but offers the same memory safeguards as protected mode. The virtual 8086 mode is the basis for the MS-DOS prompt available inside Windows. *Also called* 386, 386DX, 80386DX. *See also* protected mode, real mode, virtual real mode.

80387 *n.* The floating-point coprocessor introduced by Intel for use with the 80386 microprocessors. Available in speeds from 16 MHz to 33 MHz, the 80387 offers expanded mathematical capabilities. The 80387 operates independently of the 80386's mode, and it performs as expected regardless of whether the 80386 is running in real, protected, or virtual 8086 mode. *Also called* 387. *See also* 80386, floating-point processor.

80486 *n. See* i486DX.

80-character line length *n.* A standard line length for text mode displays, found in the earliest IBM PCs and in professional terminals of the 1970s and 1980s. Newer graphical user interfaces support longer or shorter lines depending on the fonts chosen. A message composed with longer lines using a graphical e-mail program appears broken up and difficult to read when it is viewed by a user with only a terminal emulation program and a shell account.

8.3 *n.* The standard format for filenames in MS-DOS/Windows 3.*x:* a filename with eight or fewer characters, followed by a period ("dot"), followed by a three-character file extension. *Compare* long filenames.

8-bit, 16-bit, 32-bit, 64-bit *adj.* **1.** Capable of transferring 8, 16, 32, or 64 bits, respectively, on data bus lines. *See also* 16-bit machine, 32-bit machine, 64-bit machine, 8-bit machine. **2.** Capable of transferring 8, 16, 32, or 64 bits, respectively, on the data path of a video adapter. An *n*-bit video adapter can display up to 2^n colors. For example, an 8-bit video adapter is capable of displaying up to 256 colors. *See also* video adapter.

8-bit machine *n.* A computer that works with data in groups of 8 bits at a time. A computer may be considered an 8-bit machine either because its microprocessor operates internally on 8-bit words or because its data bus can transfer 8 bits at a time. The original IBM PC was based on a microprocessor (the 8088) that worked internally on 16-bit words but transferred them 8 bits at a time. Such machines are generally called 8-bit machines because the size of the data bus limits the machine's overall speed.

8mm tape *n.* A tape cartridge format used for data backups, similar to that used for some video cameras except that the tape is rated for data storage. The capacity is 5 GB or more of (optionally compressed) data.

8-N-1 *n.* Short for **8** bits, **N**o parity, **1** stop bit. Typical default settings for serial communications, such as modem transmissions.

9,600-bps modem *n.* A modem with a maximum data transfer rate of 9,600 bits per second.

A

A: *n.* In Windows and some other operating systems, the identifier used for the first, or primary, floppy disk drive; unless otherwise specified by changing the CMOS startup instructions, this is the drive the operating system checks first for startup instructions.
ABC *n.* Acronym for **a**utomatic **b**rightness **c**ontrol. A circuit that changes the luminance of a monitor to compensate for ambient lighting conditions.
abort *vb.* To terminate abruptly, often used in reference to a program or procedure in progress.
absolute path *n.* A path specification to a file that begins from the topmost level of the identification of a disk drive (for example, C:\docs\work \contract.txt). *See also* path (definition 3). *Compare* relative path.
absolute pointing device *n.* A mechanical or physical pointing device whose location is associated with the position of the on-screen cursor. For example, if the user of a graphics tablet places the pen on the upper right corner of the tablet, the cursor moves to the upper right corner of the screen or on-screen window associated with the pen. *See also* graphics tablet. *Compare* relative pointing device.
absolute value *n.* The magnitude of a number, irrespective of its sign (+ or –). For example, 10 is the absolute value of 10 and of –10. Programming languages and spreadsheet programs commonly include functions that return the absolute value of a number.
A/B switch box *n.* An enclosure that contains a two-position selector switch. When a user selects a switch setting, the signal passing through the box may be directed either from a single input to one of two outputs, or from the selected input to a single output. *See also* switch (definition 1).
AC *n.* *See* alternating current.
AC adapter *n.* An external power supply that converts from a 110 VAC or 220 VAC domestic electric supply ("house current" or "main power") to low-voltage DC, which is required to operate solid-state electronic equipment (such as a laptop computer) that does not include an internal power supply.
accelerator *n.* **1.** In applications, a key or key combination used to perform a defined function. *Also called* shortcut key. **2.** In hardware, a device that speeds or enhances the operation of one or more subsystems, leading to improved program performance. *See also* accelerator card, Windows-based accelerator.
accelerator board *n.* *See* accelerator card.

accelerator card *n.* A printed circuit board that replaces or augments the computer's main microprocessor, resulting in faster performance. *Also called* accelerator board. *See also* expansion board, graphics accelerator.

acceptable use policy *n.* A statement issued by an Internet service provider or an online information service that indicates what activities users may or may not engage in while logged onto the service. For example, some providers prohibit users from engaging in commercial activity on the network. *Acronym:* AUP. *See also* ISP, online information service.

access[1] *n.* **1.** The act of reading data from or writing data to memory. **2.** Connection to the Internet or other network or system.

access[2] *vb.* To gain entry to memory in order to read or write data.

ACCESS.bus *n.* A bidirectional bus for connecting peripherals to a PC. The ACCESS.bus can connect up to 125 low-speed peripherals, such as printers, modems, mice, and keyboards, to the system through a single, general-purpose port. The peripherals are daisy-chained together, although the PC communicates directly with each peripheral and vice versa. When an ACCESS.bus device is connected to a system, the system automatically identifies and configures it for optimum performance and assigns it a unique address. The ACCESS.bus supports hot plugging. Developed by DEC, the ACCESS.bus competes with Intel's USB. *See also* bidirectional, bus, daisy chain, hot plugging, input/output port. *Compare* USB.

access code *n.* *See* password.

access control *n.* The mechanisms for limiting access to certain items of information or to certain controls based on users' identity and their membership in various predefined groups. Access control is typically used by system administrators for controlling user access to network resources, such as servers, directories, and files. *See also* access control list, access privileges, system administrator.

access control list *n.* A list associated with a file that contains information about which users or groups have permission to access or modify the file. *Acronym:* ACL.

accessibility *n.* The quality of a system incorporating hardware or software that makes it usable by people with one or more physical disabilities, such as restricted mobility, blindness, or deafness.

access mechanism *n.* **1.** The disk drive components that move the read/write head(s) to the proper track of a magnetic disk or optical disc. **2.** A circuit that allows one part of a computer system to send signals to another part. *See also* disk controller.

access number *n.* The telephone number used by a subscriber to gain access to an online service.

accessory *n.* *See* peripheral.

access path *n.* The route followed by an operating system to find the location of a stored file. The access path begins with a drive or volume (disk) designator, continues through a chain of directories and subdirectories, if any, and ends with the filename (for example, C:\books\diction\start.exe).

access privileges *n.* The type of operations permitted a given user for a certain system resource on a network or a file server. The system administrator can allow or disallow a variety of operations, such as the ability to access a server, open or transfer files, and create, view, modify, or delete files or directories. Assigning access privileges helps to maintain security on the system, to protect confidential information, and to allocate system resources such as disk space. *See also* file protection, file server, permission, system administrator, write access.

access provider *n. See* ISP.

access rights *n.* The permission to view, enter, or modify a file, folder, or system.

access speed *n. See* access time.

access time *n.* **1.** The amount of time it takes for data to be delivered from memory to the processor after the address for the data has been selected. **2.** The time needed for a read/write head in a disk drive to locate a track on a disk. Access time is usually measured in milliseconds and is used as a performance measure for hard disks and CD-ROM drives. *See also* read/write head, seek time, wait state.

account *n.* **1.** A record-keeping arrangement used by the vendor of an online service to identify a subscriber and to maintain a record of customer usage for billing purposes. **2.** A record kept by local area networks and multi-user operating systems for each authorized user of the system for identification, administration, and security purposes.

account policy *n.* **1.** On local area networks and multi-user operating systems, a set of rules governing whether a new user is allowed access to the system and whether an existing user's rights are expanded to include additional system resources. An account policy also generally states the rules with which the user must comply in order to maintain access privileges. **2.** In Windows NT, a set of rules controlling the use of passwords by the user accounts of a domain or of an individual computer. *See also* domain (definition 2).

ACK *n.* Short for **ack**nowledgment. A message sent by the receiving unit to the sending station or computer indicating either that the unit is ready to receive a transmission or that a transmission was received without error. *Compare* NAK.

ACL *n. See* access control list.

acoustic coupler *n.* A communications device with a built-in insulated cradle into which a telephone handset is fitted to establish a connection between sending and receiving computers. *See also* modem.

Acrobat *n.* A commercial program from Adobe that converts a fully formatted document created on a Windows, Macintosh, MS-DOS, or UNIX platform into a Portable Document Format (PDF) file that can be viewed on several different platforms. Acrobat enables users to send documents that contain distinctive typefaces, color, graphics, and photographs electronically to recipients, regardless of the application used to create the originals. Recipients need the Acrobat reader, which is available free, to view the files.

active *adj.* Pertaining to the device, program, file, or portion of the screen that is currently operational or subject to command operations. Usually the cursor or a highlighted section shows the active element on the display screen.

active cell *n.* The highlighted cell on a spreadsheet display that is the current focus of operation. *Also called* current cell, selected cell. *See also* range.

active content *n.* Material on a Web page that changes on the screen with time or in response to user action. Active content is implemented through ActiveX controls. *See also* ActiveX controls.

Active Desktop *n.* The client-side component of Microsoft's approach to Web-oriented, distributed computing. Active Desktop gives the user a single location from which to access both local and remote information in forms ranging from desktop icons to network resources and HTML-based Internet documents. Active Desktop supports language-independent scripting, and HTML and dynamic HTML technology, as well as programming tools such as Visual Basic, Java, and ActiveX for designing applications. Although native to the Windows 95 and Windows NT platforms, Active Desktop is designed to support development of applications that can run on other operating systems, including UNIX and the Apple Macintosh. *See also* ActiveX.

active file *n.* The file affected by a current command—typically a data file.

active-matrix display *n.* A liquid crystal display (LCD) made from a large array of liquid crystal cells using active-matrix technology (one cell per pixel). In the simplest active matrix there is one thin-film transistor (TFT) for each cell. Active-matrix displays are often used in laptop and notebook computers because of their thin width and are notable for their high-quality color displays, which are viewable from all angles, unlike passive-matrix displays. *Also called* TFT display, TFT LCD. *See also* liquid crystal display. *Compare* passive-matrix display.

active program *n.* The program currently in control of a microprocessor.

active window *n.* In an environment capable of displaying multiple on-screen windows, the window containing the display or document that will be affected by current cursor movements, commands, and text entry. *See also* graphical user interface. *Compare* inactive window.

ActiveX *n.* A set of technologies that enables software components to interact with one another in a networked environment, regardless of the language in which the components were created. ActiveX is built on Microsoft's Component Object Model (COM). Currently, ActiveX is used primarily to develop interactive content for the World Wide Web, although it can be used in desktop applications and other programs. *See also* ActiveX controls, COM. *Compare* applet, plug-in (definition 2).

A B C D E F G H I J K L M N O P Q R S T U V W X Y Z

ActiveX controls *n.* Reusable software components that incorporate ActiveX technology. These components can be embedded in Web pages to produce animation and other multimedia effects, interactive objects, and sophisticated applications. They can also be used to add specialized functionality to desktop applications and software development tools. ActiveX controls can be written in a variety of programming languages, including C, C++, Visual Basic, and Java. *See also* ActiveX. *Compare* helper application.
adapter or **adaptor** *n.* A printed circuit board that enables a personal computer to use a peripheral device, such as a CD-ROM drive, modem, or joystick, for which it does not already have the necessary connections, ports, or circuit boards. Commonly, a single adapter card can have more than one adapter on it. *Also called* interface card. *See also* controller, expansion board, network adapter, video adapter.
adaptive answering *n.* The ability of a modem to detect whether an incoming call is a fax or a data transmission and respond accordingly. *See also* modem.
adaptive delta pulse code modulation *n.* A class of compression encoding and decoding algorithms used in audio compression and other data compression applications. These algorithms store digitally sampled signals as a series of changes in value, adapting the range of the change with each sample as needed, thus increasing the effective bit resolution of the data. *Acronym:* ADPCM. *Compare* adaptive differential pulse code modulation.
adaptive differential pulse code modulation *n.* A digital audio compression algorithm that stores a sample as the difference between a linear combination of previous samples and the actual sample, rather than the measurement itself. The linear combination formula is modified every few samples to minimize the dynamic range of the output signal, resulting in efficient storage.
ADB *n. See* Apple Desktop Bus.
ADC *n. See* analog-to-digital converter.
A-D converter *n. See* analog-to-digital converter.
add-in *n. See* add-on.
add-on *n.* **1.** A hardware device, such as an expansion board or chip, that can be added to a computer to expand its capabilities. *Also called* add-in. *See also* open architecture (definition 2). **2.** A supplemental program that can extend the capabilities of an application. *See also* utility program.
address[1] *n.* **1.** A number specifying a location in memory where data is stored. **2.** A name or token specifying a particular site on the Internet or other network. **3.** A code used to specify an e-mail destination.
address[2] *vb.* To reference a particular storage location.
address book *n.* **1.** In an e-mail program, a reference section listing e-mail addresses and individuals' names. **2.** As a Web page, an informal e-mail or URL phone book.
Address Resolution Protocol *n. See* ARP.

ADJ *n.* Short for **adj**acent. A Boolean qualifier to indicate cases where two instances are adjacent to each other. In the case of a search string, "Microsoft ADJ Word" would return only instances where "Microsoft" and "Word" are adjacent in the string.
ADN *n. See* Advanced Digital Network.
ADP *n. See* data processing.
ADPCM *n. See* adaptive delta pulse code modulation.
ADSL *n. See* asymmetric digital subscriber line.
Advanced Digital Network *n.* A dedicated line service capable of transmitting data, video, and other digital signals with exceptional reliability, offered as a premier service by communications companies. Usually Advanced Digital Network refers to speeds at or above 56 Kbps. *See also* dedicated line.
Advanced Research Projects Agency Network *n. See* ARPANET.
Advanced RISC *n.* Short for **Advanced r**educed **i**nstruction **s**et **c**omputing. A specification for a RISC microchip architecture and system environment designed by MIPS Computer Systems to provide binary compatibility among software applications. *See also* RISC.
AFK *adv.* Acronym for **a**way **f**rom **k**eyboard. A phrase occasionally seen in live chat services as an indication that one is momentarily unable to answer. *See also* chat[1] (definition 1).
agent *n.* **1.** A program that performs a background task for a user and reports to the user when the task is done or some expected event has taken place. **2.** A program that searches through archives or other repositories of information on a topic specified by the user. Agents of this sort are used most often on the Internet and are generally dedicated to searching a single type of information repository, such as postings on Usenet groups. *Also called* intelligent agent. *See also* spider. **3.** In client/server applications, a process that mediates between the client and the server. **4.** In Simple Network Management Protocol, a program that monitors network traffic. *See also* SNMP.
AI *n. See* artificial intelligence.
.aiff *n.* The file extension that identifies audio files in the sound format originally used on Apple and Silicon Graphics (SGI) computers.
AIFF *n.* The sound format originally used on Apple and Silicon Graphics (SGI) computers. AIFF stores waveform files in an 8-bit monaural format. *See also* waveform.
alert box *n.* An on-screen box, in a graphical user interface, that is used to deliver a message or warning. *Compare* dialog box.
algorithm *n.* A finite sequence of steps for solving a logical or mathematical problem.
alias *n.* **1.** An alternative label for some object, such as a file or data collection. **2.** A name used to direct e-mail messages to a person or group of people on a network. **3.** A false signal that results from the digitization of an analog audio sample.

A B C D E F G H I J K L M N O P Q R S T U V W X Y Z

aliasing *n.* In computer graphics, the jagged appearance of curves or diagonal lines on a display screen, which is caused by low screen resolution.
align *vb.* **1.** In an application such as a word processor, to position lines of type relative to some point, such as a left or right page margin (left or right aligning), a midpoint (centering), or the decimal points in a column of numbers (decimal aligning). **2.** To adjust a device in order to position it within specified tolerances, such as the read/write head relative to a track on a disk.
alignment *n.* The arrangement of objects in fixed or predetermined positions, rows, or columns.
allocation unit *n. See* cluster.
all points addressable *n.* The mode in computer graphics in which all pixels can be individually manipulated. *Acronym:* APA. *See also* graphics mode.
alphanumeric *adj.* Consisting of letters or digits, or both, and sometimes including control characters, space characters, and other special characters. *See also* ASCII, character set, EBCDIC.
alphanumeric mode *n. See* text mode.
alphanumeric sort *n.* A method of sorting data, such as a set of records, that typically uses the following order: punctuation marks, numerals, alphabetic characters (with capitals preceding lowercase letters), and any remaining symbols.
alternating current *n.* Electric current that reverses its direction of flow (polarity) periodically according to a frequency measured in hertz (cycles per second). *Acronym:* AC. *Compare* direct current.
Alt key *n.* A key on PC and other standard keyboards that is used in conjunction with another key to produce some special feature or function.
alt. newsgroups *n.* Internet newsgroups that are part of the alt. ("alternative") hierarchy and use the prefix alt. in their names. Unlike the seven Usenet newsgroup hierarchies (comp., misc., news., rec., sci., soc., talk.) that require formal votes among users in the hierarchy before official newsgroups can be established, an alt. newsgroup can be created by anyone. Therefore, newsgroups devoted to discussions of obscure or bizarre topics are generally part of the alt. hierarchy. *See also* newsgroup.
American National Standards Institute *n. See* ANSI.
American Standard Code for Information Interchange *n. See* ASCII.
ampersand *n. See* &.
amplitude *n.* A measure of the strength of a signal, such as sound or voltage, determined by the distance from the baseline to the peak of the waveform. *See also* waveform.
analog *adj.* Pertaining to or being a device or signal having the property of continuously varying in strength or quantity, such as voltage or audio. *Compare* digital.

analog channel *n.* A communications channel, such as a voice-grade telephone line, carrying signals that vary continuously and can assume any value within a specified range.
analog computer *n.* A computer that measures data varying continuously in value, such as speed or temperature.
analog data *n.* Data that is represented by continuous variations in some physical property, such as voltage, frequency, or pressure. *Compare* digital data transmission.
analog display *n.* A video display capable of depicting a continuous range of colors or shades rather than discrete values. *Compare* digital display.
analog line *n.* A communications line, such as a standard telephone line, that carries continuously varying signals.
analog-to-digital converter *n.* A device that converts a continuously varying (analog) signal, such as sound or voltage, from a monitoring instrument to binary code for use by a computer. *Acronym:* ADC. *Also called* A-D converter. *See also* modem. *Compare* digital-to-analog converter.
analysis graphics *n. See* presentation graphics.
anchor *n.* **1.** A format code in a desktop publishing or word processing document that keeps an element in the document, such as a figure or a caption, in a certain position in the document. The anchored object is generally attached to another element in the document such as a text paragraph or a graphic. As text and other objects are added to the document, the anchored object moves relative to the object to which it is anchored or remains stationary. **2.** A tag in an HTML document that defines a section of text, an icon, or other element as a link to another element in the document or to another document or file. **3.** *See* hyperlink.
ancillary equipment *n. See* peripheral.
AND *n.* A logical operation combining the values of two bits (0, 1) or two Boolean values (false, true) that returns a value of 1 (true) if both input values are 1 (true) and returns a 0 (false) otherwise.
angle brackets *n. See* < >.
animated GIF *n.* A series of graphic images in GIF format, displayed sequentially in a single location to give the appearance of a moving picture. *See also* GIF.
animation *n.* The illusion of movement created by using a succession of static images. In computer graphics, the images can all be drawn separately, or starting and ending points can be drawn with the intervening images provided by software. *See also* 3-D graphic, surface modeling, tween, wire-frame model.
annotation *n.* A note or comment attached to some part of a document to provide related information. Some applications support voice annotations or annotations accessible by icons.
annoybot *n.* A bot on an Internet Relay Chat channel or multi-user dungeon that interacts with the user in an obnoxious way. *See also* bot, IRC, MUD.

A B C D E F G H I J K L M N O P Q R S T U V W X Y Z

anonymous *n.* On the Internet, the standard login name used to obtain access to a public FTP file archive. *See also* anonymous FTP.
anonymous FTP *n.* The ability to access a remote computer system on which one does not have an account, via the Internet's File Transfer Protocol. Although they can typically use FTP commands for such tasks as listing files and directories, users have restricted access rights with anonymous FTP and usually can only copy files to or from a public directory, often named /pub, on the remote system. A user accesses the remote system with an FTP program and generally types *anonymous* or *ftp* as a logon name. The password is usually the user's e-mail address, although a user can often skip giving a password, give a false e-mail address, or use the word anonymous. In order to maintain security, many FTP sites do not permit anonymous FTP access. *See also* FTP[1], logon, /pub.
anonymous post *n.* A message in a newsgroup or mailing list that cannot be traced to its originator. Generally this is accomplished by using an anonymous server for newsgroup posts or an anonymous remailer for e-mail. *See also* anonymous remailer.
anonymous remailer *n.* An e-mail server that receives incoming messages, replaces the headers that identify the original sources of the messages, and sends the messages to their ultimate destinations. The purpose of an anonymous remailer is to hide the identities of the senders of the e-mail messages.
ANSI *n.* Acronym for **A**merican **N**ational **S**tandards **I**nstitute. ANSI, the American representative of the International Organization for Standardization, has developed recommendations for the use of programming languages including FORTRAN, C, and COBOL. *See also* ANSI.SYS, ISO, SCSI.
ANSI.SYS *n.* An installable device driver for MS-DOS computers that uses ANSI commands to enhance the user's control of the console. *See also* ANSI, driver, install.
answer mode *n.* A setting that allows a modem to answer an incoming call automatically. It is used in all fax machines. *Also called* auto answer.
answer-only modem *n.* A modem that can receive but not originate calls.
answer/originate modem *n.* A modem that can both send and receive calls—the most common type of modem in use.
anti-aliasing *n.* A software technique for smoothing the jagged appearance of curved or diagonal lines caused by poor resolution on a display screen. Methods of anti-aliasing include surrounding pixels with intermediate shades and manipulating the size and horizontal alignment of pixels. *Also called* dejagging. *See also* dithering. *Compare* aliasing.
anti-glare *adj.* Pertaining to any measure taken to reduce reflections of external light on a monitor screen. The screen may be coated with a chemical (which may reduce its brightness), covered with a polarizing filter, or simply rotated so that external light is not reflected into the user's eyes.
antistatic device *n.* A device designed to minimize shocks caused by the buildup of static electricity, which can disrupt computer equipment or cause data loss. An antistatic device may take the form of a floor mat, a wristband

with a wire attached to the workstation, a spray, a lotion, or other special-purpose device. *See also* static[2], static electricity.

antivirus program *n.* A computer program that scans a computer's memory and mass storage to identify, isolate, and eliminate viruses and that examines incoming files for viruses as the computer receives them.

any key *n.* Any random key on a computer keyboard. Some programs prompt the user to "press any key" to continue. It does not matter which key the user presses. There is no key on the keyboard called Any.

any-to-any connectivity *n.* The property of an integrated computer network environment where it is possible to share data across multiple protocols, host types, and network topologies.

APA *n. See* all points addressable.

API *n. See* application programming interface.

app *n. See* application.

append *vb.* To place or insert as an attachment by adding data to the end of a file or database or by extending a character string. *See also* character string, file. *Compare* truncate.

Apple Desktop Bus *n.* A serial communications pathway built into Apple Macintosh and Apple IIGS computers. Typically a flexible cord, it enables low-speed input devices, such as a keyboard or mouse, to communicate with the computer. The bus functions like a simple local area network that can connect up to 16 devices to the computer. Although there are only two external ports, more than two devices can be daisy-chained together. *Acronym:* ADB. *See also* bus, daisy chain, device driver, input/output port, serial communications.

Apple key *n.* A key on Apple keyboards labeled with an outline of the Apple logo. On the Apple Extended Keyboard, this key is the same as the Command key, which functions similarly to the Control key on IBM and compatible keyboards. It is generally used in conjunction with a character key as a shortcut to making menu selections or starting a macro.

Apple Macintosh *n. See* Macintosh.

AppleShare *n.* File server software that works with the Mac OS and allows one Macintosh computer to share files with another on the same network. *See also* file server, Mac OS.

applet *n.* A small piece of code that can be transported over the Internet and executed on the recipient's machine. The term is used especially to refer to such programs embedded as objects in HTML documents on the World Wide Web.

AppleTalk *n.* An inexpensive local area network developed by Apple that can be used by Apple and non-Apple computers to communicate and share resources such as printers and file servers. Non-Apple computers must be equipped with AppleTalk hardware and suitable software.

application *n.* A program designed to assist in the performance of a specific task, such as word processing, accounting, or inventory management. *Compare* utility.

A B C D E F G H I J K L M N O P Q R S T U V W X Y Z

application-centric *adj.* Of, pertaining to, or characteristic of an operating system in which a user invokes an application to open or create documents (such as word processing files or spreadsheets). Command-line interfaces and some graphical user interfaces such as the Windows 3.*x* Program Manager are application-centric. *Compare* document-centric.
application development language *n.* A computer language designed for creating applications. The term usually refers to languages with specific high-level constructs geared toward record design, form layout, database retrieval and update, and similar tasks. *See also* application.
application file *n. See* program file.
application gateway *n.* Software running on a machine that is intended to maintain security on a secluded network yet allow certain traffic to go between the private network and the outside world. *See also* firewall.
application layer *n.* The highest of the seven layers in the ISO/OSI model for standardizing computer-to-computer communications. The application layer handles communication at the application-program level, such as file transfer or remote access to a computer. *See also* ISO/OSI model.
application processor *n.* A processor dedicated to a single application.
application program *n. See* application.
application programming interface or **application program interface** *n.* A set of routines used by an application program to direct the performance of procedures by the computer's operating system. *Acronym:* API.
application shortcut key *n.* A key or combination of keys that when pressed will quickly perform an action within an application that would normally require several user actions, such as menu selections. *Also called* keyboard shortcut.
application software *n. See* application.
application suite *n. See* suite.
arbitration *n.* A set of rules for resolving competing demands for a machine resource by multiple users or processes. *See also* contention.
.arc *n.* The file extension that identifies compressed archive files encoded using the Advanced RISC Computing Specification (ARC) format. *See also* compressed file.
arcade game *n.* **1.** A coin-operated computer game for one or more players that features high-quality screen graphics, sound, and rapid action. **2.** Any computer game designed to mimic the style of a coin-operated arcade game, such as games marketed for the home computer. *See also* computer game.
Archie *n.* An Internet utility for finding files in public archives obtainable by anonymous FTP. The master Archie server at McGill University in Montreal downloads FTP indexes from participating FTP servers, merges them into a master list, and sends updated copies of the master list to other Archie servers each day. Archie is a shortened form of the word archive. *See also* anonymous FTP, FTP[1] (definition 1). *Compare* Jughead, Veronica.

Archie server *n.* On the Internet, a server that contains Archie indexes to the names and addresses of files in public FTP archives. *See also* Archie, FTP[1] (definition 1), server (definition 2).
architecture *n.* **1.** The physical construction or design of a computer system and its components. *See also* cache, CISC, closed architecture, network architecture, open architecture, RISC. **2.** The data-handling capacity of a microprocessor. **3.** The design of application software incorporating protocols and the means for expansion and interfacing with other programs.
archive[1] *n.* **1.** A tape or disk containing files copied from another storage device and used as backup storage. **2.** A compressed file. **3.** A file directory on the Internet that is available by FTP, or an Internet directory established for dissemination of stored files.
archive[2] *vb.* **1.** To copy files onto a tape or disk for long-term storage. **2.** To compress a file.
archive bit *n.* A bit that is associated with a file and is used to indicate whether the file has been backed up. *See also* back up, bit.
archive file *n.* A file that contains a set of files, such as a program with its documentation and example input files, or collected postings from a newsgroup. Depending on the utility being used, archive files can be compressed as they are created or they can be compressed later. *See also* compress, StuffIt, tar[1].
archive site *n.* A site on the Internet that stores files. The files are usually accessed in one of the following ways: downloaded through anonymous FTP, retrieved through Gopher, or viewed on the World Wide Web. *See also* anonymous FTP, Gopher.
area search *n.* In information management, the examination of a group of documents for the purpose of identifying those that are relevant to a particular subject or category.
arithmetic operator *n.* An operator that performs an arithmetic operation: +, –, ×, or / (for addition, subtraction, multiplication, or division). *See also* logical operator, operator (definition 1).
ARP *n.* Acronym for **A**ddress **R**esolution **P**rotocol. A TCP/IP protocol for determining the hardware address of a node on a local area network connected to the Internet, when only the IP address is known. An ARP request is sent to the network, and the node that has the IP address responds with its hardware address. Although ARP technically refers only to finding the hardware address, and RARP (for Reverse ARP) refers to the reverse procedure, ARP is commonly used for both senses. *See also* IP address, TCP/IP.
ARPANET *n.* A large wide area network created in the 1960s by the U.S. Department of Defense Advanced Research Projects Agency (ARPA) for the free exchange of information between universities and research organizations, although the military also used this network for communications. In the 1980s MILNET, a separate network, was spun off from ARPANET for use

A B C D E F G H I J K L M N O P Q R S T U V W X Y Z

by the military. ARPANET was the network from which the Internet evolved. *See also* Internet, MILNET.

ARP request *n.* Short for **A**ddress **R**esolution **P**rotocol **request**. An ARP packet containing the Internet address of a host computer. The receiving computer responds with or passes along the corresponding Ethernet address. *See also* ARP, Ethernet (definition 1), IP address, packet.

arrow key *n.* Any of four keys labeled with arrows pointing up, down, left, and right, used to move the cursor vertically or horizontally on the display screen or, in some programs, to extend the highlight.

article *n.* A message that appears in an Internet newsgroup. *Also called* post. *See also* newsgroup.

artificial intelligence *n.* The branch of computer science concerned with enabling computers to simulate such aspects of human intelligence as speech recognition, deduction, inference, creative response, and the ability to learn from experience. Two common areas of artificial-intelligence research are expert systems and natural-language processing. *Acronym:* AI. *See also* expert system, natural-language processing.

artificial life *n.* The study of computer systems that simulate some aspects of the behavior of living organisms. Artificial life includes systems in which programs intended to perform some particular task compete for survival and reproduction based on their performance; the offspring can combine pieces of code and undergo random variations, and the programs so modified compete in turn, until an optimal solution is found.

.asc *n.* A filename extension most commonly indicating that the file contains ASCII text that can be processed by all types of word processing software, including MS-DOS Edit, Windows Notepad, Windows 95/NT WordPad, and Microsoft Word. Some systems may use this extension to indicate that a file contains image information. *See also* ASCII.

ascending order *n.* The arrangement of a sequence of items from lowest to highest, such as from 1 to 10 or from A to Z. The rules for determining ascending order in a particular application can be very complicated: capital letters before lowercase letters, extended ASCII characters in ASCII order, and so on.

ascending sort *n.* A sort that results in the arrangement of items in ascending order. *See also* alphanumeric sort, ascending order. *Compare* descending sort.

ASCII *n.* Acronym for **A**merican **S**tandard **C**ode for **I**nformation **I**nterchange. A coding scheme using 7 or 8 bits that assigns numeric values to up to 256 characters, including letters, numerals, punctuation marks, control characters, and other symbols. ASCII was developed in 1968 to standardize data transmission among disparate hardware and software systems and is built into most minicomputers and all personal computers. *See also* ASCII file, character, character code, control character, extended ASCII. *Compare* EBCDIC.

ASCII character set *n.* A standard 7-bit code for representing ASCII characters using binary values; code values range from 0 to 127. Most PC-based systems use an 8-bit extended ASCII code, with an extra 128 characters used to represent special symbols, foreign-language characters, and graphic symbols. *See also* ASCII, character, EBCDIC, extended ASCII.
ASCII file *n.* A document file in ASCII format, containing characters, spaces, punctuation, carriage returns, and sometimes tabs and an end-of-file marker, but no formatting information. *Also called* text file, text-only file. *See also* ASCII, text file. *Compare* binary file.
ASCII transfer *n.* The preferred mode of electronic exchange for text files. In ASCII mode, character conversions to and from the network-standard character set are performed. *See also* ASCII. *Compare* binary transfer.
aspect ratio *n.* In computer displays and graphics, the ratio of the width of an image or image area to its height. An aspect ratio of 2:1, for example, indicates that the image is twice as wide as it is high. The aspect ratio is an important factor in maintaining correct proportions when an image is printed, rescaled, or incorporated into another document.
ASR *n. See* automatic system reconfiguration.
assembler *n.* A program that converts assembly language programs, which are understandable by humans, into executable machine language. *See also* assembly language, compiler, machine code.
assembly language *n.* A low-level programming language using abbreviations or mnemonic codes in which each statement corresponds to a single machine instruction. An assembly language is translated to machine language by the assembler and is specific to a given processor. Advantages of using an assembly language include increased execution speed and direct programmer interaction with system hardware. *See also* assembler, compiler, high-level language, low-level language, machine code.
associate *vb.* To inform the operating system that a particular filename extension is linked to a specific application. When a file is opened that has an extension associated with a given application, the operating system automatically starts the application and loads the file.
asterisk *n.* **1.** The character (*) used in applications and programming languages to signify multiplication. **2.** In Windows, MS-DOS, OS/2, and other operating systems, a wildcard character that can be used in place of other characters, as in *.*, which represents any combination of filename and extension. *See also* question mark, star-dot-star, wildcard character.
asymmetrical transmission *n.* A form of transmission used by high-speed modems, typically those that operate at rates of 9,600 bps or more, that allows simultaneous incoming and outgoing transmission by dividing a telephone line bandwidth into two channels: one in the range of 300 to 450 bps and one at a speed of 9,600 bps or more.
asymmetric digital subscriber line *n.* Technology and equipment allowing high-speed digital communication, including video signals, across an

ordinary twisted-pair copper phone line, with speeds up to 9 Mbps downstream (to the customer) and up to 800 Kbps upstream. *Acronym:* ADSL. *Also called* asymmetric digital subscriber loop. *Compare* symmetric digital subscriber line.

asymmetric digital subscriber loop *n. See* asymmetric digital subscriber line.

asynchronous device *n.* A device whose internal operations are not synchronized with the timing of any other part of the system.

asynchronous operation *n.* An operation that proceeds independently of any timing mechanism, such as a clock. For example, two modems communicating asynchronously rely upon each sending the other start and stop signals in order to pace the exchange of information. *Compare* synchronous operation.

Asynchronous Protocol Specification *n.* The X.445 standard. *See* CCITT X series.

Asynchronous Transfer Mode *n. See* ATM.

asynchronous transmission *n.* In modem communication, a form of data transmission in which data is sent intermittently, one character at a time, rather than in a steady stream with characters separated by fixed time intervals. Asynchronous transmission relies on the use of a start bit and stop bit(s), in addition to the bits representing the character (and an optional parity bit), to distinguish separate characters.

ATA *n.* Acronym for **A**dvanced **T**echnology **A**ttachment. ANSI group X3T10's official name for the disk drive interface standard commonly known as Integrated Drive Electronics (IDE). *Also called* AT Attachment. *See also* IDE.

ATA hard disk drive card *n.* Expansion card used to control and interface with an ATA hard disk drive. These cards are usually ISA cards. *See also* ATA, ISA.

ATA/IDE hard disk drive *n.* A disk drive implementation designed to integrate the controller onto the drive itself, thereby reducing interface costs and making firmware implementations easier. *See also* ATA, firmware, IDE.

AT Attachment *n. See* ATA.

AT bus *n.* The electric pathway used by IBM AT and compatible computers to connect the motherboard and peripheral devices. The AT bus supports 16 bits of data, whereas the original PC bus supports only 8 bits. *Also called* expansion bus. *See also* EISA, ISA.

aTdHvAaNnKcSe *n. See* TIA.

ATDP *n.* Acronym for **At**tention **D**ial **P**ulse, a command that initiates pulse (as opposed to touch-tone) dialing in Hayes and Hayes-compatible modems. *Compare* ATDT.

ATDT *n.* Acronym for **At**tention **D**ial **T**one, a command that initiates touch-tone (as opposed to pulse) dialing in Hayes and Hayes-compatible modems. *Compare* ATDP.

ATM *n.* Acronym for **A**synchronous **T**ransfer **M**ode. A network technology capable of transmitting data, voice, video, and frame relay traffic in real time. It is currently used in local area networks involving workstations and personal computers, but it is expected that telephone companies will adopt it, to charge customers for the data they transmit rather than for their connect time.

at sign *n. See* @.

attached document *n.* An ASCII text file or a binary file, such as a document created in a word processing system, that is included with an e-mail message as an attachment. The file is generally encoded using uuencoding, MIME, or BinHex. Most e-mail programs automatically encode an attached document for transmission with a message. The recipient must have an e-mail program capable of decoding the attached document or must use a separate utility to decode it. *See also* ASCII, binary file, BinHex[1], MIME, uuencode[1].

attached processor *n.* A secondary processor attached to a computer system, such as a keyboard or video subsystem processor.

attenuation *n.* The weakening of a transmitted signal, such as a digital signal or an electrical signal, as it travels farther from its source. Attenuation is usually measured in decibels and is sometimes desirable, as when signal strength is reduced electronically, for example, by a radio volume control, to prevent overloading.

attribute *n.* **1.** In a database record, the name or structure of a field. For example, the files LASTNAME and PHONE would be attributes of each record in a PHONELIST database, as would the size of a field or the type of information it contains. **2.** In screen displays, an element of additional information stored with each character in the video buffer of a video adapter running in character mode. Such attributes control the background and foreground colors of the character, underlining, and blinking. **3.** In markup languages such as SGML and HTML, a name-value pair within a tagged element that modifies certain features of that element. *See also* HTML, SGML.

ATX *n.* A specification for PC motherboard architectures with built-in audio and video capabilities, introduced by Intel in 1995. ATX supports USB and full-length boards in all sockets. *See also* board, motherboard, specification (definition 2), USB.

audio *adj.* Relating to frequencies within the range of perception by the human ear—from about 15 to 20,000 hertz (cycles per second). *See also* audio response, synthesizer.

audio board *n. See* audio card.

audio card *n.* An expansion card that converts analog audio signals from a microphone, audio tape, or other source to digital form that can be stored as a computer audio file, and converts computer audio files to electrical signals that can be played through a speaker. Most audio cards support MIDI. Audio cards enable sounds to be heard from CD-ROMs and other storage media or over the Internet. *Also called* audio board, sound board, sound card. *See also* MIDI.

audiocast *n.* The transmission of an audio signal using IP protocols. *See also* IP.
audio compression *n.* A method of reducing the overall loudness of an audio signal, by limiting the amount of apparent distortion when the signal is played back through a speaker or transmitted through a communications link.
audio output *n.* *See* audio response.
audio output port *n.* A circuit consisting of a digital-to-analog converter that transforms signals from the computer to audible tones. It is used in conjunction with an amplifier and a speaker. *See also* digital-to-analog converter.
audio response *n.* Any sound produced by a computer; specifically, spoken output produced by a computer in response to some specific type of input. Such output may be generated using a combination of words from a digitized vocabulary or through the synthesis of words from tables of phonemes. *See also* phoneme.
Audio Video Interleaved *n.* *See* AVI.
auditing *n.* The process an operating system uses to detect and to record security-related events, such as an attempt to create, access, or delete objects such as files and directories. The records of such events are stored in a security log, a file whose contents are available only to those with the proper clearance. *See also* security log.
audit trail *n.* In reference to computing, a means of tracing all activities affecting a piece of information, such as a data record, from the time it is entered into a system to the time it is removed. An audit trail makes it possible to document, for example, who made changes to a particular record and when.
AUP *n.* *See* acceptable use policy.
authentication *n.* In a multi-user or network operating system, the process by which the system validates a user's logon information. A user's name and password are compared against an authorized list, and if the system detects a match, access is granted to the extent specified for that user in the permission list. *See also* logon, password, permission, user account, user name.
authoring language *n.* A computer language or application development system designed primarily for creating programs, databases, and materials for computer-aided instruction. *See also* CAI.
authoring system *n.* Application software that enables the operator to create and format a document for a specific kind of computer environment. An authoring system, especially for multimedia work, often consists of several applications within the framework of a single, controlling application. *See also* authoring language.
authorization *n.* In reference to computing, especially remote computers on a network, the right granted an individual to use the system and the data stored on it. Authorization is typically set up by a system administrator and verified by the computer based on some form of user identification, such as

a code number or password. *Also called* access privileges, permission. *See also* network, system administrator.
authorization code *n. See* password.
auto answer *n. See* answer mode.
autoattendant *adj.* A term used to describe a store-and-forward computer system that replaces the traditional switchboard operator to direct calls to their correct extensions or voice mailboxes. Autoattendant systems may implement voice prompts, touch-tone menus, or voice recognition features to send calls to their proper destinations. *Also called* automated attendant.
auto dial *n.* A feature enabling a modem to open a telephone line and initiate a call by transmitting a stored telephone number as a series of pulses or tones.
AUTOEXEC.BAT *n.* A special-purpose batch file containing commands that are automatically carried out by the MS-DOS operating system when the computer is started or restarted. Created by the user or (in later versions of MS-DOS) by the operating system at system installation, the file contains basic startup commands that help configure the system to installed devices and to the user's preferences.
auto-key *n. See* typematic.
automatic answering *n. See* answer mode.
automatic data processing *n. See* data processing.
automatic dialing *n. See* auto dial.
automatic error correction *n.* A process that, upon detection of an internal processing or data transmission error, invokes a routine designed to correct the error or retry the operation.
automatic system reconfiguration *n.* Automation of configuration by the system to accommodate some change in either the software or the hardware. *Acronym:* ASR.
automonitor *n.* A process or system feature capable of assessing the status of its own internal environment.
AutoPlay *n.* A feature in Windows 95 that allows it to automatically operate a CD-ROM. When a CD is inserted into a CD-ROM drive, Windows 95 looks for an AUTORUN.INF file on the CD. If the file is found, Windows 95 opens it and usually either sets up an application from the CD-ROM on the computer's hard disk or starts the application once it has been installed. If an audio CD is inserted, Windows 95 automatically launches the CD Player application and plays it.
auto-repeat *n. See* typematic.
autorestart *n.* A process or system feature that can automatically restart the system after the occurrence of certain types of errors or a power system failure.
autosave *n.* A program feature that automatically saves an open file to a disk or other medium at defined intervals or after a certain number of keystrokes to ensure that changes to a document are periodically saved.

autosizing *n.* The ability of a monitor to accept signals at one resolution and display the image at a different resolution. A monitor capable of autosizing maintains the aspect ratio of an image but enlarges or reduces the image to fit in the space available. *See also* monitor, resolution (definition 1).
autostart routine *n.* A process by which a system or device is automatically prepared for operation with the occurrence of powering up, or turning the system on, or some other predetermined event. *See also* AUTOEXEC.-BAT, autorestart, boot[2], power up.
autotrace *n.* A drawing program feature that draws lines along the edges of a bitmapped image to convert the image to an object-oriented one. *See also* bitmapped graphics, object-oriented graphics.
AUX *n.* The logical device name for auxiliary device; a name reserved by the MS-DOS operating system for the standard auxiliary device. AUX usually refers to a system's first serial port, also known as COM1.
auxiliary equipment *n. See* peripheral.
auxiliary storage *n.* Any storage medium, such as disk or tape, not directly accessed by a computer's microprocessor, as is random access memory (RAM). In current usage, such media are typically referred to as storage or permanent storage, and the RAM chips that the microprocessor uses directly for temporary storage are referred to as memory.
availability *n.* In processing, the accessibility of a computer system or a resource such as a printer, in terms of usage or of the percentage of the total amount of time the device is needed.
available time *n. See* uptime.
avatar *n.* **1.** In virtual-reality environments such as certain types of Internet chat rooms, a graphical representation of a user. An avatar typically is a generic picture or animation of a human, a photograph or caricature of the user, a picture or animation of an animal, or an object chosen by the user to depict his or her virtual-reality "identity." **2.** *See* superuser.
.avi *n.* The file extension that identifies an audiovisual interleaved data file in the Microsoft RIFF format. *See also* AVI.
AVI *n.* Acronym for **A**udio **V**ideo **I**nterleaved. A Windows multimedia file format for sound and moving pictures that uses the Microsoft RIFF (Resource Interchange File Format) specification.
axis *n.* In a chart or other two-dimensional system using coordinates, the horizontal line (*x*-axis) or vertical line (*y*-axis) that serves as a reference for plotting points. In a three-dimensional coordinate system, a third line (*z*-axis) is used to represent depth. *See also* coordinate.

B

b[1] *adj.* Short for **b**inary.
b[2] *n.* **1.** Short for **b**it. **2.** Short for **b**aud.
B *n.* Short for **b**yte.
B: *n.* **1.** Identifier for a second floppy disk drive on MS-DOS and other operating systems. **2.** Identifier for a single disk drive when used as the secondary drive.
backbone *n.* **1.** A network of communications transmission that carries major traffic between smaller networks. The backbones of the Internet, including communications carriers such as Sprint and MCI, can span thousands of miles using microwave relays and dedicated lines. **2.** The smaller networks (compared with the entire Internet) that perform the bulk of the packet switching of Internet communication. Today these smaller networks still consist of the networks that were originally developed to make up the Internet—the computer networks of the educational and research institutions of the United States. *See also* packet switching. **3.** The wires that carry major communications traffic within a network. In a local area network, a backbone may be a bus. *Also called* collapsed backbone.
back door *n.* A means of gaining access to a program or system by bypassing its security controls. Programmers often build a back door into software under development so that they can fix bugs. If the back door becomes known to anyone else, or if it is not removed before the software is released, it becomes a security risk. *Also called* trapdoor.
back end *n.* In a client/server application, the part of the program that runs on the server. *See also* client/server architecture. *Compare* front end.
back-end processor *n.* **1.** A slave processor that performs a specialized task such as providing rapid access to a database, freeing the main processor for other work. Such a task is considered "back-end" because it is subordinate to the computer's main function. **2.** A processor that manipulates data sent to it from another processor; for example, a high-speed graphics processor that paints images on a video display operates in response to commands passed "back" to it by the main processor. *Compare* coprocessor.
background[1] *adj.* In the context of processes or tasks that are part of an operating system or program, operating without interaction with the user while the user is working on another task. Background processes or tasks are assigned a lower priority in the microprocessor's allotment of time than foreground tasks and generally remain invisible to the user unless the user requests an update or brings the task to the foreground. Generally, only multitasking operating systems are able to support background processing,

although some systems that do not support multitasking may be able to perform one or more types of background tasks, such as printing. *See also* multitasking. *Compare* foreground[1].

background[2] *n.* **1.** The color against which characters and graphics are displayed, such as a white background for black characters. *Compare* foreground[2] (definition 1). **2.** The colors, textures, patterns, and pictures that make up the surface of the desktop or the surface of a Web page, upon which text, icons, buttons, menu bars, toolbars, and other items are situated. *See also* wallpaper. **3.** The condition of an open but currently inactive window in a windowing environment. *See also* inactive window. *Compare* foreground[2] (definition 2).

background noise *n.* The noise inherent in a line or circuit, independent of the presence of a signal. *See also* noise.

background printing *n.* The process of sending a document to a printer at the same time that the computer is performing one or more other tasks.

background processing *n.* The execution of certain operations by the operating system or a program during momentary lulls in the primary (foreground) task. An example of background processing is a word processor program printing a document during the time that occurs between the user's keystrokes. *See also* background[1].

background task *n. See* background[1].

back-lit display *n.* An LCD display that uses a light source behind the screen to enhance image sharpness and readability, especially in environments that are brightly lit.

back panel *n.* The panel at the rear of a computer cabinet through which most of the connections to outside power sources and peripherals are made.

backplane *n.* A circuit board or framework that supports other circuit boards, devices, and the interconnections among devices and provides power and data signals to supported devices.

backslash *n.* The character (\) used to separate directory names in MS-DOS and Windows path specifications. When used as a leading character, it means that the path specification begins from the topmost level for that disk drive. *See also* path (definition 3).

Backspace key *n.* **1.** A key that, on IBM and compatible keyboards, moves the cursor to the left, one character at a time, usually deleting each character as it moves. **2.** On Macintosh keyboards, a key (called the Delete key on some Macintosh keyboards) that deletes currently selected text or, if no text is selected, deletes the character to the left of the insertion point (cursor).

backup *n.* A duplicate copy of a program, a disk, or data, made either for archiving or for safeguarding valuable files from loss should the active copy be damaged or destroyed. A backup is an "insurance" copy. Some application programs automatically make backup copies of data files, maintaining both the current version and the preceding version on disk. *Also called* backup copy, backup file.

back up *vb.* **1.** To make a duplicate copy of a program, a disk, or data. *See also* backup. **2.** To return to a previous stable state, such as one in which a database is known to be complete and consistent.
backup and recovery *n.* A strategy available in many database management systems that allows a database to be restored to the latest complete unit of work (transaction) after a software or hardware error has rendered the database unusable. The process starts with the latest backup copy of the database. The system then reads the change file, or transaction log, and recovers logged transactions. *See also* backup, change file.
backup and restore *n.* The process of maintaining backup files and putting them back onto the source medium if necessary.
backup copy *n. See* backup.
backup file *n. See* backup.
bacterium *n.* A type of computer virus that repeatedly replicates itself, eventually taking over the entire system. *See also* virus.
bad sector *n.* A disk sector that cannot be used for data storage, usually because of media damage or imperfections. Finding, marking, and avoiding bad sectors on a disk are tasks performed by a computer's operating system. A disk-formatting utility can also find and mark bad sectors on a disk.
bad track *n.* A track on a hard disk or floppy disk that is identified as containing a faulty sector and consequently is bypassed by the operating system. *See also* bad sector.
.bak *n.* An auxiliary file, created either automatically or on command, that contains the second-most-recent version of a file and bears the same filename, with the extension .bak. *See also* backup.
band *n.* **1.** In printing graphics, a rectangular portion of a graphic sent by the computer to a printer. Dividing a graphic into bands prevents a printer from having to reconstruct an entire image in memory before printing it. **2.** In communications, a contiguous range of frequencies used for a particular purpose, such as radio or television broadcasts.
bandwidth *n.* **1.** The difference between the highest and lowest frequencies that an analog communications system can pass. For example, a telephone accommodates a bandwidth of 3,000 Hz: the difference between the lowest (300 Hz) and highest (3,300 Hz) frequencies it can carry. **2.** The data transfer capacity of a digital communications system.
bandwidth on demand *n.* In telecommunications, the capability of increasing throughput, in increments, as required by the channel to be serviced. *See also* bandwidth, channel (definition 2), throughput.
bank *n.* **1.** Any group of similar electrical devices connected together for use as a single device. For example, transistors may be connected in a row/column array inside a chip to form memory. **2.** A section of memory, usually of a size convenient for a CPU to address. For example, an 8-bit processor can address 65,536 bytes of memory; therefore, a 64-KB memory bank is the largest that the processor can address at once. *See also* bank switching, page (definition 2).

A B C D E F G H I J K L M N O P Q R S T U V W X Y Z

bank switching *n.* A method of expanding a computer's available RAM by switching between banks of RAM chips that share a range of memory addresses, which is set aside before switching begins. Only one bank is directly accessible at a time; when a bank is not active, it retains whatever is stored in it. Before another bank can be used, the operating system, driver, or program must explicitly issue a command to the hardware to make the switch. Because switching takes time, memory-intensive operations take longer with bank-switched memory than with main memory. Bank-switched memory typically takes the form of an expansion card that plugs into a slot on the motherboard.

banner *n.* A section of a Web page containing an advertisement that is usually an inch or less tall and spans the width of the Web page. The banner contains a link to the advertiser's Web site.

banner page *n.* **1.** The title page that may be added to printouts by most print spoolers. Such a page typically incorporates account ID information, job length, and print spooler information and is used primarily to separate print jobs. *See also* print spooler. **2.** In software, an initial screen used to identify a product and credit its producers.

bare bones *adj.* Purely functional; stripped or otherwise clean of features. Bare bones applications provide only the most basic functions necessary to perform a given task. By the same token, a bare bones computer provides a minimal amount of hardware or is sold at retail with no peripherals and just the operating system (and no other software).

base *n.* In mathematics, the number of digits in a particular number system. With microcomputers, four number systems are commonly used or referred to: binary, octal, decimal, and hexadecimal. Each is based on a different number of digits: 2, 8, 10, and 16, respectively. *See also* binary, hexadecimal, octal.

base-2 *adj. See* binary.

base-8 *adj. See* octal.

base-10 *adj.* Of or relating to the decimal number system.

base-16 *adj. See* hexadecimal.

baseband *adj.* Of or relating to communications systems in which the medium of transmission (such as a wire or fiber-optic cable) carries a single message at a time in digital form. Baseband communication is found in local area networks such as Ethernet and Token Ring. *See also* Ethernet (definition 1), fiber optics, Token Ring network. *Compare* broadband.

baseband network *n.* A type of local area network in which messages travel in digital form on a single transmission channel between machines connected by coaxial cable or twisted-pair wiring. Generally, machines on a baseband network transmit only when the channel is not busy. Each message travels as a packet that contains information about the source and destination machines as well as message data. Baseband networks operate over short distances (a maximum of about 2 miles) at speeds ranging from about

50 Kbps to 16 Mbps. Receiving, verifying, and converting a message add to the actual time, however, reducing throughput. *See also* coaxial cable, multiplexing, packet (definition 2), throughput, twisted-pair cable. *Compare* broadband network.

baseline *n.* In the printing and display of characters on the screen, an imaginary horizontal line with which the base of each character is aligned. *See also* font.

base memory *n.* *See* conventional memory.

base RAM *n.* *See* conventional memory.

Basic or **BASIC** *n.* Acronym for **B**eginner's **A**ll-purpose **S**ymbolic **I**nstruction **C**ode, a high-level programming language developed in the mid-1960s by John Kemeny and Thomas Kurtz. It is widely considered one of the easiest programming languages to learn. *See also* Visual Basic.

Basic Rate Interface *n.* *See* BRI.

.bat *n.* The file extension that identifies a batch program file. In MS-DOS, .bat files are executable files that contain calls to other program files. *See also* batch file.

batch *n.* A group of documents or data records that are processed as a unit. *See also* batch processing.

batch file *n.* An ASCII text file containing a sequence of operating system commands. When the user types a batch filename at the command prompt, the commands are processed sequentially. *Also called* batch program. *See also* AUTOEXEC.BAT, .bat.

batch file transmission *n.* The transmission of multiple files as the result of a single command. *Acronym:* BFT.

batch processing *n.* **1.** Execution of a batch file. *See also* batch file. **2.** The practice of acquiring programs and data sets from users, running them one or a few at a time, and then providing the results to the users. **3.** The practice of storing transactions for a period of time before they are posted to a master file, typically in a separate operation undertaken at night. *Compare* transaction processing.

batch program *n.* A program that executes without interacting with the user. *See also* batch file. *Compare* interactive program.

batch system *n.* A system that processes data in discrete groups of previously scheduled operations rather than interactively or in real time.

battery *n.* Two or more cells in a container that produces an electrical current when two electrodes within the container touch an electrolyte. In personal computers, batteries are used as an auxiliary source of power when the main power is shut off, as a power source for laptop and notebook computers (rechargeable batteries are used), and as a method of keeping the internal clock and the circuitry responsible for the part of random access memory that stores important system information always powered up. *See also* lead ion battery, lithium ion battery, nickel cadmium battery, nickel metal hydride battery, RAM.

A B C D E F G H I J K L M N O P Q R S T U V W X Y Z

battery backup *n.* **1.** A battery-operated power supply used as an auxiliary source of electricity in the event of a power failure. **2.** Any use of a battery to keep a circuit running when the main power is shut off, such as powering a computer's clock/calendar and the special RAM that stores important system information between sessions. *See also* UPS.

battery meter *n.* A device used to measure the current (capacity) of an electrical cell.

baud *n.* One signal change per second, most commonly a measure of the data transmission speed of a modem. *See also* baud rate.

baud rate *n.* The speed at which a modem can transmit data. The baud rate is the number of events, or signal changes, that occur in one second—not the number of bits per second (bps) transmitted. In high-speed digital communications, one event can actually encode more than one bit, and modems are more accurately described in terms of bits per second than baud rate. For example, a so-called 9,600-baud modem actually operates at 2,400 baud but transmits 9,600 bits per second by encoding 4 bits per event (2,400 × 4 = 9,600) and thus is a 9,600-bps modem. *Compare* bit rate, transfer rate.

bay *n.* A shelf or opening used for the installation of electronic equipment—for example, the space reserved for additional disk drives, CD-ROM drives, or other equipment in the cabinets of microcomputers. *See also* drive bay.

BBL *n.* Acronym for **be b**ack **l**ater. An expression used commonly on live chat services to indicate that a participant is temporarily leaving the discussion forum but intends to return at a later time. *See also* chat[1] (definition 1).

BBS *n.* **1.** Acronym for **b**ulletin **b**oard **s**ystem. A computer system equipped with one or more modems or other means of network access that serves as an information and message-passing center for remote users. Often BBSs are focused on special interests or topics. They can have free or fee-based access, or a combination. Users dial into a BBS and post messages to other BBS users in special areas. Many BBSs also allow users to chat online, send e-mail, download and upload files that include freeware and shareware software, and access the Internet. Many software and hardware companies run proprietary BBSs for customers that include sales information, technical support, and software upgrades and patches. **2.** Acronym for **b**e **b**ack **s**oon. A shorthand expression often seen in Internet discussion groups by a participant who wishes to bid a temporary farewell to the rest of the group.

bcc *n.* Acronym for **b**lind **c**ourtesy **c**opy. A feature of e-mail programs that allows a user to send a copy of an e-mail message to a recipient without notifying other recipients that this was done. Generally, the recipient's address is entered in a field called bcc: in the mail header. *Also called* blind carbon copy. *See also* e-mail[1] (definition 1), mail header. *Compare* cc.

bells and whistles *n.* Attractive features added to hardware or software beyond basic functionality, comparable to accessories such as electric door locks added to an automobile.

benchmark[1] *n.* A test used to measure hardware or software performance. Benchmarks for hardware use programs that test the capabilities of the equipment—for example, the speed at which a CPU can execute instructions. Benchmarks for software determine the efficiency, accuracy, or speed of a program in performing a particular task, such as recalculating data in a spreadsheet. The same data is used with each program tested, so the resulting scores can be compared to see which programs perform well and in what areas.

benchmark² *vb.* To measure the performance of hardware or software.

benign virus *n.* A program that exhibits properties of a virus, such as self-replication, but does not otherwise do harm to the computer systems that it infects.

Bernoulli box *n.* A removable floppy disk drive for personal computers that uses a nonvolatile cartridge and has high storage capacity.

beta¹ *adj.* Of or relating to software or hardware that is a beta. *See also* beta².

beta² *n.* A new software or hardware product, or one that is being updated, that is ready to be released to users for beta testing. *See also* beta test.

beta test *n.* A test of software that is still under development, accomplished by having people actually use the software. In a beta test, a software product is sent to selected potential customers and influential end users (known as beta sites), who test its functionality and report any operational or utilization errors (bugs) found. The beta test is usually one of the last steps a software developer takes before releasing the product to market.

betweening *n.* *See* tween.

Bézier curve *n.* A curve that is calculated mathematically to connect separate points into smooth, free-form curves and surfaces of the type needed for illustration programs and CAD models. Bézier curves are useful because they need only a few points to define a large number of shapes. *See also* CAD.

BFT *n.* *See* batch file transmission, binary file transfer.

bidirectional *adj.* Operating in two directions. A bidirectional printer can print from left to right and from right to left; a bidirectional bus can transfer signals in both directions between two devices.

bidirectional parallel port *n.* An interface that supports two-way parallel communication between a device and a computer.

bidirectional printing *n.* The ability of an impact or ink-jet printer to print from left to right and from right to left. Bidirectional printing improves speed substantially because no time is wasted returning the print head to the beginning of the next line, but it may lower print quality.

big red switch *n.* The power on/off switch of a computer, thought of as a kind of interrupt of last resort. On the IBM PC and many other computers, it is indeed big and red. Using the switch is an interrupt of last resort because it deletes all the data in RAM and can damage the hard drive. *Acronym:* BRS.

.bin *n.* A filename extension for a file encoded with MacBinary. *See also* MacBinary.

binary *adj.* Having two components, alternatives, or outcomes. The binary number system has 2 as its base, so values are expressed as combinations of two digits, 0 and 1. These two digits can represent the logical values true and false as well as numerals, and they can be represented in an electronic device by the two states on and off, recognized as two voltage levels. Therefore, the binary number system is at the heart of digital computing. *See also* base, binary number, bit, byte, digital computer, logic circuit. *Compare* ASCII, decimal, hexadecimal, octal.

binary chop *n. See* binary search.

binary compatibility *n.* Portability of executable programs (binary files) from one platform or flavor of operating system to another. *See also* flavor, portable (definition 1).

binary device *n.* Any device that processes information as a series of on/off or high/low electrical states. *See also* binary.

binary digit *n.* Either of the two digits in the binary number system, 0 and 1. *See also* bit.

binary file *n.* A file consisting of a sequence of 8-bit data or executable code, as distinguished from files consisting of human-readable ASCII text. Binary files are usually in a form readable only by a program, often compressed or structured in a way that is easy for a particular program to read. *Compare* ASCII file.

binary file transfer *n.* Transfer of a file containing arbitrary bytes or words, as opposed to a text file containing only printable characters (for example, ASCII characters with codes 10, 13, and 32–126). On modern operating systems a text file is simply a binary file that happens to contain only printable characters, but some older systems distinguish the two file types, requiring programs to handle them differently. *Acronym:* BFT.

binary number *n.* A number expressed in binary form. Binary numbers, which are expressed with the digits 0 and 1, are based on powers of 2. Thus, the binary number 1101 is interpreted as the sum of 1×2^3 (or 8), 1×2^2 (or 4), 0×2^1 (or 0), and 1×2^0 (or 1), which is decimal 13. *See also* binary.

binary search *n.* A type of search algorithm that seeks an item, with a known name, in an ordered list by first comparing the sought item to the item at the middle of the list's order. The search then divides the list in two, determines in which half of the order the item should be, and repeats this process until the sought item is found. *Also called* binary chop, dichotomizing search. *See also* search algorithm. *Compare* linear search.

binary synchronous protocol *n. See* BISYNC.

binary transfer *n.* The preferred mode of electronic exchange for executable files, application data files, and encrypted files. *Compare* ASCII transfer.

binaural sound *n. See* 3-D audio.

BinHex[1] *n.* **1.** A code for converting binary data files into ASCII text so they can be transmitted via e-mail to another computer or in a newsgroup post. This method can be used when standard ASCII characters are needed for transmission, as they are on the Internet. BinHex is used most frequently by Mac users. *See also* MIME. **2.** An Apple Macintosh program for converting binary data files into ASCII text and vice versa using the BinHex code. *Compare* uudecode[1], uuencode[1].

BinHex[2] *vb.* To convert a binary file into printable 7-bit ASCII text or to convert the resulting ASCII text file back to binary format using the BinHex program. *Compare* uudecode[2], uuencode[2].

BIOS *n.* Acronym for **b**asic **i**nput/**o**utput **s**ystem. On PC-compatible computers, the set of essential software routines that test hardware at startup, start the operating system, and support the transfer of data among hardware devices. The BIOS is stored in ROM so that it can be executed when the computer is turned on. Although critical to performance, the BIOS is usually invisible to computer users. *See also* CMOS setup, ROM BIOS.

BIS *n. See* business information system.

BISYNC *n.* Short for **bi**nary **sync**hronous communications protocol. A communications standard developed by IBM. BISYNC transmissions are encoded in either ASCII or EBCDIC. Messages can be of any length and are sent in units called frames, optionally preceded by a message header. BISYNC uses synchronous transmission, in which message elements are separated by a specific time interval. *Also called* BSC.

bit *n.* Short for **bi**nary digi**t**. The smallest unit of information handled by a computer. One bit expresses a 1 or a 0 in a binary numeral, or a true or false logical condition, and is represented physically by an element such as a high or low voltage at one point in a circuit or a small spot on a disk magnetized one way or the other. A single bit conveys little information a human would consider meaningful. A group of 8 bits, however, makes up a byte, which can be used to represent many types of information, such as a letter of the alphabet, a decimal digit, or other character. *See also* ASCII, binary, byte.

bit density *n.* A measure of the amount of information per unit of linear distance or surface area in a storage medium or per unit of time in a communications pipeline.

bit depth *n.* The number of bits per pixel allocated for storing indexed color information in a graphics file.

bit image *n.* A sequential collection of bits that represents in memory an image to be displayed on the screen, particularly in systems having a graphical user interface. Each bit in a bit image corresponds to one pixel (dot) on the screen. In a black-and-white display each pixel is either white or black, so it can be represented by a single bit. The "pattern" of 0s and 1s in the bit image then determines the pattern of white and black dots forming an image on the screen. *See also* bit map, pixel image.

bit map or **bitmap** *n.* A data structure in memory that represents information in the form of a collection of individual bits. A bit map is used to represent a bit image. *See also* bit image, pixel image.

#
A
B
C
D
E
F
G
H
I
J
K
L
M
N
O
P
Q
R
S
T
U
V
W
X
Y
Z

bitmapped font *n.* A set of characters in a particular size and style in which each character is described as a unique bit map (pattern of dots). *See also* downloadable font, outline font, TrueType. *Compare* PostScript font, vector font.

bitmapped graphics *n.* Computer graphics represented as arrays of bits in memory that represent the attributes of the individual pixels in an image (one bit per pixel in a black-and-white display, multiple bits per pixel in a color or gray-scale display). Bitmapped graphics are typical of paint programs, which treat images as collections of dots rather than as shapes. *See also* bit image, bit map, pixel image. *Compare* object-oriented graphics.

BITNET *n.* Acronym for **B**ecause **I**t's **T**ime **Net**work. A wide area network operated by the Corporation for Research and Educational Networking in Washington, D.C., used to provide e-mail and file transfer services between mainframe computers at educational and research institutions in North America, Europe, and Japan. BITNET uses the IBM NJE protocol rather than TCP/IP, but it can exchange e-mail with the Internet. The LISTSERV software for maintaining mailing lists originated on BITNET.

bit. newsgroups *n.* A hierarchy of Internet newsgroups that mirror the content of some BITNET mailing lists. *See also* BITNET.

bit-oriented protocol *n.* A communications protocol in which data is transmitted as a steady stream of bits rather than as a stream of characters. Because the bits transmitted have no inherent meaning in terms of a particular character set (such as ASCII), a bit-oriented protocol uses special sequences of bits rather than reserved characters for control purposes.

bit plane *n.* One of a set of bit maps that collectively make up a color image. Each bit plane contains the values for one bit of the set of bits that describe a pixel. One bit plane allows two colors (usually black and white) to be represented; two bit planes, four colors; three bit planes, eight colors; and so on. These sections of memory are treated as if they were separate layers that stack one upon another to form the complete image. By contrast, in a chunky pixel image, the bits describing a given pixel are stored contiguously within the same byte. *See also* layering. *Compare* color bits.

bit rate *n.* The speed at which binary digits are transmitted. *See also* transfer rate.

bits per inch *n.* A measure of data storage capacity; the number of bits that fit into an inch of space on a disk or a tape. On a disk, bits per inch are measured based on inches of circumference of a given track. *Acronym:* BPI.

bits per second *n.* *See* bps.

bit stream *n.* **1.** A series of binary digits representing a flow of information transferred through a given medium. **2.** In synchronous communications, a continuous flow of data in which characters in the stream are separated from one another by the receiving station rather than by markers, such as start and stop bits, inserted into the data.

bit transfer rate *n.* *See* transfer rate.

biz. newsgroups *n.* Usenet newsgroups that are part of the biz. hierarchy, use the .biz prefix in their names, and are devoted to discussions related to business. Unlike most other newsgroup hierarchies, biz. newsgroups permit users to post advertisements and other marketing material. *See also* newsgroup.

black box *n.* A unit of hardware or software whose internal structure is unknown but whose function is documented. The internal mechanics of the function do not matter to a designer who uses a black box to obtain that function. For example, many people use memory chips and design them into computers, but generally only memory chip designers need to understand their internal operation.

blank[1] *n.* The character entered by pressing the Spacebar. *See also* space character.

blank[2] *vb.* To not show or not display an image on part or all of the screen.

blanking *n.* The brief suppression of a display signal as the electron beam in a raster-scan video monitor is moved into position either horizontally or vertically to display a new line. The beam must be turned off to avoid overwriting the line just displayed or marking the screen with the retrace path. *See also* retrace.

blind carbon copy *n. See* bcc.

blind courtesy copy *n. See* bcc.

blind search *n.* A search for data in memory or on a storage device with no foreknowledge of the data's order or location. *See also* linear search. *Compare* binary search, indexed search.

blink *vb.* To flash on and off. Cursors, insertion points, menu choices, warning messages, and other displays on a computer screen that are intended to catch the eye are often made to blink. The rate of blinking in a graphical user interface can sometimes be controlled by the user.

bloatware *n.* Software whose files occupy an extremely large amount of storage space on a user's hard disk, especially in comparison with previous versions of the same product.

block[1] *n.* **1.** A section of random access memory temporarily assigned (allocated) to a program by the operating system. **2.** A unit of transmitted information consisting of identification codes, data, and error-checking codes. **3.** A collection of consecutive bytes of data that are read from or written to a device (such as a disk) as a group. **4.** A rectangular grid of pixels that are handled as a unit. **5.** A segment of text that can be selected and acted upon as a whole in an application.

block[2] *vb.* **1.** To distribute a file over fixed-size blocks in storage. **2.** To prevent a signal from being transmitted. **3.** To select a segment of text, by using a mouse, menu selection, or cursor key, to be acted upon in some way—for example, to format or delete the segment.

block cipher *n.* A private key encryption method that encrypts data in blocks of a fixed size (usually 64 bits). The encrypted data block contains the same number of bits as the original. *See also* encryption, private key.

block cursor *n.* An on-screen cursor that has the same width and height in pixels as a text-mode character cell. A block cursor is used in text-based applications, especially as the mouse pointer when a mouse is installed in the system. *See also* character cell, cursor (definition 1), mouse pointer.

block device *n.* A device, such as a disk drive, that moves information in blocks—groups of bytes—rather than one character (byte) at a time. *Compare* character device.

block move *n.* Movement of a number of items of data together to a different location, as in reorganizing documents with a word processor or moving the contents of cell ranges in a spreadsheet. Most CPUs have instructions that easily support block moves.

block size *n.* The declared size of a block of data transferred internally within a computer, via FTP, or by modem. The size is usually chosen to make the most efficient use of all the hardware devices involved. *See also* FTP[1] (definition 1).

block transfer *n.* The movement of data in discrete blocks (groups of bytes).

blow up *vb.* To terminate abnormally, as when a program crosses some computational or storage boundary and cannot handle the situation on the other side, as in, "I tried to draw outside the window, and the graphics routines blew up." *See also* abort.

.bmp *n.* The file extension that identifies raster graphics stored in bit map file format. *See also* bit map.

BNC connector *n.* A connector for coaxial cables that locks when one connector is inserted into another and rotated 90 degrees. *See also* coaxial cable.

board *n.* An electronic module consisting of chips and other electronic components mounted on a flat, rigid substrate on which conductive paths are laid between the components. A personal computer contains a main board, called the motherboard, which usually has the microprocessor on it, and slots into which other, smaller boards, called cards or adapters, can be plugged to expand the functionality of the main system by, for example, connecting to monitors, disk drives, or a network. *See also* adapter, card, motherboard.

board computer *n.* *See* single-board.

board level *n.* A level of focus in troubleshooting and repair that involves tracking down a problem in a computer to a circuit board and replacing the board. This is in contrast to the component level, which involves repairing the board itself. *See also* circuit board.

body *n.* In e-mail and Internet newsgroups, the content of a message. The body of a message follows the header, which contains information about the sender, origin, and destination of the message. *See also* mail header.

BOF *n.* Acronym for **b**irds **o**f a **f**eather. Meetings of special interest groups at trade shows, conferences, and conventions. BOF sessions provide an opportunity for people working on the same technology at different companies or research institutions to meet and exchange their experiences.

boilerplate *n.* Recyclable text; a piece of writing or code, such as an organization's mission statement or the graphics code that prints a company's logo, which can be used over and over in many different documents.
boldface *n.* A type style that makes the text to which it is applied appear darker and heavier than the surrounding text. Some applications allow the user to apply a Bold command to selected text; other programs require that special codes be embedded in the text before and after words that are to be printed in boldface. **This sentence appears in boldface.**
bomb[1] *n.* A program planted surreptitiously, with intent to damage or destroy a system in some way—for example, to erase a hard disk or cause it to be unreadable to the operating system. *See also* Trojan horse, virus, worm.
bomb[2] *vb.* To fail abruptly and completely, without giving the user a chance to recover from the problem short of restarting the program or system. *See also* bug (definition 1), crash[2] (definition 1), hang.
bookmark *n.* A marker inserted at a specific point in a document to which the user may wish to return for later reference.
Boolean *adj.* Of, pertaining to, or characteristic of logical (true, false) values. Many programming languages directly support a Boolean data type, with predefined values for true and false; others use integer data types to implement Boolean values, usually (although not always) with 0 equaling false and "not 0" equaling true. *See also* Boolean operator, data type.
Boolean operator *n.* An operator designed to work with Boolean values. The four most common Boolean operators are AND (logical conjunction), OR (logical inclusion), XOR (exclusive OR), and NOT (logical negation). Boolean operators are often used as qualifiers in database searches—for example, *find all records where DEPARTMENT = "marketing" OR DEPARTMENT = "sales" AND SKILL = "word processing"*. *Also called* logical operator. *See also* AND, exclusive OR, NOT, OR.
Boolean search *n.* A database search that uses Boolean operators. *See also* Boolean operator.
boot[1] *n.* The process of starting or resetting a computer. When first turned on or reset, the computer executes the software that loads and starts the computer's more complicated operating system and prepares it for use. Thus, the computer can be said to pull itself up by its own bootstraps. *Also called* bootstrap. *See also* BIOS, bootstrap loader, cold boot, warm boot.
boot[2] *vb.* **1.** To start or reset a computer by turning the power on, by pressing a reset button on the computer case, or by issuing a software command to restart. *Also called* bootstrap, boot up. *See also* reboot. **2.** To execute the bootstrap loader program. *Also called* bootstrap. *See also* bootstrap loader.
bootable *adj.* Containing the system files necessary for booting a PC and running it. *See also* boot[2].
bootable disk *n.* *See* boot disk.
boot disk *n.* A floppy disk that can boot, or start, the PC and that contains key system files from a PC-compatible operating system. A boot disk must be inserted in the primary floppy disk drive (usually drive A:) and is used

when there is some problem with starting the PC from the hard disk, from which the computer generally boots. *Also called* bootable disk. *See also* A:, boot², boot drive, hard disk.

boot drive *n.* In a PC-compatible computer, the disk drive that the BIOS uses to automatically load the operating system when the computer is turned on. Generally, the default boot drive is the primary floppy disk drive A: in PC-compatible computers with MS-DOS, Windows 3.*x*, or Windows 95 operating systems. If a floppy disk is not found in that drive, the BIOS will check the primary hard disk next, which is drive C:. The BIOS for these operating systems can be reconfigured to search drive C: first by using the BIOS setup program. *See also* A:, BIOS, disk drive, hard disk.

boot failure *n.* The inability of a computer to locate or activate the operating system and thus boot, or start, the computer. *See also* boot².

boot loader *n.* *See* bootstrap loader.

boot partition *n.* The partition on a hard disk that contains the operating system and support files that the system loads into memory when the computer is turned on or restarted.

boot sector *n.* The portion of a disk reserved for the bootstrap loader (the self-starting portion) of an operating system. The boot sector typically contains a short machine language program that loads the operating system.

bootstrap¹ *n.* *See* boot¹.

bootstrap² *vb.* *See* boot².

bootstrap loader *n.* A program that is automatically run when a computer is switched on (booted). After first performing a few basic hardware tests, the bootstrap loader loads and passes control to a larger loader program, which typically then loads the operating system. The bootstrap loader generally resides in the computer's read-only memory (ROM).

boot up *vb.* *See* boot².

border *n.* **1.** In programs and working environments that feature on-screen windows, the edge surrounding the user's workspace. Window borders provide a visible frame around a document or graphic. Depending on the program, they can also represent an area in which the cursor or a mouse pointer takes on special characteristics. For example, clicking the mouse on a window border can enable the user to resize the window or split the window in two. **2.** In printing, a decorative line or pattern along one or more edges of a page or illustration.

boss screen *n.* A false display screen usually featuring business-related material that can be substituted for a game display when the boss walks by. Boss screens were popular with MS-DOS games, where it was difficult to switch to another application quickly. However, games designed for the Mac or Windows 95 generally don't need them because switching is faster and easier.

bot *n.* **1.** Short for ro**bot**. A displayed representation of a person or other entity whose actions are based on programming. **2.** A program that performs some task on a network, especially a repetitive or time-consuming task. **3.** On the Internet, a program that performs a repetitive or time-consuming task, such as searching Web sites and newsgroups for information and indexing it in a record-keeping system, automatically posting articles to multiple newsgroups, or keeping IRC channels open. *Also called* Internet robot. *See also* IRC, newsgroup, spam[1], spambot, spider.

bounce *vb.* To return to the sender, used in reference to undeliverable e-mail.

bound *adj.* Limited in performance or speed; for example, an input/output-bound system is limited by the speed of its input and output devices (keyboard, disk drives, and so on), even though the processor or program is capable of performing at a higher rate.

bounding box *n. See* graphic limits.

bozo *n.* A slang term used frequently on the Internet, particularly in newsgroups, for a foolish or eccentric person.

bozo filter *n.* On the Internet, slang for a feature in some e-mail clients and newsgroup readers or a separate utility that allows the user to block, or filter out, incoming e-mail messages or newsgroup articles from specified individuals. Generally these individuals are ones that the user does not want to hear from, such as bozos. *Also called* kill file. *See also* bozo.

BPI *n. See* bits per inch, bytes per inch.

bps *n.* Short for **b**its **p**er **s**econd. The speed at which a device such as a modem can transfer data. Speed in bps is not the same as baud rate. *See also* baud, baud rate.

braindamaged *adj.* Performing in an erratic or destructive manner. A braindamaged application or utility program may have a mysterious and unintuitive user interface, fail to respond predictably to commands, fail to release unused memory, fail to close open files, or use "reserved" elements of the operating system, resulting in a fatal error. Braindamaged programs are also often responsible for causing problems across local area networks. *Compare* kludge.

brain dump *n.* A large, unorganized mass of information, presented in response to a query via e-mail or a newsgroup article, that is difficult to digest or interpret.

branch *n.* **1.** A node intermediate between the root and the leaves in some types of logical tree structure, such as the directory tree in Windows or a tape distribution organization. **2.** Any connection between two items such as nodes in a network.

BRB Acronym for **b**e **r**ight **b**ack. An expression used commonly on live chat services by participants signaling their temporary departure from the group. *See also* chat[1] (definition 1).

break *n.* **1.** Interruption of a program caused by the user pressing the Break key or its equivalent. **2.** Interruption of a communications transmission that occurs when the receiving station interrupts and takes over control of the line or when the transmitting station prematurely halts transmission.

#
A
B
C
D
E
F
G
H
I
J
K
L
M
N
O
P
Q
R
S
T
U
V
W
X
Y
Z

Break key *n.* A key or combination of keys used to tell a computer to halt, or break out of, whatever it is doing. On IBM PCs and compatibles under DOS, pressing the Pause/Break or Scroll Lock/Break key while holding down the Ctrl key issues the break command (just as pressing Ctrl-C does). On Macintosh computers, the key combination that sends a break code is Command-period.

breakout box *n.* A small hardware device that can be attached between two devices normally connected by a cable (such as a computer and a modem) to display and, if necessary, change the activity through individual wires of the cable.

BRI *n.* Acronym for **B**asic **R**ate **I**nterface. An ISDN service that uses two B (64 Kbps) channels and one D (64 Kbps) channel to transmit voice, video, and data signals. *See also* ISDN, PRI.

bridge *n.* **1.** A device that connects networks using the same communications protocols so that information can be passed from one to the other. *Compare* gateway. **2.** A device that connects two local area networks, whether or not they use the same protocols. A bridge operates at the ISO/OSI data-link layer. *See also* data-link layer. *Compare* router.

bridge router *n.* A device that supports the functions of both a bridge and router. A bridge router links two segments of a local or wide area network, passing packets of data between the segments as necessary, and uses Level 2 addresses for routing. *Also called* Brouter. *See also* bridge (definition 2), router.

bridgeware *n.* Hardware or software designed to convert application programs or data files to a form that can be used by a different computer.

brightness *n.* The perceived quality of radiance or luminosity of a visible object. Although its subjective value cannot be measured with physical instruments (a burning candle in the dark appears brighter than the same candle under incandescent lights), brightness can be measured as luminance (radiant energy). The brightness component of a color is different from its color (the hue) and from the intensity of its color (the saturation). *See also* color model, HSB.

broadband *adj.* Of or relating to communications systems in which the medium of transmission (such as a wire or fiber-optic cable) carries multiple messages at a time, each message modulated on its own carrier frequency by means of modems. Broadband communication is found in wide area networks. *Compare* baseband.

broadband modem *n.* A modem for use on a broadband network. Broadband technology allows several networks to coexist on a single cable. Traffic from one network does not interfere with traffic from another, since the conversations are carried on different frequencies, rather like the commercial radio system. *See also* broadband network.

broadband network *n.* A local area network on which transmissions travel as radio-frequency signals over separate inbound and outbound channels. Stations on a broadband network are connected by coaxial or fiber-optic cable, which can carry data, voice, and video simultaneously over multiple transmission channels that are distinguished by frequency. A broadband network is capable of high-speed operation (20 megabits or more), but it is more expensive than a baseband network and can be difficult to install. *Also called* wideband transmission. *Compare* baseband network.

broadcast[1] *adj.* Sent to more than one recipient. In communications and on networks, a broadcast message is one distributed to all stations. *See also* e-mail[1] (definition 1).

broadcast[2] *n.* As in radio or television, a transmission sent to more than one recipient.

broadcast storm *n.* A network broadcast that causes multiple hosts to respond simultaneously, overloading the network. A broadcast storm may occur when old TCP/IP routers are mixed with routers that support a new protocol. *Also called* network meltdown. *See also* communications protocol, router, TCP/IP.

Brouter *See* bridge router.

browse *vb.* To scan a database, a list of files, or the Internet, either for a particular item or for general interest. Generally, browsing implies observing, rather than changing, information. In unauthorized computer hacking, browsing is a (presumably) nondestructive means of finding out about an unknown computer after illegally gaining entry.

browser *n. See* Web browser.

BRS *n. See* big red switch.

BSC *n. See* BISYNC.

BTW or **btw** Acronym for **b**y **t**he **w**ay. An expression often used to preface remarks in e-mail and Internet newsgroup articles.

bubble-jet printer *n.* A form of nonimpact printer that uses a mechanism similar to that used by an ink-jet printer to shoot ink from nozzles to form characters on paper. A bubble-jet printer uses special heating elements to prepare the ink. *See also* ink-jet printer, nonimpact printer. *Compare* laser printer.

bubble memory *n.* Memory formed by a series of persistent magnetic "bubbles" in a thin film substrate. In contrast to ROM, information can be written to bubble memory. In contrast to RAM, data written to bubble memory remains there until it is changed, even when the computer is turned off. For this reason, bubble memory has had some application in environments in which a computer system must be able to recover with minimal data loss in the event of a power failure. Bubble memory has been largely superseded by flash memory, which is less expensive and easier to produce. *See also* flash memory, nonvolatile memory.

bubble sort *n.* A sorting algorithm that starts at the end of a list with *n* elements and moves all the way through, testing the value of each adjacent pair of items and swapping them if they aren't in the right order. The process is then repeated until the list is completely sorted, with the largest value at the end of the list. A bubble sort is so named because the "lightest" item in a list (the smallest) will figuratively "bubble up" to the top of the list first; then the next-lightest item bubbles up to its position, and so on. *Also called* exchange sort. *See also* algorithm, sort. *Compare* insertion sort, merge sort, quicksort.

bubble storage *n. See* bubble memory.

buffer¹ *n.* A region of memory reserved for use as an intermediate repository in which data is temporarily held while waiting to be transferred between two locations, as between an application's data area and an input/output device. A device or its adapter may in turn use a buffer to store data awaiting transfer to the computer or processing by the device.

buffer² *vb.* To use a region of memory to hold data that is waiting to be transferred, especially to or from input/output devices such as disk drives and serial ports.

bug *n.* **1.** An error in coding or logic that causes a program to malfunction or to produce incorrect results. Minor bugs, such as a cursor that does not behave as expected, can be inconvenient or frustrating but do not damage information. More severe bugs can require the user to restart the program or the computer, losing unsaved work. Worse yet are bugs that damage saved data without alerting the user. Because of the potential risk to important data, commercial application programs are tested and debugged as completely as possible before release. *See also* beta test, bomb², crash² (definition 1), debug, debugger, hang. **2.** A recurring physical problem that prevents a system or set of components from working together properly.

buggy *adj.* Full of flaws, or bugs, in reference to software. *See also* bug (definition 1).

built-in check *n. See* hardware check, power-on self test.

built-in font *n. See* internal font.

bulk eraser *n.* A device for eliminating all information from a storage medium, such as a floppy disk or a tape, by generating a strong magnetic field that scrambles the alignment of the ferrous materials in the media that encode stored data.

bullet *n.* A typographical symbol, such as a filled or empty circle, diamond, box, or asterisk, used to set off a small block of text or each item in a list. *See also* dingbat.

bulletin board system *n. See* BBS (definition 1).

bulletproof *adj.* Capable of overcoming hardware problems that, in another system, could lead to interruption of the task in progress.

bundled software *n.* **1.** Programs sold with a computer as part of a combined hardware/software package. **2.** Smaller programs sold with larger programs to increase the latter's functionality or attractiveness.

burn in *vb.* To make a permanent change in the phosphor coating on the inside of a monitor screen by leaving the monitor on and keeping a bright, unchanging image on the screen for extended periods. Such an image will remain visible after the monitor is turned off. Burning in was a danger with older PC monitors; it is no longer a concern with most new PC monitors. *Also called* ghosting.

burst[1] *n.* Transfer of a block of data all at one time without a break. Certain microprocessors and certain buses have features that support various types of burst transfers. *See also* burst speed (definition 1).

burst[2] *vb.* To break fanfold continuous-feed paper apart at its perforations, resulting in a stack of separate sheets.

burst mode *n.* A method of data transfer in which information is collected and sent as a unit in one high-speed transmission. In burst mode, an input/output device takes control of a multiplexer channel for the time required to send its data. In effect, the multiplexer, which normally merges input from several sources into a single data stream, temporarily becomes a channel dedicated to the needs of one device. Burst mode is used both in communications and between devices in a computer system. *See also* burst[1].

burst rate *n.* *See* burst speed (definition 1).

burst speed *n.* **1.** The fastest speed at which a device can operate without interruption. For example, various communications devices (as on networks) can send data in bursts, and the speed of such equipment is sometimes measured as the burst speed (the speed of data transfer while the burst is being executed). *Also called* burst rate. **2.** The number of characters per second that a printer can print on one line without a carriage return or linefeed. Burst speed does not include the time taken to advance paper or to move the print head. Almost always, the speed claimed by the manufacturer is the burst speed. By contrast, throughput, the number of characters per second when one or more entire pages of text are being printed, is a more practical measurement of printer speed in real-life situations.

bursty *adj.* Transmitting data in spurts, or bursts, rather than in a continuous stream.

bus *n.* A set of hardware lines (conductors) used for data transfer among the components of a computer system. A bus is essentially a shared highway that connects different parts of the system—including the microprocessor, disk-drive controller, memory, and input/output ports—and enables them to transfer information. The bus consists of specialized groups of lines that carry different types of information, such as data, memory addresses where data items are to be found, and control signals. Buses are characterized by the number of bits they can transfer at a single time, equivalent to the number of wires within the bus. A computer with a 32-bit address bus and a 16-bit data bus, for example, can transfer 16 bits of data at a time from any of 2^{32} memory locations. Most microcomputers contain one or more expansion slots into which additional boards can be plugged to connect them to the bus.

bus extender *n.* A device that expands the capacity of a bus. *See also* bus.

business graphics *n.* *See* presentation graphics.

business information system *n.* A combination of computers, printers, communications equipment, and other devices designed to handle data. A

A B C D E F G H I J K L M N O P Q R S T U V W X Y Z

completely automated business information system receives, processes, and stores data; transfers information as needed; and produces reports or printouts on demand. *Acronym:* BIS. *See also* management information system.

business software *n.* Any computer application designed primarily for use in business, as opposed to scientific use or entertainment. In addition to the well-known areas of word processing, spreadsheets, databases, and communications, business software for microcomputers also encompasses such applications as accounting, payroll, financial planning, project management, decision and support systems, personnel record maintenance, and office management.

bus mouse *n.* A mouse that attaches to the computer's bus through a special card or port rather than through a serial port. *See also* mouse. *Compare* serial mouse.

bus network *n.* A topology (configuration) for a local area network in which all nodes are connected to a main communications line (bus). On a bus network, each node monitors activity on the line. Messages are detected by all nodes but are accepted only by the node(s) to which they are addressed. A malfunctioning node ceases to communicate but does not disrupt operation (as it might on a ring network). To avoid conflicts that occur when two or more nodes try to use the line at the same time, bus networks commonly rely on collision detection or token passing to regulate traffic. *See also* collision detection, contention, token bus network, token passing. *Compare* ring network, star network.

bus system *n.* The interface circuitry that controls the operations of a bus and connects it with the rest of the computer system. *See also* bus.

bus topology *n. See* bus network.

button *n.* **1.** A graphic element in a dialog box that, when activated, performs a specified function. The user activates a button by clicking on it with a mouse or, if the button has the focus, by pressing the Return or Enter key. **2.** On a mouse, a movable piece that is pressed to activate some function. Older mouse models have only one button; newer models typically have two or more.

button bomb *n.* A button on Web pages with the image of a bomb.

button help *n.* Help information displayed via the selection of buttons or icons. Applications such as the World Wide Web, multimedia kiosks, and computer-aided instruction often use button help icons to ease system navigation.

bypass *n.* In telecommunications, the use of communication pathways other than the local telephone company, such as satellites and microwave systems.

byte *n.* Abbreviated B. Short for **b**inar**y te**rm. A unit of data, today almost always consisting of 8 bits. A byte can represent a single character, such as a letter, a digit, or a punctuation mark. Because a byte represents only a small amount of information, amounts of computer memory and storage are usually given in kilobytes, megabytes, or gigabytes. *See also* bit, gigabyte, kilobyte, megabyte. *Compare* word.

byte-oriented protocol *n.* A communications protocol in which data is transmitted as a string of characters in a particular character set, such as ASCII, rather than as a stream of bits as in a bit-oriented protocol. To express control information, a byte-oriented protocol relies on control characters, most of which are defined by the coding scheme used. The asynchronous communications protocols commonly used with modems and IBM's BISYNC protocol are byte-oriented protocols. *Compare* bit-oriented protocol.

bytes per inch *n.* The number of bytes that fit into an inch of length on a disk track or a tape. *Acronym:* BPI.

C

C *n.* A structured programming language developed by Dennis Ritchie at Bell Laboratories in 1972. Its close association with the UNIX operating system, its enormous popularity, and its standardization by ANSI have made C perhaps the closest thing to a standard programming language in the microcomputer/workstation marketplace. *See also* C++, compiled language, structured programming.

C++ *n.* An object-oriented version of the C programming language, developed by Bjarne Stroustrup in the early 1980s at Bell Laboratories and adopted by a number of vendors, including Apple Computer and Sun Microsystems, Inc. *See also* C, object-oriented programming.

CA *n.* *See* certificate authority.

.cab *n.* A file extension for cabinet files, which are multiple files compressed into one, extractable with the extract.exe utility. Such files are frequently found on Microsoft software distribution disks.

cabinet *n.* The box in which the main components of a computer (CPU, hard drive, floppy and CD-ROM drives, and expansion slots for peripheral devices such as monitors) are located. *See also* central processing unit, expansion slot.

cable *n.* A collection of wires shielded within a protective tube, used to connect peripheral devices to a computer. A mouse, a keyboard, and a printer might all be connected to a computer with cables.

cable connector *n.* The connector on either end of a cable. *See also* DB connector, DIN connector, RS-232-C standard, RS-422/423/449.

cable matcher *n.* A device that allows the use of a cable whose wire connections differ slightly from those required by the device(s) to which it is attached.

cable modem *n.* A modem that sends and receives data through a coaxial cable television network instead of through telephone lines as a conventional modem does. Cable modems, which have speeds of 500 Kbps, can generally transmit data faster than current conventional modems. *See also* coaxial cable, modem.

cabling diagram *n.* A plan that shows the path of cables that attach computer system components or peripherals. Cabling diagrams are important for explaining the connection of disk drives to a disk controller.

cache *n.* A special memory subsystem in which frequently used data values are duplicated for quick access. A memory cache stores the contents of frequently accessed RAM locations and the addresses where these data items are stored. When the processor references an address in memory, the cache checks to see whether it holds that address. If it does hold the address, the data is returned to the processor; if it does not, a regular memory access occurs. A cache is useful when RAM accesses are slow compared with the microprocessor speed, because cache memory is always faster than main RAM memory. *See also* wait state.

cache card *n.* An expansion card that increases a system's cache memory. *See also* cache, expansion board.

cache memory *n.* *See* cache.

CAD *n.* Acronym for **c**omputer-**a**ided **d**esign. A system of programs and workstations used in designing engineering, architectural, and scientific models ranging from simple tools to buildings, aircraft, and molecules. Various CAD applications create objects in two or three dimensions, presenting the results as wire-frame "skeletons," as more substantial models with shaded surfaces, or as solid objects. Some programs can also rotate or resize models, show interior views, and generate lists of materials required for construction. CAD programs rely on mathematics, often requiring the computing power of a high-performance workstation.

caddy *n.* A plastic carrier that holds a CD-ROM and is inserted into a CD-ROM drive. The CD-ROM drives of some older-model personal computers require the use of a caddy, although most current CD-ROM drives do not.

CAI *n.* Acronym for **c**omputer-**a**ided (or **c**omputer-**a**ssisted) **i**nstruction. An educational program designed to serve as a teaching tool. CAI programs typically use tutorials, drills, and question-and-answer sessions to present a topic and to test the student's comprehension. CAI programs are excellent aids for presenting factual material and for allowing students to pace their learning speed. *Compare* CBT, CMI.

calendar program *n.* An application in the form of an electronic calendar, commonly used for highlighting dates and scheduling appointments. A calendar/scheduler program might show blocks of dates or, like an appointment book, single days divided into blocks of time, with room for notes. Some programs allow the user to set an alarm as a reminder of important events. Other programs can coordinate the calendars of different people on the same network.

callback *n.* A user authentication scheme used by computers running dial-in services. A user dials in to a computer and types a logon ID and password. The computer breaks the connection and automatically calls the user back at a preauthorized number. This security measure usually prevents unauthorized access to an account even if an individual's logon ID and password have been stolen. *See also* authentication.

callback modem *n.* A modem that, instead of answering an incoming call, requires the caller to enter a touch-tone code and hang up so that the modem can return the call. The modem checks the caller's code against a list of

#
A
B
C
D
E
F
G
H
I
J
K
L
M
N
O
P
Q
R
S
T
U
V
W
X
Y
Z

authorized phone numbers. If it matches, the modem dials the number and then opens a connection for the original caller. Callback modems can help to protect data from unauthorized intruders.

cancel *n.* A control character used in communication with printers and other computers, commonly designated as CAN. It usually means that the line of text being sent should be canceled. In ASCII, this is represented internally as character code 24.

cancelbot *n.* Short for **cancel** ro**bot**. A program that identifies articles in newsgroups based on a set of criteria and cancels the distribution of those articles. Although the criteria for cancellation are set by the owner of the cancelbot, most cancelbots exist to identify and eliminate spam messages posted to multiple newsgroups. *See also* spam[1].

cancel message *n.* A message sent to Usenet news servers indicating that a certain article is to be canceled or deleted from the server. *See also* article, news server, Usenet.

canned software *n.* Off-the-shelf software, such as word processors and spreadsheet programs.

capacity *n.* The amount of information a computer or an attached device can process or store. *See also* computer.

caps *n.* Short for **cap**ital letter**s**. *Compare* lowercase.

Caps Lock key *n.* A toggle key that, when on, shifts the alphabetic characters on the keyboard to uppercase. The Caps Lock key does not affect numbers, punctuation marks, or other symbols.

capture *vb.* In communications, to transfer received data into a file for archiving or later analysis.

capture board *n. See* video capture card.

capture card *n. See* video capture card.

carbon copy *n. See* cc.

card *n.* A printed circuit board or adapter that can be plugged into a computer to provide added functionality or new capability. These cards provide specialized services, such as mouse support and modem capabilities, that are not built into the computer. *See also* adapter, board, printed circuit board.

card cage *n.* An enclosure area for holding printed circuit boards (cards). Most computers have an area with protective metal and mounting brackets where cards are installed.

caret *n.* The small, upward-pointing symbol (^) typically found over the 6 key on the top row of a microcomputer keyboard. The caret is used to represent the Control key on the keyboard. For example, ^Z means "hold the Control key down and press the Z key."

careware *n.* Software developed by an individual or a small group and distributed freely, with the proviso that users make a donation to a charity if they continue to use the software after trying it out. The charity is usually one designated by the software creator.

carpal tunnel syndrome *n.* A form of repetitive strain injury to the wrist and hand. Making the same small motions over and over can cause swelling and scarring of the soft tissue of the wrist, which then compresses the main nerve leading to the hand. Symptoms of carpal tunnel syndrome include pain and tingling in the fingers; in advanced cases, sufferers can lose functionality of the hands. Typing at a computer keyboard without proper wrist support is a common cause of carpal tunnel syndrome. *Acronym:* CTS. *See also* repetitive strain injury, wrist support.

carriage return *n.* A control character that tells a computer or printer to return to the beginning of the current line. A carriage return is similar to the return on a typewriter but does not automatically advance to the beginning of a new line. In the ASCII character set, the carriage-return character has the decimal value 13 (hexadecimal 0D).

carrier *n.* **1.** In communications, a specified frequency that can be modulated to convey information. **2.** A company that provides telephone and other communications services to consumers.

Carrier Detect *n. See* CD (definition 1).

carrier frequency *n.* A radio-frequency signal, such as those used with modems and on networks, used to transmit information. A carrier frequency is a signal that vibrates at a fixed number of cycles per second, or hertz (Hz), and is modulated in either frequency or amplitude to enable it to carry intelligible information.

carrier system *n.* A communications method that uses different carrier frequencies to transfer information along multiple channels of a single path. Transmission involves modulating the signal on each frequency at the originating station and demodulating the signal at the receiving station.

cartridge *n.* Any of various container devices that usually consist of some form of plastic housing. *See also* disk cartridge, ink cartridge, memory cartridge, ROM cartridge, tape cartridge, toner cartridge.

cartridge font *n.* A font contained in a plug-in cartridge, used to add fonts to laser, ink-jet, or high-end dot-matrix printers. Cartridge fonts are distinguished both from internal fonts, which are contained in ROM in the printer and are always available, and from downloadable fonts, which reside on disk and can be sent to the printer as needed. *See also* font cartridge. *Compare* internal font.

cascade *n.* **1.** Additional elements displayed by a menu item or list box from which the user can choose in order to interact with other screen elements. **2.** In newsgroup articles, the accumulation of quotation marks (often angle brackets) added by newsgroup readers each time an article is replied to. Most newsgroup readers copy the original article in the body of a reply; after several replies, this material will have several quotation marks. *See also* article, newsgroup, newsreader.

cascading menu *n.* A hierarchical graphical menu system in which a side menu of subcategories is displayed when the pointer is placed on the main category.

Cascading Style Sheet mechanism *n. See* cascading style sheets.
cascading style sheets *n.* An HTML specification that allows authors of HTML documents and users to attach style sheets to HTML documents. The style sheets include typographical information on how the page should appear, such as the text font. This specification also directs the way in which the style sheets of the HTML document and the user's style will blend. *Also called* Cascading Style Sheet mechanism, CSS, CSS1. *See also* HTML, style sheet (definition 2).
cascading windows *n.* A sequence of successive, overlapping windows in a graphical user interface, displayed so that the title bar of each is visible. *Also called* overlaid windows.
case *n.* In text processing, an indication of whether one or more alphabetic characters are capitalized (uppercase) or not (lowercase). A case-sensitive program or routine distinguishes between uppercase and lowercase letters—for example, it treats the word *cat* as distinct from either *Cat* or *CAT*.
case-sensitive search *n.* A search in a database in which capitalization of key words must exactly match the capitalization of words in the database. A case-sensitive search for *north and south* would fail to find a database entry for *North and South*.
case sensitivity *n.* Discrimination between lowercase and uppercase characters. *See also* case.
CAT *n.* **1.** Acronym for **c**omputer-**a**ided **t**esting. A procedure used by engineers for checking or analyzing designs, especially those created with CAD programs. **2.** Acronym for **c**omputer-**a**ssisted **t**eaching. *See* CAI.
catalog *n.* **1.** In a computer, a list containing specific information, such as name, length, type, and location of files or of storage space. **2.** In a database, the data dictionary. *See also* data dictionary.
cathode-ray tube *n. See* CRT.
CBT *n.* Acronym for **c**omputer-**b**ased **t**raining. The use of computers and specially developed tutorial programs for teaching. CBT uses color, graphics, and other aids to help maintain interest, and it has both simple and sophisticated applications. A software developer, for example, might include a series of CBT lessons for new users with an application; a consultant might use a longer, detailed CBT program as a tool in a management-training seminar.
cc *n.* Acronym for **c**ourtesy **c**opy. A directive to an e-mail program to send a complete copy of a given piece of mail to another individual. The use of cc addressing, as opposed to directly addressing the mail to a person, generally implies that the recipient is not required to take any action; the message is for information only. The cc directive is printed in the mail header and is thus seen by all other recipients. *Also called* carbon copy. *See also* e-mail[1] (definition 1), mail header. *Compare* bcc.
CCITT *n.* Acronym for **C**omité **C**onsultatif **I**nternational **T**élégraphique et **T**éléphonique. Also known as the **I**nternational **T**elegraph and **T**elephone

Consultative Committee. An organization based in Geneva, Switzerland, and established as part of the United Nations International Telecommunications Union (ITU). Its functions have been taken over by the ITU. The ITU recommends use of communications standards that are recognized throughout the world. Protocols established by the ITU are applied to modems, networks, and facsimile transmission. *See also* CCITT V series, CCITT X series.

CCITT V series *n.* A set of recommendations developed by the CCITT and adopted by the ISO and the Telecommunication Standardization Sector of the ITU (ITU-T) for standardizing modem design and operations. Those recommendations most relevant to computer users are briefly described as follows in terms of the modems they standardize:

- V.26: 2,400-bps modems used with four-wire leased lines; full-duplex transmission.
- V.26bis: 1,200/2,400-bps modems used with dial-up lines; full-duplex transmission.
- V.26ter: 2,400-bps modems used with dial-up and two-wire leased lines; DPSK modulation; fallback to 1,200 bps; echo canceling to remove phone-line echo; full-duplex transmission.
- V.27: 4,800-bps modems used with leased lines; manual equalizer; full-duplex transmission.
- V.27bis: 2,400/4,800-bps modems used with leased lines; automatic equalizer; full-duplex transmission.
- V.27ter: 2,400/4,800-bps modems used with dial-up lines; full-duplex transmission.
- V.29: 9,600-bps modems used with point-to-point leased circuits; half-duplex transmission or full-duplex transmission.
- V.32: 9,600-bps modems used with dial-up lines; echo canceling to remove phone-line echo; full-duplex transmission.
- V.32bis: 4,800/7,200/9,600/12,000/14,400-bps modems used with dial-up lines; echo canceling; full-duplex transmission.
- V.33: 12,000/14,400-bps modems used with four-wire leased lines; synchronous; QAM modulation; time-division multiplexing; full-duplex transmission.
- V.34: 28,800-bps modems; full-duplex transmission.
- V.35: Group band modems, which combine the bandwidth of more than one telephone circuit.

CCITT X series *n.* A set of recommendations adopted by the International Telecommunications Union Telecommunication Standardization Sector (ITU-T), formerly the CCITT, and the ISO for standardizing equipment and protocols used in both public-access and private computer networks. Some of the recommendations in the X series include the following:

- X.25 documents the interface required to connect a computer to a packet-switched network such as the Internet.
- The X.200 series of recommendations documents the widely accepted seven-layer set of protocols known as the ISO/OSI (International Organization for Standardization Open Systems Interconnection) model for standardizing computer-to-computer connections.
- X.400 documents the format at the ISO/OSI application layer for e-mail messages over various network transports, including Ethernet, X.25, and TCP/IP. Gateways must be used to translate e-mail messages between the X.400 and Internet formats.
- X.445, also known as the Asynchronous Protocol Specification, governs the transmission of X.400 messages over dial-up telephone lines.
- X.500 documents protocols for client/server systems that maintain and access directories of users and resources in X.400 form.

cd *n.* Acronym for **c**hange **d**irectory. In MS-DOS, UNIX, and FTP client programs, the command that changes the current directory to the directory whose path follows the command. *See also* directory, path (definition 3).

CD *n.* **1.** Acronym for **C**arrier **D**etect. A signal sent from a modem to the attached computer to indicate that the modem is on line. *See also* DCD. **2.** Acronym for **c**ompact **d**isc. *See* CD-I, CD-ROM, compact disc.

CD burner *n. See* CD recorder.

CD-E *n. See* compact disc–erasable.

cdev *n.* Short for **c**ontrol panel **dev**ice. A Macintosh utility that allows basic system settings to be customized. In Macintosh computers running System 6, a cdev is a utility program placed in the System folder. Keyboard and mouse cdevs are preinstalled. Other cdevs are provided with software packages and utilities. In System 7, cdevs are called control panels. *See also* control panel, System folder. *Compare* INIT.

CD-I *n.* Acronym for **c**ompact **d**isc–**i**nteractive. A hardware and software standard for a form of optical disc technology that can combine audio, video, and text on high-capacity compact discs. CD-I includes such features as image display and resolution, animation, special effects, and audio. *See also* CD-ROM.

CDPD *n. See* Cellular Digital Packet Data.

CD Plus *n.* A compact disc encoding format that allows mixing of audio recordings and computer data on the same CD, without the possibility of audio equipment becoming damaged by attempting to play the data sections.

CD-R *n.* Acronym for **c**ompact **d**isc–**r**ecordable. A type of CD-ROM that can be written on a CD recorder and read on a CD-ROM drive. *See also* CD recorder, CD-ROM.

CD-R/E *n. See* compact disc–recordable and erasable.
CD recorder *n.* A device used to write CD-ROMs. Because a disc can be written only once on these machines, they are used most commonly to create CD-ROMs for data archives or to produce CD-ROM masters that can be duplicated for mass distribution. *Also called* CD-R machine, CD-ROM burner. *See also* CD-ROM.
CD-R machine *n. See* CD recorder.
CD-ROM *n.* **1.** Acronym for **c**ompact **d**isc **r**ead-**o**nly **m**emory. A form of storage characterized by high capacity (roughly 650 MB) and the use of laser optics, rather than magnetic means, for reading data. Although CD-ROM drives are strictly read-only, they are similar to CD-R drives (write once, read many) and optical read-write drives. *See also* CD-I, CD-R, worm. **2.** An individual compact disc designed for use with a computer and capable of storing up to 650 MB of data. *See also* compact disc, disc.
CD-ROM burner *n. See* CD recorder.
CD-ROM drive *n.* A disk storage device that uses compact disc technology. *See also* CD-ROM, compact disc.
CD-ROM jukebox *n.* A CD-ROM player that can contain up to 200 CD-ROMs and is connected to a CD-ROM drive in a personal computer or workstation. A user can request data from any of the CD-ROMs in the jukebox, and the device will locate and play the disc that contains the data. If multiple jukeboxes are each connected to separate CD-ROM drives that are daisy-chained together to the computer, more than one CD-ROM can be used at a time. *See also* CD-ROM, CD-ROM drive, daisy chain.
CD-RW *n. See* compact disc–rewritable.
CDV *n.* **1.** Acronym for **c**ompressed **d**igital **v**ideo. The compression of video images for high-speed transmission. **2.** Acronym for **c**ompact **d**isc **v**ideo. A 5-inch videodisc. *See also* videodisc.
CD Video *n. See* CDV (definition 2).
cell *n.* The intersection of a row and a column in a spreadsheet. Each row and each column in a spreadsheet is unique, so each cell can be uniquely identified—for example, cell B17, at the intersection of column B and row 17. Each cell is displayed as a rectangular space that can hold text, a value, or a formula.
cell animation or **cel animation** *n.* A process performed by software that emulates traditional cell animation, which uses transparent celluloid sheets ("cells" or "cels" for short) to overlay active elements in an animation frame onto a static background. Computer cell animation is quite efficient because images can be quickly reproduced and manipulated.
Cellular Digital Packet Data *n.* A wireless standard providing two-way, 19.2-Kbps packet data transmission over existing cellular telephone channels. *Acronym:* CDPD. *See also* packet (definition 2), wireless.
censorship *n.* The action of preventing material that a party considers objectionable from circulating within a system of communication over which that party has some power. The Internet as a whole is not censored, but

some parts of it come under varying degrees of control. A news server, for example, often is set to exclude any or all of the alt. newsgroups, which are unmoderated and tend to be controversial. The moderator of a moderated newsgroup or mailing list will usually delete highly controversial and obscene content or content unrelated to the topic followed by the newsgroup. The owners of online services often take some responsibility for what reaches their users' computer screens. In some countries, censorship of certain political or cultural Web sites is a matter of national policy.

censorware *n.* Software that imposes restrictions on which Internet sites, newsgroups, or files may be accessed by the user.

center *vb.* To align characters around a point located in the middle of a line, page, or other defined area; in effect, to place text an equal distance from each margin or border. *See also* align (definition 1).

central office *n.* In communications, the switching center where interconnections between customers' communications lines are made.

central processing unit *n.* The computational and control unit of a computer. The central processing unit—or microprocessor (a single-chip central processing unit), in the case of a microcomputer—has the ability to fetch, decode, and execute instructions and to transfer information to and from other resources over the computer's main data-transfer path, the bus. By definition, the central processing unit is the chip that functions as the "brain" of a computer. In some instances, however, the term encompasses both the processor and the computer's memory or, even more broadly, the main computer console (as opposed to peripheral equipment). *Acronym:* CPU. *See also* microprocessor.

CERT *n.* Acronym for **C**omputer **E**mergency **R**esponse **T**eam. An organization (http://www.cert.org/) that provides a round-the-clock security consultation service for Internet users and provides advisories whenever new virus programs and other computer security threats are discovered.

certificate authority *n.* An issuer of digital certificates, the cyberspace equivalent of identity cards. A certificate authority may be an external issuing company or an internal company authority that has installed its own server for issuing and verifying certificates. A certificate authority is responsible for providing and assigning the unique strings of numbers that make up the "keys" used in digital certificates for authentication and to encrypt and decrypt sensitive or confidential online information. *Acronym:* CA. *Also called* certification authority. *See also* digital certificate, encryption.

certification *n.* **1.** The act of awarding a document to demonstrate a computer professional's competence in a particular field. Some hardware and software suppliers, such as Microsoft and Novell, offer certification in the use of their products; other organizations, such as the Institute for Certification of Computer Professionals (ICCP), offer more general certification. **2.** The act of awarding a document to demonstrate that a hardware or software product meets some specification, such as being able to work with a certain other product. **3.** The issuance of a notice that a user or site is trusted for the purpose of security and computer authentication. Often certification is used with Web sites.

CGI *n.* **1.** Acronym for **C**ommon **G**ateway **I**nterface. The specification that defines communications between information servers and resources on the server's host computer, such as databases and other programs. For example, when a user submits a form through a Web browser, the HTTP server executes a program (often called a CGI script) and passes the user's input information to that program via CGI. The program then returns information to the server via CGI. Use of CGI can make a Web page much more dynamic and add interactivity for the user. *See also* CGI script, HTTP server (definition 1). **2.** *See* Computer Graphics Interface.

cgi-bin *n.* Short for **C**ommon **G**ateway **I**nterface–**bin**aries. A file directory that holds external applications to be executed by HTTP servers via CGI. *See also* CGI (definition 1).

CGI script *n.* Short for **C**ommon **G**ateway **I**nterface **script**. An external application that is executed by an HTTP server in response to a request by a client, such as a Web browser. Generally, the CGI script is invoked when the user clicks on an element on a Web page, such as a link or an image. Communication between the script and the server is carried out via the CGI specification. Although CGI scripts can be written in many programming languages, the most frequently used language is Perl, a small but robust language that is common on the UNIX platform. CGI scripts are used to provide interactivity on a Web page, including such features as forms that users can fill out, image maps that contain links to other Web pages or resources, and links that users can click on to send e-mail to a specified address. *See also* CGI (definition 1), cgi-bin, image map, Perl. *Compare* ActiveX controls, Java applet.

chain printer *n.* *See* line printer.

chalkware *n.* *See* vaporware.

change file *n.* A file that records transactional changes occurring in a database, providing a basis for updating a master file and establishing an audit trail. *Also called* transaction log.

channel *n.* **1.** A path or link through which information passes between two devices. A channel can be either internal or external to a microcomputer. *See also* bus. **2.** In communications, a medium for transferring information. Depending on its type, a communications channel can carry information (data, sound, and/or video) in either analog or digital form. It can be a physical link, such as the cable connecting two stations in a network, or it can consist of electromagnetic transmission on one or more frequencies within a bandwidth in the electromagnetic spectrum, as in radio and television. *Also called* circuit, line. *See also* analog, band, bandwidth, cable, digital.

#
A
B
C
D
E
F
G
H
I
J
K
L
M
N
O
P
Q
R
S
T
U
V
W
X
Y
Z

channel access *n.* A method used in networked systems to gain access to the data communications channel that links two or more computers. Common methods of channel access are contention and the token ring network. *See also* channel, contention, token ring network.

channel adapter *n.* A device that enables hardware using two different types of communications channels to communicate.

channel capacity *n.* The speed at which a communications channel can transfer information, measured in bits per second or in baud.

channel hop *vb.* To switch repeatedly from one IRC channel to another. *See also* IRC.

channel op *n.* Short for **channel op**erator. A user on an IRC channel who has the privilege of expelling undesirable participants. *See also* IRC.

character *n.* A letter, number, punctuation mark, or other symbol or control code that is represented to a computer by one unit—1 byte—of information. A character is not necessarily visible, either on the screen or on paper; a space, for example, is as much a character as is the letter *a*. Because computers must manage both so-called printable characters and the formatting and transfer of electronically stored information, a character can also indicate a carriage return or a paragraph mark in a word-processed document, or it can be a signal to sound a beep or begin a new page. *See also* ASCII, control character, EBCDIC.

character cell *n.* A rectangular block of pixels that represents the space in which a given character is drawn on the screen. Computer displays use different numbers of pixels as character cells. Character cells are not always the same size for a given font, however; for proportionally spaced fonts, the height within a given font remains the same, but the width varies with each character.

character code *n.* A specific code that represents a particular character in a set such as the ASCII character set. The character code for a given key depends on whether another key, such as Shift, is pressed at the same time. For example, pressing the A key alone normally generates the character code for a lowercase *a*. Pressing Shift plus the A key normally generates the character code for an uppercase *A*. *Compare* key code.

character density *n.* In printing or screen display, a measure of the number of characters per unit of area or of linear distance. *See also* pitch (definition 1).

character device *n.* **1.** A computer device, such as a keyboard or printer, that receives or transmits information as a stream of characters, one character at a time. The characters can be transferred either bit by bit (serial transmission) or byte by byte (parallel transmission) but are not moved in blocks (groups of bytes). *Compare* block device. **2.** In reference to video displays, a device that handles text but not graphics. *See also* text mode.

character mode *n.* *See* text mode.

character-oriented protocol *n.* *See* byte-oriented protocol.

character printer *n.* **1.** A printer that operates by printing one character at a time, such as a standard dot-matrix printer. *Compare* line printer, page printer. **2.** A printer that cannot print graphics. Such a printer simply receives character codes from the controlling system and prints the appropriate characters. *Compare* graphics printer.

character recognition *n.* The process of applying pattern-matching methods to character shapes that have been read into a computer to determine which alphanumeric characters or punctuation marks the shapes represent. Because different typefaces and text treatments, such as bold and italic, can make big differences in the way characters are shaped, character recognition can be prone to error. Some systems work only with known typefaces and sizes, with no text treatments. These systems achieve very high accuracy, but they can work only with text specifically printed for them. Other systems use sophisticated pattern-matching techniques to learn new typefaces and sizes, achieving fairly good accuracy. *See also* magnetic-ink character recognition, optical character recognition.

character set *n.* A grouping of alphabetic, numeric, and other characters that have some relationship in common. For example, the standard ASCII character set includes letters, numbers, symbols, and control codes that make up the ASCII coding scheme.

characters per inch *n.* A measurement for the number of characters of a particular size and font that can fit into a line one inch long. This number is affected by the type's point size and the width of the letters in the font being measured. In monospace fonts, every character is the same width, so figuring out the number of characters per inch is a simple task. In proportional fonts, characters have varying widths, so the number of characters per inch must be calculated as an average of the different widths. *Acronym:* cpi. *See also* monospace font, pitch (definition 1), proportional font.

characters per second *n.* **1.** A measure of the speed of a nonlaser printer, such as a dot-matrix or an ink-jet printer. **2.** A measure of the rate at which a device, such as a disk drive, can transfer data. In serial communications, the speed of a modem in bits per second can generally be divided by 10 for a rough determination of the number of characters per second transmitted. *Acronym:* CPS.

character string *n.* A set of characters treated as a unit and interpreted by a computer as text rather than numbers. A character string can contain any sequence of elements from a given character set, such as letters, numbers, control characters, and extended ASCII characters. *Also called* string. *See also* ASCII, control character, extended ASCII.

character style *n.* Any attribute, such as boldface, italic, underline, or small caps, applied to a character. *See also* font, font family.

character user interface *n.* A user interface that displays only text characters. *Acronym:* CUI. *See also* user interface. *Compare* graphical user interface.

#
A
B
C
D
E
F
G
H
I
J
K
L
M
N
O
P
Q
R
S
T
U
V
W
X
Y
Z

chart *n.* A graphic or diagram that displays data or the relationships between sets of data in pictorial rather than numeric form.
chassis *n.* A metal frame on which electronic components, such as printed circuit boards, fans, and power supplies, are mounted.
chat¹ *n.* **1.** Real-time conversation via computer. When a participant types a line of text and then presses the Enter key, that participant's words appear on the screens of the other participants, who can then respond in kind. Most online services support chat; on the Internet, IRC is the usual system. *See also* IRC. **2.** An Internet utility program that supports chat. IRC has largely superseded it.
chat² *vb.* To carry on a real-time conversation with other users by computer. *See also* IRC.
chat room *n.* The informal term for a data communications channel that links computers and permits users to "converse," often about a particular subject of interest, by sending text messages to one another in real time, as on the channels provided by IRC. Chat rooms are supported by online services and some electronic bulletin board systems. They can also be set up by individuals who have appropriate software. *Also called* room. *See also* BBS (definition 1), chat¹, chat², IRC.
Cheapernet *n. See* 10Base2.
check bit *n.* One of a set of bits added to a data message at its origin and scrutinized by the receiving process to determine whether an error has occurred during transmission. The simplest example is a parity bit. *See also* data integrity, parity bit.
check box *n.* An interactive control often found in graphical user interfaces. A check box is used to enable or disable one or more features or options from a set. When the user chooses an option, an × or a check mark appears in the box. *See also* control (definition 2). *Compare* radio button.
check digit *n.* A digit added to an account number or other identifying key value and then recomputed when the number is used. This process determines whether an error occurred when the number was entered. *See also* checksum.
checksum *n.* A calculated value used to test data for errors that can occur when data is transmitted or written to disk. The checksum is calculated for a chunk of data by sequentially combining all the bytes of data with a series of arithmetic or logical operations. After the data is transmitted or stored, a new checksum is calculated in the same way using the transmitted or stored data. If the two checksums do not match, an error has occurred and the data should be transmitted or stored again. Checksums cannot detect all errors, and they cannot be used to correct erroneous data.
child *n.* **1.** A process initiated by another process (the parent). This initiating action is frequently called a fork. The parent process often sleeps (is suspended) until the child process stops executing. **2.** In a tree structure, the relationship of a node to its immediate predecessor. *See also* tree structure.

child directory *n. See* subdirectory.
child menu *n. See* submenu.
chimes of doom *n.* In Macintosh computers, a series of chimes that sound as a result of serious system failure.
chip *n. See* integrated circuit.
chip set *n.* A collection of chips designed to function as a unit in the performance of some common task. The term most commonly refers to the set of integrated circuits that support a CPU together with the CPU itself. Often a chip set will fit on one chip. *See also* central processing unit, integrated circuit.
choose *vb.* To pick a command or option from within a graphical user interface—for example, by clicking a button in a dialog box or a command name on a menu. *Compare* select.
chroma *n.* The quality of a color that combines hue and saturation. *See also* hue, saturation.
churn rate *n.* The rate of customer subscription turnover. In online businesses, customers who drop their monthly subscriptions can create a churn rate as high as 2 or 3 percent per month. High churn rates are costly to companies because attracting new subscribers through advertising and promotion is expensive.
CIM *n.* Acronym for **c**omputer-**i**nput **m**icrofilm. A process in which information stored on microfilm is scanned and the data (both text and graphics) converted into codes that can be used and manipulated by a computer. *Compare* COM (definition 4).
cipher *n.* **1.** A code. **2.** An encoded character. **3.** A zero.
circuit *n.* **1.** Any path that can carry electrical current. **2.** A combination of electrical components interconnected to perform a particular task. At one level, a computer consists of a single circuit; at another, it consists of hundreds of interconnected circuits.
circuit board *n.* A flat piece of insulating material, such as epoxy or phenolic resin, on which electrical components are mounted and interconnected to form a circuit. Most modern circuit boards use patterns of copper foil to interconnect the components. The foil layers may be on one or both sides of the board and, in more advanced designs, in several layers within the board. A printed circuit board is one in which the pattern of copper foil is laid down by a printing process such as photolithography. *See also* board, printed circuit board.
circuit breaker *n.* A switch that opens and cuts off the flow of current when the current exceeds a certain level. Circuit breakers are placed at critical points in circuits to protect against damage that could result from excessive current flow, which is typically caused by component failure. Circuit breakers are often used in place of fuses because they need only to be reset rather than replaced. *Compare* surge protector.
circuit card *n. See* circuit board.

circuit switching *n.* A method of opening communications lines by creating a physical link between the initiating and receiving parties. In circuit switching, the connection is made at a switching center, which physically connects the two parties and maintains an open line between them for as long as needed. Circuit switching is typically used on the dial-up telephone network and, on a smaller scale, in private communications networks. *Compare* message switching, packet switching.

CISC *n.* Acronym for **c**omplex **i**nstruction **s**et **c**omputing. The implementation of complex instructions in a microprocessor design so that they can be invoked at the assembly language level. The instructions can be very powerful, allowing for complicated and flexible ways of calculating such elements as memory addresses. The added power, however, comes at the cost of the additional time the microprocessor takes to execute each instruction. *Compare* RISC.

Class A network *n.* An Internet network that can define a maximum of 16,777,215 hosts. Class A networks are best suited for sites with few networks but numerous hosts and are usually designated for use by large government or educational institutions. *See also* host.

clean boot *n.* Booting or starting a computer using the minimum system files in the operating system. The clean boot is used as a troubleshooting method for isolating problems associated with software that may be calling on the same system resources at the same time, thus causing conflicts that lower the performance of the system, make some programs inoperable, or crash the computer. *See also* boot[1].

clean install *n.* Reinstallation of software in a manner that ensures that no application or system files from a previous installation will remain. The procedure prevents "smart" installer programs from skipping file installations where a file already exists, which could potentially keep a problem from being removed.

clean interface *n.* A user interface with simple features and intuitive commands. *See also* user interface.

Clear key *n.* A key in the upper left corner of the numeric keypad on some keyboards. In many applications, it clears the current menu choice or deletes the current selection.

Clear To Send *n. See* CTS.

click *vb.* To press and release a mouse button once without moving the mouse. Clicking is usually performed to select or deselect an item or to activate a program or program feature. *See also* right click. *Compare* double-click, drag.

clickable maps *n. See* image map.

click speed *n.* The maximum interval between two mouse clicks that will still identify these actions as a double-click to the computer as opposed to two single-clicks. *See also* click, double-click, mouse.

clickstream *n.* The path a user takes while browsing a Web site. Each distinct selection made on a Web page adds one click to the stream. The further down the clickstream the user goes without finding the sought item, the more likely he or she is to depart to another Web site. Analysis of such usage patterns helps Web site designers create user-friendly site structures, links, and search facilities. *See also* Web site.

client *n.* **1.** A process, such as a program or task, that requests a service provided by another program—for example, a word processor that calls on a sort procedure built into another program. The client process uses the requested service without having to "know" any working details about the other program or the service itself. *Compare* child (definition 1). **2.** On a local area network or the Internet, a computer that accesses shared network resources provided by another computer (called a server). *See also* client/server architecture, server.

client error *n.* A problem reported by the HTTP client module as the result of difficulty in interpreting a command or the inability to connect properly to a remote host.

client/server architecture *n.* An arrangement used on local area networks that makes use of distributed intelligence to treat both the server and the individual workstations as intelligent, programmable devices, thus exploiting the full computing power of each. This is done by splitting the processing of an application between a "front-end" client and a "back-end" server. The client component is a complete, stand-alone personal computer (not a "dumb" terminal), and it offers the user its full range of power and features for running applications. The server component can be a personal computer, minicomputer, or mainframe that provides the traditional strengths offered by minicomputers and mainframes in a time-sharing environment: data management, information sharing between clients, and sophisticated network administration and security features. The client and server machines work together, not only increasing the processing power available over older architectures but also using that power more efficiently. The client portion of the application is typically optimized for user interaction, whereas the server portion provides the centralized, multi-user functionality.

client-side image maps *n.* A Web page user selection device whereby a user can click regions of an image to indicate selections from a collection of options, comparable to clicking an icon of the desired item on a menu. Client-side image maps do not transmit the mouse click coordinates to the Web server for processing but perform the processing completely within the client program (the Web browser) itself, generally improving the speed of response to the user. *See also* image map.

clip *vb.* **1.** To cut off the portion of a displayed image that lies beyond a certain boundary, such as the edge of a window. Certain graphics programs also support clipping as a means of masking everything but a certain object so that painting tools, for example, can be applied to the object alone. **2.** To cut a photograph, drawing, or other illustration from a clip art collection. *See also* clip art.

clip art *n.* A collection—either in a book or on a disk—of proprietary or public-domain photographs, diagrams, maps, drawings, and other graphics that can be "clipped" from the collection and incorporated into other documents.

clipboard *n.* **1.** A special memory resource maintained by windowing operating systems. The clipboard stores a copy of the last information that was "copied" or "cut." A "paste" operation passes data from the clipboard to the current program. A clipboard allows information to be transferred from one program to another, if the second program can read data generated by the first. Data copied using the clipboard is static and will not reflect later changes. *See also* cut and paste, DDE. *Compare* scrap. **2.** A computer that uses a pen as the primary input device. *See also* clipboard computer, pen computer.

clipboard computer *n.* A portable computer whose overall appearance and operation resemble that of a traditional clipboard. A clipboard computer has an LCD or similar flat display and has a pen for user input instead of a keyboard or mouse. The user operates it by touching the pen to the display. Data entered in a clipboard computer is generally transferred to another computer via a cable or a modem. Like a traditional clipboard, a clipboard computer is used in field work, data collection, or meetings. *See also* pen computer, portable computer.

Clipper Chip *n.* An integrated circuit that implements the SkipJack algorithm, an encryption algorithm created by the National Security Agency that encrypts 64-bit blocks of data with an 80-bit key. The Clipper is manufactured by the U.S. government to encrypt telephone data. It has the added feature that it can be decrypted by the U.S. government, which has tried unsuccessfully to make the chip compulsory in the United States. *See also* encryption.

clipping path *n.* A polygon or curve that is used to mask an area in a document. Only what is inside the clipping path appears when the document is printed. *See also* PostScript.

clobber *vb.* To destroy data, generally by inadvertently writing other data over it.

clock *n.* **1.** The electronic circuit in a computer that generates a steady stream of timing pulses—the digital signals that synchronize every operation. The clock rate of a computer is one of the prime determinants of its overall processing speed, and it can go as high as the other components of the computer allow. *Also called* system clock. **2.** The battery-backed circuit that keeps track of the time and date in a computer—not the same as the system clock. *Also called* clock/calendar.

clock/calendar *n.* An independent timekeeping circuit used within a microcomputer to maintain the correct time and calendar date. A clock/calendar circuit is battery powered, so it continues running even when the computer is turned off. The time and date kept by the clock/calendar can be used by the operating system (for example, to "stamp" files with the date and time of creation or revision) and by applications (for example, to insert the date or time in a document). *Also called* clock, internal clock.

clocking *n. See* synchronization (definition 3).

clock rate *n.* The rate at which the clock in an electronic device, such as a computer, oscillates. The clock rate is normally given in hertz, kilohertz, or megahertz. Clock rates in personal computers increased from about 5 MHz to about 50 MHz between 1981 and 1995. *Also called* clock speed, hertz time. *See also* clock (definition 1).

clock speed *n. See* clock rate.

clone *n.* A copy; in microcomputer terminology, a look-alike, act-alike computer that contains the same microprocessor and runs the same programs as a better-known, more prestigious, and often more expensive machine.

close[1] *n.* An FTP command that instructs the client to close the current connection with a server. *See also* FTP[1] (definition 1), Web site.

close[2] *vb.* **1.** To end an application's relationship with an open file so that the application will no longer be able to access the file without opening it again. **2.** To end a computer's connection with another computer on a network.

close box *n.* In the Macintosh graphical user interface, a small box in the left corner of a window's title bar. Clicking on the box closes the window. *Compare* close button.

close button *n.* In the graphical user interface for Windows 95, Windows NT, and the X Window System, a square button in the right corner (left corner in X Windows) of a window's title bar with an × mark on it. Clicking on the button closes the window. *Also called* X button. *Compare* close box.

closed architecture *n.* **1.** Any computer design whose specifications are not freely available. Such proprietary specifications make it difficult or impossible for third-party vendors to create ancillary devices that work correctly with a closed-architecture machine; usually only its original maker can build peripherals and add-ons for such a machine. *Compare* open architecture (definition 1). **2.** A computer system that provides no expansion slots for adding new types of circuit boards within the system unit. *Compare* open architecture (definition 2).

closed file *n.* A file not being used by an application. An application must open such a file before reading or writing to it and must close it afterward. *Compare* open file.

closed system *n. See* closed architecture (definition 2).

cluster *n.* **1.** An aggregation, such as a group of data points on a graph. **2.** A communications computer and its associated terminals. **3.** In data storage, a disk-storage unit consisting of a fixed number of sectors (storage segments on the disk, each holding a certain number of bytes) that the operating system uses to read or write information. **4.** A group of independent network servers that operate—and appear to clients—as if they were a single unit. Clustering is designed to improve network capacity by, among other

A B C D E F G H I J K L M N O P Q R S T U V W X Y Z

A B C D E F G H I J K L M N O P Q R S T U V W X Y Z

things, enabling the servers within a cluster to shift work in order to balance the load. By enabling one server to take over for another, clustering also enhances network stability and minimizes or eliminates down time caused by application or system failure.

cluster controller *n.* An intermediary device that is situated between a computer and a group (cluster) of subsidiary devices, such as terminals on a network, and is used to control the cluster.

CMI *n.* Acronym for **c**omputer-**m**anaged **i**nstruction. Any type of teaching that uses computers as educational tools. *See also* CAI, CBT.

CMOS *n.* **1.** Acronym for **c**omplementary **m**etal-**o**xide **s**emiconductor. A semiconductor technology in which pairs of metal-oxide semiconductor field effect transistors (MOSFETs) are integrated on a single silicon chip. Generally used for RAM and switching applications, these devices have very high speed and extremely low power consumption. **2.** The battery-backed memory (presumably made with CMOS technology) used to store the clock/calendar time and the parameter values needed to boot IBM PCs and compatibles, such as the type of disks and the amount of memory.

CMOS RAM *n.* Random access memory made using CMOS technology. CMOS chips consume very little power and have high tolerance for noise from the power supply. These characteristics make CMOS chips, including CMOS RAM chips, very useful in hardware components that are powered by batteries, such as most microcomputer clocks and certain types of scratchpad RAM maintained by the operating system. *See also* CMOS (definition 1), PRAM, RAM.

CMOS setup *n.* A system configuration utility, accessible at boot time, for setting up certain system options, such as the date and time, the kind of drives installed, and port configuration. *See also* CMOS (definition 2).

CMS *n. See* color management system.

CMY *n.* Acronym for **c**yan-**m**agenta-**y**ellow. A model for describing colors that are produced by absorbing light, as by ink on paper, rather than by emitting light, as on a video monitor. The three kinds of cone cells in the eye respond to red, green, and blue light, which are absorbed (removed from white light) by cyan, magenta, and yellow pigments, respectively. Percentages of pigments in these subtractive primary colors can therefore be mixed to get the appearance of any desired color. Absence of any pigment leaves white unchanged; adding 100 percent of all three pigments turns white to black. *Compare* CMYK, RGB.

CMYK *n.* Acronym for **c**yan-**m**agenta-**y**ellow-blac**k**. A color model that is similar to the CMY color model but produces black with a separate black component rather than by adding 100 percent of cyan, magenta, and yellow. *See also* CMY.

coaxial cable *n.* A two-conductor cable consisting of a center wire inside a grounded cylindrical shield, typically made of braided wire, that is insulated from the center wire. The shield prevents signals transmitted on the center wire from affecting nearby components and prevents external interference from affecting the signal carried on the center wire.

COBOL *n.* Acronym for **Co**mmon **B**usiness-**O**riented **L**anguage. A verbose, English-like, compiled programming language developed between 1959 and 1961 and still in widespread use today, especially in business applications typically run on mainframes. *See also* compiled language.

cobweb site *n.* A Web site that is far out of date.

code¹ *n.* **1.** Program instructions. Source code consists of human-readable statements written by a programmer in a programming language. Machine code consists of numerical instructions that the computer can recognize and execute and that were converted from source code. *See also* data, program. **2.** A system of symbols used to convert information from one form to another. A code for converting information in order to conceal it is often called a cipher. **3.** One of a set of symbols used to represent information.

code² *vb.* To write program instructions in a programming language. *See also* program.

codec *n.* **1.** Short for **co**der/**dec**oder. Hardware that can convert audio or video signals between analog and digital forms. **2.** Short for **co**mpressor/**dec**ompressor. Hardware or software that can compress and uncompress audio or video data. *See also* compress, uncompress. **3.** Hardware that combines the functions of definitions 1 and 2.

coder *n.* *See* programmer.

cold boot *n.* A startup process that begins with turning on the computer's power. Typically, a cold boot involves some basic hardware checking by the system, after which the operating system is loaded from disk into memory. *See also* boot¹. *Compare* warm boot.

cold fault *n.* A fatal error that occurs immediately upon or shortly after startup as a result of the misalignment of components in the system. The process of running and shutting down any computer induces a series of thermal expansions and contractions in its internal components. Over time, these changes in the dimensions of components can create a microscopic crack in a chip or loosen a pin in a socket; thus, the system crashes when cold, but the problem seems to disappear after the machine is warm. For this reason some users leave the system unit (but not the monitor) of a computer running from day to day, rather than turning the machine on only when needed.

cold link *n.* A link established upon a request for data. Once the request is filled, the link is broken. The next time data is required, a link from the client to the server must be reestablished. In a client/server architecture cold links are useful when the linked item consists of a large amount of data. Dynamic Data Exchange, used in applications such as Microsoft Excel, uses cold links for data exchange. *See also* client/server architecture, DDE. *Compare* hot link.

cold start *n.* *See* cold boot.

A B C D E F G H I J K L M N O P Q R S T U V W X Y Z

collapsed backbone *n. See* backbone (definition 3).

collate *vb.* In data handling, to merge items from two or more similar sets to create a combined set that maintains the order or sequence of items in the original sets.

collating sort *n.* A sort that proceeds by continuous merging of two or more files to produce a certain sequence of records or data items.

collation sequence *n.* The ordering relationship (sequence) among objects that is to be established by a collating sort. *See also* collating sort.

collision *n.* The result of two devices or network workstations trying to transmit signals at the exact same time on the same channel. The typical outcome is a garbled transmission.

collision detection *n.* **1.** The process by which a node on a local area network monitors the communications line to determine when a collision has occurred; that is, when two nodes have attempted to transmit at the same time. When a collision occurs, the two nodes involved usually wait a random amount of time before attempting to retransmit. *See also* contention. **2.** The process by which a game or simulation program determines whether two objects on the screen are touching each other. This is a time-consuming, often complicated procedure; some computers optimized for graphics and games have special hardware built in specifically to detect collisions.

color *n.* In physics, the component of the human perception of light that depends on frequency. For light of a single frequency, color ranges from violet at the high-frequency end of the visible-light band to red at the low-frequency end. In computer video, color is produced by a combination of hardware and software. Software manipulates combinations of bits that represent the distinct shades of color that are destined for particular positions on the screen (pixels). The video adapter hardware translates these bits into electrical signals, which in turn control the brightnesses of different-colored phosphors at the corresponding positions on the screen. The user's eye unites the light from the phosphors to perceive a single color. *See also* color model, color monitor, CRT, HSB, monitor, RGB, video, video adapter.

color bits *n.* A predetermined number of bits assigned to each displayable pixel that determine its color when it is displayed on a monitor. For example, two color bits are required for four colors; eight color bits are required for 256 colors. *See also* pixel image. *Compare* bit plane.

color burst *n.* A technique used to encode color in a composite video signal. The color burst consists of a combination of the red, green, and blue intensities (used by black-and-white displays) and two color-difference signals that determine separate red, green, and blue intensities (used by color displays). *See also* color look-up table.

color cycling *n.* A technique used in computer graphics for changing the color of one or more pixels on the screen by changing the color palette used by the video adapter rather than by changing the color bits for each pixel. For example, to cause a red circle to fade away to a black background color, the program need only change the set of signal values corresponding to "red" in the video adapter's color look-up table, periodically making it darker until it matches the black background. At each step, the apparent color of the whole circle changes instantly; it appears to fade rather than to be painted over and over.

color look-up table *n.* A table stored in a computer's video adapter, containing the color signal values that correspond to the different colors that can be displayed on the computer's monitor. When color is displayed indirectly, a small number of color bits are stored for each pixel and are used to select a set of signal values from the color look-up table. *Also called* color map, color table, video look-up table. *See also* color, color bits, palette (definition 2), pixel.

color management system *n.* A technology developed by Kodak and licensed to many other software vendors that is designed to calibrate and match colors that appear on video monitors and computer monitors and those that appear in any printed form. *Acronym:* CMS.

color map *n. See* color look-up table.

color model *n.* Any method or convention for representing color in desktop publishing and graphic arts. In graphic arts and printing, the Pantone system is often used. In computer graphics, colors can be described using any of several color systems: HSB, CMY, and RGB. *See also* CMY, HSB, Pantone Matching System, process color, RGB.

color monitor *n.* A video display device designed to work with a video card or adapter to produce text or graphics images in color. A color monitor, unlike a monochrome display, has a screen coated internally with patterns of three phosphors that glow red, green, and blue when struck by an electron beam. To create colors such as yellow, pink, and orange, the three phosphors are lighted together in varying degrees. A video card that uses large groups of bits (6 or more) to describe colors and that generates analog (continuously variable) signals is capable of generating an enormous potential range of colors on a color monitor. *See also* color, color model.

color palette *n. See* palette (definition 1).

color plane *n. See* bit plane.

color printer *n.* A computer printer that can print full-color output. Most color printers can also produce black-and-white output.

color saturation *n.* The amount of a hue contained in a color; the more saturation, the more intense the color. *See also* HSB.

color scanner *n.* A scanner that converts images to a digitized format and is able to interpret color. Depth of color depends on the scanner's bit depth—its ability to transform color into 8, 16, 24, or 32 bits. High-end color scanners, commonly used when output is to be printed, are able to encode information at a high resolution. Low-end color scanners encode information at a resolution of 72 dots per inch and are commonly used for computer screen images not intended for printing. *See also* resolution (definition 1), scanner.

color table *n. See* color look-up table.

A B C D E F G H I J K L M N O P Q R S T U V W X Y Z

column *n.* **1.** A series of items arranged vertically within some type of framework—for example, a continuous series of cells running from top to bottom in a spreadsheet, a vertical line of pixels on a video screen, or a set of values aligned vertically in a table or matrix. *Compare* row. **2.** In a relational database management system, the name for an attribute. The collection of column values that form the description of a particular entity is called a tuple or row. A column is equivalent to a field in a record in a nonrelational file system. *See also* field (definition 1), row, table (definition 1).

.com *n.* **1.** In the Internet's Domain Name System, the top-level domain that identifies addresses operated by commercial organizations. The designation .com appears as a suffix at the end of the address. *See also* DNS (definition 1), domain (definition 3). *Compare* .edu, .gov, .mil, .net, .org. **2.** In MS-DOS, the file extension that identifies a command file. *See also* COM (definition 3).

COM *n.* **1.** A name reserved by the MS-DOS operating system for serial communications ports. For example, if a modem is connected to one serial port and a serial printer to another, the devices are identified as COM1 and COM2 by the operating system. **2.** Acronym for **C**omponent **O**bject **M**odel. A specification developed by Microsoft for building software components that can be assembled into programs or add functionality to existing programs running on Windows platforms. COM components can be written in a variety of languages. COM is the foundation of the OLE, ActiveX, and DirectX specifications. *See also* ActiveX, DirectX, OLE. **3.** The extension reserved by MS-DOS for a type of executable binary (program) file limited to a single 64-KB segment. COM files are often used for utility programs and short routines. They are not supported in OS/2. **4.** Acronym for **c**omputer-**o**utput **m**icrofilm. Microfilm that can record data from a computer.

COM1 *n.* A serial communications port in Wintel systems. COM1 is usually specified by the I/O range 03F8H, is usually associated with interrupt request line IRQ4, and in many systems is used to connect an RS-232 serial mouse. *See also* IRQ.

COM2 *n.* A serial communications port in Wintel systems. COM2 is usually specified by the I/O range 02F8H, is usually associated with interrupt request line IRQ3, and in many systems is used to connect a modem. *See also* IRQ.

COM3 *n.* A serial communications port in Wintel systems. COM3 is usually specified by the I/O range 03E8H, is usually associated with interrupt request line IRQ4, and in many systems is used as an alternative to COM1 or COM2 if the latter is being used by some other peripheral. *See also* IRQ.

Comité Consultatif International Télégraphique et Téléphonique *n.* *Also called* International Telegraph and Telephone Consultative Committee. *See* CCITT.

comma-delimited file *n.* A data file consisting of fields and records, stored as text, in which the fields are separated from each other by commas. Use of comma-delimited files allows communication between database systems that use different formats. If the data in a field contains a comma, the field is further surrounded with quotation marks.

command *n.* An instruction to a computer program that, when issued by the user, causes an action to be carried out. Commands are usually either typed at the keyboard or chosen from a menu.

command button *n.* A control shaped like a pushbutton in a dialog box in a graphical user interface. By clicking a command button, the user causes the computer to perform some action, such as opening a file that has just been selected using the other controls in the dialog box.

COMMAND.COM *n.* The command interpreter for MS-DOS. *See also* command interpreter.

command-driven *adj.* Accepting commands in the form of code words or letters, which the user must learn. *Compare* menu-driven.

command-driven system *n.* A system in which the user initiates operations by a command entered from the console. *Compare* graphical user interface.

command interpreter *n.* A program, usually part of the operating system, that accepts typed commands from the keyboard and performs tasks as directed. The command interpreter is responsible for loading applications and directing the flow of information between applications. In OS/2 and MS-DOS, the command interpreter also handles simple functions, such as moving and copying files and displaying disk directory information. *See also* shell.

Command key *n.* On the original Macintosh keyboard, a key labeled with the special symbol, sometimes called the propeller or puppy foot ⌘. This key is found on one side or both sides of the Spacebar, depending on the version of the Apple keyboard. The key serves some of the same functions as the Control key on IBM keyboards. *See also* Control key.

command language *n.* The set of keywords and expressions accepted as valid by the command interpreter. *See also* command interpreter.

command line *n.* A string of text written in the command language and passed to the command interpreter for execution. *See also* command language.

command-line interface *n.* A form of interface between the operating system and the user in which the user types commands, using a special command language. Although systems with command-line interfaces are considered more difficult to learn and use than those with graphical interfaces, command-based systems are usually programmable; this gives them flexibility unavailable in graphics-based systems that do not have a programming interface. *Compare* graphical user interface.

command mode *n.* A mode of operation in which a program waits for a command to be issued. *Compare* edit mode, insert mode.

command processing *n.* *See* command-driven system.

command processor *n.* *See* command interpreter.

command shell *n.* *See* shell.

A B C D E F G H I J K L M N O P Q R S T U V W X Y Z

command state *n.* The state in which a modem accepts commands, such as a command to dial a telephone number. *Compare* online state.

commerce server *n.* An HTTP server designed for conducting online business transactions. Data is transferred between the server and Web browser in an encrypted form to keep information such as credit card numbers reasonably secure. Commerce servers are typically used by online stores and companies that are set up for mail order business. These stores or companies present their wares on Web sites and allow users to order directly from the sites. *See also* HTTP server (definition 1), Secure Sockets Layer, Web browser.

commercial access provider *n. See* ISP.

common carrier *n.* A communications company (such as a telephone company) that provides service to the public and is regulated by governmental organizations.

Common Gateway Interface *n. See* CGI (definition 1).

communications *n.* The discipline encompassing the methods, mechanisms, and media involved in information transfer. In computer-related areas, communications involves data transfer from one computer to another through a communications medium, such as a telephone, microwave relay, satellite link, or physical cable. Two primary methods of computer communications exist: temporary connection of two computers through a switched network, such as the public telephone system; and permanent or semipermanent linking of multiple workstations or computers in a network. *See also* asynchronous transmission, CCITT, channel (definition 2), communications protocol, IEEE, ISDN, ISO/OSI model, LAN, modem, network, synchronous transmission. *Compare* data transmission, telecommunications, teleprocess.

communications channel *n. See* channel (definition 2).

communications controller *n.* A device used as an intermediary in transferring communications to and from the host computer to which it is connected. By performing the tasks of sending, receiving, deciphering, and checking transmissions for errors, a communications controller helps to free the host computer's processing time for noncommunications tasks. A communications controller can be either a programmable machine or a nonprogrammable device designed to follow certain communications protocols. *See also* front-end processor (definition 2).

communications link *n.* The connection between computers that enables data transfer.

communications network *n. See* network.

communications parameter *n.* Any of several settings required in order to enable computers to communicate. In asynchronous communications, for example, modem speed, number of data bits and stop bits, and type of parity are parameters that must be set correctly to establish communication between two modems.

communications port *n. See* COM (definition 1).

communications program *n.* A software program that enables a computer to connect with another computer and to exchange information. For initiating communications, communications programs perform such tasks as maintaining communications parameters, storing and dialing phone numbers, executing logon procedures, and repeatedly dialing busy lines. Once a connection is made, these programs can also be instructed to save incoming messages on disk or to find and transmit disk files. During communication, such programs can encode data, coordinate transmissions to and from the distant computer, and check incoming data for transmission errors.

communications protocol *n.* A set of rules or standards designed to enable computers to connect with one another and to exchange information with as little error as possible. The protocol generally accepted for standardizing overall computer communications is a seven-layer set of hardware and software guidelines known as the ISO/OSI (International Organization for Standardization Open Systems Interconnection) model. The word *protocol* is often used, sometimes confusingly, in reference to a multitude of standards affecting different aspects of communication, such as file transfer, handshaking, and network transmissions. *See also* ISO/OSI model.

communications satellite *n.* A satellite stationed in geosynchronous orbit that acts as a microwave relay station, receiving signals sent from a ground-based station, amplifying them, and retransmitting them on a different frequency to another ground-based station. Communications satellites can be used for high-speed transmission of computer data. Two factors affecting this use, however, are propagation delay (the time lag caused by the distance the signal travels) and security concerns. *See also* downlink, uplink.

communications server *n.* A gateway that translates packets on a local area network into asynchronous signals, such as those used on telephone lines or in RS-232-C serial communications, and allows all nodes on the LAN access to its modems or RS-232-C connections. *See also* gateway, RS-232-C standard.

communications slot *n.* On many models of the Apple Macintosh, a dedicated expansion slot for network interface cards. *Acronym:* CS.

communications software *n.* The software that controls the modem in response to user commands. Generally such software includes terminal emulation as well as file transfer facilities. *See also* modem, terminal emulation.

communications system *n.* The combination of hardware, software, and data transfer links that make up a communications facility.

Communications Terminal Protocol *n.* A terminal protocol that enables a user at a remote location to access a computer as if the remote computer were directly connected (hardwired) to the computer. *Acronym:* CTERM.

compact disc *n.* **1.** An optical storage medium for digital data, usually audio. A compact disc is a nonmagnetic, polished metal disc with a protective plastic coating with the capacity to hold up to 74 minutes of high-fidelity recorded sound. The disc is read by an optical scanning mechanism that uses a high-intensity light source, such as a laser, and mirrors. *Also called* optical disc.

2. A technology that forms the basis of media such as CD-ROM, CD-I, CD-R, and PhotoCD. These media are all compact disc–based but store various types of digital information and have different read/write capabilities. *Acronym:* CD. *See also* CD-I, CD-R, CD-ROM, PhotoCD.

compact disc–erasable *n.* A technological improvement in compact discs whereby information can be repeatedly changed on the CD. Contemporary CDs are "write once, read many," in that the information originally written cannot be changed, although new information can be appended. *Acronym:* CD-E.

compact disc–interactive *n. See* CD-I.

compact disc–recordable and erasable *adj.* Of or pertaining to hardware and software for interfacing computers with both compact disc–recordable and compact disc–erasable devices.

compact disc–rewritable *n.* The technology, equipment, software, and media used in the production of multiple-write compact discs. *Acronym:* CD-RW.

compaction *n.* The process of gathering and packing the currently allocated regions of memory or auxiliary storage into as small a space as possible, so as to create as much continuous free space as possible. *Compare* fragmentation.

compatibility *n.* **1.** The degree to which one computer, attached device, data file, or program can work with or understand the same commands, formats, or language as another. True compatibility means that any operational differences are invisible to people and programs alike. **2.** The extent to which two machines can work in harmony—communicating, sharing data, or running the same programs. **3.** The extent to which a piece of hardware conforms to an accepted standard (for example, IBM-compatible or Hayes-compatible). **4.** In reference to software, harmony on a task-oriented level among computers and computer programs. Computers deemed software-compatible can run programs originally designed for other makes or models. Compatible programs can work together and share data—for example, different programs, such as a word processor and a drawing program, are compatible if each can incorporate images or files created using the other. *See also* downward compatibility, upward-compatible.

compatibility mode *n.* A mode in which hardware or software in one system supports operations of software from another system. The term often refers to the ability of advanced operating systems designed for Intel microprocessors to run MS-DOS software or to the ability of some UNIX workstations and some Apple Macintosh systems to run MS-DOS software.

compile *vb.* To translate all the source code of a program from a high-level language into object code prior to execution of the program. Object code is executable machine code or a variation of machine code. *See also* compiler, high-level language, machine code, source code. *Compare* interpret.

compiled language *n.* A language that is translated into machine code prior to any execution, as opposed to an interpreted language, which is

translated and executed statement by statement. *See also* compiler. *Compare* interpreted language.
compiler *n.* A program that translates all the source code of a program written in a high-level language into object code prior to execution of the program. *See also* assembler, compile, high-level language, interpreted language, object code.
complementary metal-oxide semiconductor *n. See* CMOS.
complementary operation *n.* In Boolean logic, an operation that produces the opposite result from that of another operation performed on the same data. For example, if A is true, NOT A (its complement) is false.
complex instruction set computing *n. See* CISC.
comp. newsgroups *n.* Usenet newsgroups that are part of the comp. hierarchy, use the comp. prefix in their names, and are devoted to discussions of computer hardware, software, and other aspects of computer science. *See also* newsgroup, traditional newsgroup hierarchy, Usenet.
Component Object Model *n. See* COM (definition 2).
component software *n.* Modular software routines, or components, that can be combined with other components to form an overall program. A programmer can use and reuse an existing component, without having to understand its inner workings, simply by knowing how to have another program or component call it and pass data to and from it. *Also called* componentware. *See also* program, routine.
componentware *n. See* component software.
COM port or **comm port** *n.* Short for **com**munications **port**. The logical address assigned by MS-DOS (versions 3.3 and higher) and Windows (including Windows 95 and Windows NT) to each of the four serial ports on an IBM PC or compatible. COM ports also have come to be known as the actual serial ports on a PC's CPU where peripherals, such as printers and external modems, are plugged in. *See also* COM (definition 1), input/output port, serial port.
composite display *n.* A display, characteristic of television monitors and some computer monitors, that is capable of extracting an image from a composite signal (also called an NTSC signal). A composite display signal carries on one wire not only the coded information required to form an image on the screen but also the pulses needed to synchronize horizontal and vertical scanning as the electron beam sweeps across the screen. Composite displays can be either monochrome or color. Composite color monitors are less readable than either monochrome monitors or the RGB color monitors that use separate signals (and wires) for the red, green, and blue components of the image. *See also* color monitor, monochrome display, NTSC, RGB monitor.
compound document *n.* A document that contains different types of information, each type created with a different application. For example, a report containing both charts (created with a spreadsheet) and text (created with a word processor) is a compound document. Although a compound document is visually a single, seamless unit, it is actually formed of discrete

objects (blocks of information) that are created in their own applications. Either these objects can be physically embedded in the destination document or they can be linked to it while remaining in the originating file. Both embedded and linked objects can be edited. Linked objects, however, can be updated to reflect changes made to the source file. *See also* ActiveX, OLE, OpenDoc.

compress *vb.* To reduce the size of a set of data, such as a file or a communications message, so that it can be stored in less space or transmitted with less bandwidth. Data can be compressed by removing repeated patterns of bits and replacing them with some form of summary that takes up less space; restoring the repeated patterns decompresses the data. *See also* lossless compression, lossy compression.

compressed digital video *n. See* CDV (definition 1).

compressed disk *n.* A hard disk or floppy disk whose apparent capacity to hold data has been increased through the use of a compression utility. *See also* data compression.

compressed drive *n.* A hard disk whose apparent capacity has been increased through the use of a compression utility. *See also* compressed disk, data compression.

compressed file *n.* A file whose contents have been compressed by a special utility program so that it occupies less space on a disk or other storage device than in its uncompressed (normal) state. *See also* installation program, utility program.

compression *n. See* data compression.

compressor *n.* A device that limits some aspect of a transmitted signal, such as volume, in order to increase efficiency.

compute *vb.* **1.** To perform calculations. **2.** To use a computer or cause it to do work.

computer *n.* Any machine that accepts structured input, processes it according to prescribed rules, and produces the results as output. Ways to categorize computers are described in the following list.

- Class: Computers can be classified as supercomputers, mainframes, superminicomputers, minicomputers, workstations, or microcomputers. All else (for example, the age of the machine) being equal, this categorization provides some indication of the computer's speed, size, cost, and abilities.

- Generation: First-generation computers of historic significance, such as UNIVAC, introduced in the early 1950s, were based on vacuum tubes. Second-generation computers, appearing in the early 1960s, were those in which transistors replaced vacuum tubes. In third-generation computers, dating from the 1960s, integrated circuits replaced transistors. In fourth-generation computers such as microcomputers, which first appeared in the mid-1970s, large-scale integration enabled thousands of circuits to be incorporated on one chip. Fifth-generation computers are expected to combine very-large-scale integration with sophisticated approaches to computing, including artificial intelligence and true distributed processing. *See also* integrated circuit.

- Mode of processing: Computers are either analog or digital. Analog computers, generally used in scientific pursuits, represent values by continuously variable signals that can have any of an infinite number of values within a limited range at any particular time. Digital computers, the type most people think of as computers, represent values by discrete signals—the bits representing the binary digits 0 and 1. *See also* analog, digital.

computer-aided design *n. See* CAD.
computer-aided instruction *n. See* CAI.
computer-aided testing *n. See* CAT (definition 1).
computer art *n.* A broad term that can refer either to art created on a computer or to art generated by a computer, the difference being whether the artist is human or electronic. Human artists create computer art with painting programs that offer a range of line-drawing tools, brushes, shapes, patterns, and colors. Some programs also offer predrawn figures and animation capabilities.
computer-assisted instruction *n. See* CAI.
computer-assisted teaching *n. See* CAI.
computer-based training *n. See* CBT.
computer conferencing *n.* Person-to-person interaction through the use of computers located in different places but connected through communications facilities.
computer control console *n. See* console, system console.
computer crime *n.* The illegal use of a computer by an unauthorized individual, either for pleasure (as by a computer hacker) or for profit (as by a thief). *See also* hacker (definition 2).
computer-dependent *adj. See* hardware-dependent.
Computer Emergency Response Team *n. See* CERT.
computer engineering *n.* The discipline that involves the design and underlying philosophies involved in the development of computer hardware.
computer family *n.* A term commonly used to indicate a group of computers that are built around the same microprocessor or around a series of related microprocessors and that share significant design features. For example, the Apple Macintosh computers, from the original Macintosh to the Quadra, represent a family designed by Apple around the Motorola 68000, 68020, 68030, and 68040 microprocessors. Computer families tend to parallel microprocessor families, but this is not always the case. For instance, Macintoshes are no longer made with 680x0 processors, and the Macintosh family has "extended" to another generation: the Power Macs, based on the PowerPC microprocessor.

A B C D E F G H I J K L M N O P Q R S T U V W X Y Z

computer game *n.* A class of computer program in which one or more users interact with the computer as a form of entertainment. Computer games run the gamut from simple alphabet games for toddlers to chess, treasure hunts, war games, and simulations of world events. The games are controlled from a keyboard or with a joystick or other device and are supplied on disks, on CD-ROMs, as game cartridges, or as arcade devices.

computer graphics *n.* The display of "pictures," as opposed to only alphabetic and numeric characters, on a computer screen. Computer graphics encompasses different methods of generating, displaying, and storing information. Thus, computer graphics can refer to the creation of business charts and diagrams; the display of drawings, italic characters, and mouse pointers on the screen; or the way images are generated and displayed on the screen. *See also* graphics mode, presentation graphics, raster graphics, vector graphics.

Computer Graphics Interface *n.* A software standard applied to computer graphics devices, such as printers and plotters. Computer Graphics Interface is an offshoot of the Graphical Kernel System, a widely recognized graphics standard that provides applications programmers with standard methods of creating, manipulating, and displaying or printing computer graphics. *Acronym:* CGI. *See also* Graphical Kernel System.

computer-input microfilm *n. See* CIM.

computer instruction *n.* **1.** An instruction that a computer can recognize and act on. **2.** The use of a computer in teaching. *See also* CAI.

computer interface unit *n. See* interface (definition 3).

computerized mail *n. See* e-mail[1].

computer language *n.* An artificial language that specifies instructions to be executed on a computer. The term covers a wide spectrum, from binary-coded machine language to high-level languages. *See also* assembly language, high-level language, machine code.

computer letter *n. See* form letter.

computer literacy *n.* Knowledge and an understanding of computers combined with the ability to use them effectively. On a basic level, computer literacy involves knowing how to start and stop simple application programs and save and print information. At higher levels, it can involve manipulating complex applications, programming, or acquiring specialized knowledge of electronics and assembly language.

computer-managed instruction *n. See* CMI.

computer name *n.* In computer networking, a name that uniquely identifies a computer to the network. A computer name differs from a user name in that the computer name is used to identify a particular computer and all its shared resources to the rest of the system so that they can be accessed. *Compare* alias (definition 2), user name.

computer network *n. See* network.

computer-output microfilm *n. See* COM (definition 4).

computerphile *n.* A person who is immersed in the world of computing, who collects computers, or whose hobby involves computing.

computer power *n.* The ability of a computer to perform work. If defined as the number of instructions the machine can carry out in a given time, computer power is measured in millions of instructions per second (MIPS) or millions of floating-point operations per second (MFLOPS). By users or purchasers of computers, power is often considered in terms of the machine's amount of RAM, the speed at which the processor works, or the number of bits (8, 16, 32, and so on) handled by the computer at one time. *See also* access time (definition 2), benchmark[1], MIPS.

computer program *n.* A set of instructions in a computer language, intended to be executed on a computer to perform a task. The term usually implies a self-contained entity, as opposed to a routine. *See also* computer language. *Compare* routine.

computer-readable *adj.* Of, pertaining to, or characteristic of information that can be interpreted and acted on by a computer. Two types of information are referred to as computer-readable: bar codes, magnetic tape, and other formats that can be scanned in some way and read as data by a computer; and machine code, the form in which instructions and data reach the computer's microprocessor.

computer science *n.* The study of computers, including their design, operation, and use in processing information. Computer science combines both theoretical and practical aspects of engineering, electronics, information theory, mathematics, logic, and human behavior. Aspects of computer science range from programming and computer architecture to artificial intelligence and robotics.

computer security *n.* The steps taken to protect a computer and the information it contains. On large systems or those handling financial or confidential data, computer security requires professional supervision that combines legal and technical expertise. On a microcomputer, data can be protected by backing up and storing copies of files in a separate location, assigning passwords to files, marking files "read-only" to avoid changes, physically locking a hard disk, storing sensitive information on floppy disks kept in locked cabinets, and installing special programs to protect against viruses. On a computer to which many people have access, security can be maintained by requiring passwords and by limiting access to sensitive information. *See also* bacterium, encryption, virus.

computer simulation *n.* *See* simulation.

computer system *n.* The configuration that includes all functional components of a computer and its associated hardware. A basic microcomputer system includes a console, or system unit, with one or more disk drives, a monitor, and a keyboard. Additional hardware, called peripherals, can include such devices as a printer, a modem, and a mouse. Software is usually not considered part of a computer system, although the operating system that runs the hardware is known as system software.

computer telephone integration *n.* A process allowing computer applications to answer incoming calls, provide database information on-screen as a call comes in, route and reroute calls by drag-and-drop, dial and speed-dial outgoing calls from a computer-resident database, and identify incoming customer calls and transfer them to predetermined destinations. *See also* drag-and-drop.

computer users' group *n. See* user group.

computer utility *n. See* utility.

computer virus *n. See* virus.

computer vision *n.* The processing of visual information by a computer. Computer vision is a form of artificial intelligence that creates a symbolic description of images that are generally input from a video camera or sensor in order to convert the images to digital form. *Acronym:* CV. *See also* artificial intelligence.

COM recorder *n.* Short for **c**omputer **o**utput **m**icrofilm **recorder**. A device that records computer information on microfilm.

CON *n.* The logical device name for *console;* reserved by the MS-DOS operating system for the keyboard and the screen. The input-only keyboard and the output-only screen together make up the console and represent the primary sources of input and output in an MS-DOS computer system.

concatenate *vb.* To join sequentially (for example, to combine the two strings "hello" and "there" into the single string "hello there"). *See also* character string.

concatenated data set *n.* A group of separate sets of related data treated as a single unit for processing.

concordance *n.* A list of words that appear in a document, along with the contexts of the appearances.

concurrent *adj.* Of, pertaining to, or characteristic of a computer operation in which two or more processes (programs) have access to the microprocessor's time and are therefore carried out nearly simultaneously. Because a microprocessor can work with much smaller units of time than people can perceive, concurrent processes appear to be occurring simultaneously but in reality are not.

condensed *adj.* Of, pertaining to, or characteristic of a font style, supported in some applications, that reduces the width of each character and then sets the characters closer together than their normal spacing. Many dot-matrix printers have a feature that causes the printer to reduce the width of each character and print the characters closer together, fitting more of them on a single line. *Compare* expanded.

conditioning *n.* The use of special equipment to improve the ability of a communications line to transmit data. Conditioning controls or compensates for signal attenuation, noise, and distortion. It can be used only on leased lines, where the path from sending to receiving computer is known in advance.

CONFIG.SYS *n.* A special text file that controls certain aspects of operating system behavior in MS-DOS and OS/2. Commands in the CONFIG.SYS file enable or disable system features, set limits on resources (for example, the maximum number of open files), and extend the operating system by loading device drivers that control hardware specific to an individual computer system.

configuration *n.* **1.** In reference to a single microcomputer, the sum of a system's internal and external components, including memory, disk drives, keyboard, video, and add-on hardware, such as a mouse or printer. Software (the operating system and various device drivers), the user's choices (established through configuration files), and sometimes hardware (switches and jumpers) are needed to "configure the configuration" to work correctly. Although system configuration can be changed, as by adding more memory or disk capacity, the basic structure of the system—its architecture—remains the same. *See also* AUTOEXEC.BAT, CONFIG.SYS. **2.** In relation to networks, the entire interconnected set of hardware, or the way in which a network is laid out—the manner in which elements are connected.

configuration file *n.* A file that contains machine-readable operating specifications for a piece of hardware or software or that contains information on another file or on a specific user.

connect charge *n.* The amount of money a user must pay for connecting to a commercial communications system or service. Some services calculate the connect charge as a flat rate per billing period. Others charge a varying rate based on the type of service or the amount of information being accessed. Still others base their charges on the number of time units used, the time or distance involved per connection, the bandwidth of each connected session, or some combination of the preceding criteria. *See also* connect time.

connection *n.* A physical link via wire, radio, fiber-optic cable, or other medium between two or more communications devices.

connectionless *adj.* In communications, of, pertaining to, or characteristic of a method of data transmission that does not require a direct connection between two nodes on one or more networks. Connectionless communication can be achieved by passing, or routing, data packets, each of which contains a source and destination address, through the nodes until the destination is reached. *See also* node (definition 2), packet (definition 2). *Compare* connection-oriented.

connection-oriented *adj.* In communications, of, pertaining to, or characteristic of a method of data transmission that requires a direct connection between two nodes on one or more networks. *Compare* connectionless.

connectivity *n.* **1.** The nature of the connection between a user's computer and another computer, such as a server or a host computer on the Internet or a network. This may describe the quality of the circuit or telephone line, the degree of freedom from noise, or the bandwidth of the communications devices. **2.** The ability of hardware devices or software packages to transmit data between other devices or packages. **3.** The ability of hardware devices, software packages, or a computer itself to work with network devices or with other hardware devices, software packages, or a computer over a network connection.

connector *n.* In hardware, a coupler used to join cables or to join a cable to a device (for example, an RS-232-C connector used to join a modem cable to a computer). A male connector is characterized by one or more exposed pins; a female connector is characterized by one or more receptacles designed to accept the pins on the male connector. *See also* DB connector, DIN connector.

connect time *n.* The amount of time during which a user is actively connected to a remote computer. On commercial systems, the connect time is one means of calculating the user's bill. *See also* connect charge.

console *n.* A control unit, such as a terminal, through which a user communicates with a computer. In microcomputers, the console is the cabinet that houses the main components and controls of the system, sometimes including the screen, the keyboard, or both. *See also* CON, system console.

contact manager *n.* A type of specialized database that allows a user to maintain a record of personal communication with others. *See also* database.

contention *n.* On a network, competition among stations for the opportunity to use a communications line or network resource. In one sense, contention applies to a situation in which two or more devices attempt to transmit at the same time, thus causing a collision on the line. In a somewhat different sense, contention also applies to a free-for-all method of controlling access to a communications line, in which the right to transmit is awarded to the station that wins control of the line. *Compare* token passing.

context-dependent *adj.* Of, pertaining to, or characteristic of a process or a set of data characters whose meaning depends on the surrounding environment.

context-sensitive help *n.* A form of assistance in which a program that provides on-screen help shows information to the user concerning the current command or operation being attempted.

context-sensitive menu *n.* A menu that highlights options as available or unavailable depending on the context. The menus on the Windows menu bar, for example, are context sensitive; commands such as Copy are grayed out if nothing is selected.

context switching *n.* A type of multitasking; the act of turning the central processor's "attention" from one task to another, rather than allocating increments of time to each task in turn. *See also* multitasking.

contextual search *n.* A search operation in which the user can direct a program to search specified files for a particular set of text characters.

contiguous *adj.* Having a shared boundary; being immediately adjacent. For example, contiguous sectors on a disk are data-storage segments physically located next to one another.

continuous carrier *n.* In communications, a carrier signal that remains on throughout the transmission, whether or not it is carrying information.
continuous-form paper *n.* Paper in which each sheet is connected to the sheets before and after it, for use with most impact and ink-jet printers and other printing devices with an appropriate paper-feed mechanism. The paper usually has holes punched along each side so that it can be pulled by a tractor-feed device. *Also called* fanfold paper, z-fold paper. *See also* pin feed, sprocket feed, tractor feed.
continuous processing *n.* The processing of transactions as they are input to the system. *Compare* batch processing (definition 3).
continuous-tone image *n.* An image, such as a photograph, in which color or varying shades of gray are reproduced as gradients rather than as clustered or variably sized dots, as in traditional book or newspaper printing. Continuous-tone images can be viewed on an analog monitor (such as a television monitor), which accepts input as a continuously variable signal. They cannot be viewed on a digital monitor, which requires input broken into discrete units, nor can they be printed in books or newspapers. *See also* scan (definition 2), video digitizer. *Compare* halftone.
continuous-tone printer *n.* A printer that produces an image using smoothly blended levels of continuous ink for gradations of gray or color. *Compare* dithering.
contouring *n.* **1.** In computer graphics, such as CAD models, the representation of the surface of an object—its bumps and crannies. **2.** In image processing, the loss of detail that occurs in a shaded image when too few gradations of gray are used to reproduce a graphic, such as a photograph. In graphic arts, this phenomenon is sometimes called posterization.
contrast *n.* **1.** The degree of difference between light and dark extremes of color on a monitor or on printed output. **2.** The control knob by which the contrast of a monitor is changed.
control *n.* **1.** Management of a computer and its processing abilities so as to maintain order as tasks and activities are carried out. Control applies to measures designed to ensure error-free actions carried out at the right time and in the right order relative to other data-handling or hardware-based activities. *See also* control bus. **2.** In a graphical user interface, an object on the screen that can be manipulated by the user to perform an action. The most common controls are buttons and scroll bars.
control break *n.* A transition in control of the computer that typically gives control of the CPU to the user console or to some other program.
Control-Break *n.* *See* Break key.
control bus *n.* The set of lines (conductors) within a computer that carry control signals between the CPU and other devices. For example, a control bus line is used to indicate whether the CPU is attempting to read from memory or to write to it.
control character *n.* **1.** Any of the first 32 characters in the ASCII character set (0 through 31 in decimal representation), each of which is defined as

having a standard control function, such as carriage return, linefeed, or backspace. **2.** Any of the 26 characters Control-A through Control-Z (1 through 26 in decimal representation) that can be typed at the keyboard by holding the Control key down and typing the appropriate letter. The six remaining characters with control functions, such as Escape (ASCII 27), cannot be typed using the Control key. *Compare* control code.

control code *n.* One or more nonprinting characters used by a computer program to control the actions of a device, used in printing, communications, and management of display screens. Control codes are mainly employed by programmers or by users to control a printer when an application does not support the printer or one of its specialized features. In video, control codes are sent from a computer to a display unit to manipulate the appearance of text or a cursor on the screen. *Also called* setup string. *See also* control character.

control console *n.* *See* console, system console.

Control key *n.* A key that, when pressed in combination with another key, gives the other key an alternative meaning. In many applications, pressing Control (labeled CTRL or Ctrl on a PC keyboard) plus another key is used as a command for special functions. *See also* control character (definition 2).

controller *n.* A device on which other devices rely for access to a computer subsystem. A disk controller, for example, controls access to one or more disk drives, managing physical and logical access to the drive or drives.

control panel *n.* In Windows and Macintosh systems, a utility that allows the user to control aspects of the operating system or hardware, such as system time and date, keyboard characteristics, screen colors, mouse movements, and networking options.

control sequence *n.* *See* control code.

control strip *n.* **1.** An equipment calibration tool used to determine the corrections needed to restore accuracy by comparing recorded data against known values. **2.** A utility that groups shortcuts to commonly used items or information, such as time, battery power level, desktop items, and programs, in an easily accessible place. *See also* shortcut.

conventional memory *n.* The amount of RAM addressable by an IBM PC or compatible machine operating in real mode, typically 640 KB. Without the use of special techniques, conventional memory is the only kind of RAM accessible to MS-DOS programs. *See also* low memory, protected mode, real mode. *Compare* expanded memory, extended memory.

convergence *n.* A coming together. Convergence can occur between different disciplines and technologies, as when telephone communications and computing converge in the field of telecommunications. It can also occur within a program, such as a spreadsheet, when a circular set of formulas are repeatedly recalculated (iterated), with the results of each iteration coming closer to a true solution.

#
A
B
C
D
E
F
G
H
I
J
K
L
M
N
O
P
Q
R
S
T
U
V
W
X
Y
Z

conversational *adj.* Of, pertaining to, or characteristic of the mode of operation, typical of microcomputers, in which the computer user and the system engage in a dialogue of commands and system responses. *See also* interactive.

conversational interaction *n.* Interaction in which two or more parties alternately transmit and receive messages from each other. *See also* interactive processing.

conversational mode *n.* *See* conversational.

conversion *n.* The process of changing from one form or format to another; where information is concerned, a changeover that affects form but not substance. Types of conversion include the following:

- Data conversion: Changing the way information is represented—for example, changing binary representation to decimal or hexadecimal.
- File conversion: Changing a file from one format to another. Another, more detailed, type of file conversion involves changing character coding from one standard to another, as in converting EBCDIC characters (used primarily with mainframes) to ASCII characters. *See also* ASCII, EBCDIC.
- Hardware conversion: Changing all or part of a computer system to work with new or different devices.
- Media conversion: Transferring data from one storage medium to another—for example, from disk to tape or from 3.5-inch Apple Macintosh disk to 5.25-inch MS-DOS disk.
- Software conversion: Changing or moving a program designed to run on one computer to run on another. Usually this involves detailed (professional) work on the program itself.
- System conversion: Changing from one operating system to another—for example, from MS-DOS to UNIX or OS/2.

conversion table *n.* A table listing a set of characters or numbers and their equivalents in another coding scheme. Common examples of conversion tables include ASCII tables, which list characters and their ASCII values, and decimal-to-hexadecimal tables.

converter *n.* Any device that changes electrical signals or computer data from one form to another. For example, an analog-to-digital converter translates analog signals to digital signals.

cookie *n.* **1.** A block of data that a server returns to a client in response to a request from the client. **2.** On the World Wide Web, a block of data that a Web server stores on a client system. When a user returns to the same Web site, the browser sends a copy of the cookie back to the server. Cookies are used to identify users, to instruct the server to send a customized version of the requested Web page, to submit account information for the user, and for other administrative purposes. **3.** Originally an allusion to "fortune cookie," a UNIX program that outputs a different message, or "fortune," each time it is used. On some systems, the cookie program is run during user logon.

cookie filtering tool *n.* A utility that prevents a cookie on a Web browser from relaying information about the user requesting access to a Web site. *See also* cookie (definition 2).

cooperative multitasking *n.* A type of multitasking in which one or more background tasks are given processing time during idle times in the foreground task only if the foreground task allows it. This is the primary mode of multitasking in the Macintosh operating system. *See also* background[1], context switching, foreground[1], multitasking. *Compare* preemptive multitasking.

coordinate *n.* Any element in a group of references to a particular location, such as the intersection of a certain row and column. In computer graphics and displays, coordinates specify such elements as points on a line, the corners of a square, or the location of a pixel on the screen. In other computer applications, coordinates specify cells on a spreadsheet, data points on a graph, locations in memory, and so on.

coordinated universal time format *n. See* Universal Time Coordinate.

coprocessor *n.* A processor, distinct from the main microprocessor, that performs additional functions or assists the main microprocessor. The most common type is the floating-point coprocessor, which is designed to perform numeric calculations faster and better than the general-purpose microprocessors used in personal computers. *See also* floating-point processor.

copy *vb.* To duplicate information and reproduce it in another part of a document, in a different file or memory location, or in a different medium. A copy operation can affect data ranging from a single character to large segments of text, a graphics image, or one to many data files. In most cases, a copy procedure leaves the original information in place. *See also* copy program. *Compare* cut and paste, move.

copy disk *n.* An MS-DOS command to duplicate the contents of a floppy disk on a second disk.

copy holder *n.* An inclined clipboard or other such device designed to hold printed material so that it can be easily viewed by someone working at a computer keyboard.

copyleft *n. See* General Public License.

copy program *n.* **1.** A program designed to duplicate one or more files to another disk or directory. **2.** A program that disables or circumvents the copy-protection device on a computer program so that the software can be copied, often illegally, to another disk. *See also* copy protection.

copy protection *n.* A software "lock" placed on a computer program by its developer to prevent the product from being copied and distributed without approval or authorization.

copyright *n.* A method of protecting the rights of an originator of a creative work, such as a text, a piece of music, a painting, or a computer program, through law. Unauthorized copying and distribution of copyrighted material can lead to severe penalties, whether done for profit or not. Copyrights affect the computer community in three ways: the copyright protection of software, the copyright status of material (such as song lyrics) distributed over a network such as the Internet, and the copyright status of original material distributed over a network (such as a newsgroup post). Legislation protecting the information disseminated through electronic media is still evolving. *See also* fair use, General Public License.

CORBA *n.* Acronym for **C**ommon **O**bject **R**equest **B**roker **A**rchitecture. A specification developed by the Object Management Group in 1992 in which pieces of programs (known as objects) communicate with other objects in other programs, even if the two programs are written in different programming languages and are running on different platforms. CORBA is designed to work in object-oriented environments. *See also* object (definition 2), object-oriented.

core *n.* One of the types of memory built into computers before random access memory was available or affordable. Some people still use the term to refer to the main memory of any computer system, as in the phrase "core dump"—a listing of the raw contents of main memory at the moment of a system crash. *Compare* RAM.

core program *n.* A program or program segment that is resident in RAM.

coresident *adj.* Of or pertaining to a condition in which two or more programs are loaded in memory at the same time.

correspondence quality *n. See* print quality.

corruption *n.* A process wherein data in memory or on disk is unintentionally changed, with its meaning thereby altered or obliterated.

counter *n.* A device that keeps track of the number of visitors to a World Wide Web site.

country code *n. See* major geographic domain.

country-specific *adj.* Of, pertaining to, or characteristic of hardware or software that uses characters or conventions unique to a particular country or group of countries. The term does not necessarily refer to spoken languages, although it does allow for special characters (such as accent marks) that are language-specific. The features considered country-specific generally include keyboard layout (including special-character keys), time and date conventions, financial and monetary symbols, decimal notation (decimal point or comma), and alphabetic sorting order. Such features are handled either by the operating system or by applications that offer options for tailoring documents to a particular set of national or international conventions.

courseware *n.* Software dedicated to education or training.

courtesy copy *n. See* cc.

cpi *n. See* characters per inch.

cps *n. See* characters per second.

CPU *n. See* central processing unit.

CPU cache *n.* A section of fast memory linking the CPU and main memory, which temporarily stores data and instructions the CPU needs to execute upcoming commands and programs. Considerably faster than main memory, the CPU cache contains data that is transferred in blocks, thereby speeding execution. *Also called* cache memory, memory cache. *See also* cache, central processing unit.

CPU cycle *n.* **1.** The smallest unit of time recognized by the CPU—typically a few hundred-millionths of a second. **2.** The time required for the CPU to perform the simplest instruction, such as fetching the contents of a register. *Also called* clock tick.

CPU fan *n.* An electric fan usually placed directly on a CPU or on the CPU's heat sink to help dissipate heat from the chip by circulating air around it. *See also* central processing unit, heat sink.

CPU speed *n.* A relative measure of the data-processing capacity of a particular CPU, usually measured in megahertz. *See also* central processing unit.

CPU time *n.* In multiprocessing, the amount of time during which a particular process has active control of the CPU. *See also* central processing unit, multiprocessing.

CR *n. See* carriage return.

cracker *n.* A person who overcomes the security measures of a computer system and gains unauthorized access. The goal of some crackers is to obtain information illegally from a computer system or use computer resources. However, the goal of the majority is merely to break into the system. *See also* hacker (definition 2).

crash¹ *n.* The failure of either a program or a disk drive. A program crash results in the loss of all unsaved data and can leave the operating system unstable enough to require restarting the computer. A disk drive crash, sometimes called a disk crash, leaves the drive inoperable and can cause loss of data. *See also* head crash.

crash² *vb.* **1.** For a system or program, to fail to function correctly, resulting in the suspension of operation. **2.** For a magnetic head, to hit a recording medium, with possible damage to one or both.

crash recovery *n.* The ability of a computer to resume operation after a disastrous failure, such as the failure of a hard drive. Ideally, recovery can occur without any loss of data, although usually some, if not all, data is lost. *See also* crash¹.

crawler *n. See* spider, Web browser.

CRC *n.* Acronym for **c**yclical (or **c**yclic) **r**edundancy **c**heck. A procedure used in checking for errors in data transmission. CRC error checking uses a complex calculation to generate a number based on the data transmitted. The sending device performs the calculation before transmission, and the receiving device repeats the same calculation after transmission. If both devices obtain the same result, it is assumed that the transmission was error-free.

creeping featurism *n.* The process in which software developers add features to each new release of a program, in an effort to enhance its competitive advantage, until the program becomes unduly cumbersome and difficult to use.
crippled version *n.* A scaled-down or functionally reduced version of hardware or software, distributed for demonstration purposes. *See also* demo.
critical error *n.* An error that suspends processing until the condition can be corrected either by software or by user intervention (for example, an attempt to read to a nonexistent disk, an out-of-paper condition on the printer, or a checksum fault in a data message).
crop *vb.* In computer graphics, to cut off part of an image, such as unneeded sections of a graphic or extra white space around the borders. As in preparing a photograph for traditional printing, cropping is used to refine or clean up a graphic for placement in a document.
crop marks *n.* **1.** Lines drawn at the edges of pages to mark where the paper will be cut to form pages in the final document. *See also* registration marks. **2.** Lines drawn on photographs or illustrations to indicate where they will be cropped, or cut. *See also* crop.
cross development *n.* The use of one system to develop programs for a different type of system, often because the software development tools of the development system are superior to those of the target system.
cross hairs *n.* Intersecting lines used by some computer input devices to locate a particular *x-y*-coordinate.
cross-hatching *n.* Shading made up of regularly spaced, intersecting lines, used to fill in areas of a graphic.
cross-linked files *n.* In Windows 95, Windows 3.*x*, and MS-DOS, a file-storage error occurring when one or more sections, or clusters, of the hard drive or a floppy disk have been erroneously allocated to more than one file in the file allocation table. Like lost clusters, cross-linked files can result from the ungraceful exit (messy or abrupt termination) of an application program. *See also* file allocation table, lost cluster.
cross-platform *adj.* Of, pertaining to, or characteristic of a software application or hardware device that can be run or operated on more than one system platform.
cross-post *vb.* To copy a message or news article from one newsgroup, conference topic, e-mail system, or other communications channel to another—for example, from a Usenet newsgroup to a CompuServe forum or from e-mail to a newsgroup.
crosstalk *n.* Interference caused by a signal transferring from one circuit to another, as on a telephone line.
CRT *n.* Acronym for **c**athode-**r**ay **t**ube. The basis of the standard microcomputer display screen. A CRT display is built around a vacuum tube containing one or more electron guns whose electron beams rapidly sweep horizontally across the inside of the front surface of the tube, which is coated with a material that glows when irradiated. Each electron beam moves from left to

right, top to bottom, one horizontal scan line at a time. To keep the screen image from flickering, the electron beam refreshes the screen 30 times or more per second. The clarity of the image is determined by the number of pixels on the screen. *See also* pixel, raster, resolution (definition 1).

CRT controller *n.* The part of a video adapter board that generates the video signal, including the horizontal and vertical synchronization signals. *See also* video adapter.

cruise *vb.* *See* surf.

crunch *vb.* To process information. *See also* number cruncher.

cryptoanalysis *n.* The decoding of electronically encrypted information for the purpose of understanding encryption techniques. *See also* cryptography, encryption.

cryptography *n.* The use of codes to convert data so that only a specific recipient will be able to read it, using a key. The persistent problem of cryptography is that the key must be transmitted to the intended recipient and may be intercepted. Public key cryptography is a recent significant advance. *See also* code[1] (definition 2), encryption, PGP, private key, public key.

CSO *n.* Acronym for **C**omputing **S**ervices **O**ffice. An Internet directory service that matches users' own names with e-mail addresses, generally at colleges and universities. The CSO service can be reached through Gopher.

CSO name server *n.* A facility that provides e-mail directory information through the CSO system. *See also* CSO.

CSS or **CSS1** *n.* *See* cascading style sheets.

CTERM *n.* *See* Communications Terminal Protocol.

CTI *n.* Acronym for **c**omputer-**t**elephony **i**ntegration. The practice of using a computer to control one or more telephone and communications functions.

CTL *n.* Short for **contr**o**l.** *See* control character (definition 2), Control key.

CTRL or **Ctrl** *n.* Short for **contr**o**l**. A designation used to label the Control key on computer keyboards. *See also* control character (definition 2), Control key.

Ctrl-Alt-Delete *n.* A three-key combination used with IBM and compatible computers to restart (reboot) the machine. Pressing Ctrl-Alt-Delete causes a warm boot in MS-DOS—the computer restarts but does not go through all the internal checks involved when power to the system is switched on (cold boot). In Windows 95 and Windows NT, Ctrl-Alt-Delete provides a dialog box from which the user may choose to shut down the computer or end any current tasks.

Ctrl-C *n.* The keyboard shortcut recognized by many programs (such as Windows) as an instruction to copy the currently selected item.

Ctrl-S *n.* **1.** On systems in which a software handshake is used between terminals and a central computer, the key combination used to suspend output. Ctrl-Q will resume output after a Ctrl-S suspension. *See also* handshake, XON/XOFF. **2.** A keyboard shortcut recognized by many programs as an instruction to save the current document or file.

CTS *n.* Acronym for **C**lear **T**o **S**end. In serial communications, a signal sent, as from a modem to its computer, to indicate that transmission can proceed. *Compare* RTS.
CUI *n.* *See* character user interface.
CUL8R A fanciful shorthand notation meaning "See you later," sometimes seen in Internet discussion groups as a farewell by a participant temporarily leaving the group.
curly quotes *n.* *See* smart quotes.
current cell *n.* *See* active cell.
current directory *n.* The disk directory at the end of the active directory path—the directory that is searched first for a requested file, and the one in which a new file is stored unless another directory is specified. *See also* path (definition 3).
cursor *n.* **1.** A special on-screen indicator, such as a blinking underline or rectangle, that marks the place at which a keystroke will appear when typed. **2.** In reference to digitizing tablets, the stylus (pointer or "pen"). **3.** In applications and operating systems that use a mouse, the arrow or other on-screen icon that moves with movements of the mouse.
cursor blink speed *n.* The rate at which a cursor on screen flashes on and off. *See also* cursor (definition 1).
cursor control *n.* The ability of a computer user to move the cursor to a specified location on the screen. Keys dedicated to cursor control include the arrow keys and others such as Backspace, Home, and End. Pointing devices such as the mouse can also control cursor movements, often helping the user move the cursor long distances in a document.
cursor key *n.* *See* arrow key.
CUSeeMe *n.* A video conferencing program developed at Cornell University. It was the first program to give Windows and Mac OS users the ability to engage in real-time video conferencing over the Internet, but it requires a lot of bandwidth (at least 128 Kbps speed) to function properly.
customize *vb.* To modify or assemble hardware or software to suit the needs or preferences of the user.
custom software *n.* Any type of program developed for a particular client or to address a special need. Certain products, such as dBASE and Lotus 1-2-3, are designed to provide the flexibility and tools required for the production of tailor-made applications.
cut *vb.* To remove part of a document, usually placing it temporarily in memory so that the cut portion can be inserted (pasted) elsewhere. *Compare* delete.
cut and paste *n.* A procedure in which the computer acts as an electronic combination of scissors and glue for reorganizing a document or for compiling a document from different sources. In cut and paste, the portion of a document to be moved is selected, removed to storage in memory or on disk, and then reinserted into the same or a different document.

CV *n. See* computer vision.

cybercafe or **cyber café** *n.* **1.** A coffee shop or restaurant that offers access to personal computers or other terminals that are connected to the Internet, usually for a per-hour or per-minute fee. **2.** A virtual café on the Internet, generally used for social purposes. Users interact by means of a chat program or by posting messages through a BBS, as in a newsgroup or on a Web site.

cybercash *n. See* e-money.

cyberchat *n. See* IRC.

cybercop *n.* A person who investigates criminal acts committed online, especially fraud and harassment.

cybernaut *n.* One who spends copious time online, exploring the Internet. *Also called* Internaut. *See also* cyberspace.

cyberpunk *n.* **1.** A genre of near-future science fiction in which conflict and action take place in virtual-reality environments maintained on global computer networks in a worldwide culture of dystopian alienation. The prototypical cyberpunk novel is William Gibson's *Neuromancer* (1982). **2.** A category of popular culture that resembles the ethos of cyberpunk fiction. **3.** A person or fictional character who resembles the heroes or central characters of cyberpunk fiction.

cybersex *n.* Communication via electronic means, such as e-mail, chat, or newsgroups, for the purpose of sexual stimulation or gratification. *See also* chat[1] (definition 1), newsgroup.

cyberspace *n.* **1.** The advanced shared virtual-reality network imagined by William Gibson in his novel *Neuromancer* (1982). **2.** The universe of environments, such as the Internet, in which persons interact by means of connected computers. A defining characteristic of cyberspace is that communication is independent of physical distance.

cyberspeak *n.* Terminology and language (often jargon, slang, and acronyms) relating to the Internet environment, that is, cyberspace. Most words prefixed by cyber- have the same meaning as their "real-world" counterparts, but the prefix specifically indicates their use in the online culture of the Internet and the Web—for example, cybercash, cybercop.

cybrarian *n.* Software used at some libraries that allows one to query a database through the use of an interactive search engine.

cycle power *vb.* To turn the power to a machine off and back on in order to clear something out of memory or to reboot after a hung or crashed state.

D

DA *n. See* desk accessory.
DAC *n. See* digital-to-analog converter.
daemon *n.* A program associated with UNIX systems that performs a housekeeping or maintenance utility function without being called by the user. A daemon sits in the background and is activated only when needed, for example, to correct an error from which another program cannot recover.
daisy chain *n.* A set of devices connected in series. In order to eliminate conflicting requests to use the channel (bus) to which all the devices are connected, either each device is given a different priority or, as in the Apple Desktop Bus, each device monitors the channel and transmits only when the line is clear.
DARPANET *n.* Short for **D**efense **A**dvanced **R**esearch **P**rojects **A**gency **Net**work. *See* ARPANET.
DASD *n.* Acronym for **d**irect **a**ccess **s**torage **d**evice. A data storage device by which information can be accessed directly, instead of by passing sequentially through all storage areas. For example, a disk drive is a DASD, but a tape unit, where data is stored as a linear sequence, is not. *See also* direct access. *Compare* sequential access.
.dat *n.* A generic file extension for a data file.
DAT *n. See* digital audio tape.
data *n.* Plural of the Latin *datum,* meaning an item of information. In practice, the term data is often used as the singular as well as the plural form of the noun. *Compare* information.
data aggregate *n.* A collection of data records. A data aggregate usually includes a description of the placement of the data blocks and their relation to the entire set.
data bank *n.* Any substantial collection of data.
database *n.* A file composed of records, each containing fields together with a set of operations for searching, sorting, recombining, and other functions. *Acronym*: DB. *See also* flat-file database, hierarchical database, relational database.
database administrator *n.* One who manages a database. The administrator determines the content, internal structure, and access strategy for a database, defines security and data integrity, and monitors performance. *Acronym:* DBA. *Also called* database manager.
database engine *n.* The program module or modules that provide access to a database management system.

#
A
B
C
D
E
F
G
H
I
J
K
L
M
N
O
P
Q
R
S
T
U
V
W
X
Y
Z

database machine *n.* **1.** A peripheral that executes database tasks, thereby relieving the main computer from performing them. **2.** A database server that performs only database tasks.
database management system *n.* A software interface between the database and the user. A database management system handles user requests for database actions and allows control of security and data integrity requirements. *Acronym:* DBMS. *Also called* database manager. *See also* database engine.
database manager *n.* *See* database administrator, database management system.
database publishing *n.* The use of desktop publishing or Internet technology to produce reports containing information obtained from a database.
database server *n.* A network node, or station, dedicated to storing and providing access to a shared database. *Also called* database machine.
database structure *n.* A general description of the format of records in a database, including the number of fields, specifications regarding the type of data that can be entered in each field, and the field names used.
data bit *n.* In asynchronous communications, one of a group of from 5 to 8 bits that represents a single character of data for transmission. Data bits are preceded by a start bit and followed by an optional parity bit and one or more stop bits. *See also* asynchronous transmission, bit, communications parameter.
data bus *n.* *See* bus.
data cable *n.* Fiber-optic or wire cable used to transfer data from one device to another.
data capture *n.* **1.** The collection of information at the time of a transaction. **2.** The process of saving on a storage medium a record of interchanges between a user and a remote information utility.
data carrier *n.* *See* carrier (definition 1).
Data Carrier Detected *n.* *See* DCD.
data channel *n.* *See* channel.
data collection *n.* **1.** The process of acquiring source documents or data. **2.** The grouping of data by means of classification, sorting, ordering, and other organizing methods.
datacom *n.* Short for **data com**munications. *See* communications.
data communications *n.* *See* communications.
data compaction *n.* *See* data compression.
data compression *n.* A means of reducing the amount of space or bandwidth needed to store or transmit a block of data, used in data communications, facsimile transmission, and CD-ROM publishing. *Also called* data compaction.
data conferencing *n.* Simultaneous data communication among geographically separated participants in a meeting. Data conferencing involves whiteboards and other software that enable a single set of files at one loca-

tion to be accessed and modified by all participants. *See also* desktop conferencing, whiteboard. *Compare* video conferencing.

data control *n.* The aspect of data management concerned with tracking how and by whom data is used, accessed, altered, owned, and reported on.

data corruption *n. See* corruption.

data definition language *n.* A language that defines all attributes and properties of a database, especially record layouts, field definitions, key fields, file locations, and storage strategy. *Acronym:* DDL.

data description language *n.* A language designed specifically for declaring data structures and files. *See also* data definition language.

data dictionary *n.* A database containing data about all the databases in a database system. Data dictionaries store all the various schema and file specifications and their locations. They also contain information about which programs use which data and which users are interested in which reports.

data directory *n. See* catalog, data dictionary.

data encryption *n. See* encryption.

data encryption key *n.* A sequence of data that is used to encrypt and decrypt other data. *Acronym:* DEK. *See also* decryption, encryption, key (definition 3).

data encryption standard *n. See* DES.

data entry *n.* The process of writing new data to computer memory.

data/fax modem *n.* A modem that can handle both serial data and facsimile images to either send or receive transmissions.

data field *n.* A well-defined portion of a data record, such as a column in a database table.

data file *n.* A file consisting of data in the form of text, numbers, or graphics, as distinct from a program file of commands and instructions. *Compare* program file.

data flow or **dataflow** *n.* **1.** The movement of data through a system, from entry to destination. **2.** In parallel processing, a design in which a calculation is made either when all necessary data is available (data-driven processing) or when other processors request the data (demand-driven processing). *See also* parallel processing.

data fork *n.* In Macintosh files, the part of a stored document that contains user-supplied information, such as the text of a word processing document. A Macintosh file can have a data fork, a resource fork, and a header. The operating system uses all three parts in file management and storage. *See also* resource (definition 2), resource fork.

data format *n.* The structure applied to data by an application to provide a context in which the data can be interpreted.

data glove *n.* A data input device or controller in the form of a glove fitted with sensors that convert movement of the hand and fingers into commands. *See also* virtual reality.

A B C D E F G H I J K L M N O P Q R S T U V W X Y Z

data independence *n.* The separation of data in a database from the programs that manipulate it. Data independence makes stored data as accessible as possible.

data integrity *n.* The accuracy of data and its conformity to its expected value, especially after being transmitted or processed.

data library *n.* A cataloged collection of data files on disk or in another storage medium.

data link *n.* A connection between any two devices capable of sending and receiving information, such as a computer and a printer or a main computer and a terminal. The term can also describe equipment, such as a modem, that enables transmitting and receiving. *See also* data-link layer, DCE, DTE.

data link escape *n.* In data transmission, a control character that changes the meaning of the characters immediately following it.

data-link layer *n.* The second of the seven layers in the ISO/OSI model for standardizing computer-to-computer communications. The data-link layer is one layer above the physical layer. Its concern is packaging and addressing data and managing the flow of transmissions. It is the lowest of the three layers (data-link, network, and transport) involved in actually moving data between devices. *See also* ISO/OSI model.

data management *n.* The control of data from acquisition and input through processing, output, and storage. For example, applications manage data by receiving and processing input and sending results to an output device or to disk storage. The user also manages data by acquiring it, organizing disks, backing up data, archiving files, and removing unneeded material.

data manipulation *n.* The processing of data by means of programs that accept user commands, offer ways to handle data, and tell the hardware what to do with the data.

data manipulation language *n.* In database management systems, a language that is used to insert data in, update, and query a database. Data manipulation languages can often perform mathematical and statistical calculations that facilitate generating reports. *Acronym:* DML. *See also* structured query language.

data medium *n.* The physical material on which computer data is stored.

data migration *n.* The process of moving data from one repository or source, such as a database, to another, usually via automated scripts or programs. Often data migration involves transferring data from one type of computer system to another.

data model *n.* A collection of related object types, operators, and integrity rules that form the abstract entity supported by a database management system. Thus, one speaks of a relational DBMS, a network DBMS, and so on, depending on the data model that a DBMS supports.

data network *n.* A network designed for transferring data encoded as digital signals, as opposed to a voice network, which transmits analog signals.

data packet *n.* *See* packet.

data processing *n.* **1.** The general work performed by computers. **2.** More specifically, the manipulation of data to transform it into some desired result. *Acronym:* DP. *Also called* ADP, automatic data processing, EDP, electronic data processing. *See also* distributed processing.
data rate *n.* The speed at which a circuit or communications line can transfer information, usually measured in bits per second.
data record *n.* *See* record[1].
data reduction *n.* The process of converting raw data to a more useful form by scaling, smoothing, ordering, or other editing procedures.
data set *n.* **1.** A collection of related information made up of separate elements that can be treated as a unit in data handling. **2.** In communications, a modem. *See also* modem.
Data Set Ready *n.* *See* DSR.
data sharing *n.* The use of a single file by more than one person or computer. Data sharing can be done by physically transferring a file from one computer to another or, more commonly, by networking and computer-to-computer communications.
data signal *n.* The information transmitted over a line or circuit. It consists of binary digits and can include actual information or messages and other elements such as control characters or error-checking codes.
data sink *n.* **1.** Any recording medium where data can be stored until needed. **2.** In communications, the portion of a DTE device that receives transmitted data.
data source *n.* **1.** The originator of computer data, frequently an analog or a digital data collection device. **2.** In communications, the portion of a DTE device that sends data.
data stream *n.* An undifferentiated, byte-by-byte flow of data.
data structure *n.* An organizational scheme, such as a record, that can be applied to data to facilitate interpreting the data or performing operations on it.
data switch *n.* A device in a computer system that routes incoming data to various locations.
Data Terminal Ready *n.* *See* DTR.
data traffic *n.* The exchange of electronic messages—control and data—across a network. Traffic capacity is measured in bandwidth; traffic speed is measured in bits per unit of time.
data transfer *n.* The movement of information from one location to another, either within a computer (as from a disk drive to memory), between a computer and an external device (as between a file server and a computer on a network), or between separate computers.
data transfer rate *n.* *See* data rate.
data transmission *n.* The electronic transfer of information from a sending device to a receiving device.
data type *n.* In programming, a definition of a set of data that specifies the possible range of values of the set, the operations that can be performed on

the values, and the way in which the values are stored in memory. Defining the data type—such as integer, character, or Boolean, for example—allows a computer to manipulate the data appropriately. *See also* variable.

data validation *n.* The process of testing the accuracy of data.

data value *n.* The literal or interpreted meaning of a data item, such as an entry in a database.

data warehouse[1] *n.* A database, accessible through a server and often very large, that can access all of a company's information. The warehouse can be distributed over several computers, and it may contain several databases, data from various sources in various formats, and data about how the warehouse is organized. Despite this complexity, users can retrieve and analyze all the information with simple commands. *See also* database, server (definition 1), transparent (definition 1).

data warehouse[2] *vb.* To acquire, collect, manage, and disseminate information gathered from various sources into a single location, or to implement an informational database used to store sharable data.

date stamping *n.* A software feature that automatically inserts the current date into a document.

datum *n.* Singular of *data;* a single item of information. *See also* data.

daughterboard *n.* A circuit board that attaches to another, such as the main system board (motherboard), to add extra capabilities. *See also* motherboard.

DAV connector *n. See* digital audio/video connector.

dB *n. See* decibel.

DB *n. See* database.

DBA *n. See* database administrator.

DB connector *n.* Any of various connectors that facilitate parallel input and output. The initials DB (for data bus) are followed by a number that indicates the number of lines (wires) within the connector. For example, a DB-9 connector supports up to nine lines, each of which can connect to a pin on the connector.

.dbf *n.* A file extension for a dBASE database file.

DBMS *n. See* database management system.

DC *n. See* direct current.

DCD *n.* Acronym for **D**ata **C**arrier **D**etected. A signal in serial communications that is sent from a modem to its computer to indicate that the modem is ready for transmitting. *Also called* RLSD (Received Line Signal Detect).

DCE *n.* Acronym for **D**ata **C**ommunications **E**quipment. One of two types of hardware connected by an RS-232-C serial connection, the other being a DTE device. A DCE is an intermediary device that often transforms input from a DTE before sending it to a recipient. A modem, for example, is a DCE that modulates data from a microcomputer (DTE) and sends it along a telephone connection. *See also* RS-232-C standard. *Compare* DTE.

DCOM *n.* Acronym for **D**istributed **C**omponent **O**bject **M**odel. The version of Microsoft's Component Object Model (COM) specification that stipulates

how components communicate over Windows-based networks. *Also called* Distributed COM. *See also* COM (definition 2).
DDBMS *n. See* distributed database management system.
DDE *n.* Acronym for **D**ynamic **D**ata **E**xchange. An interprocess communication method featured in Windows and OS/2. DDE allows two or more programs that are running simultaneously to exchange data and commands. DDE has been largely supplanted by OLE, which is an extension of DDE, and by ActiveX. *See also* ActiveX, interprocess communication, OLE.
DDL *n. See* data definition language.
dead halt *n.* A machine stop with no hope of recovery by either the program or the operating system. The only choice after a dead halt is to reboot. *Also called* drop-dead halt. *See also* hang. *Compare* reboot.
dead key *n.* A key on the keyboard that is used with another key to create an accented character. When pressed, a dead key produces no visible character, but the accent mark it represents will be combined with the next key pressed. *See also* key (definition 1).
dead-letter box *n.* In e-mail or message systems, a file to which undeliverable messages are sent.
deadlock *n.* **1.** A situation that occurs when two programs or devices are each waiting for a response from the other before continuing. *Also called* deadly embrace. **2.** In operating systems, a situation in which two or more processes are prevented from continuing while each waits for resources to be freed by the continuation of the other.
deadly embrace *n. See* deadlock (definition 1).
deblock *vb.* To remove one or more logical records (units of stored information) from a block, often to make specific units of information available for processing. *Compare* block[2] (definition 1).
debug *vb.* To detect, locate, and correct logical or syntactical errors in a program or malfunctions in hardware. *See also* bug, debugger, troubleshoot.
debugger *n.* A program designed to aid in debugging another program by allowing the programmer to step through the program, examine the data, and monitor conditions. *See also* bug (definition 1), debug.
decibel *n.* Abbreviated dB. One tenth of a bel, a unit used in electronics and other fields to measure the strength of a sound or signal.
decimal *adj.* Of or pertaining to the base-10 number system. *See also* base.
deck *n.* A storage device, such as a tape deck, or a group of such devices.
declarative markup language *n.* In the processing of text, a system of text-formatting codes that indicates only that a unit of text is a certain part of a document. Document formatting is then done by another program, called a parser. SGML and HTML are examples of declarative markup languages. *Acronym:* DML. *See also* HTML, SGML.
decompiler *n.* A program that attempts to generate high-level source code from assembly language code or machine code. *See also* disassembler. *Compare* compiler.

decompress *vb. See* uncompress.
decrement[1] *n.* The amount by which a number is decreased. *Compare* increment[1].
decrement[2] *vb.* To decrease a number by a given amount. *Compare* increment[2].
decryption *n.* The process of restoring encrypted data to its original form. *Compare* encryption.
dedicated *adj.* Of, pertaining to, or being a device, program, or procedure devoted to a single task or function.
dedicated channel *n.* A communications link reserved for a particular use or a particular user.
dedicated line *n.* **1.** A communications channel that permanently connects two or more locations. Dedicated lines are private or leased lines, rather than public ones. T1 lines, used by many organizations for Internet connectivity, are examples of dedicated lines. *Also called* leased line, private line. *Compare* switched line. **2.** A telephone line used for one purpose only, such as to receive or send faxes or to serve as a modem line.
default[1] *n.* A choice made by a program when the user does not specify an alternative. Defaults are built into a program when a value or option must be assumed for the program to function.
default[2] *vb.* In reference to programs, to make a choice when the user does not specify an alternative.
default button *n.* The control that is automatically selected when a window is introduced by an application or operating system, typically activated by pressing the Enter key.
default drive *n.* The disk drive that an operating system reads to and writes from when no alternative is specified.
default home page *n.* On a Web server, the file that is returned when a directory is referenced without a specific filename. This is specified by the Web server software and is typically the file called index.html or index.htm.
default printer *n.* The printer to which a computer sends documents for printing unless an alternative is specified.
Defense Advanced Research Projects Agency *n.* The U.S. government agency that provided the original support for the development of the interconnected networks that later grew into the Internet. *Acronym:* DARPA. *See also* ARPANET.
defragmentation *n.* The process of rewriting parts of a file to contiguous sectors on a hard disk to increase the speed of access and retrieval, usually accomplished by using a defragmentation utility (defragger). As files are added to and deleted from the computer's hard disk, the amount of continuous available space on the hard disk decreases. If a file saved to the hard disk is larger than the largest available block of space, the computer splits the file among sectors of the hard disk. When files are thus "fragmented," the computer must search the hard disk each time the file is accessed to find all the file's parts, which slows response time. *Compare* fragmentation.

#
A
B
C
D
E
F
G
H
I
J
K
L
M
N
O
P
Q
R
S
T
U
V
W
X
Y
Z

degausser *n.* A device used to remove magnetization from a video monitor or tape recorder head and to erase information from magnetic storage media, such as tapes and disks.

degradation *n.* **1.** In communications, a deterioration of signal quality, as from line interference. **2.** In computer systems, a reduction in level of performance or service. Degradation in microcomputer performance is indicated by slow response times or frequent pauses for disk access because memory is insufficient to hold an entire program plus the data the program is using.

deinstall *vb. See* uninstall.

dejagging *n.* Smoothing of the jagged, "stairstep" appearance of diagonal lines and curves in graphical images. *Also called* anti-aliasing. *Compare* aliasing.

DEK *n. See* data encryption key.

delete *vb.* To eliminate text, a file, or any part of a document. Deleting tells the computer that data or a file is no longer needed; a deletion usually indicates that the information should be removed permanently. In many cases, however, deleted data can be reinstated by choosing an Undo command within the application being used. A deleted file usually remains stored (and is recoverable) until the operating system reuses the space containing the deleted material. *See also* file recovery. *Compare* erase, undelete[1].

Delete key *n.* **1.** On IBM and PC-compatible computers, a key that removes the character following the insertion point. On the MS-DOS command line, it removes the character under the cursor. In some applications, it can also remove selected text or graphics. **2.** On Apple Macintosh computers, a key on the ADB and Extended keyboards that removes the character preceding the insertion point or deletes highlighted text or graphics.

deletia *n.* Omitted material. The term is used in responses to Usenet or mailing list messages to indicate that some unnecessary material has been excluded from the incorporated message being answered.

delimiter *n.* A special character that sets off, or separates, individual items in a program or set of data. For example, commas serve as delimiters separating the fields in this database record (each non-numeric field is enclosed by double quotation marks):

"Jones", "718 Harbor Drive", "Bayview", "WA", 98077;

See also field (definition 1), record[1].

Del key *n. See* Delete key.

demo *n.* **1.** Short for **demo**nstration. A partial or limited version of a software package distributed free of charge for advertising purposes. Demos often consist of animated presentations that describe or demonstrate the program's features. *See also* crippled version. **2.** A computer in a store that is available for customers to test.

demodulation *n.* In communications, the means by which a modem converts data from modulated carrier waves over a telephone line to the digital

A B C D E F G H I J K L M N O P Q R S T U V W X Y Z

form needed by a computer, with as little distortion as possible. *Compare* modulation.

demonstration program or **demo program** *n.* **1.** A prototype that shows the on-screen look and sometimes the proposed capabilities of a program under development. *See also* prototyping. **2.** A scaled-down version of a proprietary program offered as a marketing tool.

denizen *n.* A participant in a Usenet newsgroup.

dependence *n.* The state in which an entity is dependent on specific hardware or software or specific events for its own definition or functionality. *See also* context-dependent, device dependence, hardware-dependent, software-dependent.

derived font *n.* A font that has been scaled or modified from a previously existing font. *See also* font. *Compare* intrinsic font.

DES *n.* Acronym for **D**ata **E**ncryption **S**tandard. A specification for encryption of computer data developed by IBM and adopted by the U.S. government as a standard in 1976. DES uses a 56-bit key. *See also* encryption, key (definition 3).

descending sort *n.* A sort that arranges items in descending order—for example, with Z preceding A and higher numbers preceding lower ones. *See also* alphanumeric sort. *Compare* ascending sort.

descriptor *n.* In information retrieval, a word, similar to an index entry in a book, that identifies a significant topic or element in a stored document or group of documents. It is used as a key in rapid search and retrieval of information. *See also* keyword (definition 1).

deselect *vb.* To reverse the action of selecting an option, a range of text, a graphic, and so on. *Compare* select.

desk accessory *n.* A type of small program on Macintosh computers and in windowing programs for IBM PCs and compatibles that acts as the electronic equivalent of a clock, calendar, calculator, or other small appliance found on a typical desktop. Desk accessories can be activated when needed and then either put away or moved to a small part of the screen. *Acronym:* DA. *Also called* desktop accessory.

desktop *n.* An on-screen work area that uses icons and menus to simulate the top of a desk. A desktop is characteristic of the Apple Macintosh and of windowing systems such as Windows. It enables users to move pictures of objects and to start and stop tasks much as they would if they were working on a physical desktop. *See also* graphical user interface.

desktop accessory *n.* *See* desk accessory.

desktop computer *n.* A computer that fits conveniently on the surface of a business desk. Most personal computers as well as some workstations can be considered desktop computers. *Compare* portable computer.

desktop conferencing *n.* The use of computers for simultaneous communication among geographically separated participants in a meeting. This communication may include input to and display from application programs as well as audio and video communication. *See also* data conferencing, teleconferencing, video conferencing.

desktop enhancer *n.* Software that adds functionality to a windows-based operating system such as Windows or the Mac OS—for example, an enhanced file browser, clipboard, or multimedia player.

Desktop file *n.* A hidden file maintained on a particular volume (roughly equivalent to a disk) by the Macintosh operating system for storing information about the files on the volume, such as version data, lists of icons, and file references.

desktop publishing *n.* The use of a computer and specialized software to combine text and graphics to create a document that can be printed on either a laser printer or a typesetting machine. The original text and illustrations are generally produced with software such as word processors and drawing and painting programs and with photograph-scanning equipment and digitizers. The finished product is then transferred to a page-layout program, which enables the user to lay out text and graphics on screen; for refining the document, these programs often also include word processing and graphics features. *Acronym:* DTP.

desktop video *n.* The use of a personal computer to display video images, which may be recorded on video tape or on a laser disc or may be live footage from a video camera. Live video images can be transmitted in digital form over a network in video conferencing. *Acronym:* DTV.

destination *n.* The location (drive, folder, or directory) to which a file is copied or moved. *Compare* source.

detail file *n.* *See* transaction file.

detection *n.* Discovery of a certain condition that affects a computer system or the data with which it works.

device *n.* A generic term for a computer subsystem. Printers, serial ports, and disk drives are often referred to as devices; such subsystems frequently require their own controlling software, called device drivers. *See also* device driver.

device control character *n.* *See* control character.

device controller *n.* *See* input/output controller.

device dependence *n.* The requirement that a particular device be present or available for the use of a program, interface, or protocol. Device dependence in a program is often considered unfortunate because the program either is limited to one system or requires adjustments for every other type of system on which it is to run. *Compare* device independence.

device driver *n.* A software component that permits a computer system to communicate with a device. In most cases, the driver also manipulates the hardware in order to transmit the data to the device. Many devices, especially video adapters on PC-compatible computers, will not work properly—if at all—without the correct device drivers installed in the system.

A B C D E F G H I J K L M N O P Q R S T U V W X Y Z

#
A
B
C
D
E
F
G
H
I
J
K
L
M
N
O
P
Q
R
S
T
U
V
W
X
Y
Z

device independence *n.* A characteristic of a program, interface, or protocol that supports software operations that produce similar results on a wide variety of hardware. For example, PostScript is a device-independent page-description language because programs issuing PostScript drawing and text commands need not be customized for each potential printer. *Compare* device dependence.

device-independent bit map *n.* *See* DIB (definition 1).

device name *n.* The label by which a computer system component is identified by the operating system. MS-DOS, for example, uses the device name COM1 to identify the first serial communications port.

device resolution *n.* *See* resolution (definition 1).

DFS *n.* *See* distributed file system.

dialect *n.* A variant of a language or protocol. For example, Transact-SQL is a dialect of SQL.

dialog *n.* **1.** In computing, the exchange of human input and machine responses that forms a "conversation" between an interactive computer and the person using it. **2.** The exchange of signals by computers communicating on a network.

dialog box *n.* In a graphical user interface, a special window displayed by the system or application to solicit a response from the user. *See also* windowing environment.

dial-up *adj.* Of, pertaining to, or being a connection that uses the public switched telephone network rather than a dedicated circuit or some other type of private network.

dial-up access *n.* Connection to a data communications network through a public switched telecommunication network.

dial-up service *n.* A telephone connection provider for a local or worldwide public switched telephone network that provides Internet or intranet access, advertisement via a Web page, access to news services, or access to the stock market and other resources.

DIB *n.* **1.** Acronym for **d**evice-**i**ndependent **b**it map. A file format designed to ensure that bitmapped graphics created using one application can be loaded and displayed in another application exactly the way they appeared in the originating application. *See also* bitmapped graphics. **2.** Acronym for **D**irectory **I**nformation **B**ase. A directory of user and resource names in an X.500 system. *Also called* white pages. *See also* CCITT X series.

dichotomizing search *n.* *See* binary search.

dictation software *n.* Computer programs that can recognize spoken words as input; used as alternatives to keyboard input. Dictation software cannot comprehend the spoken language; it can only convert and transmit the sounds to the computer. *Also called* voice recognition software. *See also* voice recognition.

digerati *n.* Cyberspace populace that can be roughly compared to "literati." Digerati are people renowned as or claiming to be knowledgeable about topics and issues related to the digital revolution; more specifically, they are people "in the know" about the Internet and online activities. *See also* guru, techie, wizard (definition 1).

digest *n.* **1.** An article in a moderated newsgroup that summarizes multiple posts submitted to the moderator. *See also* moderator, newsgroup. **2.** A message in a mailing list that is sent to subscribers in place of the multiple individual posts that the digest contains. If the mailing list is moderated, the digest may be edited.

digicash *n.* *See* e-money.

digit *n.* One of the characters used to indicate a whole number (unit) in a number system. In any number system, the number of possible digits is equal to the base used. For example, the decimal (base-10) system has 10 digits, 0 through 9; the binary (base-2) system has 2 digits, 0 and 1; and the hexadecimal (base-16) system has 16 digits, 0 through 9 and A through F.

digital *adj.* In computing, analogous to the term binary because the computers familiar to most people process information coded as combinations of binary digits (bits). *Compare* analog.

digital audio disc *n.* *See* compact disc.

digital audio tape *n.* A magnetic tape storage medium for recording digitally encoded audio information. *Acronym:* DAT.

digital audio/video connector *n.* An interface on some high-end video cards or TV tuner cards that allows the simultaneous transmission of digital audio and video signals. *Also called* DAV connector. *See also* interface (definition 3), video adapter.

digital camera *n.* A type of camera that captures and stores photographed images electronically instead of on traditional film. After the image has been captured, it is downloaded by cable to the computer using software supplied with the camera. Once stored in the computer, the image can be manipulated and processed much like the image from a scanner or related input device.

digital cash *n.* *See* e-money.

digital certificate *n.* **1.** An assurance that software downloaded from the Internet comes from a reputable source. A digital certificate provides information about the software, such as the identity of the author and the date on which the software was registered with a certificate authority, as well as a measure of tamper-resistance. **2.** A user identity card or "driver's license" for cyberspace. Issued by a certificate authority, a digital certificate is an electronic credential that authenticates a user on the Internet and intranets. Digital certificates ensure the legitimate online transfer of confidential information, money, or other sensitive materials by means of public encryption technology. *Also called* digital cert, digital ID. *See also* certificate authority, encryption, private key, public key.

digital communications *n.* Exchange of communications in which all information is transmitted in binary-encoded (digital) form.

digital computer *n.* A computer in which operations are based on two or more discrete states. Binary digital computers are based on two states, logical

A B C D E F G H I J K L M N O P Q R S T U V W X Y Z

"on" and "off," represented by two voltage levels, arrangements of which are used to represent all types of information—numbers, letters, graphics symbols, and program instructions. Within such a computer, the states of various circuit components change continuously to move, operate on, and save this information. *Compare* analog computer.

digital data transmission *n.* The transfer of information encoded as a series of bits rather than as a fluctuating (analog) signal in a communications channel.

digital display *n.* A video display capable of rendering only a fixed number of colors or gray shades. *Compare* analog display.

digital line *n.* A communications line that transmits information only in binary-encoded (digital) form. To minimize distortion and noise interference, a digital line regenerates the signal periodically during transmission. *Compare* analog line.

digital photography *n.* Photography by means of a digital camera, which captures and stores each image electronically rather than using the conventional silver halide–based film. *See also* digital camera.

digital recording *n.* The storage of information in binary-encoded (digital) format. Digital recording converts information—text, graphics, sound, or pictures—to strings of 1s and 0s that can be physically represented on a storage medium. Digital recording media include computer disks and tapes, optical (or compact) discs, and the ROM cartridges used for some software and many computer games.

digital satellite system *n.* A high-powered satellite system with the ability to deliver high-quality transmissions of hundreds of channels directly to television receivers. *Acronym:* DSS.

digital signal *n.* A signal, such as one transmitted within or between computers, in which information is represented by discrete states—for example, high and low voltages—rather than by fluctuating levels in a continuous stream, as in an analog signal.

digital signal processor *n.* An integrated circuit designed for high-speed data manipulation and used in audio, communications, image manipulation, and other data acquisition and data control applications. *Acronym:* DSP.

digital signature *n.* A personal authentication method based on encryption and secret authorization codes used for "signing" electronic documents.

digital sort *n.* A type of ordering process in which record numbers or their key values are sorted digit by digit, beginning with the least significant (rightmost) digit.

digital speech *n. See* speech synthesis.

digital subscriber line *n.* An ISDN Basic Rate Interface line or channel. *Acronym:* DSL. *See also* BRI, ISDN.

digital-to-analog converter *n.* A device that translates digital data to an analog signal. A digital-to-analog converter takes a succession of discrete digital values as input and creates an analog signal whose amplitude corresponds, moment by moment, to each digital value. *Acronym:* DAC. *Compare* analog-to-digital converter.

digital versatile disc *n. See* digital video disc.

digital video disc *n.* The next generation of optical disc storage technology. With digital video disc technology, video, audio, and computer data can be encoded onto a compact disc (CD). A digital video disc can store greater amounts of data than a traditional CD—as much as 17 GB in the case of a double-sided digital video disc. A digital video disc player is needed to read digital video discs; this player is also equipped to read older optical storage technologies. Advocates of digital video disc technology intend to replace current digital storage formats, such as laser disc, CD-ROM, and audio CD, with the single digital format of the digital video disc. *Acronym:* DVD. *Also called* digital versatile disc. *See also* digital video disc–ROM.

digital video disc–erasable *n.* A proposed extension to the digital video disc recording format to allow multiple re-recording by a consumer. *Acronym:* DVD-E. *See also* digital video disc–ROM.

digital video disc–recordable *n.* A proposed extension to the digital video disc recording format to allow one-time recording by a consumer. *Acronym:* DVD-R.

digital video disc–ROM *n.* A computer-readable version of a digital video disc containing either 4.7 or 8.5 GB of storage per side. *Acronym:* DVD-ROM. *See also* digital video disc.

digitize *vb.* To convert any continuously varying (analog) source of input, such as the lines in a drawing or a sound signal, to a series of discrete units represented in a computer by the binary digits 0 and 1. Analog-to-digital converters are commonly used to perform this translation. *See also* analog-to-digital converter.

digitizing tablet *n. See* graphics tablet.

dimensioning *n.* In CAD programs, a means of specifying and possibly controlling the measurements and spatial relationships of elements in a modeled object, such as using lines, arrows, and text (that is, measurements) to indicate the length, height, and thickness of each of the walls in a modeled room or house. *See also* CAD.

dimmed *adj.* Shown on the screen in gray characters instead of black characters on white or white characters on black. Menu options are dimmed in a graphical user interface when they are not available under current circumstances—for example, "Cut" is dimmed when no text has been highlighted, and "Paste" is dimmed when there is no text in the clipboard to paste.

DIN connector *n.* A multipin connector conforming to the specification of the German national standards organization (Deutsch Industrie Norm). DIN connectors are used to link various components in personal computers.

dingbat *n.* A small graphical element used for decorative purposes in a document. Some fonts, such as Zapf Dingbats, are designed to present sets of dingbats. *See also* font. *Compare* bullet.

A B C D E F G H I J K L M N O P Q R S T U V W X Y Z

DIP *n.* **1.** Acronym for **d**ual **i**n-line **p**ackage. A standard for packaging integrated circuits in which the electronic circuits etched on a silicon wafer are enclosed in a rectangular housing of plastic or ceramic and connected to downward-pointing pins protruding from the longer sides of the chip. This design does not work well for modern chips requiring very large numbers of connections. *Compare* SIP, surface-mount technology. **2.** *See* document image processing.

DIP switch *n.* One or more small rocker- or sliding-type switches contained in the housing of a dual in-line package (DIP) connected to a circuit board. Each switch on a DIP switch can be set to one of two positions, closed or open, to control options on the circuit board. *See also* DIP.

dir *n.* An MS-DOS command that instructs a computer to display a list of files and subdirectories in the current directory or folder. If the command is followed by a path, the computer displays a list of files and subdirectories in the specified directory or folder. *See also* path (definition 3).

direct access *n.* The ability of a computer to find and go straight to a particular storage location in memory or on disk to retrieve or store an item of information. Note that direct access is not the same as direct memory access. *See also* random access. *Compare* direct memory access.

direct access storage device *n.* *See* DASD.

direct cable connection *n.* A link between the I/O ports of two computers that uses a single cable rather than a modem or other active interface device. In most cases, a direct cable connection requires a null modem cable.

direct-connect modem *n.* A modem that uses standard telephone wire and connectors and plugs directly into a telephone jack, eliminating the need for an intermediary telephone. *Compare* acoustic coupler.

direct current *n.* Electrical current whose direction of flow does not reverse. The current may stop or change amplitude, but it always flows in the same direction. *Acronym:* DC. *Compare* alternating current.

direction key *n.* *See* arrow key.

direct memory access *n.* Memory access that does not involve the microprocessor and is frequently used for data transfer directly between memory and an "intelligent" peripheral device, such as a disk drive. *Acronym:* DMA.

directory *n.* A catalog for filenames and other directories stored on a disk. A directory is a way of organizing and grouping files. Depending on how an operating system supports directories, filenames in a directory can be viewed and ordered in various ways—for example, alphabetically, by date, by size, or as icons in a graphical user interface. In the Macintosh and Windows 95 operating systems, directories are called folders. *See also* root directory, subdirectory.

directory path *n.* *See* pathname.

directory service *n.* A service on a network that returns mail addresses of other users or enables a user to locate hosts and services.

directory tree *n.* A graphics display listing the directories and subdirectories on a hard disk in tree form, with subdirectories shown as branches of the main directory. *See also* branch (definition 1), directory, tree structure.

DirectX *n.* Windows 95 software that gives applications direct access to a computer's sound and graphics hardware.

dirty *adj.* Of, pertaining to, or characteristic of a communications line that is hampered by excessive noise, degrading the quality of the signal. *See also* noise (definition 2).

dirty power *n.* A power source that can cause damage to electronic components, as a result of noise, voltage spikes, or incorrect voltage levels.

disable *vb.* To suppress something or to prevent it from happening. Disabling is a method of controlling system functions by disallowing certain activities. For example, a program might temporarily disable nonessential requests from system devices to prevent interruptions during a critical point in processing. *Compare* enable.

disassembler *n.* A program that converts machine code to assembly language source code. Most debuggers contain some kind of built-in disassembler that allows the programmer to view an executable program in terms of human-readable assembly language. *See also* decompiler. *Compare* assembler.

disassociate *vb.* In Windows 95 and NT, to remove an association between a file and some application. *Compare* associate.

disc *n.* A round, flat piece of nonmagnetic, shiny metal encased in a plastic coating, designed to be read from and written to by optical (laser) technology. It is now standard practice to use the spelling *disc* for optical discs and *disk* in all other computer contexts, such as floppy disk, hard disk, and RAM disk. *See also* compact disc.

disconnect *vb.* To break a communications link.

discretionary hyphen *n.* *See* hyphen.

discussion group *n.* Any of a variety of online forums in which people communicate about subjects of common interest. Forums for discussion groups include electronic mailing lists, Internet newsgroups, and IRC channels.

disk *n.* A round, flat piece of flexible plastic (floppy disk) or inflexible metal (hard disk) coated with a magnetic material that can be electrically influenced to hold information recorded in digital (binary) form. In most computers a disk is the primary means of storing data on a permanent or semipermanent basis. Floppy disks are encased in a protective plastic jacket; a hard disk is enclosed in a rigid case and can be exposed only in a dust-free environment. Types of disks used with microcomputers include floppy disks, microfloppy disks, hard disks, and removable cartridges that can be used with some hard disk drives and data storage units such as Bernoulli boxes. *Compare* compact disc, disc.

disk access time *n.* *See* access time (definition 2).

#
A
B
C
D
E
F
G
H
I
J
K
L
M
N
O
P
Q
R
S
T
U
V
W
X
Y
Z

disk cartridge *n.* A removable disk enclosed in a protective case. A disk cartridge can be used by certain types of hard disk drives and related devices, such as the external data storage units known as Bernoulli boxes.

disk controller *n.* A special-purpose chip and associated circuitry that directs and controls reading from and writing to a computer's disk drive. A disk controller handles such tasks as positioning the read/write head, mediating between the drive and the microprocessor, and controlling the transfer of information to and from memory. Disk controllers are used with floppy disk drives and hard disks and can either be built into the system or be part of a card that plugs into an expansion slot.

disk copy *n.* The process of duplicating a source disk's data and the data's organizational structure onto a target disk. *See also* backup.

disk crash *n.* The failure of a disk drive. *See also* crash[1].

disk directory *n.* An index of the files on a disk. A disk directory includes information about the files, such as their names, sizes, dates of creation, and physical locations on the disk. *See also* directory.

disk drive *n.* An electromechanical device that reads from and writes to disks. Floppy disk drives are designed to accept removable disks in either 5.25-inch or 3.5-inch format; hard disk drives are faster, high-capacity storage units that are completely enclosed in a protective case.

disk driver *n.* A device driver added to a system to support a specific manufacturer's disk device. *See also* device driver.

disk envelope *n.* The paper container that holds a 5.25-inch floppy disk and its attached jacket. The disk envelope protects exposed surfaces of the disk from dust and other foreign material that can scratch and otherwise damage the surface, resulting in the loss of recorded data. *See also* disk jacket.

diskette *n.* *See* floppy disk.

disk jacket *n.* The protective plastic sheath that covers a floppy disk.

diskless workstation *n.* A station on a computer network that is not equipped with a disk drive and that uses files stored in a file server. *See also* file server.

disk memory *n.* *See* virtual memory.

disk operating system *n.* *See* DOS.

disk partition *n.* A logical compartment on a physical disk drive. A single disk might have two or more logical disk partitions, each referenced with a different disk drive name. Multiple partitions are divided into a primary (boot) partition and one or more extended partitions.

disk server *n.* A node on a local area network that acts as a remote disk drive shared by network users. Unlike a file server, which performs the more sophisticated tasks of managing network requests for files, a disk server functions as a storage medium on which users can read and write files. A disk server can be divided into sections (volumes), each of which appears to be a separate disk. *Compare* file server.

disk unit *n.* A disk drive or its housing.
display *n.* The visual output device of a computer, commonly a CRT-based video display. With portable and notebook computers, the display is usually an LCD-based or a gas plasma–based flat-panel display. *See also* flat-panel display, liquid crystal display, video adapter, video display.
display adapter *n.* *See* video adapter.
display attribute *n.* A quality assigned to a character or image displayed on the screen. Display attributes include such features as color, intensity, and blinking.
display background *n.* In computer graphics, the portion of an on-screen image that remains static while other elements change—for example, window borders on a screen.
display board *n.* *See* video adapter.
display card *n.* *See* video adapter.
display device *n.* *See* display.
display frame *n.* One image in an animation sequence. *See also* frame (definition 3).
display image *n.* The collection of elements displayed together at a single time on a computer screen.
display port *n.* An output port on a computer that provides a signal for a display device such as a video monitor.
Display PostScript *n.* An extended version of the PostScript language, intended for device-independent imaging (including monitors and printers) in a multitasking environment. Display PostScript has been adopted by some hardware manufacturers as the standard imaging approach for both screens and printers. *See also* PostScript.
display screen *n.* The part of a video unit on which images are shown. *See also* CRT.
display terminal *n.* *See* terminal.
distortion *n.* An undesirable change in the waveform of a signal. Distortion can occur during signal transmission or when a signal passes through a circuit. Distortion often results in loss of information. It is mainly a problem in analog signals; digital signals are not affected by moderate distortion.
distribute *vb.* To allocate among locations or facilities, such as in a data-processing function that is performed by a collection of computers and other devices linked together by a network.
distributed bulletin board *n.* A collection of newsgroups distributed to all computers in a wide area network. *See also* newsgroup, Usenet.
Distributed COM *n.* *See* DCOM.
Distributed Component Object Model *n.* *See* DCOM.
distributed computing *n.* *See* distributed processing.
distributed database *n.* A database implemented on a network. The component partitions are distributed over various nodes of the network. Depending on the specific update and retrieval traffic, distributing the database can significantly enhance overall performance. *See also* partition (definition 2).

A B C D E F G H I J K L M N O P Q R S T U V W X Y Z

distributed database management system *n.* A database management system capable of managing a distributed database. *Acronym:* DDBMS. *See also* distributed database.

distributed file system *n.* A file management system in which files may be located on multiple computers connected over a local or wide area network.

distributed network *n.* A network in which processing, storage, and other functions are handled by separate units (nodes) rather than by a single main computer.

distributed processing *n.* A form of information processing in which work is performed by separate computers linked through a communications network.

distributed transaction processing *n.* Transaction processing that is shared by one or more computers communicating over a network. *Acronym:* DTP. *See also* distributed processing, transaction processing.

distributed workplace *n.* An environment other than the traditional office or factory, in which work is carried out on a regular basis. The flexibility afforded by the combination of communications and computing technologies enables workers to conduct business anywhere the appropriate computer and data communications infrastructure has been set up. *Also called* distributed office, virtual office. *See also* SOHO, telecommute.

distribution list *n.* A list of recipients on an e-mail mailing list. This can be in the form of either a mailing list program, such as LISTSERV, or an alias in an e-mail program for all recipients of an e-mail message. *See also* alias (definition 2), LISTSERV, mailing list.

distributive sort *n.* An ordering process in which a list is separated into parts and then reassembled in a particular order. *See also* sort algorithm. *Compare* bubble sort, insertion sort, merge sort, quicksort.

dithering *n.* A technique used in computer graphics to create the illusion of varying shades of gray on a monochrome display or printer, or additional colors on a color display or printer. By treating areas of an image as groups of dots that are colored in different patterns, dithering takes advantage of the eye's tendency to blur spots of different colors by averaging their effects and merging them into a single perceived shade or color. Dithering is used to add realism to computer graphics and to soften jagged edges in curves and diagonal lines at low resolutions. *See also* aliasing, halftone.

divergence *n.* A moving apart or separation. On computer displays, divergence occurs when the red, green, and blue electron beams in a color monitor do not collectively light the same spot on the screen. Within a program, such as a spreadsheet, divergence can occur when a circular set of formulas are repeatedly recalculated (iterated), with the results of each iteration moving further from a stable solution. *Compare* convergence.

.dl_ *n.* A file extension indicating a compressed .dll file, used in a Windows setup procedure. *See also* .dll.

.dll *n.* A file extension for a dynamic-link library. *See also* dynamic-link library.

DLL *n. See* dynamic-link library.
DMA *n. See* direct memory access.
DML *n. See* data manipulation language.
DNS *n.* **1.** Acronym for **D**omain **N**ame **S**ystem. The system by which hosts on the Internet have both domain name addresses (such as bluestem.prairienet.org) and IP addresses (such as 192.17.3.4). The domain name address is used by human users and is automatically translated into the numerical IP address, which is used by the packet-routing software. *See also* domain name address, IP address. **2.** Acronym for **D**omain **N**ame **S**ervice. The Internet utility that implements the Domain Name System (see definition 1). *See also* DNS server.
DNS server *n.* A computer that can answer Domain Name Service queries. The DNS server keeps a database of host computers and their corresponding IP addresses. Presented with the name apex.com, for example, the DNS server would return the IP address of the hypothetical company Apex. *Also called* name server. *See also* DNS (definition 2), IP address.
.doc *n.* A file extension that identifies document files formatted for a word processor. This is the default file extension for Microsoft Word document files.
dock *vb.* **1.** To connect a laptop or notebook computer to a docking station. *See also* docking station, laptop, portable computer. **2.** To move a toolbar to the edge of an application window so that it attaches to and becomes a feature of that window.
docking mechanism *n.* The portion of a docking station that physically connects the portable computer with the station. *See also* docking station.
docking station *n.* A unit for housing a laptop or notebook computer that contains a power connection, expansion slots, and connections to peripherals, such as a monitor, printer, full-size keyboard, and mouse. The purpose of a docking station is to turn the laptop or notebook computer into a desktop machine and allow users the convenience of using peripherals. *See also* expansion slot, laptop, peripheral, portable computer.
document *n.* Any self-contained piece of work created with an application and, if saved on disk, given a unique filename by which it can be retrieved. To a computer, data is merely a collection of characters, so a spreadsheet or a graphic is as much a document as any word-processed material. In the Macintosh environment in particular, a document is any user-created work named and saved as a separate file.
documentation *n.* The set of instructions shipped with a program or a piece of hardware. Documentation usually includes necessary information about the type of computer system required, setup instructions, and instructions on the use and maintenance of the product.
document-centric *adj.* Of, pertaining to, or characteristic of an operating system in which the user opens document files and thus automatically invokes the applications (such as word processors or spreadsheet programs) that process them. Many graphical user interfaces, such as the Macintosh

A B C D E F G H I J K L M N O P Q R S T U V W X Y Z

A B C D E F G H I J K L M N O P Q R S T U V W X Y Z

Finder, as well as the World Wide Web, are document-centric. *Compare* application-centric.
document file *n.* A user-created file that represents the output of a program. *Also called* data file. *Compare* program file.
document image processing *n.* A system for storing and retrieving information for an enterprise in the form of bitmapped images of paper documents input with a scanner rather than in the form of text and numeric files. Document image processing takes more memory than purely electronic data processing, but it more readily incorporates signatures, drawings, and photographs and can be more familiar to users without computer training. *Acronym:* DIP.
document management *n.* The full spectrum of electronic document creation and distribution within an organization.
document processing *n.* The act of retrieving and manipulating a document. In terms of the way a computer works, document processing involves creating or retrieving a data file, using a program to manipulate the data, and storing the modified file.
document reader *n.* A device that scans printed text and uses character recognition methods to convert it to computer text files. *See also* character recognition.
document source *n.* The plain-text HTML form of a World Wide Web document, with all tags and other markup displayed as such rather than being formatted. *Also called* source, source document. *See also* HTML.
document window *n.* In windowing environments such as the Apple Macintosh and Windows, an on-screen window (enclosed work area) in which the user can create, view, or work on a document.
domain *n.* **1.** In database design and management, the set of valid values for a given attribute. For example, the domain for the attribute AREA-CODE might be the list of all valid three-digit numeric telephone area codes in the United States. *See also* attribute (definition 1). **2.** For Windows NT Advanced Server, a collection of computers that share a common domain database and security policy. Each domain has a unique name. **3.** In the Internet and other networks, the highest subdivision of a domain name in a network address, which identifies the type of entity owning the address (for example, .com for commercial users or .edu for educational institutions) or the geographical location of the address (for example, .fr for France). The domain is the last part of the address (for example, www.acm.org). *See also* domain name.
domain name *n.* An address of a network connection that identifies the owner of that address in a hierarchical format: *server.organization.type*. For example, www.whitehouse.gov identifies the Web server at the White House, which is part of the U.S. government.
domain name address *n.* The address of a device connected to the Internet or any other TCP/IP network, in the hierarchical system that uses

words to identify servers, organizations, and types, such as www.logos.net. *See also* TCP/IP.

domain name server *n. See* DNS server.

Domain Name Service *n. See* DNS (definition 2).

Domain Name System *n. See* DNS (definition 1).

Domain Naming System *n. See* DNS (definition 1).

dongle *n. See* hardware key.

DOS *n.* Acronym for **d**isk **o**perating **s**ystem. A generic term describing any operating system that is loaded from disk devices when the system is started or rebooted. *See also* MS-DOS, PC-DOS.

DOS extender *n.* A program designed to extend the 640 KB of conventional memory available for use by DOS and DOS-based applications. A DOS extender works by claiming a portion of reserved memory (memory used by other parts of the system, such as the video adapter, the ROM BIOS, and the I/O ports).

DOS prompt *n.* The visual indication from the MS-DOS command processor that the operating system is ready to accept a new command. The default DOS prompt is a path followed by a greater-than sign (for example, C:>); the user can also design a custom prompt with the PROMPT command.

dot *n.* **1.** In UNIX, MS-DOS, OS/2, and other operating systems, the character that separates a filename from an extension, as in TEXT.DOC (pronounced "text-dot-doc"). **2.** In computer graphics and printing, a small spot combined with others in a matrix of rows and columns to form a character or a graphic element in a drawing or design. The dots forming an image on the screen are called pixels. The resolution of a display or printing device is often expressed in dots per inch. *See also* pixel, resolution (definition 1). *Compare* spot. **3.** In an Internet address, the character that separates the different parts of the domain name, such as the entity name from the domain. *See also* domain (definition 3), domain name.

dot address *n.* An IP address in dotted quad form. *See also* IP address.

dot-addressable mode *n.* A mode of operation in which a computer program can address ("point to") individual dots on the screen or in a printed character. *See also* all points addressable.

dot com *n. See* .com (definition 1).

dot-matrix[1] *adj.* Referring to video and print hardware that forms character and graphical images as patterns of dots.

dot matrix[2] *n.* The rectangular grid, or matrix, of tiny "cells" in which dots are displayed or printed in the patterns required to form text characters, circles, squares, and other graphical images. *See also* dot-matrix printer, raster graphics.

dot-matrix printer *n.* Any printer that produces characters made up of dots using a wire-pin print head. The quality of output from a dot-matrix printer might be low enough to show individual dots or might be high enough to approach the look of fully formed characters. Dot-matrix printers

A B C D E F G H I J K L M N O P Q R S T U V W X Y Z

are often categorized by the number of pins in the print head—typically 9, 18, or 24. *Compare* laser printer.

dot pitch *n.* **1.** In printers, the distance between dots in a dot matrix. *See also* dot matrix[2]. **2.** In video displays, a measure of image clarity. A video display's dot pitch is the vertical distance, expressed in millimeters, between like-colored pixels. A smaller dot pitch generally means a crisper image. *See also* CRT, display.

dots per inch *n.* A measure of screen and printer resolution that is expressed as the number of dots that a device can print or display per linear inch. *Acronym:* dpi.

double-click *vb.* To press and release a mouse button twice without moving the mouse. Double-clicking is a means of rapidly selecting and activating a program or program feature. *Compare* click, drag.

double-density disk *n.* A disk created to hold data at twice the density (bits per inch) of a previous generation of disks. Early IBM PC floppy disks held 180 KB of data. Double-density disks increased that capacity to 360 KB. *See also* floppy disk, microfloppy disk. *Compare* high-density disk.

double-sided disk *n.* A floppy disk that can hold data on both its top and bottom surfaces.

double-strike *n.* On an impact printer, the process of printing twice over a word, producing text that appears darker and heavier than it normally appears. On dot-matrix printers, double striking with a slight offset can be used to fill in the space between the dots, producing smoother and darker characters.

down *adj.* Not functioning, in reference to computers, printers, communications lines on networks, and other such hardware.

downlink *n.* The transmission of data from a communications satellite to an earth station.

download *vb.* **1.** In communications, to transfer a copy of a file from a remote computer to the requesting computer by means of a modem or network. **2.** To send a block of data, such as a PostScript file, to a dependent device, such as a PostScript printer. *Compare* upload[2].

downloadable font *n.* A set of characters stored on disk and sent (downloaded) to a printer's memory when needed for printing. Downloadable fonts are most commonly used with laser printers and other page printers, although many dot-matrix printers can accept some of them. *Also called* soft font.

downsizing *n.* In computing, the practice of moving from larger computer systems, such as mainframes and minicomputers, to smaller systems in an organization, generally to save costs and to update to newer software. The smaller systems are usually client/server systems composed of a combination of PCs, workstations, and some legacy system such as a mainframe, connected in one or more local area networks or wide area networks. *See also* client/server architecture, legacy system.

downstream *adv.* or *adj.* The term applied to data moving from a remote network to an individual computer. In some Internet-related communications technologies, data flows more quickly downstream than upstream; cable modems, for example, can transfer data as fast as 30 Mbps downstream but support much slower rates, from 128 Kbps to around 2 Mbps, upstream. *Compare* upstream.
downtime *n.* The amount or percentage of time a computer system or associated hardware remains nonfunctional. Although downtime can occur because hardware fails unexpectedly, it can also be a scheduled event, as when a network is shut down to allow time for maintenance.
downward compatibility *n.* The capability of source code or programs developed on a more advanced system or compiler version to be executed or compiled by a less advanced (older) system or version. *Compare* upward-compatible.
DP *n.* *See* data processing.
dpi *n.* *See* dots per inch.
draft mode *n.* A high-speed, relatively low-quality print mode offered by most dot-matrix printers. *See also* dot-matrix printer, draft quality, print quality.
draft quality *n.* A low grade of printing generated by the draft mode on dot-matrix printers. Draft quality varies among printers, ranging from suitable for most purposes to nearly useless. *See also* draft mode, print quality.
drag *vb.* In a graphical user interface, to move an object on the screen by "grabbing" it and pulling it to a new location using the mouse. The user positions the mouse pointer over the object and presses and holds down the mouse button while moving the mouse to the new location.
drag-and-drop *vb.* To perform operations in a graphical user interface by dragging objects on the screen with the mouse. For example, to delete a document in the Mac OS, a user can drag the document icon across the screen and drop it on the trashcan icon. *See also* drag.
DRAM *n.* *See* dynamic RAM.
drawing interchange format *n.* *See* DXF.
drawing program *n.* A program for manipulating object-oriented graphics, as opposed to manipulating pixel images. In a drawing program, for example, the user can manipulate an element, such as a line or a circle, as an independent object simply by selecting the object and moving it. *See also* object-oriented graphics, pixel image, vector graphics.
dribbleware *n.* Updates, patches, and new drivers for a software product that are released one at a time, as they become available, rather than being issued together in a new version of the product. A company using the dribbleware technique may distribute new and replacement files on disk or CD-ROM or may make them available for download through the Internet or a private network. *See also* driver, patch[1].

A B C D E F G H I J K L M N O P Q R S T U V W X Y Z

drill down *vb.* To start at a top-level or general menu, directory, or Web page and pass through several intermediate menus, directories, or linked pages, until the specific file, page, menu command, or other item being sought is reached. Drilling down is common practice in searching for files or information on the Internet.

drive *n. See* disk drive.

drive bay *n.* A hollow, rectangular area in a computer chassis designed to hold a disk drive. The side walls of a drive bay generally contain holes to facilitate installation of a disk drive. Some drive bays, such as those for hard disks, are not visible to the user. Most drives are located on the front of the chassis so that the user can interact with the drive.

drive letter *n.* The naming convention for disk drives on IBM and compatible computers. Drives are named by letter, beginning with A, followed by a colon.

drive mapping *n.* The assignment of a letter or name to a disk drive so that the operating system or network server can identify and locate it. For example, in PCs, the primary drive mappings are A: and B: for floppy disk drives and C: for the hard disk. *See also* A:, B:, disk drive, hard disk.

drive number *n.* The naming convention for Macintosh disk drives. For example, a two-drive system calls its drives 0 and 1.

driver *n.* A hardware device or a program that controls or regulates another device. A device driver, for example, is a device-specific control program that enables a computer to work with a particular device, such as a printer or a disk drive. *See also* device driver.

drop cap *n.* A large capital letter at the beginning of a text block that occupies the vertical depth of two or more lines of regular text.

drop-dead halt *n. See* dead halt.

drop-down menu *n.* A menu that drops from the menu bar when requested and remains open without further action until the user closes it or chooses a menu item. *Compare* pull-down menu.

drop in *vb.* To read a spurious signal during a data read/write operation, producing erroneous data.

drop out *vb.* To lose the signal momentarily during a data read/write operation, thus producing erroneous data.

drum *n.* A rotating cylinder used with some printers and plotters. *See also* drum plotter, laser printer.

drum plotter *n.* A plotter in which paper is wrapped around a large revolving drum, with a pen that moves back and forth at the uppermost point on the drum. The paper is rolled with the drum to align the correct point on the paper with the pen. Drums take up a fraction of the space required by flatbed plotters that can handle the same paper size. They also effectively have no limit on the length of the paper they can handle. *See also* plotter. *Compare* flatbed plotter, pinch-roller plotter.

drum scanner *n.* A type of scanner where the medium being scanned, such as a sheet of paper, is rotated around a stationary scan head. *See also* scanner. *Compare* flatbed scanner, handheld scanner, sheet-fed scanner.

.drv *n.* The file extension for a driver file. *See also* driver.

dry run *n.* Running a program intended to have a dramatic effect, such as formatting a disk or printing a book, with the effect disabled, thus avoiding formatting a disk with data on it or wasting paper.

DSL *n. See* digital subscriber line.

DSP *n. See* digital signal processor.

DSR *n.* Acronym for **D**ata **S**et **R**eady. A signal used in serial communications sent, for example, by a modem to the computer to which it is attached, to indicate that it is ready to operate. *Compare* CTS.

DSS *n. See* digital satellite system.

DTE *n.* Acronym for **D**ata **T**erminal **E**quipment. In the RS-232-C hardware standard, any device, such as a microcomputer or a terminal, that has the ability to transmit information in digital form over a cable or a communications line. *See also* RS-232-C standard. *Compare* DCE.

DTP *n. See* desktop publishing, distributed transaction processing.

DTR *n.* Acronym for **D**ata **T**erminal **R**eady. A signal used in serial communications sent, for example, by a computer to its modem to indicate that the computer is ready to accept incoming transmission.

DTV *n.* Acronym for **d**esk**t**op **v**ideo. The use of digital cameras over a network for video conferencing. *See also* video conferencing.

dual boot *n.* A computer configuration that allows a user to boot one of a choice of two operating systems on a PC. Some possible dual boot combinations include Windows 95/Windows NT, Windows NT/OS/2, and Windows 95/Linux. Some operating systems, such as Windows 95 and OS/2, include a multiple boot option. Older operating systems, such as Windows 3.*x* and DOS, require the use of a boot utility to perform a dual boot. *See also* boot[1].

dual density *adj.* Of, pertaining to, or characteristic of floppy disk drives that can read from and write to disks in more than one density format.

dual disk drive *adj.* Of, pertaining to, or characteristic of a computer that has two floppy disk drives.

dual in-line package *n. See* DIP (definition 1).

dual processors *n.* Two processors used in a computer to speed its operation—one processor to control memory and the bus, and another to manage input/output. Many personal computers use a second processor to perform complex mathematical operations. *See also* coprocessor, floating-point processor.

dual-scan display *n.* A passive-matrix LCD-type display used in laptop computers. The screen refresh rate is twice as fast in dual-scan displays as in standard passive-matrix displays. Compared with active-matrix displays, dual-scan displays are more economical in terms of power consumption but have less clarity and a smaller viewing angle. *See also* passive-matrix display, refresh rate.

dual-sided disk drive *n.* A disk drive that can read or write information to both the top and bottom sides of a double-sided disk. Dual-sided disk drives have two read/write heads, one for each disk surface.

dumb quotes *n.* Quotation marks that have the same appearance (usually upright, like the apostrophe ' and the quotation marks " on a typewriter) whether they stand before or after the material being quoted. *Compare* smart quotes.

dumb terminal *n.* A terminal that does not contain an internal microprocessor. Dumb terminals are typically capable of displaying only characters and numbers and responding to simple control codes. *See also* terminal. *Compare* smart terminal.

dummy *n.* A placeholder, usually a character, a record, or a variable, that is used to reserve space until the intended item is available.

duplex^{1} *adj.* Capable of carrying information in both directions over a communications channel. A system is full-duplex if it can carry information in both directions at once; it is half-duplex if it can carry information in only one direction at a time.

duplex^{2} *n.* **1.** Simultaneous communications, in both directions, between the sender and receiver. *Also called* duplex transmission, full-duplex transmission. *See also* half-duplex transmission. **2.** Photographic paper on which an image can be printed on both sides.

duplex channel *n.* A communications link that allows for duplex (two-way) transmission.

duplex printer *n.* A printer capable of printing on both sides of the page.

duplex system *n.* A system of two computers, one of which is active while the other remains on standby, ready to take over processing if the active machine malfunctions.

duplex transmission *n.* *See* duplex^{2} (definition 1).

duplicate key *n.* A value assigned to an indexed field in one record in a database that duplicates a value assigned to the same field in another record in the database. For example, a key composed of ZIP-CODE would contain duplicate values if the file contained a number of addresses from a single Zip code. A field in which duplicate values are permitted cannot serve as a primary key because the primary key must be unique. *See also* field (definition 1), key (definition 2), primary key.

DVD *n.* *See* digital video disc.

DVD-E *n.* *See* digital video disc–erasable.

DVD-R *n.* *See* digital video disc–recordable.

DVD-ROM *n.* *See* digital video disc–ROM.

Dvorak keyboard *n.* A keyboard layout developed as an alternative to the popular QWERTY keyboard. The Dvorak keyboard was designed to speed typing by placing the characters on the keyboard for easiest access to the most frequently typed letters. *See also* ergonomic keyboard, keyboard. *Compare* QWERTY keyboard.

DXF *n.* Short for drawing interchange format. A computer-aided design file format originally developed for use with the AutoCAD program to facilitate transfer of graphics files between applications.

dye-diffusion printer *n. See* continuous-tone printer.

dye-sublimation printer *n. See* continuous-tone printer.

dynalink *n.* Short for **dyna**mic **link.** *See* dynamic-link library.

dynamic *adj.* Occurring immediately and concurrently. For both hardware and software, the term describes some action or event that occurs when and as needed. In dynamic memory management, for example, a program is able to negotiate with the operating system when it needs more memory.

Dynamic Data Exchange *n. See* DDE.

dynamic HTML *n.* A technology designed to add interactivity and graphical interest to Web pages by allowing those pages to change and update themselves dynamically—that is, in response to user actions, without the need for repeated downloads from a server. Dynamic HTML enables client-side scripts (programs that affect elements on a Web page) produced with languages such as VBScript and JavaScript to control and manipulate elements such as fonts and graphics by means of HTML tags. For the user, dynamic HTML produces the type of interactivity and relatively rapid download times associated with multimedia CD-ROM products. *See also* HTML.

dynamic keys *n.* An encryption technique in which messages are encrypted differently for each transmission based on different keys so that if a key is captured and decrypted, it will never be useful again. *See also* encryption, key (definition 3).

dynamic-link library *n.* A feature of the Windows family of operating systems and OS/2 that allows executable routines to be stored separately as files with DLL extensions and to be loaded only when needed by a program. *Acronym:* DLL.

dynamic page *n.* An HTML document that contains animated GIFs, Java applets, or ActiveX controls. *See also* ActiveX controls, animated GIF, HTML, Java applet.

dynamic RAM *n.* A form of semiconductor RAM. Dynamic RAMs store information in integrated circuits containing capacitors. Because capacitors lose their charge over time, dynamic RAM boards must include logic to refresh (recharge) the RAM chips continuously. While a dynamic RAM is being refreshed, it cannot be read by the processor. Despite being slower, dynamic RAMs are more common than RAMs because their circuitry is simpler and because they can hold up to four times as much data. *Acronym:* DRAM. *See also* RAM. *Compare* static RAM.

dynamic random access memory *n. See* dynamic RAM.

#
A
B
C
D
E
F
G
H
I
J
K
L
M
N
O
P
Q
R
S
T
U
V
W
X
Y
Z

dynamic SLIP *n.* Short for **dynamic S**erial **L**ine **I**nternet **P**rotocol. Internet access under SLIP in which the user's IP address is not permanent but instead is reassigned from a pool each time the user connects. The number of IP addresses an Internet service provider needs to offer is reduced to the number of connections that can be in use at one time, rather than the total number of subscribers. *See also* IP address, ISP, SLIP.

dynamic storage *n.* Information storage systems whose contents will be lost if power is removed from the system. RAM systems are the most common form of dynamic storage; both dynamic RAM and static RAM are considered forms of dynamic storage. *See also* dynamic RAM, static RAM. *Compare* permanent storage.

dynamic Web page *n.* A Web page that has fixed form but variable content, allowing it to be tailored to a customer's search criteria.

E

EAROM *n.* Acronym for **e**lectrically **a**lterable **r**ead-**o**nly **m**emory. *See* EEPROM.

Easter egg *n.* A hidden feature of a computer program. It may be a hidden command, an animation, a humorous message, or a list of credits for the people who developed the program. To display an Easter egg, a user often must enter an obscure series of keystrokes.

EBCDIC *n.* Acronym for **E**xtended **B**inary **C**oded **D**ecimal **I**nterchange **C**ode. An IBM code that uses 8 bits to represent 256 possible characters. It is used primarily in IBM mainframes, whereas personal computers use ASCII. *Compare* ASCII.

e-bomb *n.* Short for **e**-mail **bomb.** A technique used by some hackers in which a target is put on a large number of mailing lists so that network traffic and storage are tied up by e-mail sent by other mailing list subscribers to the lists' recipients.

e-cash *n.* *See* e-money.

ECC *n.* *See* error-correcting code.

echo[1] *n.* In communications, a signal transmitted back to the sender that is distinct from the original signal. Network connections can be tested by sending an echo back to the main computer.

echo[2] *vb.* To transmit a received signal back to the sender. Data communications circuits may echo text back to the originating terminal to confirm that it has been received.

echo cancellation *n.* A technique for eliminating unwanted incoming transmissions in a modem that are echoes of the modem's own transmission. The modem sends a modified, reversed version of its transmission on its receiving path, thus erasing echoes while leaving incoming data intact. Echo cancellation is standard in V.32 modems.

echo check *n.* In communications, a method for verifying the accuracy of transmitted data by retransmitting it to the sender, which compares the echoed signal with the original.

echoplex *n.* In communications, a technique for error detection. The receiving station retransmits data back to the sender's screen, where it can be displayed visually to check for accuracy.

echo suppressor *n.* In communications, a method for preventing echoes in telephone lines. Echo suppressors inhibit signals from the listener to the speaker, creating a one-way channel. For modems that transmit and receive on the same frequency, the echo suppressor must be disabled to allow two-way transmission. This disabling produces the high-pitched tone heard in modem-to-modem connections.

A B C D E F G H I J K L M N O P Q R S T U V W X Y Z

e-commerce *n. See* electronic commerce.

e-credit *n. See* electronic credit.

edge connector *n.* The set of wide, flat metallic contacts on an expansion board that is inserted into a personal computer's expansion slot or a ribbon cable's connector. The edge connector connects the board with the system's shared data pathway, or bus, by means of a series of printed lines that connect to the circuits on the board. *See also* expansion board, ribbon cable.

EDI *n.* Acronym for **e**lectronic **d**ata **i**nterchange. A set of standards for the transfer of business documents, such as purchase orders and invoices, between computers, with the goal of eliminating paperwork and improving response time. For EDI to be effective, users must agree on standards for formatting and exchanging information, such as the X.400 protocol. *See also* CCITT X series, standard (definition 1).

edit *vb.* **1.** To make a change to an existing file or document. Changes are saved in memory or in a temporary file but are not added to the document until the program is instructed to save them. Editing programs typically provide safeguards against inadvertent changes, for example, by requesting confirmation before saving under an existing filename or by allowing the user to assign a password to a file. **2.** To run software that makes extensive, predictable changes to a file automatically, such as a linker or a filter for graphics.

editing keys *n.* A set of keys on some keyboards that assist in editing. Located between the main keyboard and the numeric keypad, editing keys consist of three pairs: Insert and Delete, Home and End, and Page Up and Page Down.

edit key *n.* In a software application, a predefined key or combination of keys that, when pressed, causes the application to enter edit mode.

edit mode *n.* The mode of a program in which a user can make changes to a document, as by inserting or deleting data or text. *Compare* command mode.

editor *n.* A program that creates files or makes changes to existing files. An editor is usually less powerful than a word processor, lacking the latter's text formatting capability. Text or full-screen editors allow the user to move through the document using direction arrows; line editors require that the user indicate the line number on which text is to be edited.

EDO DRAM *n.* Acronym for **e**xtended **d**ata **o**ut **d**ynamic **r**andom **a**ccess **m**emory. A type of memory that allows for faster read times (and faster overall system performance) than DRAM of comparable speed by allowing a new read cycle to begin while data is being read from a previous cycle. *Compare* dynamic RAM, EDO RAM.

EDO RAM *n.* Acronym for **e**xtended **d**ata **o**ut **r**andom **a**ccess **m**emory. A type of dynamic RAM that keeps data available for the CPU while the next memory access is being initialized, resulting in increased speed. *See also* central processing unit, dynamic RAM. *Compare* EDO DRAM.

EDP *n.* Acronym for **e**lectronic **d**ata **p**rocessing. *See* data processing.

.edu *n.* In the Internet's Domain Name System, the top-level domain that identifies addresses operated by four-year, degreed educational institutions. The designation .edu appears as a suffix at the end of the address. *See also* DNS (definition 1), domain (definition 3), .k12.us. *Compare* .com, .gov, .mil, .net, .org.

edutainment *n.* Multimedia content—in software, on CD-ROM, or on a Web site—that purports to educate the user as well as entertain. *See also* multimedia.

EEMS *n.* Acronym for **E**nhanced **E**xpanded **M**emory **S**pecification. A superset of the original Expanded Memory Specification. EMS version 3.0 allowed only storage of data and supported 4 page frames. EEMS allowed up to 64 page frames along with executable code to be stored in expanded memory. The features of EEMS were included in EMS version 4.0. *See also* EMS, page frame.

EEPROM *n.* Acronym for **e**lectrically **e**rasable **p**rogrammable **r**ead-**o**nly **m**emory. A type of EPROM that can be erased with an electrical signal. It is useful for stable storage for long periods without electricity while still allowing reprogramming. EEPROMs contain less memory than RAM, take longer to reprogram, and can be reprogrammed only a limited number of times before wearing out. *See also* EPROM, ROM.

e-form *n.* Short for **e**lectronic **form**. An online document that contains blank spaces for a user to fill in with requested information and that can be submitted through a network to the organization requesting the information. On the Web, e-forms are often coded in CGI script and secured via encryption. *See also* CGI (definition 1), encryption.

EIDE *n.* *See* Enhanced IDE.

EISA *n.* Acronym for **E**xtended **I**ndustry **S**tandard **A**rchitecture. A bus standard for the connection of add-on cards to a PC motherboard, such as video cards, internal modems, and cards that support other peripherals. EISA has a 32-bit data path, and it uses connectors that can accept ISA cards. However, EISA cards are compatible only with EISA systems. EISA can operate at much higher frequencies than the ISA bus and provides much faster data throughput than ISA. *See also* ISA.

electroluminescent *adj.* Giving off light when electric current is applied. Electroluminescent panels are used in portable computers to backlight the liquid crystal displays. *See also* liquid crystal display.

electroluminescent display *n.* A type of flat-panel display used in laptops. Electroluminescent displays provide a sharp, clear image and a wide viewing angle. They were replaced by active-matrix LCD screens. *See also* flat-panel display, liquid crystal display, passive-matrix display. *Compare* active-matrix display.

electronic bulletin board *n.* *See* BBS (definition 1).

electronic cash *n.* *See* e-money.

electronic circuit *n. See* circuit.
electronic commerce *n.* Commercial activity that takes place by means of connected computers. Electronic commerce can occur between vendor and customer computers through EDI or between a user and a vendor through an online information service, the Internet, or a bulletin board system. *Also called* e-commerce. *See also* EDI.
electronic credit *n.* A form of electronic commerce involving credit card transactions carried out over the Internet. *Also called* e-credit. *See also* electronic commerce.
electronic data interchange *n. See* EDI.
electronic data processing *n. See* data processing.
electronic form *n. See* e-form.
electronic journal *n. See* journal.
electronic mail *n. See* e-mail[1].
electronic mail services *n.* Services that allow users, administrators, or daemons to send, receive, and process e-mail. *See also* daemon.
electronic mall *n.* A virtual collection of online businesses that affiliate with the intention of increasing the exposure of each business through the fellow businesses.
electronic money *n. See* e-money.
electronic music *n.* Music created with computers and electronic devices. *See also* MIDI, synthesizer.
electronic photography *n. See* digital photography.
electronic publishing *n.* A general term for distributing information via electronic media, such as communications networks or CD-ROM.
electronics *n.* The branch of physics dealing with electrons, electronic devices, and electrical circuits.
electronic software distribution *n.* A means of directly distributing software to users online over the Internet. Electronic software distribution is analogous to direct-mail ordering. *Acronym:* ESD.
electronic spreadsheet *n. See* spreadsheet program.
electronic storefront *n.* A business that displays its merchandise on the Internet and has provisions for contact or online sales.
electronic text *n. See* e-text.
electrophotographic printers *n.* Printers in a category including laser, LED, and LCD printers. In such a printer, an electrically charged, photosensitive drum develops a pattern of electrostatic charge on its surface representing the photo negative of the image to be printed. Toner adheres to the charged areas of the drum, the drum presses the ink onto the paper, and then heat binds the toner to the paper. The printer types vary mainly in how they charge the drum. *See also* laser printer, LCD printer, LED printer.
electrophotography *n.* The production of photographic images using electrostatic charges. This method is used in photocopiers and laser printers. *Also called* xerography. *See also* electrophotographic printers.

electrostatic *adj.* Of or relating to electric charges that are not flowing along a conducting path. Electrostatic charges are used in copiers and laser printers to hold toner particles on a photoconducting drum and in flatbed plotters to hold the plot medium in place.

electrostatic discharge *n.* The discharge of static electricity from an outside source, such as human hands, into an integrated circuit, often resulting in damage to the circuit. *Acronym:* ESD.

electrostatic plotter *n.* A plotter that creates an image from a dot pattern on specially coated paper. The paper is electrostatically charged and exposed to toner, which adheres to the dots. Electrostatic plotters can be up to 50 times faster than pen plotters but are more costly. Color models produce images through multiple passes with cyan, magenta, yellow, and black. *See also* plotter. *Compare* electrophotographic printers, pen plotter.

electrostatic printer *n. See* electrostatic plotter.

element *n.* **1.** Any stand-alone item within a broader context. For example, a picture element (pixel) is one single dot on a computer screen or in a computer graphic. **2.** In markup languages such as HTML and SGML, the combination of a set of tags, any content contained between the tags, and any attributes the tags may have. Elements can be nested, one within the other. *See also* attribute (definition 3), HTML, markup language, SGML.

elevator *n.* The square box within a scroll bar that can be moved to change the position of text or an image on the screen. *Also called* scroll box, thumb. *See also* scroll bar.

ellipsis *n.* A set of three dots (...) used to convey incompleteness. In many windowing applications, selecting a command that is followed by an ellipsis will produce a submenu or a dialog box. *See also* dialog box.

e-mail[1] or **email** or **E-mail** *n.* **1.** The exchange of text messages and computer files over a communications network, such as a local area network or the Internet, usually between computers or terminals. **2.** An electronic text message.

e-mail[2] or **email** or **E-mail** *vb.* To send an e-mail message.

e-mail address *n.* A string that identifies a user so that the user can receive Internet e-mail. An e-mail address typically consists of a name that identifies the user to the mail server, followed by an at sign (@) and the host name and domain name of the mail server. For example, if Anne E. Oldhacker has an account on the machine called baz at Foo Enterprises, she might have the e-mail address aeo@baz.foo.com.

e-mail filter *n.* Reading software that automatically sorts incoming e-mail into folders or mailboxes based on information contained in the message. For example, all mail from a user's Uncle Joe might be placed in a folder labeled "Uncle Joe." Filters may also be used either to block or accept e-mail from designated sources.

embedded hyperlink *n.* A link to a resource, embedded within text or associated with an image or an image map. *See also* hyperlink, image map.

A B C D E F G H I J K L M N O P Q R S T U V W X Y Z

embedded interface *n.* An interface built into a hardware device's drive and controller board so that the device can be directly connected to the computer's system bus. *See also* controller, interface (definition 3). *Compare* ESDI, SCSI.

em dash *n.* A punctuation mark (—) used to indicate a break or interruption in a sentence. It is named for the em, a typographical unit of measure that in some fonts equals the width of a capital M. *Compare* en dash, hyphen.

EMM *n. See* Expanded Memory Manager.

e-money or **emoney** *n.* Short for **e**lectronic **money**. A generic name for the exchange of money through the Internet. *Also called* cybercash, digicash, digital cash, e-cash.

emotag *n.* In an e-mail message or newsgroup article, a letter, word, or phrase that is encased in angle brackets and that, like an emoticon, indicates the attitude the writer takes toward what he or she has written. Often emotags have opening and closing tags, similar to HTML tags, that enclose a phrase or one or more sentences. For example: <joke>You didn't think there would really be a joke here, did you?</joke>. Some emotags consist of a single tag, such as <grin>. *See also* emoticon, HTML.

emoticon *n.* A string of text characters that, when viewed sideways, form a face expressing a particular emotion. An emoticon is often used in an e-mail message or newsgroup post as a comment on the text that precedes it. Some common emoticons are shown here:

:-) or :)	"I'm smiling at the joke here"
;-)	"I'm winking and grinning at the joke here"
:-(	"I'm sad about this"
:-7	"I'm speaking with tongue in cheek"
:D or :-D	big smile; "I'm overjoyed"
:-O	either a yawn of boredom or a mouth open in amazement

Compare emotag.

EMS *n.* Acronym for **E**xpanded **M**emory **S**pecification. A technique for adding memory to PCs that allows for increasing memory beyond the Intel 80x86 microprocessor real-mode limit of 1 MB. In earlier versions of microprocessors, EMS bypassed this limit with 16-KB banks of RAM that could be accessed by software. In later versions of Intel microprocessors, including the 80386 and 80486 models, EMS is converted from extended memory by software memory managers. Now EMS is used mainly for older MS-DOS applications because Windows and other applications running in protected mode on 80386 and higher microprocessors are free of the 1-MB limit. *Also called* LIM EMS. *See also* expanded memory, protected mode. *Compare* conventional memory, extended memory.

em space *n.* A typographical unit of measure that is equal in width to the point size of a particular font. For many fonts, this is equal to the width of a capital M. *Compare* en space, fixed space.

emulate *vb.* For a hardware or software system to behave in the same manner as another hardware or software system. In a network, for example, microcomputers often emulate mainframes or terminals so that two machines can communicate.
emulator *n.* Hardware or software designed to make one type of computer or component act as if it were another. By means of an emulator, a computer can run software written for another machine. In a network, microcomputers might emulate mainframes or terminals so that two machines can communicate.
enable *vb.* To activate or turn on. *Compare* disable.
encapsulate *vb.* To treat a collection of structured information as a whole without affecting or taking notice of its internal structure.
Encapsulated PostScript *n. See* EPS.
encipher *vb. See* encryption.
encode *vb.* **1.** In data security, to encrypt. *See also* encryption. **2.** In programming, to put something into code.
encryption *n.* The process of encoding data to prevent unauthorized access, especially during transmission. Encryption is usually based on a key that is essential for decoding. The U.S. National Bureau of Standards created a complex encryption standard (DES), which provides almost unlimited ways to encrypt documents. *See also* DES.
encryption key *n.* A sequence of data that is used to encrypt other data and that, consequently, must be used for the data's decryption. *See also* decryption, encryption.
en dash *n.* A punctuation mark (–) used in ranges of dates and numbers, such as 1990–92, and in certain compound adjectives, such as pre–Civil War. The en dash is named after a typographical unit of measure, the en space, which is half the width of an em space. *See also* em space. *Compare* em dash, hyphen.
End key *n.* A cursor-control key that moves the cursor to a certain position, usually to the end of a line, the end of a screen, or the end of a file, depending on the program.
end mark *n.* A symbol that designates the end of some entity, such as a file or word processing document.
end-of-text *n.* In data transmission, a character used to mark the end of a text file. End-of-text does not necessarily signify the end of transmission; other information, such as error-checking or transmission control characters, can be included at the end of the file. In ASCII, end-of-text is represented by the decimal value 3 (hexadecimal 03). *Acronym:* ETX.
end-of-transmission *n.* A character representing the end of a transmission. In ASCII, the end-of-transmission character has the decimal value 4 (hexadecimal 04). *Acronym:* EOT.
endpoint *n.* The beginning or end of a line segment.
end user *n.* The ultimate user of a computer or computer application in its finished, marketable form.

A B C D E F G H I J K L M N O P Q R S T U V W X Y Z

End-User License Agreement *n.* A legal agreement between a software manufacturer and the software's purchaser with regard to terms of distribution, resale, and restricted use. *Acronym:* EULA.

Energy Star *n.* A symbol affixed to systems and components that denotes lower power-consumption design. Energy Star is the name of an Environmental Protection Agency program that encourages personal computer manufacturers to build systems that are energy efficient. Requirements dictate that systems or monitors be capable of automatically entering a "sleep state" or lower power-consumption state (defined as 30 watts or less) while the unit is inactive. Systems and monitors that comply with these guidelines are marked with an Energy Star sticker.

engine *n.* A processor or portion of a program that determines how the program manages and manipulates data. The term is most often used in relation to a specific program; for example, a database engine contains the tools for manipulating a database. *Compare* back-end processor, front-end processor.

Enhanced Expanded Memory Specification *n. See* EEMS.

Enhanced IDE *n.* Short for **Enhanced I**ntegrated **D**rive **E**lectronics. An extension of the IDE standard, Enhanced IDE is a hardware interface standard for the design of disk drives that house control circuits in the drives themselves. It allows for standardized interfaces to the system bus while providing for advanced features such as burst data transfer and direct data access. Enhanced IDE accommodates drives as large as 8.4 GB. Most PCs have Enhanced IDE drives, which are cheaper than SCSI drives and provide much of the same functionality. *Acronym:* EIDE. *See also* IDE (definition 1), SCSI.

enhanced keyboard *n.* An IBM 101/102-key keyboard that replaced the PC and AT keyboards. It features 12 function keys across the top, extra Control and Alt keys, and a bank of cursor and editing keys between the main keyboard and number pad.

enhanced parallel port *n.* A connection port for peripheral devices, most often used for printers, external disk drives, or tape drives. Enhanced parallel ports utilize high-speed circuits for faster data throughput. Data and communications control lines are wired in parallel; each data line corresponds to 1 data bit. Data is transferred across all lines in sync. *Acronym:* EPP. *See also* input/output port.

enhanced serial port *n.* A connection port for peripheral devices, commonly used for mice and external modems. Enhanced serial ports utilize high-speed UART circuits for faster data throughput. Data is transferred as a sequence of bits and bytes on a pair of lines, either synchronously (data flows in one direction only) or asynchronously (data flows each way in turn). *Acronym:* ESP. *See also* input/output port, UART.

Enhanced Small Device Interface *n. See* ESDI.

enlarge *vb.* In Windows and other graphical user interfaces, to increase the size of a window. *See also* maximize. *Compare* minimize, reduce.

en space *n.* A typographical unit of measure that is equal in width to half the point size of a particular font. *Compare* em space, fixed space.

Enter key *n.* The key used at the end of a line or command to instruct the computer to process the command or text. In word processing programs, the Enter key is used at the end of a paragraph. *Also called* Return key.

enterprise computing *n.* In a large enterprise such as a corporation, the use of computers in a network or series of interconnected networks that generally encompasses a variety of platforms, operating systems, protocols, and network architectures. *Also called* enterprise networking.

enterprise network *n.* In a large enterprise such as a corporation, the network (or interconnected networks) of computer systems owned by the enterprise, which fills the enterprise's computing needs. This network can span diverse geographical locations and usually encompasses a range of platforms, operating systems, protocols, and network architectures.

enterprise networking *n. See* enterprise computing.

entry *n.* **1.** A unit of information treated as a whole by a computer program. **2.** The process of inputting information.

environment *n.* **1.** The configuration of resources available to the user. The term refers to the hardware and the operating system running on it. For example, Windows and the Apple Macintosh are called windowing environments because they are based on screen regions called windows. **2.** In microcomputing, a definition of the specifications, such as command path, in which a program operates.

EOL *n.* Acronym for **e**nd **o**f **l**ine. A control (nonprinting) character that signals the end of a data line in a data file.

EOT *n. See* end-of-transmission.

EPP *n. See* enhanced parallel port.

EPROM *n.* Acronym for **e**rasable **p**rogrammable **r**ead-**o**nly **m**emory. A nonvolatile memory chip that is programmed after it is manufactured. EPROMs can also be reprogrammed. Though EPROMS are more expensive than PROM chips, they can be more cost-effective if many changes are required. *Also called* reprogrammable read-only memory (RPROM). *See also* EEPROM, PROM, ROM.

.eps *n.* The file extension that identifies Encapsulated PostScript files. *See also* EPS.

EPS *n.* Acronym for **E**ncapsulated **P**ost**S**cript. A PostScript file format that can be used as an independent entity. The EPS image must be incorporated into the PostScript output of an application such as a desktop publisher. Many high-quality clip-art packages consist of such images. *See also* PostScript.

EPSF *n.* Acronym for **E**ncapsulated **P**ost**S**cript **f**ile. *See* EPS.

erasable programmable read-only memory *n. See* EPROM.

erasable storage *n.* Storage media that can be used repeatedly because the user has the ability to erase whatever data was previously there. Most forms of magnetic storage, such as tape and disk, are erasable.

#
A
B
C
D
E
F
G
H
I
J
K
L
M
N
O
P
Q
R
S
T
U
V
W
X
Y
Z

erase *vb.* To remove data permanently from a storage medium. This is usually done by replacing existing data with zeros or meaningless text or, in magnetic media, by disturbing the magnetic particles' physical arrangement, either with the erase head or with a large magnet. Erasing differs from deleting in that deleting merely tells the computer that data or a file is no longer needed; the data remains stored and is recoverable until the operating system reuses the space containing the deleted file. Erasing, on the other hand, removes data permanently. *Compare* delete.

ergonomic keyboard *n.* A keyboard designed to reduce the risk of wrist and hand injuries that result from prolonged use or repetitive movement. It can include such features as alternative key layouts and palm rests. *See also* carpal tunnel syndrome, Dvorak keyboard, keyboard.

ergonomics *n.* The study of people (their physical characteristics and the ways they function) in relation to their working environment (the furnishings and machines they use). The goal of ergonomics is to incorporate comfort, efficiency, and safety into the design of keyboards, computer desks, chairs, and other items in the workplace.

error *n.* A value or condition that is not consistent with the true, specified, or expected value or condition. In computers, an error results when an event does not occur as expected or when impossible or illegal maneuvers are attempted. In data communications, an error occurs when there is a discrepancy between the transmitted and received data. *See also* critical error, error message, error rate, error ratio, fatal error, hard error, intermittent error, machine error, parity error, read error, recoverable error, system error, write error. *Compare* fault.

error checking *n.* A method for detecting discrepancies between transmitted and received data during file transfer.

error-correcting code *n.* A code, designed for transmission of electronic data, that encodes data in such a way that transmission errors may be detected and corrected by examination of the encoded data on the receiving end. Error-correcting codes are used by most modems. *Acronym:* ECC. *See also* modem.

error detection and correction *n.* A method for discovering and resolving errors during file transfer. Some programs only detect errors; others detect and attempt to fix them.

error file *n.* A file that records the time and type of data processing and transmission errors.

error message *n.* A message from the system or program indicating that an error requiring resolution has occurred.

error rate *n.* In communications, the ratio of the number of bits or other elements that arrive incorrectly during transmission to the total number of bits or elements. For a 1,200-bps modem, a typical error rate would be 1 in every 200,000 bits. *See also* parity, parity bit, Xmodem, Ymodem.

error ratio *n.* The ratio of errors to the number of units of data processed. *See also* error rate.

Escape key *n.* A key on a computer keyboard that sends the escape (ESC) character to the computer. In many applications, the Escape key moves the user back one level in the menu structure or exits the program. *See also* Clear key.
Esc key *n. See* Escape key.
ESD *n. See* electronic software distribution, electrostatic discharge.
ESDI *n.* Acronym for **E**nhanced **S**mall **D**evice **I**nterface. A device that allows disks to communicate with computers at high speeds. ESDI drives typically transfer data at about 10 Mbps, but they are capable of doubling that speed.
ESP *n. See* enhanced serial port.
e-text *n.* Short for **e**lectronic **text**. A book or other text-based work that is available online in an electronic media format. An e-text can be read online or downloaded to a user's computer for offline reading. *See also* ezine.
Ethernet *n.* **1.** An IEEE 802.3 standard for contention networks. Ethernet uses a bus or star topology and relies on the form of access known as Carrier Sense Multiple Access with Collision Detection to regulate communications line traffic. Network nodes are linked by coaxial cable, by fiber-optic cable, or by twisted-pair wiring. The Ethernet standard provides for baseband transmission at 10 Mbps. *See also* 10Base2, 10Base5, 10BaseF, 10BaseT, baseband, bus network, coaxial cable, contention, IEEE, star network, twisted-pair cable. **2.** A widely used local area network system developed by Xerox in 1976, from which the IEEE 802.3 standard was developed.
etiquette *n. See* netiquette.
ETX *n. See* end-of-text.
EULA *n. See* End-User License Agreement.
even parity *n. See* parity.
event *n.* An action or occurrence, often generated by the user, to which a program might respond—for example, a key press, a button click, or a mouse movement. *See also* event-driven programming.
event-driven *adj.* Of, pertaining to, or being software that accomplishes its purpose by responding to externally caused events, such as the user pressing a key or clicking a mouse button. For example, an event-driven data entry form allows the user to click on and edit any field at any time rather than forcing the user to step through a fixed sequence of prompts.
event-driven programming *n.* A type of programming in which the program constantly evaluates and responds to sets of events, such as key presses or mouse movements. Event-driven programs are typical of most graphical user interfaces. *See also* event.
exchangeable disk *n. See* removable disk.
exchange sort *n. See* bubble sort.
exclusive OR *n.* A Boolean operation that yields a result of true (1) if and only if one of its operands is true (1) and the other is false (0). *Acronym:* EOR. *Also called* XOR. *See also* Boolean operator, truth table. *Compare* AND, OR.

.exe *n.* In MS-DOS, a filename extension indicating that a file is an executable program. To run an executable program, the user types the filename without the .exe extension at the prompt and presses Enter. *See also* executable program.

executable[1] *adj.* Of, pertaining to, or being a program file that can be run. Executable files have extensions such as .bat, .com, and .exe.

executable[2] *n.* A program file that can be run, such as file0.bat, file1.exe, or file2.com.

executable program *n.* A program that can be run. The term usually applies to a compiled program translated into machine code in a format that can be loaded into memory and run by a computer's processor. *See also* code[1] (definition 1), compiler, computer program, interpreter, source code.

execute *vb.* To perform an instruction. In programming, execution implies loading the machine code of the program into memory and then performing the instructions.

executive *n. See* operating system.

expanded *adj.* A font style that sets characters farther apart than the normal spacing. *Compare* condensed.

expanded memory *n.* A type of memory, up to 8 MB, that can be added to IBM PCs. Its use is defined by the Expanded Memory Specification (EMS). Expanded memory is not accessible to programs in MS-DOS, so the Expanded Memory Manager maps pages (blocks) of bytes from expanded memory into accessible memory areas. *See also* EEMS, EMS, Expanded Memory Manager.

Expanded Memory Manager *n.* A driver that implements the software portion of the Expanded Memory Specification to make expanded memory accessible in IBM and compatible PCs. *Acronym:* EMM. *See also* EMS, expanded memory, extended memory.

Expanded Memory Specification *n. See* EMS.

expansion *n.* A way of increasing a computer's capabilities by adding hardware that performs tasks that are not part of the basic system. Expansion is usually achieved by plugging printed circuit boards (expansion boards) into openings (expansion slots) inside the computer. *See also* expansion board, expansion slot, open architecture (definition 2), PC Card, PCMCIA slot.

expansion board *n.* A circuit board that is plugged into a computer's bus (main data transfer path) to add extra functions or resources to the computer. Typical expansion boards add memory, disk drive controllers, video support, parallel and serial ports, or internal modems. For laptops and other portable computers, expansion boards come in credit card–size devices called PC Cards that plug into a slot in the side or back of the computer. *Also called* expansion card, extender board. *See also* expansion slot, PC Card, PCMCIA slot.

expansion bus *n. See* AT bus.

expansion card *n. See* expansion board.
expansion slot *n.* A socket in a computer, designed to hold expansion boards and connect them to the system bus. Expansion slots are a means of adding to or enhancing the computer's features and capabilities. In laptop and other portable computers, expansion slots come in the form of PCMCIA slots designed to accept PC Cards. *See also* expansion board, PC Card, PCMCIA slot.
expert system *n.* An application that makes decisions or solves problems in a particular field, such as finance or medicine, by using knowledge and analytical rules defined by experts in the field. It uses two components, a knowledge base and an inference engine, to form conclusions. *See also* artificial intelligence, inference engine, intelligent database, knowledge base.
expiration date *n.* The date on which a shareware, beta, or trial version of a program stops functioning, pending purchase of the full version or the entry of an access code.
expire *vb.* To stop functioning in whole or in part. Beta versions of software are often programmed to expire when a new version is released. *See also* beta^2.
exploded view *n.* A form of display that shows a structure with its parts separated but depicted in relation to each other.
export *vb.* To move information from one system or program to another. Files that consist only of text can be exported in ASCII (plain-text format). For files with graphics, however, the receiving system or program must offer support for the exported file's format. *See also* EPS, PICT, TIFF. *Compare* import.
extended ASCII *n.* Any set of characters assigned to ASCII values between decimal 128 and 255 (hexadecimal 80 through FF). The specific characters assigned to the extended ASCII codes vary between computers and between programs, fonts, or graphics characters. Extended ASCII adds capability by allowing for 128 additional characters, such as accented letters, graphics characters, and special symbols. *See also* ASCII.
Extended Binary Coded Decimal Interchange Code *n. See* EBCDIC.
extended characters *n.* Any of the 128 additional characters in the extended ASCII (8-bit) character set. *See also* extended ASCII.
extended data out random access memory *n. See* EDO RAM.
eXtended Graphics Array *n.* An advanced standard for graphics controller and display mode design. This standard supports 640×480 resolution with 65,536 colors, or 1,024×768 resolution with 256 colors, and is used mainly on workstation-level systems. *Acronym:* XGA.
Extended Industry Standard Architecture *n. See* EISA.
extended memory *n.* System memory beyond 1 MB in computers based on the Intel 80×86 processors. This memory is accessible only when an 80386 or higher-level processor is operating in protected mode or in emulation on the 80286. To use extended memory, MS-DOS programs need either the aid

#
A
B
C
D
E
F
G
H
I
J
K
L
M
N
O
P
Q
R
S
T
U
V
W
X
Y
Z

of software that temporarily places the processor into protected mode or the use of features in the 80386 or higher-level processors to remap portions of extended memory into conventional memory. Programs running under Windows, OS/2, and other operating systems that run on Intel processors and use the protected mode of the 80386 and higher-level processors can access all system memory in the same way. *See also* EMS, extended memory specification, protected mode.

extended memory specification *n.* A specification that defines a software interface allowing real-mode applications to use extended memory and areas of memory not managed by MS-DOS. Memory is managed by an installable device driver, the Expanded Memory Manager. The application must use the driver to access the additional memory. *Acronym:* XMS. *See also* Expanded Memory Manager, extended memory.

extended VGA *n. See* SVGA.

extender board *n. See* expansion board.

eXtensible Markup Language *n. See* XML.

extension *n.* **1.** A set of characters added to a filename that serves to extend or clarify its meaning or to identify a file as a member of a category. An extension may be assigned by the user or by a program. For example, the extension .com or .exe is used for executable programs that MS-DOS can load and run. **2.** A supplemental set of codes used to include additional characters in a particular character set. **3.** On the Macintosh, a program that alters or augments the functionality of the operating system. There are two types: system extensions, such as QuickTime, and Chooser extensions, such as printer drivers. When a Macintosh is turned on, the extensions in the Extensions folder within the System folder are loaded into memory. *See also* QuickTime, System folder.

extension manager *n.* On the Macintosh, a utility that allows the user to determine which extensions are loaded when the computer is turned on. *See also* extension (definition 3).

external command *n.* A program included in an operating system that is loaded into memory and executed only when its name is entered at the system prompt. Although an external command is a program in its own right, it is called a command because it is included with the operating system. *See also* XCMD.

external hard disk *n.* A free-standing hard disk with its own case and power supply, connected to the computer with a data cable and used mainly as a portable unit. *See also* hard disk.

external modem *n.* A stand-alone modem that is connected via cable to a computer's serial port. *Compare* internal modem.

external storage *n.* A storage medium for data, such as a disk or tape unit, that is external to a computer's memory.

external viewer *n.* A separate application used to view documents of a type that cannot be handled by the current application. *See also* helper program.

extra-high-density floppy disk *n.* A 3.5-inch floppy disk capable of holding 4 MB of data and requiring a special disk drive that has two heads rather than one. *See also* floppy disk.

extranet *n.* An extension of a corporate intranet using World Wide Web technology to facilitate communication with the corporation's suppliers and customers. An extranet allows customers and suppliers to gain limited access to a company's intranet. *See also* intranet.

ezine *n.* Short for **e**lectronic maga**zine**. A digital production available on the Internet, a BBS, or other online service, often free of charge.

F

F2F *adv.* Short for face-to-face. In person, rather than over the Internet. The term is used in e-mail.

face *n.* **1.** In computer graphics, one side of a solid object, such as a cube. **2.** In printing and typography, short for type**face**.

facsimile *n. See* fax.

failback *n.* In a cluster network system (one with two or more interconnected servers), the process of restoring resources and services to their primary server after they have been temporarily relocated to a backup system while repairs were implemented on the original host. *See also* cluster (definition 4), failover.

failover *n.* The automatic relocation of a failed or malfunctioning resource or service in a cluster system (one with two or more interconnected servers) to the backup resource or system. Failover ensures uninterrupted service to the user by detecting any failure or malfunction of a server, network adapter, disk drive, and so on and automatically switching to the backup component. *Also called* fault tolerance. *See also* cluster (definition 4), failback.

fail over *vb.* In a cluster network system (one with two or more interconnected servers), to relocate an overloaded or failed resource, such as a server, disk drive, or network, to its backup component. For example, when one server in a two-server system stops processing because of a power outage or other malfunction, the system automatically "fails over" to the second server, with little or no disruption to the users. *See also* cluster (definition 4), failback.

fail-safe system *n.* A computer system designed to continue operating when part of the system breaks down or seriously malfunctions, without loss of or damage to programs and data. *Compare* fail-soft system.

fail-soft system *n.* A computer system designed to fail gracefully over a period of time when an element of hardware or software malfunctions. A fail-soft system terminates nonessential functions and remains operating at a diminished capacity until the problem has been corrected. *Compare* fail-safe system.

failure *n.* The inability of a computer system or related device to operate reliably or to operate at all. A common cause of system failure is loss of power, which can be minimized with a battery-powered backup source until all devices can be shut down.

failure rate *n.* The number of failures in a specified time period. Failure rate is a means of measuring the reliability of a device, such as a hard disk. *See also* MTBF.

fair use *n.* A legal doctrine describing the boundaries of legitimate use of copyrighted software or other published material.
family *n.* A series of hardware or software products that have some properties in common, such as a series of personal computers from the same company or a series of CPU chips from the same manufacturer that all use the same instruction set.
fan[1] *n.* The cooling mechanism built into computer cabinets, laser printers, and other devices to prevent malfunction as a result of heat buildup. Fans are the main source of the continuous humming associated with computers and other hardware.
fan[2] *vb.* To flip through a stack of printer paper to ensure that the pages are loose and will not stick together or jam the printer.
fanfold paper *n. See* continuous-form paper.
fan-in *n.* The maximum number of signals that can be fed to a given electronic device at one time without risking signal corruption. The fan-in rating of a device depends on the device's type and method of construction. *Compare* fan-out.
fan-out *n.* The maximum number of electronic devices that can be fed by a given electronic device at one time without the signal becoming too weak. The fan-out rating of a device depends on the device's type and method of construction. *Compare* fan-in.
fanzine *n.* A magazine, distributed online or by mail, that is produced by and devoted to fans of a particular group, person, or activity. *See also* ezine.
FAQ *n.* Acronym for **f**requently **a**sked **q**uestions. A document listing common questions and answers on a particular subject. FAQs are often posted on Internet newsgroups where new participants ask the same questions that regular readers have answered many times.
Fast Ethernet *n.* Ethernet capable of supporting 100 Mbps. *See also* Ethernet (definition 1).
fast infrared port *n. See* FIR port.
fast packet *n.* A standard for high-speed network technology that utilizes fast switching of fixed-length cells or packets for real-time transmission of data. *Also called* Asynchronous Transfer Mode, ATM. *See also* packet (definition 2), packet switching.
FAT *n. See* file allocation table.
fatal error *n.* An error that causes the system or application program to crash—that is, to fail abruptly with no hope of recovery.
fatal exception error *n.* A message used in Windows to signal that an unrecoverable error has occurred, one that causes the system to halt. Data being processed when the error occurs is usually lost, and the computer must be rebooted. *Also called* exception error, fatal error.
fat application *n.* An application that can be used on both PowerPC processor–based Macintosh computers and 680x0-based Macintosh computers.
fatbits *n.* **1.** Originally (as FatBits), a feature of the Apple MacPaint program in which a small portion of a drawing can be enlarged and modified

#
A
B
C
D
E
F
G
H
I
J
K
L
M
N
O
P
Q
R
S
T
U
V
W
X
Y
Z

one pixel (FatBit) at a time. **2.** A similar feature in any program that allows pixel-by-pixel modification through a zoom feature.

fat client *n.* In a client/server architecture, a client machine that performs most or all of the processing, with little or none performed by the server. The client handles presentation and functions, and the server manages data and access to it. *See also* client (definition 2), client/server architecture, server (definition 2), thin server. *Compare* fat server, thin client.

FAT file system *n.* The system used by MS-DOS to organize and manage files. MS-DOS creates a FAT (file allocation table) on a disk when the disk is formatted. When MS-DOS stores a file on a formatted disk, it places information about the file in the FAT so that the file can be retrieved later upon request. The FAT is the only file system MS-DOS can use; OS/2, Windows NT, and Windows 95 can use the FAT file system in addition to their own file systems. *See also* file allocation table.

father *n. See* father file, generation (definition 1).

father file *n.* A file that is the last previously valid set of a changing set of data. The father file is immediately preceded by a grandfather file and immediately succeeded by its son. The pairs father and son, parent and child (or descendant), and independent and dependent are synonymous. *See also* generation (definition 1).

fat server *n.* In a client/server architecture, a server machine that performs most of the processing, with little or none performed by the client. Applications logic and data reside on the server, and presentation services are handled by the client. *See also* client (definition 2), client/server architecture, server (definition 2), thin client. *Compare* fat client, thin server.

fatware *n.* Software that monopolizes hard disk space and power because of an overabundance of features or inefficient design. *Also called* bloatware.

fault *n.* A physical defect, such as a loose connection, that prevents a system or device from operating as it should.

fault tolerance *n.* The ability of a computer or an operating system to respond to a catastrophic event or fault, such as a power outage or a hardware failure, in a way that ensures that no data is lost and work in progress is not corrupted. This can be accomplished with, for example, a battery-backed power supply, backup hardware, or provisions in the operating system. In a fault-tolerant network, the system can either continue operation without loss of data or shut down and restart, recovering all processing that was in progress when the fault occurred.

fax *n.* Short for facsimile. The transmission of text or graphics over telephone lines in digitized form. Conventional fax machines scan an original document, transmit an image of the document as a bit map, and reproduce the received image on a printer. Fax images can also be sent and received by microcomputers equipped with fax hardware and software.

fax machine *n.* Short for facsimile machine. A device that scans pages, converts the images of those pages to a digital format consistent with the international facsimile standard, and transmits the image through a telephone line. A fax machine also receives such images and prints them on paper. *See also* scan (definition 2).

fax modem *n.* A modem that sends (and possibly receives) data encoded in a fax format, which a fax machine or another modem decodes and converts to an image. The image must already have been encoded on the host computer. Text and graphics documents can be converted to fax format by special software usually provided with the modem; paper documents must first be scanned in. Fax modems may be internal or external and may combine fax and conventional modem capabilities. *See also* fax, modem.

fax on demand *n.* An automated system that makes information available for request by telephone. When a request is made, the system faxes the information to the telephone number given in the request. *Acronym:* FOD.

fax program *n.* A computer application that allows the user to send, receive, and print fax transmissions. *See also* fax.

fax server *n.* A computer on a network capable of sending and receiving fax transmissions to and from other computers on the network. *See also* fax, server (definition 1).

F connector *n.* A coaxial connector, used primarily in video applications, that requires a screw-on attachment.

feature extraction *n.* The selection of significant aspects of a computer image for use as guidelines in computerized pattern matching and image recognition. *See also* image processing.

Federal Internet Exchange *n. See* FIX.

feed[1] *n. See* news feed.

feed[2] *vb.* **1.** To advance paper through a printer. **2.** To supply media to a recording device, as by inserting disks into a disk drive.

feed scanner *n. See* sheet-fed scanner.

female connector *n.* A connector that has one or more receptacles for the insertion of pins. Female connector part numbers often include an F (female), an S (socket), a J (jack), or an R (receptacle). For example, a female DB-25 connector might be labeled DB-25S or DB-25F. (Although the letter F can denote a female connector, it does not have that meaning in the term F connector, which is a type of coaxial connector.) *Compare* male connector.

FEP *n. See* front-end processor.

ferric RAM *n. See* FRAM.

FF *n. See* form feed.

fiber optics *n.* A technology for the transmission of light beams along optical fibers. A light beam, such as that produced in a laser, can be modulated to carry information. A single fiber-optic channel can carry significantly more information than most other means of transmission. Optical fibers are essentially immune to electromagnetic interference. *See also* optical fiber.

Fidonet *n.* **1.** A protocol for sending e-mail, newsgroup postings, and files over telephone lines. The protocol originated on the Fido BBS. Maintaining low costs has been a factor in its subsequent development. Fidonet can exchange e-mail with the Internet. **2.** The network of BBSs, private companies,

#
A
B
C
D
E
F
G
H
I
J
K
L
M
N
O
P
Q
R
S
T
U
V
W
X
Y
Z

NGOs (nongovernment organizations), and individuals that use the Fidonet protocol.

.fidonet.org *n.* On the Internet, the major domain specifying that an address is located on Fidonet.

field *n.* **1.** A location in a record in which a particular type of data is stored. For example, EMPLOYEE-RECORD might contain fields to store Last-Name, First-Name, Address, Zip-Code, Hire-Date, Title, and so on. A field is characterized by its maximum length and the type of data (for example, alphabetic or numeric) that can be placed in it. In a relational DBMS, fields are called columns. **2.** A space in an on-screen form where the user can enter a specific item of information.

field separator *n.* Any character that separates one field of data from another. *See also* delimiter, field (definition 1).

FIFO *n. See* first in, first out.

fifth-generation computer *n. See* computer.

fifth normal form *n.* Abbreviated 5NF. *See* normal form.

file *n.* A complete, named collection of information, such as a program, a set of data used by a program, or a user-created document. A file is the basic unit of storage that enables a computer to distinguish one set of information from another. It constitutes a coherent unit that a user can retrieve, change, delete, save, or send to an output device.

file allocation table *n.* A table or list maintained by some operating systems to manage disk space used for file storage. Files on a disk are stored, as space allows, in fixed-size groups of bytes rather than as contiguous strings of text or numbers. A single file can thus be scattered in pieces over many separate storage areas. A file allocation table maps available disk storage space so that it can mark and avoid flawed segments and can find and link the pieces of a file. In MS-DOS, the file allocation table is commonly known as the FAT.

file attribute *n.* A restrictive label attached to a file that describes and regulates its use—for example, hidden, system, read-only, archive. In MS-DOS, this information is stored as part of the file's directory entry.

file backup *n. See* backup.

file compression *n.* The process of reducing the size of a file for transmission or storage. *See also* data compression.

file conversion *n.* The process of transforming the data in a file from one format to another without altering its contents—for example, converting a file from a word processor's format to its ASCII equivalent.

file extension *n. See* extension (definition 1).

file format *n.* The structure of a file that defines the way it is stored and laid out on the screen or in print. The format can be fairly simple, as for files stored as "plain" ASCII text, or it can be complex and include various control instructions and codes used by programs, printers, and other devices. Examples include RTF (Rich Text Format), PICT, DXF, TIFF (Tagged Image File Format), and EPSF (Encapsulated PostScript Format).

file fragmentation *n.* **1.** *See* fragmentation. **2.** In a database, a situation in which records are not stored in their optimal access sequence because of accumulated additions and deletions of records. Most database systems offer or contain utility programs that resequence records to improve efficiency of access and to aggregate free space.

file header *n.* *See* header (definition 2).

file layout *n.* In data storage, the organization of records within a file. Frequently, descriptions of the record structure are also included within the file layout.

file librarian *n.* A person or process responsible for maintaining, archiving, copying, and providing access to a collection of data.

file maintenance *n.* The process of changing information in a file, altering a file's control information or structure, or copying and archiving files.

file manager *n.* A module of an operating system or environment that controls the physical placement of and access to a group of program files.

filename *n.* The set of letters, numbers, and allowable symbols assigned to a file to distinguish it from all other files in a particular directory on a disk. A filename is the handle by which a computer user saves and requests a block of information. Both programs and data have filenames and often extensions that further identify the type or purpose of the file. Naming conventions, such as maximum length and allowable characters of a filename, vary from one operating system to another. *See also* 8.3, directory, long filenames, path (definition 3).

filename extension *n.* *See* extension (definition 1).

file protection *n.* A process or device by which the existence and integrity of a file are maintained. Methods of file protection range from allowing read-only access and assigning passwords to covering the write-protect notch on a disk and locking away floppy disks that hold sensitive files.

file recovery *n.* The process of reconstructing lost or unreadable files on disk. File recovery involves the use of utility programs that attempt to rebuild on-disk information about the storage locations of inadvertently deleted files. Because deletion makes the file's disk space available but does not remove the data, data that has not yet been overwritten can be recovered. In the case of damaged files or disks, recovery programs read whatever raw data they can find and save it to a new disk or file in ASCII or numeric form. In some instances, however, such reconstructed files contain so much extraneous or mixed information that they are unreadable. The best way to recover a file is to restore it from a backup copy.

file retrieval *n.* The act of transferring a data file from a storage location to the machine where it is to be used.

file server *n.* A file storage device on a local area network that is accessible to all users on the network. Unlike a disk server, a file server is a sophisticated device that not only stores files but manages them and maintains order as users request and change files. To handle multiple—sometimes simultaneous—requests, a file server contains a processor and controlling software

A B C D E F G H I J K L M N O P Q R S T U V W X Y Z

as well as a disk drive for storage. A file server is often a computer with a large hard disk that is dedicated only to managing shared files. *Compare* disk server.

file sharing *n.* The use of computer files on networks, wherein files are stored on a central computer or a server and are requested, reviewed, and modified by more than one individual. When a file is used with different programs or different computers, file sharing can require conversion to a mutually acceptable format. Access to a file can be regulated through such means as password protection, security clearances, or file locking.

file size *n.* The length of a file, typically given in bytes.

filespec *n. See* file specification (definition 1).

file specification *n.* **1.** Abbreviated filespec. The path to a file, from a disk drive through a chain of directory files to the filename that serves to locate the particular file. **2.** A filename containing wildcard characters that indicate which files among a group of similarly named files are requested. **3.** A document that describes the organization of data within a file.

file structure *n.* A description of a file or a group of files that are to be treated together. Such a description includes the file layout and the location for each file.

file system *n.* In an operating system, the overall structure in which files are named, stored, and organized. A file system consists of files, directories, and the information needed to locate and access these items. The term can also refer to the portion of an operating system that translates requests for file operations from an application into low-level, sector-oriented tasks that can be understood by the drivers controlling the disk drives. *See also* driver.

file transfer *n.* The process of moving or transmitting a file from one location to another, as between two programs or over a network.

File Transfer Protocol *n. See* FTP[1] (definition 1).

file type *n.* A designation of the operational or structural characteristics of a file. A file's type is often identified in the filename. With MS-DOS, a file's type is usually reflected in the filename extension. *See also* file format.

fill *n.* In computer graphics, to "paint" the inside of an enclosed figure, such as a circle, with color or a pattern. The portion of the shape that can be colored or patterned is the fill area.

film at 11 A phrase sometimes seen in newsgroups. An allusion to a brief TV newsbreak that promises to cover a top news story in full on the 11 o'clock news, it is used sarcastically to ridicule a previous article's lack of timeliness or newsworthiness. *See also* newsgroup.

film recorder *n.* A device for capturing on 35-mm film the images displayed on a computer screen.

filter *n.* **1.** A program or set of features within a program that reads designated input, transforms it in some way, and then writes the output to its designated destination. A database filter, for example, might flag information of a certain age. **2.** In communications and electronics, hardware or software that selectively passes certain elements of a signal and eliminates or minimizes others. **3.** A pattern or mask through which data is passed to weed out specified items. For instance, an e-mail filter can allow a user to filter out messages from specific other users. *See also* e-mail filter. **4.** In computer graphics, a special effect applied to bitmapped images; for example, making elements of the image transparent or distorting the image. Some filters are built into a graphics program; others are separate software packages that plug into the program. *See also* bitmapped graphics.

filtering program *n.* A program that filters information and presents only results that match the qualifications defined in the program.

find *vb.* *See* search[2].

Finder *n.* The standard interface to the Macintosh operating system, allowing the user to view the contents of directories (folders); to move, copy, and delete files; and to launch applications. Items in the system are often represented as icons, and a mouse or similar pointing device is used to manipulate these items. The Finder was the first commercially successful graphical user interface. *See also* MultiFinder.

finger[1] *n.* An Internet utility, originally limited to UNIX but now available on many platforms, that enables a user to obtain information on other users who may be at other sites (if those sites permit access by finger). Given an e-mail address, finger returns the user's full name, an indication of whether the user is currently logged on, and any other information the user has supplied as a profile. Given a first or last name, finger returns the logon names of users whose first or last names match.

finger[2] *vb.* To obtain information on a user by means of the finger program.

firewall *n.* A security system intended to protect an organization's network against external threats, such as hackers, coming from another network, such as the Internet. A firewall prevents computers in the organization's network from communicating directly with computers external to the network and vice versa. Instead, all communication is routed through a proxy server outside the organization's network, and the proxy server decides whether it is safe to let a particular message or file pass through to the organization's network.

firmware *n.* Software routines stored in read-only memory (ROM). Unlike RAM, ROM stays intact even in the absence of electrical power. Startup routines and low-level input/output instructions are stored in firmware. It falls between software and hardware in terms of ease of modification. *See also* RAM, ROM.

FIR port *n.* Short for **f**ast **i**nfra**r**ed **port**. A wireless I/O port, most common on a portable computer, that exchanges data with an external device using infrared light. *See also* infrared, input/output port.

first-generation computer *n.* *See* computer.

first in, first out *n.* A method of processing a queue, in which items are removed in the same order in which they were added—the first in is the first out. Such an order is typical of a list of documents waiting to be printed. *Acronym:* FIFO. *See also* print queue. *Compare* last in, first out.

first normal form *n.* Abbreviated 1NF. *See* normal form.

FIX *n.* Acronym for **F**ederal **I**nternet **Ex**change. A connection point between the U.S. government's various internets and the Internet.

fixed disk *n. See* hard disk.

fixed-pitch spacing *n. See* monospacing.

fixed space *n.* A set amount of horizontal space used to separate characters in text—often, the width of a numeral in a given font. *See also* em space, en space.

fixed spacing *n. See* monospacing.

fixed storage *n.* Any nonremovable storage, such as a large disk that is sealed permanently in its drive.

fixed-width font *n. See* monospace font.

fixed-width spacing *n. See* monospacing.

F keys *n. See* function key.

flag *n.* Broadly, a marker of some type used by a computer in processing or interpreting information; a signal indicating the existence or status of a particular condition. Flags are used in such areas as communications and information processing.

flame[1] *n.* An abusive or personally insulting e-mail message or newsgroup posting.

flame[2] *vb.* **1.** To send an abusive or personally insulting e-mail message or newsgroup posting. **2.** To criticize personally by means of e-mail messages or newsgroup postings.

flame bait *n.* A posting to a mailing list, newsgroup, or other online discussion that is likely to provoke flames, often because it expresses a controversial opinion on a highly emotional topic. *See also* flame[1], flame war. *Compare* troll.

flamefest *n.* A series of inflammatory messages or articles in a newsgroup or other online forum.

flamer *n.* A person who sends or posts abusive messages via e-mail, in newsgroups and other online forums, and in online chats. *See also* chat[1] (definition 1), newsgroup.

flame war *n.* A discussion in a mailing list, newsgroup, or other online forum that has turned into a protracted exchange of flames. *See also* flame[1].

flash memory *n.* A type of nonvolatile memory. Flash memory is similar to EEPROM memory in function, but it must be erased in blocks, whereas EEPROM can be erased one byte at a time. Flash memory is commonly used as a supplement to or replacement for hard disks in portable computers. In this context, flash memory either is built into the unit or, more commonly, is available as a PC Card that can be plugged into a PCMCIA slot. A disadvantage of flash memory is that its block-oriented nature prevents it from being practically used as main memory (RAM) because a computer must write to memory in single-byte increments. *See also* EEPROM, nonvolatile memory, PC Card, PCMCIA slot.

flash ROM *n. See* flash memory.

flatbed plotter *n.* A plotter in which paper is held on a flat platform and a pen moves along both axes, traveling across the paper to draw an image. This method is slightly more accurate than that used by drum plotters but requires more space. Flatbed plotters can also accept a wider variety of media, such as vellum and acetate, because the material does not need to be flexible. *See also* plotter. *Compare* drum plotter, pinch-roller plotter.

flatbed scanner *n.* A scanner with a flat transparent surface that holds the image to be scanned, which is generally a book or other paper document. A scan head below the surface moves across the image. Some flatbed scanners can also reproduce transparent media, such as slides. *Compare* drum scanner, handheld scanner, sheet-fed scanner.

flat file *n.* A file consisting of records of a single record type in which there is no embedded structure information that governs relationships between records.

flat-file database *n.* A database that takes the form of a table, where only one table can be used for each database. A flat-file database can work with only one file at a time. *Compare* relational database.

flat file directory *n.* A directory that cannot contain subdirectories but simply contains a list of filenames. *Compare* hierarchical file system.

flat file system *n.* A filing system with no hierarchical order, in which no two files on a disk may have the same name, even if they exist in different directories. *Compare* hierarchical file system.

flat-panel display *n.* A video display with a shallow physical depth, based on technology other than the CRT; typically used in laptop computers. Common types of flat-panel displays are electroluminescent, gas-discharge, and LCD displays.

flat screen *n. See* flat-panel display.

flavor *n.* One of several varieties of a system, having its own details of operation. UNIX in particular is found in distinct flavors, such as BSD UNIX or AT&T UNIX System V.

flexible disk *n. See* floppy disk.

.fli *n.* The file extension that identifies animation files in the FLI file format.

flicker *n.* Rapid, visible fluctuation in a screen image, as on a computer monitor. Flicker occurs when the image is refreshed (updated) too infrequently or too slowly for the eye to perceive a steady level of brightness.

flight simulator *n.* A computer-generated re-creation of the experience of flying. Sophisticated flight simulators can provide pilot training, simulating emergency situations. Flight simulator software running on personal computers simulates flight less realistically but provides entertainment and practice in navigation and instrument reading.

floating-point processor *n.* A coprocessor for performing arithmetic on floating-point numbers (numbers represented by a mantissa and an exponent according to a given base, for example, 2.33×10^{23}). Adding a floating-point processor to a system can speed up the processing of mathematical calculations and graphics dramatically if the software is designed to recognize and use it. The i486DX and 68040 and higher microprocessors have built-in floating-point processors. *Also called* math coprocessor, numeric coprocessor.

floppy disk *n.* A round piece of flexible plastic film coated with ferric oxide particles that can hold a magnetic field. When placed inside a disk drive, the floppy disk rotates to bring different sectors of the disk surface under the drive's read/write head, which can detect and alter the orientation of the particles' magnetic fields to represent binary 1s and 0s. A 5.25-inch floppy disk is encased in a flexible plastic jacket and has a large hole in the center, which fits around a spindle in the disk drive; such a disk can hold from a few hundred thousand to over one million bytes of data. A 3.5-inch disk encased in rigid plastic is also called a microfloppy disk. *See also* microfloppy disk.

floppy disk controller *n.* *See* disk controller.

floppy disk drive *n.* An electromechanical device that reads data from and writes data to floppy or microfloppy disks. *See also* floppy disk.

flush[1] *adj.* Aligned in a certain way on the screen or on paper. Flush left, for example, means aligned on the left side; flush right means aligned on the right side. *See also* align (definition 1).

flush[2] *vb.* To clear a portion of memory. For example, to flush a disk file buffer is to save its contents on disk and then clear the buffer for filling again.

FOD *n.* *See* fax on demand.

folder *n.* In the Mac OS, Windows 95, and other operating systems, a container for programs and files in graphical user interfaces, symbolized on the screen by a graphical image (icon) of a file folder. This container is called a directory in other systems, such as MS-DOS and UNIX. A folder is a means of organizing programs and documents on a disk and can hold both files and additional folders. *See also* directory.

follow-up *n.* A post to a newsgroup that replies to an article. The follow-up has the same subject line as the original article, with the prefix "Re:" attached. An article and all its follow-ups, in the order they were received, constitute a thread, which a user can read together using a newsreader.

font *n.* A set of characters of the same typeface and size (such as 10-point Garamond). The typeface defines the design of the letters, the style (such as italic), and the weight (such as bold); the font additionally defines the size. Fonts are used by computers for on-screen displays and by printers for hard-copy output. In both cases, the fonts are stored either as bit maps (patterns of dots) or as outlines (defined by a set of mathematical formulas). *See also* bit map.

font card *n.* *See* font cartridge, ROM card.

font cartridge *n.* A plug-in unit available for some printers that contains fonts in several styles and sizes. Font cartridges, like downloadable fonts, enable a printer to produce characters in sizes and styles other than those created by the fonts built into it. *Also called* font card. *See also* ROM cartridge.

font editor *n.* A utility program that enables the user to modify existing fonts or to create and save new ones. Such an application commonly works with a screen representation of the font, with a representation that can be downloaded to a PostScript or other printer, or with both. *See also* PostScript font, screen font.

font family *n. See* typeface.

font number *n.* The number by which an application or operating system internally identifies a given font. *See also* font.

font size *n.* The point size of a set of characters in a particular typeface. *See also* point[1] (definition 1).

footer *n.* One or more identifying lines printed at the bottom of a page. A footer may contain a page number, a date, the author's name, and the document title. *Also called* running foot. *Compare* header (definition 1).

footprint *n.* The surface area occupied by a personal computer or other device.

foreground[1] *adj.* Currently having control of the system and responding to commands issued by the user. *See also* multitasking. *Compare* background[1].

foreground[2] *n.* **1.** The color of displayed characters and graphics. *Compare* background[2] (definition 1). **2.** The condition of the program or document currently in control and affected by commands and data entry in a windowing environment. *Compare* background[2] (definition 3).

fork[1] *n.* One of the two parts of a file recognized by the Mac OS. A Macintosh file has a data fork and a resource fork. Most or all of a typical user-produced document is in the data fork; the resource fork usually contains application-oriented information, such as fonts, dialog boxes, and menus. *See also* data fork, resource fork.

fork[2] *vb.* To initiate a child process in a multitasking system after a parent process has been started. *See also* multitasking.

form *n.* **1.** A structured document with spaces reserved for entering information and often containing special coding as well. **2.** In some applications (especially databases), a structured window, box, or other self-contained presentation element with predefined areas for entering or changing information. A form is a visual "filter" for the underlying data it is presenting, generally offering the advantages of better data organization and greater ease of viewing.

format[1] *n.* **1.** In general, the structure or appearance of a unit of data. **2.** The arrangement of data within a document file that typically permits the document to be read or written by a certain application. Many applications can store a file in a more generic format, such as plain ASCII text. **3.** The layout of data storage areas (tracks and sectors) on a disk. **4.** The order and types of fields in a database. **5.** The attributes of a cell in a spreadsheet, such as its being alphabetic or numeric, the number of digits, the use of commas, and the use of currency signs. **6.** The specifications for the placement of text on a page or in a paragraph.

format² *vb.* **1.** To change the appearance of selected text or the contents of a selected cell in a spreadsheet. **2.** To prepare a disk for use by organizing its storage space into a collection of data "compartments," each of which can be located by the operating system so that data can be sorted and retrieved. When a previously used disk is formatted, any preexisting information on it is lost.

format bar *n.* A toolbar within an application used for modifying the format of the document being displayed, such as changing font size or type.

formatting *n.* **1.** The elements of style and presentation that are added to documents through the use of margins, indents, and different sizes, weights, and styles of type. **2.** The process of initializing a disk so that it can be used to store information. *See also* initialize.

form feed *n.* A printer command that tells a printer to move to the top of the next page. In the ASCII character set, the form-feed character has the decimal value 12 (hexadecimal 0C). Because its purpose is to begin printing on a new page, form feed is also known as the page-eject character. *Acronym:* FF.

form letter *n.* A letter created for printing and distribution to a group of people whose names and addresses are taken from a database and inserted by a mail-merge program into a single basic document. *See also* mail merge.

formula *n.* A mathematical statement that describes the actions to be performed on numeric values. A formula sets up a calculation without regard to the actual values it is to act upon, such as $A + B$, with A and B representing whatever values the user designates. Through formulas, users of applications such as spreadsheets gain the power to perform "what-if" calculations simply by changing selected values and having the program recalculate the results.

fortune cookie *n.* A proverb, prediction, joke, or other phrase chosen at random from a collection of such items and output to the screen by a program. Fortune cookies are sometimes displayed at logon and logoff times by UNIX systems.

forum *n.* A medium provided by an online service or BBS for users to carry on written discussions of a particular topic by posting messages and replying to them. On the Internet, the most widespread forums are the newsgroups in Usenet.

forward *vb.* In e-mail, to send a received message, either modified or in its entirety, to a new recipient.

forward error correction *n.* In communications, a means of controlling errors by inserting extra (redundant) bits into a stream of data transmitted to another device. The redundant bits are used by the receiving device in detecting and, where possible, correcting errors in the data.

fourth-generation computer *n.* *See* computer.

fourth normal form *n.* Abbreviated 4NF. *See* normal form.

FPD *n.* *See* full-page display.

fractal *n.* A class of shapes characterized by irregularity, but in a way that evokes a pattern. Computer graphics technicians often use fractals to generate naturelike images such as landscapes, clouds, and forests. The distinguishing characteristic of fractals is that they are "self-similar"; any piece of a fractal, when magnified, has the same character as the whole. *See also* graftal.

fractional T1 *n.* A shared connection to a T1 line, in which only a fraction of the 24 T1 voice or data channels are used. *Acronym:* FT1. *See also* T1.

fragmentation *n.* The scattering of parts of the same disk file over different areas of the disk. Fragmentation occurs as files on a disk are deleted and new files are added. Such fragmentation slows disk access and degrades the overall performance of disk operations, although usually not severely. Utility programs are available for rearranging file storage on fragmented disks. *Compare* defragmentation.

FRAM *n.* Acronym for **f**erromagnetic **r**andom **a**ccess **m**emory. A form of data storage technology in which data is recorded semipermanently on small cards or strips of material coated with a ferric oxide magnetic film. As with tape or disk, the data persists without power; as with semiconductor RAM, a computer can access the data in any order.

frame *n.* **1.** In asynchronous serial communications, a unit of transmission that is sometimes measured in elapsed time and begins with the start bit that precedes a character and ends with the last stop bit that follows the character. **2.** In synchronous communications, a package of information transmitted as a single unit. Every frame follows the same basic organization and contains control information, such as synchronizing characters, station address, and an error-checking value, as well as a variable amount of data. **3.** A single screen-sized image that can be displayed in sequence with other, slightly different, images to create animated drawings. **4.** The storage required to hold one screen-sized image of text, graphics, or both. **5.** A rectangular space containing, and defining the proportions of, a graphic. **6.** The part of an on-screen window (title bar and other elements) that is controlled by the operating system rather than by the application running in the window. **7.** A rectangular section of the page displayed by a Web browser that is a separate HTML document from the rest of the page. Web pages can have multiple frames. Associated with each frame are the same capabilities as for an unframed Web page, including scrolling and linking to another frame or Web site; these capabilities can be used independently of other frames on the page. Frames are often used as a table of contents for one or more HTML documents on a Web site. Most current Web browsers support frames, although older ones do not. *See also* HTML document, Web browser.

frame buffer *n.* A portion of a computer's display memory that holds the contents of a single screen image.

frame grabber *n.* *See* video digitizer.

frame rate *n.* **1.** The speed at which full, single-screen images are transmitted to and displayed by a raster-scan monitor. Frame rate is calculated as the

#
A
B
C
D
E
F
G
H
I
J
K
L
M
N
O
P
Q
R
S
T
U
V
W
X
Y
Z

number of times per second (hertz) the electron beam sweeps the screen. **2.** In animation, the number of times per second an image is updated. When the frame rate exceeds about 14 frames per second, animation seems to blend into smooth motion. *See also* animation.

frame source *n.* In the HTML frames environment, a contents document that will look for the source document to display within a frame drawn by the local browser. *See also* frame (definition 7), HTML.

frames per second *n.* *See* frame rate.

freenet or **free-net** *n.* A community-based computer BBS and Internet service provider, usually operated by volunteers and providing free access to subscribers in the community or access for a very small fee. Many freenets are operated by public libraries or universities. *See also* ISP.

.freenet.edu *n.* On the Internet, the major domain specifying that an address is located on a freenet. *See also* freenet.

free software *n.* Software, complete with source code, that is distributed freely to users who are in turn free to use, modify, and distribute it, provided that all alterations are clearly marked and that the name and copyright notice of the original author are not deleted or modified in any way. Unlike freeware, free software is protected by a license agreement. *Compare* freeware, public-domain software, shareware.

free space *n.* Space on a floppy disk or a hard drive not currently occupied by data. *See also* floppy disk, hard disk.

freeware *n.* A computer program given away free of charge and often made available on the Internet or through user groups. An independent program developer might offer a product as freeware either for personal satisfaction or to assess its reception among interested users. Freeware developers often retain all rights to their software, and users are not necessarily free to copy or distribute it further. *Compare* free software, public-domain software, shareware.

freeze-frame video *n.* Video in which the image changes only once every few seconds. *Compare* full-motion video.

frequently asked questions *n.* *See* FAQ.

friction feed *n.* A means of moving paper through a printer in which the paper is pinched either between the printer's platen and pressure rollers or between two sets of rollers. Friction feed is available on most printers, for use with paper that does not have pin-feed holes. In printers that also have tractor feed, the friction-feed mechanism should be disengaged when the tractor is being used, to avoid stress on the tractor gears. *See also* platen. *Compare* pin feed, tractor feed.

friendly *adj.* Referring to features built into hardware or software that make a computer or a program easy to learn and easy to use. *See also* user-friendly.

fringeware *n.* Freeware whose reliability and value are questionable. *See also* freeware.

front end *n.* In applications, software or a feature of software that provides an interface to another application or tool. Front ends are often used to supply a common interface for a range of tools produced by a software manufacturer. A front end generally offers a more user-friendly interface than that of the application running "behind" it.

front-end processor *n.* **1.** Generally, a computer or processing unit that produces and manipulates data before another processor receives it. *Compare* back-end processor (definition 2). **2.** In communications, a computer that is located between communications lines and a main (host) computer and is used to relieve the host of housekeeping chores related to communications (such as error detection, receiving and transmitting messages, and managing the lines that run to and from other devices); sometimes considered synonymous with communications controller. *See also* communications controller.

front panel *n.* The faceplate of a computer cabinet through which the control knobs, switches, and lights are available to an operator. *See also* console.

FT1 *n. See* fractional T1.

FTAM *n.* Acronym for **F**ile-**T**ransfer **A**ccess and **M**anagement. A communications standard for transferring files between different makes and models of computer.

FTP[1] *n.* **1.** Acronym for **F**ile **T**ransfer **P**rotocol, the protocol used for copying files to and from remote computer systems on a network using TCP/IP, such as the Internet. This protocol also allows users to use FTP commands to work with files, such as listing files and directories on the remote system. *See also* TCP/IP. **2.** A common logon ID for anonymous FTP. *See also* anonymous FTP.

FTP[2] *vb.* To download files from or upload files to remote computer systems, via the Internet's File Transfer Protocol. The user needs an FTP client to transfer files to and from the remote system, which must have an FTP server. Generally, the user also needs to establish an account on the remote system to FTP files, although many FTP sites permit the use of anonymous FTP. *See also* FTP client, FTP server.

FTP client or **ftp client** *n.* A program that enables the user to upload and download files to and from an FTP site over a network, such as the Internet, using the File Transfer Protocol. *See also* FTP[1] (definition 1). *Compare* FTP server.

FTP commands *n.* Commands that are part of the File Transfer Protocol. *See also* FTP[1] (definition 1).

FTP program or **ftp program** *n. See* FTP client.

FTP server *n.* A file server that uses the File Transfer Protocol to permit users to upload or download files through the Internet or any other TCP/IP network. *See also* file server, FTP[1] (definition 1), TCP/IP. *Compare* FTP client.

FTP site *n.* **1.** The collection of files and programs residing on an FTP server. *See also* FTP[1] (definition 1), FTP server. **2.** *See* FTP server.

full-duplex *adj. See* duplex[1].
full-duplex transmission *n. See* duplex[2] (definition 1).
full justification *n.* The process of aligning text evenly along both the left and right margins of a column or page. *See also* justify (definition 2).
full-motion video *n.* Digital video that is displayed at 30 frames per second. *Compare* freeze-frame video.
full-motion video adapter *n.* An expansion card for a computer that can convert motion video from devices such as a video cassette recorder to a digital format that a computer can use, such as AVI, MPEG, or Motion JPEG. *See also* AVI, Motion JPEG, MPEG.
full name *n.* A user's complete name, usually consisting of last name, first name, and middle initial. The full name is often maintained by the operating system as part of the information that identifies and defines a user account. *See also* user account.
full-page display *n.* A video display with sufficient size and resolution to show at least one 8½-by-11-inch image; useful for desktop publishing applications. *Acronym:* FPD. *See also* portrait monitor.
full path *n.* A pathname containing all the possible components of a path, including the drive, root directory, any subdirectories, and the file or object name. *See also* path (definitions 2 and 3), pathname, root directory, subdirectory. *Compare* relative path.
full-screen *adj.* Capable of using or being displayed on the full area of a display screen. Applications running in windowing environments commonly allocate different areas to different windows, any of which can be enlarged to fill the entire screen.
full-text search *n.* A search for one or more documents, records, or strings based on all of the actual text data rather than on an index containing a limited set of keywords. For example, a full-text search can locate a document containing the words "albatrosses are clumsy on land" by searching files for just those words without the need of an index containing the keyword "albatross." *See also* index[1].
fully populated board *n.* A printed circuit board whose integrated circuit sockets are all occupied. Memory boards in particular may have fewer than the maximum possible number of memory chips, leaving some IC sockets empty; such a board is said to be partially populated.
function *n.* **1.** The purpose of, or the action carried out by, a program or routine. **2.** A general term for a routine. **3.** In some programming languages, a routine that returns a value. *See also* procedure, routine.
function key *n.* Any of the 10 or more keys labeled F1, F2, F3, and so on, that appear along the left side or across the top of a keyboard (or both) and are used for special tasks. The meaning of a function key is defined by a program or, in some instances, by the user. Function keys are used in applications or the operating system to provide either a shortcut for a series of common instructions (such as calling up a program's on-screen help) or a

feature not otherwise available. *Compare* Command key, Control key, Escape key.

fuse *n.* A circuit element that burns out or breaks when the current passing through it exceeds a certain level. A fuse protects a circuit from damage caused by excess current. It performs the same function as a circuit breaker, but it cannot be reset, so it must be replaced if it breaks.

FWIW *adv.* Acronym for **f**or **w**hat **i**t's **w**orth. An expression used in e-mail and newsgroups.

FYI *n.* **1.** Acronym for **f**or **y**our **i**nformation. An expression used in e-mail and newsgroups to introduce information thought to be useful to the reader. **2.** An electronic document distributed through InterNIC, as an RFC is, but intended to explain an Internet standard or feature to users rather than defining it for developers, as an RFC does. *See also* InterNIC. *Compare* RFC.

G

G *prefix See* giga-.
game *n. See* computer game.
game card *n. See* ROM card.
game cartridge *n. See* ROM cartridge.
Game Control Adapter *n.* In IBM PCs and compatibles, a circuit that processes input signals at a game port. Devices such as joysticks and game paddles use potentiometers (circuit elements that can be adjusted to provide varying amounts of resistance) to represent their positions as varying voltage levels; the Game Control Adapter converts these levels to numbers using an analog-to-digital converter. *See also* analog-to-digital converter, game port.
game port *n.* In IBM PCs and compatibles, an I/O port for devices such as joysticks and game paddles. The game port is often included with other I/O ports on a single expansion board. *See also* expansion board, Game Control Adapter.
garbage *n.* Incorrect or corrupted data.
garbage in, garbage out *n.* A computing axiom meaning that if the data put into a process is incorrect, the data output by the process will also be incorrect. *Acronym:* GIGO.
gas-discharge display *n.* A type of flat-panel display, used on some portable computers, containing neon between a horizontal and a vertical set of electrodes. When one electrode in each set is charged, the neon glows where the two electrodes intersect, representing a pixel. *Also called* gas-plasma display. *See also* flat-panel display, pixel.
gas-plasma display *n. See* gas-discharge display.
gated *adj.* Transmitted through a gateway to a subsequent network or service. For example, a mailing list on BITNET may be gated to a newsgroup on the Internet.
gateway *n.* A device that connects networks using different communications protocols so that information can be passed from one to the other. A gateway both transfers information and converts it to a form compatible with the protocols used by the receiving network. *Compare* bridge.
GB *n. See* gigabyte.
Gbps *n. See* gigabits per second.
GDI *n.* Acronym for **G**raphical **D**evice **I**nterface. In Windows, a graphics display system used by applications to display or print bitmapped text (TrueType fonts), images, and other graphical elements. The GDI is responsible for drawing dialog boxes, buttons, and other elements in a consistent

style on screen by calling the appropriate screen drivers and passing them the information on the item to be drawn. The GDI also works with GDI printers (which have limited ability to prepare a page for printing) by calling the appropriate printer drivers and moving the image or document directly to the printer rather than reformatting it in PostScript or another printer language. *See also* bitmapped font, dialog box, driver, PostScript.

geek *n.* **1.** Generally, a person who enjoys cerebral activities (such as wordplay, computer programming, and use of the Internet) more than the mainstream population does. Geeks in this sense increasingly claim the word with pride, but it may give offense when used by others, suggesting inadequacy in normal social relationships. **2.** A computer expert or specialist. For issues of etiquette, see definition 1. *Compare* guru, techie.

gender bender *n.* *See* gender changer.

gender changer *n.* A device for joining two connectors that are either both male (having pins) or both female (having sockets). *Also called* gender bender.

General Protection Fault *n.* The error condition that occurs in an 80386 or higher processor running in protected mode (such as Windows 3.1) when an application attempts to access memory outside of its authorized memory space or when an invalid instruction is issued. *Acronym:* GPF. *See also* protected mode.

General Public License *n.* The agreement under which software is distributed by the Free Software Foundation. Anyone who has a copy of such a program may redistribute it to another party and may charge for distribution and support services, but may not restrict the other party from doing the same. A user may modify the program, but if the modified version is distributed, it must be clearly identified as such and is also covered under the General Public License. A distributor must also either provide source code or indicate where source code can be obtained. *Acronym:* GPL. *Also called* copyleft. *See also* free software.

general-purpose computer *n.* A computer that can perform any computational task. Each task depends on specific software.

general-purpose controller *n.* A controller designed for multiple uses. *See also* controller.

generation *n.* **1.** A concept used to distinguish stored versions of a set of files. The oldest is called the grandfather, the next oldest is the father, and the newest is the son. **2.** A category that distinguishes products, such as computers or programming languages, according to the technological advances they represent. *See also* computer.

generic icon *n.* An icon on a Macintosh screen that identifies a file only as a document or an application. Ordinarily the icon for an application is specific to that application, and the icon for a document is specific to the application that opens it. If a generic icon appears instead, the information that the Macintosh Finder uses to identify the application has been damaged. *See also* Finder, icon, Macintosh.

A B C D E F G H I J K L M N O P Q R S T U V W X Y Z

geographic information system *n.* An application or suite of applications for viewing and creating maps. Generally, geographic information systems contain a viewing system (sometimes allowing users to view maps with a Web browser), an environment for creating maps, and a server for managing maps and data for real-time online viewing. *Acronym:* GIS.

GeoPort *n.* A fast serial I/O port on a Macintosh Centris 660AV, Quadra 660AV, Quadra 840AV, or PowerMac computer. Any Macintosh-compatible serial device can be connected to a GeoPort, but with GeoPort-specific hardware and software the GeoPort can transmit data at up to 2 Mbps and can handle voice, fax, data, and video transmission.

get *n.* An FTP command that instructs the server to transfer a specified file to the client. *See also* FTP client, FTP commands, FTP server.

ghost[1] *n.* A dim, secondary image that is displaced slightly from the primary image on a video display (as a result of signal reflection in transmission) or on a printout (as a result of unstable printing elements).

ghost[2] *vb.* **1.** To produce a duplicate, such as duplicating an application in memory. **2.** To display an option on a menu or on a submenu in faint type to show that it cannot be selected at the present time. *See also* dimmed.

ghosting *n. See* burn in.

.gif *n.* The file extension that identifies GIF bit map images. *See also* GIF.

GIF *n.* **1.** Acronym for **G**raphics **I**nterchange **F**ormat. A graphics file format used for transmitting raster images on the Internet. An image may contain up to 256 colors, including a transparent color. The size of the file depends on the number of colors actually used. The LZW compression method is used to reduce the file size. *See also* raster graphics. **2.** A graphic stored as a file in the GIF format.

giga- *prefix* Abbreviated G. **1.** A prefix meaning one billion (10^9). **2.** In computer-related terms, a prefix meaning either 2^{30} (that is, 1,024 × 1,048,576) or 1,000 × 1,048,576.

gigabits per second *n.* Abbreviated Gbps. A measurement of data transfer speed, as on a network, in multiples of 1,073,741,824 (2^{30}) bits per second.

gigabyte *n.* Abbreviated GB. A data unit of 1,024 megabytes (2^{30} bytes); sometimes interpreted as 1,000 megabytes.

gigahertz *n.* Abbreviated GHz. A measure of frequency equivalent to 1 billion hertz, or 1 billion (1,000 million) cycles per second. *See also* hertz.

GIGO *n. See* garbage in, garbage out.

GIS *n. See* geographic information system.

GKS *n. See* Graphical Kernel System.

glare filter *n.* A transparent mask placed over the screen of a video monitor to reduce or eliminate light reflected from its glass surface.

glitch *n.* **1.** A problem, usually minor. **2.** A brief surge in electrical power.

global *adj.* Pertaining to an entire document, file, or program rather than to a restricted segment of it. *Compare* local.

global operation *n.* An operation, such as a search and replace, that affects an entire document, program, or other object such as a disk.

global search and replace *n.* A search and replace operation that finds and changes all instances of the selected string throughout a document. *See also* search and replace.
gnomon *n.* In computer graphics, a representation of the three-dimensional (*x*-*y*-*z*) axis system.
Good Times virus *n.* A purported e-mail virus alluded to in a warning that has been propagated widely across the Internet as well as by fax and standard mail. The warning claims that reading an e-mail message with the subject "Good Times" will damage the user's system. In fact, it is currently impossible to harm a system by reading an e-mail message, although it is possible to include a virus in a file that is attached to an e-mail message. Information on such hoaxes and on real viruses can be obtained from CERT (http://www.cert.org/). *See also* urban legend, virus.
Gopher or **gopher** *n.* An Internet utility for finding textual information and presenting it to the user in the form of hierarchical menus, from which the user selects submenus, files, or documents that can be downloaded and displayed. One Gopher client may access all available Gopher servers, so the user accesses a common "Gopherspace." Gopher is being subsumed by the World Wide Web.
.gov *n.* In the Internet's Domain Name System, the top-level domain that identifies addresses operated by government agencies. The designation .gov appears as a suffix at the end of the address. In the United States, only nonmilitary federal government agencies may use the .gov domain. State governments in the United States use the top-level domain of .state.us, with .us preceded by the two-letter abbreviation for the state, or just .us; other regional governments in the United States are registered under the .us domain. *See also* DNS (definition 1), domain (definition 3). *Compare* .com, .edu, .mil, .net, .org.
GPF *n.* *See* General Protection Fault.
GPL *n.* *See* General Public License.
grabber *n.* **1.** A device for capturing graphical image data from a video camera or another full-motion video source and putting it into memory. *See also* video digitizer. **2.** Any device for capturing data. **3.** Software that takes a "snapshot" of the currently displayed screen image by transferring a portion of video memory to a file on disk. **4.** In certain graphics-based applications, a special type of mouse pointer.
graceful exit *n.* The methodical termination of a process, even under error conditions, that allows the operating system or parent process to regain normal control, leaving the system in a state of equilibrium. This is expected behavior. *See also* fail-soft system.
grade *n.* In communications, the range of frequencies available for transmission on a single channel. For example, voice-grade telephone frequencies range from about 300 Hz through 3,400 Hz.
grade of service *n.* The probability that a user of a shared communications network, such as a public telephone system, will receive an "all channels

A B C D E F G H I J K L M N O P Q R S T U V W X Y Z

busy" signal. The grade of service is used as a measure of the network's ability to handle traffic and is usually applied to a specific period, such as the peak traffic hour.

graftal *n.* One of a family of geometric forms, similar to fractals but easier to compute. Graftals are often used in the special-effects industry to create synthetic images of structures such as trees and plants. *See also* fractal.

grammar checker *n.* A software accessory that checks text for errors in grammatical construction.

grandfather *n.* *See* generation (definition 1).

grandfather/father/son *adj.* *See* generation (definition 1).

granularity *n.* A description, from "coarse" to "fine," of a computer activity or feature (such as screen resolution or searching and sorting) in terms of the size of the units it handles (pixels or sets of data). The larger the pieces, the coarser the granularity.

Graphical Device Interface *n.* *See* GDI.

graphical interface *n.* *See* graphical user interface.

Graphical Kernel System *n.* A computer graphics standard, recognized by ANSI and ISO, that specifies methods of describing, manipulating, storing, and transferring graphical images. *Acronym:* GKS.

graphical user interface *n.* A type of environment that represents programs, files, and options by means of icons, menus, and dialog boxes on the screen. The user can select and activate these options by pointing and clicking with a mouse or, often, by using the keyboard. To the user, a particular item (such as a scroll bar) works the same way in all applications because the interface provides standard software routines to handle these elements and report the user's actions (such as a click on a particular icon or a key press); applications make use of these routines rather than attempting to reproduce them from scratch. *Acronym:* GUI.

graphic character *n.* Any character that is represented by a visible symbol, such as an ASCII character. *Compare* graphics character.

graphic limits *n.* On a computer screen, the boundary of a graphical image in a graphics software program, including all the area enclosed within the graphic. In some graphics environments, the limits of a graphic consist of the smallest rectangle that can completely enclose it, called its bounding rectangle or bounding box.

graphics accelerator *n.* A video adapter that contains a graphics coprocessor. A graphics accelerator can update the video display much more quickly than the CPU can, and it frees the CPU for other tasks. A graphics accelerator is a necessity for modern software such as graphical user interfaces and multimedia applications. *See also* graphics coprocessor, video adapter.

graphics adapter *n.* A video adapter capable of displaying graphics as well as alphanumeric characters. Almost all video adapters in common use today are graphics adapters.

graphics card *n. See* video adapter.
graphics character *n.* A character that can be combined with others to create simple graphics such as lines, boxes, and shaded or solid blocks. *Compare* graphic character.
Graphics Controller *n.* The part of the VGA video adapter that allows the computer to access the video buffer (the memory on a video adapter that is used to store data to be shown on the display). *See also* VGA.
graphics coprocessor *n.* A specialized microprocessor, included in some video adapters, that can generate graphical images such as lines and filled areas in response to instructions from the CPU, freeing the CPU for other work.
graphics engine *n.* **1.** A display adapter that handles high-speed graphics-related processing, freeing the CPU for other tasks. *Also called* graphics accelerator, video accelerator. **2.** Software that, based on commands from an application, sends instructions for creating graphical images to the hardware that actually creates the images. Examples are Macintosh QuickDraw and Windows GDI.
Graphics Interchange Format *n. See* GIF.
graphics interface *n. See* graphical user interface.
graphics mode *n.* **1.** On computers such as the IBM PC, the display mode in which lines and characters on the screen are drawn pixel by pixel. Because graphics mode creates images from individual dots on the screen, programs have more flexibility in creating images than they do in text (character) mode. Thus, the computer can display a mouse pointer as an arrowhead or other shape rather than as a blinking square or rectangle, and it can display character attributes, such as boldface and italics, as they will appear in print rather than using conventions such as highlighting, underlining, or alternate colors. *Compare* text mode. **2.** A particular set of color and resolution values, often related to a particular video adapter, such as VGA color with 16 colors and 640×480 pixels on the screen. *See also* high resolution, low resolution, resolution (definition 1).
graphics primitive *n.* A drawing element, such as a text character, an arc, or a polygon, that is drawn and manipulated as a single unit and is combined with other primitives to create an image.
graphics printer *n.* A printer, such as a laser or an ink-jet printer, that can produce graphics formed pixel by pixel and not merely text characters. Nearly all printers currently used with personal computers are graphics printers. *Compare* character printer.
graphics processor *n. See* graphics coprocessor.
graphics tablet *n.* A device used to input graphics position information in engineering, design, and illustration applications. A flat rectangular plastic board is equipped with a puck or a stylus (pen) and with sensing electronics that report the position of the puck or stylus to the computer, which translates that data into a cursor position on the screen. *Also called* digitizing tablet. *See also* puck, stylus.

graphics terminal *n.* A terminal capable of displaying graphics as well as text. Such terminals usually interpret graphics control commands rather than receiving streams of already-processed pixels.
gray scale *n.* A sequence of shades ranging from black through white, used in computer graphics to add detail to images or to represent a color image on a monochrome output device. Grays may be represented by actual gray shades, by halftone dots, or by dithering. *See also* dithering, halftone.
greater than *adj. See* relational operator.
greater than or equal to *adj. See* relational operator.
greeking *n.* **1.** The use of gray bars or other graphics to represent lines of characters too small to be drawn legibly on a screen at the chosen resolution, such as when viewing the layout of a whole page. **2.** The use of nonsense words to represent the text of a document in design samples. Greeking does not involve substituting the Greek alphabet for the Roman one.
greek text *n. See* greeking.
green PC *n.* A computer system designed to conserve energy. For example, some computers shut off power to nonessential systems when no input has been detected for a certain amount of time, a condition known as sleep mode. Green PCs may also be distinguished by the use of minimal packaging materials and replaceable components, such as toner cartridges, that are recyclable.
grep[1] *n.* Acronym for **g**lobal **r**egular **e**xpression **p**rint. A UNIX command used to search a file or files by keyword.
grep[2] *vb.* To search text, especially with the UNIX grep utility.
grid *n.* Two sets of lines or linear elements at right angles to each other. A spreadsheet is a grid of rows and columns; a graphics screen is a grid of horizontal and vertical lines of pixels.
grok *vb.* To understand deeply and appreciatively. The term comes from Robert A. Heinlein's novel *Stranger in a Strange Land,* where it is also a Martian word for "to drink" and implies the kind of devoted interest that a Martian—native of a dry planet—would have in water. Hackers often use the word in reference to computer expertise.
ground *n.* A conducting path from an electrical circuit to earth or to a conducting body serving in place of earth, usually used as a safety device. *See also* grounding.
grounding *n.* The connection of sections of an electrical circuit to a common conductor, called the ground, which serves as the reference for the other voltages in the circuit. The ground conductor on installed circuit boards is usually connected to the chassis, or metal frame, holding the electronic parts; the chassis is in turn usually connected to the third (round) prong on the power plug, which connects to a ground circuit that is, in fact, connected to the earth. This is important to avoid creating a shock hazard.
group[1] *n.* A collection of elements that can be treated as a whole, such as a collection of records in a database report or a collection of objects that can be moved and transformed as a single object in a drawing program. In vari-

ous multi-user operating systems, a group is a set of user accounts, sometimes referred to as members; if privileges are specified for the group, each member will then have those privileges. *See also* user account.

group[2] *vb.* In a drawing program, to transform a number of objects into a group. *See also* drawing program.

groupware *n.* Software intended to enable a group of users on a network to collaborate on a particular project. Groupware may provide services for communication (such as e-mail), collaborative document development, scheduling, and tracking.

guest *n.* A common name for a login account that can be accessed without a password. BBSs and service providers often maintain such an account so that prospective subscribers can sample the services offered.

GUI *n. See* graphical user interface.

guru *n.* A technical expert who is available to help solve problems and to answer questions in an intelligible way. *See also* techie, wizard (definition 1).

gutter *n.* The blank space or inner margin between two facing pages of a bound document.

H

hack[1] *n.* **1.** A modification to the code in a program, often made without taking the time to find an elegant solution. **2.** A sloppy job. *See also* kludge (definition 2), patch[2].
hack[2] *vb.* **1.** To apply creative ingenuity to a problem or project. **2.** To alter the behavior of an application or an operating system by modifying its code rather than by running the program and selecting options.
hacker *n.* **1.** A computerphile; a person who is totally engrossed in computer technology and computer programming or who likes to examine the code of operating systems and other programs to see how they work. **2.** A person who uses computer expertise for illicit ends, such as by gaining access to computer systems without permission and tampering with programs and data. *Also called* cracker.
HAGO Acronym for **h**ave **a** **g**ood **o**ne. An expression used to conclude e-mail messages or to sign off from a chat session.
hairline *n.* The smallest amount of visible space or the narrowest line that is displayable on a printed page. *See also* rule (definition 1).
half-card *n. See* short card.
half-duplex transmission *n.* Two-way electronic communication that takes place in only one direction at a time. *Compare* duplex[2] (definition 1), simplex transmission.
half router *n.* A device that connects a local area network to a communications line (such as one to the Internet) using a modem and controls the routing of data to individual stations on the LAN.
halftone *n.* A printed reproduction of a photograph or other illustration, using evenly spaced spots of varying diameter to produce apparent shades of gray. The darker the shade at a particular point in the image, the larger the corresponding spot in the halftone. *See also* dithering, gray scale.
handheld computer *n.* A computer small enough to be held in one hand while being operated. Usually built to perform specific tasks, handheld computers are commonly used in transportation and other field service industries. They often have restricted specialized keyboards rather than the standard QWERTY layout, smaller displays, input devices such as bar code readers, and communications devices for sending their data to a central computer; they rarely have disk drives. Their software is usually proprietary and stored in ROM. *See also* QWERTY keyboard, ROM. *Compare* handheld PC, PDA.
handheld PC *n.* A computer that is small enough to fit in a jacket pocket and that is able to run, for example, Windows CE (a scaled-down version of

Windows 95) and applications made for that operating system. *Acronym:* HPC. *Compare* handheld computer, PDA.

handheld scanner *n.* A type of scanner in which the scan head is contained within a handheld unit. The user passes the scan head over the medium being scanned, such as a piece of paper. *See also* scan head, scanner. *Compare* drum scanner, flatbed scanner, sheet-fed scanner.

handle *n.* One of several small squares displayed around a graphical object in a drawing program. The user can move or reshape the object by clicking on a handle and dragging.

handshake *n.* A series of signals acknowledging that communication or the transfer of information can take place between computers or other devices. A hardware handshake is an exchange of signals over specific wires (other than the data wires), in which each device indicates its readiness to send or receive data. A software handshake consists of signals transmitted over the same wires used to transfer data, as in modem-to-modem communications over telephone lines.

hands-on *adj.* Involving interactive work with a computer or a computer program. A hands-on tutorial, for example, would teach a skill (such as the use of a program) by means of practice sessions and question-and-answer dialogues.

handwriting recognition *n.* **1.** The ability of a computer to identify a user by recognizing features of handwriting, especially a signature. **2.** The ability of a computer to translate handwritten text into character data for input. This technology, which is still under development, could be useful in PDAs, whose keyboards are sometimes too small for data entry, and in software designed for Asian countries whose languages have so many characters that a keyboard becomes cumbersome for entering text. *See also* PDA. *Compare* optical character recognition.

hang *vb.* To stop responding. A hung program or computer system does not respond to user input, but the screen looks as if everything is running normally. The program or system might be waiting for something—for example, information from a network—or it might have terminated abnormally. It might resume running normally on its own, or the user might need to terminate and restart the program or reboot the computer. A hung computer system is said to be locked up.

hanging indent *n.* Placement of the beginning of the first line of a paragraph farther to the left than the subsequent lines. *Also called* outdent. *Compare* indent[1].

hard *adj.* Permanent, fixed, or physically defined; unchangeable by the ordinary operation of a computer system. *See also* hard copy, hard error, hard return. *Compare* soft.

hard card *n.* A circuit board, carrying a hard disk and containing its controller, that plugs into an expansion slot and uses the expansion bus for power as well as for data and control signals. By contrast, a hard disk in a drive bay communicates with a separate controller card by a ribbon cable and has a direct cable to the computer's main power supply. *See also* controller, drive bay, expansion slot, ribbon cable.

hard-coded *adj.* **1.** Designed to handle a specific situation only. **2.** Depending on values embedded in the program code rather than on values that can be input and changed by the user.

hard copy *n.* Printed output on paper, film, or other permanent medium. *Compare* soft copy.

hard disk *n.* A device containing one or more inflexible platters coated with material in which data can be recorded magnetically, together with their read/write heads, the head-positioning mechanism, and the spindle motor in a sealed case that protects against outside contaminants. Compared to a floppy disk, much more data can be stored on a hard disk, and the data can be accessed much more quickly. Most hard disks contain from two to eight platters. *Also called* hard disk drive. *Compare* floppy disk.

hard disk drive *n. See* hard disk.

hard disk type *n.* One or more numbers that inform a computer about the characteristics of a hard disk, such as the number of read/write heads and the hard disk's capacity. The hard disk type numbers are usually marked on a label attached to the disk and must be input to the computer when the hard disk is installed, often by means of the computer's CMOS setup program. *See also* CMOS setup.

hard error *n.* **1.** An error caused by a hardware failure or by accessing incompatible hardware. *See also* hard failure. *Compare* soft error. **2.** An error that prevents a program from returning to normal operation. *See also* fatal error.

hard failure *n.* A cessation of function from which no recovery is possible, usually requiring a call to a repair service to correct. *Also called* hardware failure.

hard hyphen *n. See* hyphen.

hard return *n.* A character input by the user to indicate that the current line of text is to end and a new line is to begin. In word processing programs that automatically break lines within the margins of a page, a hard return indicates the end of a paragraph. In text-entry programs that lack wordwrap, a hard return is required to end each line; often two or more hard returns are needed to end a paragraph. *See also* wordwrap. *Compare* soft return.

hard space *n. See* nonbreaking space.

hardware *n.* The physical components of a computer system, including any peripheral equipment such as printers, modems, and mouse devices. *Compare* firmware, software.

hardware check *n.* An automatic check performed by hardware to detect internal errors or problems.

hardware-dependent *adj.* Of or pertaining to programs, languages, or computer components and devices that are tied to a particular computer system or configuration. Assembly language, for example, is hardware-

dependent because it is created for and works only with a particular make or model of microprocessor.
hardware failure *n.* A malfunction of a physical component in a computer system, such as a disk head crash or memory error. *See also* hard failure.
hardware handshake *n. See* handshake.
hardware key *n.* **1.** A security device connected to an I/O port to permit the use of a particular software package on that computer. The use of the hardware key permits backup copying of software but prevents its unlicensed use on additional computers. *Also called* dongle. **2.** Any physical device used to secure a computer system from unauthorized access, such as a lock on the front of the cabinet.
hardware profile *n.* A set of data that describes the configuration and characteristics of a given piece of computer equipment. Such data is typically used to configure computers for use with peripheral devices.
hardwired *adj.* **1.** Built into a system using hardware such as logic circuits, rather than accomplished through programming. **2.** Physically connected to a system or a network, as by means of a network connector board and cable.
hash *n.* In many FTP client programs, a command that instructs the FTP client to display a pound sign (#) each time it sends or receives a block of data. *See also* FTP client.
Hayes-compatible *adj.* Responding to the same set of commands as the modems manufactured by Hayes Microcomputer Products. This command set has become the de facto standard for microcomputer modems.
HDBMS *n. See* hierarchical database management system.
HDF *n. See* Hierarchical Data Format.
HDSL *n. See* high-bit-rate digital subscriber line.
head *n.* The read/write mechanism in a disk or tape drive. It converts changes in the magnetic field of the material on the disk or tape surface to changing electrical signals and vice versa. Disk drives usually contain one head for each surface that can be read from and written to.
head-cleaning device *n.* An apparatus for applying a small amount of cleaning fluid to a magnetic head to remove accumulated debris.
head crash *n.* A hard disk failure in which a read/write head, normally supported on a thin cushion of air, comes into contact with the platter, damaging the magnetic coating in which data is recorded. A head crash can be caused by mechanical failure or by heavy shaking of the disk drive. If the crash occurs on a directory track, the whole disk may become instantly unreadable.
header *n.* **1.** In word processing or printing, text that is to appear at the top of pages. A header might be specified for the first page, all pages after the first, even pages, or odd pages. It can include the page number, the date, the title, or other document information. *Also called* heading, running head. *Compare* footer. **2.** An information structure that precedes and identifies the information that follows, such as a block of bytes in communications, a file on a disk, a set of records in a database, or an executable program.

A B C D E F G H I J K L M N O P Q R S T U V W X Y Z

header record *n.* The first record in a sequence of records.
heading *n. See* header (definition 1).
head slot *n.* The oblong opening in the jacket of a floppy disk that provides access to the magnetic surface of the disk for the read/write head.
heat pipe *n.* A cooling device consisting of a sealed metal tube containing a liquid and a wick. The liquid evaporates at the hot end, taking some heat with it; the vapor spreads along the tube to the cold end, where it condenses onto the wick; the liquid flows back along the wick to the hot end by capillary action. Heat pipes have been used in Pentium-based laptop computers, which have high cooling requirements and little room for conventional heat sinks. *Compare* heat sink.
heat sink *n.* A device that absorbs and dissipates heat produced by an electrical component, such as an integrated circuit, to prevent overheating. Heat sinks are usually made of metal and often have fins that assist in transferring heat to the atmosphere. *Compare* heat pipe.
help *n.* **1.** The ability of many applications to display advice or instructions for using their features when so requested by the user. The user can access help by, for example, clicking a screen button, choosing a menu item, or pressing a function key. Some help facilities are context-sensitive, meaning that the user receives information specific to the task or command being attempted. *Also called* online help. **2.** In some applications (for instance, in many FTP programs), a command that displays an explanation of another command that follows it.
Help *n.* An item on a menu bar in a graphical user interface that enables the user to access the help feature of the current application. *See also* graphical user interface, help (definition 1), menu bar.
help desk *n.* **1.** Technical support staff who help solve users' problems with hardware or software systems or refer such problems to those who can solve them. Help desks are typically run by larger organizations such as corporations or universities, or vendors to corporations, to assist users in the organization. **2.** A software application for tracking problems with hardware and software and their solutions.
helper application *n.* An application intended to be launched by a Web browser when the browser downloads a file that it is not able to process itself. Examples of helper applications are sound and movie players. Helper applications generally must be obtained and installed by users; they usually are not included in the browser itself. Many current Web browsers no longer require helper applications for common multimedia file formats. *Also called* helper program. *Compare* ActiveX controls, plug-in (definition 2).
helper program *n. See* helper application.
Help key *n.* A key on the keyboard that the user can press to request help. *See also* function key, help (definition 1).
help screen *n.* A screen of information that is displayed when the user requests help. *See also* help (definition 1).

hertz *n.* Abbreviated Hz. The unit of frequency measurement; one cycle (of a periodic event such as a waveform) per second. Frequencies of interest in computers and electronic devices are often measured in kilohertz (kHz, or 1,000 Hz), megahertz (MHz, or 1,000 kHz), gigahertz (GHz, or 1,000 MHz), or terahertz (THz, or 1,000 GHz).

hertz time *n. See* clock rate.

heterogeneous environment *n.* A computing milieu, usually within an organization, in which hardware and software from two or more manufacturers are used. *Compare* homogeneous environment.

hex *adj. See* hexadecimal.

hexadecimal *adj.* Of or pertaining to the base-16 number system. The hexadecimal system uses the digits 0 through 9 and A through F (uppercase or lowercase) to represent the decimal numbers 0 through 15. One hexadecimal digit is equivalent to 4 bits, and 1 byte can be expressed by two hexadecimal digits. For example, binary 0101 0011 corresponds to hexadecimal 53. To prevent confusion with decimal numbers, hexadecimal numbers in programs or documentation are usually followed by the letter H or preceded by the symbol &, $, or 0x. Thus, 10H = decimal 16; 100H = decimal 16^2 = decimal 256. *Also called* hex.

HFS *n. See* Hierarchical File System.

HHOK Acronym for **h**a, **h**a, **o**nly **k**idding. An indication of humor or facetiousness often used in e-mail and online communications.

hidden file *n.* A file that is not shown in the normal listing of the files contained in a directory, in order to protect the file from deletion or modification. A hidden file is often used to store code or data critical to the operating system.

hidden line *n.* In any application, such as a CAD program, that represents solid three-dimensional objects, a line in a drawing that would (or should) be hidden if the object were perceived as a solid construction. The process of removing such lines in an application is called hidden-line removal. *See also* CAD, hidden surface.

hidden surface *n.* A surface of a solid three-dimensional object, such as one represented in a CAD program, that would not be visible when the object is viewed from a particular angle—for example, the underside of the wing of an airplane viewed from the top. *See also* CAD, hidden line.

hide *vb.* To defer the display of an application's active window while leaving the application running. Windows that have been hidden are returned to active display by issuing the appropriate command to the operating system.

hierarchical computer network *n.* **1.** A network in which one host computer controls a number of smaller computers, which may in turn act as hosts to a group of PC workstations. **2.** A network in which control functions are organized according to a hierarchy and in which data processing tasks may be distributed.

hierarchical database *n.* A database in which records are grouped in such a way that their relationships form a branching, treelike structure. This type of database structure is well suited for organizing information that breaks down logically into successively greater levels of detail. The organization of records in such a database should reflect the most common or the most time-critical types of access expected.

hierarchical database management system *n.* A database management system that supports a hierarchical model. *Acronym:* HDBMS. *See also* hierarchical model.

Hierarchical Data Format *n.* A file format for storing multiple types of graphical and numerical data and transferring them between different types of machines, together with a library of functions for handling such files in a uniform way. Hierarchical Data Format files are supported on most common types of computers. *Acronym:* HDF.

hierarchical file system *n.* A system for organizing files on a disk in which files are contained in directories or folders, each of which can contain other directories as well as files. The main directory for the disk is called the root; the chain of directories from the root to a particular file is called the path. *See also* hierarchy, path (definitions 2 and 3), root. *Compare* flat file system.

Hierarchical File System *n.* A tree-structured file system used on the Apple Macintosh in which folders can be nested within other folders. *Acronym:* HFS. *See also* hierarchy, path (definitions 2 and 3), root. *Compare* flat file system.

hierarchical menu *n.* A menu that has one or more submenus. Such an arrangement is hierarchical because each level subsumes the next.

hierarchical model *n.* A model used in database management in which each record may be the "parent" of one or more "child" records, which may or may not have the same structure as the parent; a record can have no more than one parent. Conceptually, therefore, a hierarchical model can be, and usually is, regarded as a tree. The individual records are not necessarily contained in the same file. *See also* tree.

hierarchy *n.* A type of organization that, like a tree, branches into more specific units, each of which is "owned" by the higher-level unit immediately above. Hierarchies are characteristic of several aspects of computing because they provide organizational frameworks that can reflect logical links, or relationships, between separate records, files, or pieces of equipment. For example, hierarchies are used in organizing related files on a disk, related records in a database, and related (interconnected) devices on a network. *See also* hierarchical file system.

high-bit-rate digital subscriber line *n.* A protocol for digital transmission of data over standard copper telecommunications lines as opposed to fiber-optic lines. *Acronym:* HDSL. *Also called* high-data-rate digital subscriber line.

high-capacity CD-ROM *n.* *See* digital video disc.

high-data-rate digital subscriber line *n.* *See* high-bit-rate digital subscriber line.

high-density disk *n.* **1.** A 3.5-inch floppy disk that can hold 1.44 MB. *Compare* double-density disk. **2.** A 5.25-inch floppy disk that can hold 1.2 MB. *Compare* double-density disk.

high DOS memory *n. See* high memory area.

high-end *adj.* A descriptive term for something that uses the latest technology to maximize performance. There is usually a direct correlation between high-end technology and higher prices.

high-level language *n.* A computer language that provides a level of abstraction from the underlying machine language. Statements in a high-level language generally use keywords similar to English and translate into more than one machine-language instruction. In practice, every computer language above assembly language is a high-level language. *Also called* high-order language. *Compare* assembly language.

highlight *vb.* To alter the appearance of displayed characters as a means of calling attention to them, as by displaying them in reverse video or with greater intensity. Highlighting is used to indicate an item, such as a menu option or a section of text, that is to be acted on in some way. *See also* reverse video.

high memory *n.* Memory locations addressed by the largest numbers. *See also* high memory area, UMA. *Compare* low memory.

high memory area *n.* In IBM PCs and compatibles, the 64-KB range of addresses immediately above 1 MB. By means of the file HIMEM.SYS, MS-DOS (versions 5.0 and later) can move portions of itself into the high memory area, thereby increasing the amount of conventional memory available for applications. *Acronym:* HMA. *See also* conventional memory, expanded memory.

high-order language *n. See* high-level language.

High Performance Serial Bus (1394) *n.* A serial bus interface for both the PC and the Macintosh that can support transmission speeds of 100, 200, or 400 Mbps and allows daisy-chaining of up to 63 devices in a branched form. Devices connected in such a way are able to draw power directly through the interface.

high resolution *n.* The capability of reproducing text and graphics with relative clarity and fineness of detail. High resolution is achieved by using a large number of pixels (for screen displays) or dots (for printers) to create an image in a given area. *Also called* hi-res. *See also* resolution (definition 1).

high tech *n.* **1.** Cutting-edge applied science and engineering, usually involving computers and electronics. **2.** Sophisticated, often complex, specialized technical innovation.

hi-res *n. See* high resolution.

history *n.* A list of the user's actions within a program, such as commands entered in an operating system shell, menus passed through using Gopher, or links followed using a Web browser.

#
A
B
C
D
E
F
G
H
I
J
K
L
M
N
O
P
Q
R
S
T
U
V
W
X
Y
Z

hit *n.* **1.** A successful retrieval of data from a cache rather than from the slower hard disk or RAM. *See also* cache. **2.** A successful retrieval of a record matching a query in a database. *See also* query (definition 1). **3.** Retrieval of a document, such as a home page, from a Web site.
HLS *n.* Acronym for **h**ue-**l**ightness-**s**aturation. *See* HSB.
HMA *n. See* high memory area.
holy war *n.* **1.** A widespread and acrimonious debate among computer professionals over some aspect of the computer field. **2.** An argument in a mailing list, newsgroup, or other forum over some emotional and controversial topic, such as abortion or Northern Ireland. Introducing a holy war that is off the purported topic of the forum is considered a violation of netiquette. *See also* netiquette.
home *n.* A beginning position, such as the top left corner of a character-based display, the left end of a line of text, cell A1 of a spreadsheet, or the top of a document.
homebrew *n.* Hardware or software developed by an individual at home or by a company for its own use rather than as a commercial product, such as hardware developed by electronics hobbyists when microcomputers first appeared in the 1970s.
home computer *n.* A personal computer designed and priced for use in the home.
home directory *n.* A directory associated with a user account under UNIX. The home directory is the current directory when the user logs in, and the user can return to it by entering the cd (change directory) command without a pathname. The user's files are ordinarily stored in the home directory and its descendants.
homegrown software *n.* Software developed by an individual at home rather than in a professional environment. Most public-domain and shareware programs are created this way.
Home key *n.* A key, found on most keyboards, whose function usually involves sending the cursor to some type of home position in an application. *See also* home.
home page *n.* **1.** A document intended to serve as a starting point in a hypertext system, especially the World Wide Web. **2.** An entry page for a set of Web pages and other files in a Web site.
home record *n. See* header record.
homogeneous environment *n.* A computing milieu, usually within an organization, in which only one manufacturer's hardware and one manufacturer's software are used. *Compare* heterogeneous environment.
homogeneous network *n.* A network on which all the hosts are similar and only one protocol is used.
horizontal market software *n.* Applications, such as word processors, that can be used in all types of business, as opposed to those geared for a certain industry.

horizontal scrolling *n.* Movement right or left in a displayed document. *See also* scroll, scroll bar.

host *n.* The main computer in a system of computers or terminals connected by communications links.

host adapter *n.* A device for connecting a peripheral to the main computer, typically in the form of an expansion board. *Also called* controller, host bus adapter.

host name *n.* A unique name that identifies a computer on a network. On the Internet, the host name is a string consisting of a local part and a domain, as in compxyz.eng.com. The host name is translated into an Internet address that usually has a dot notation, such as 123.12.4.27. A single computer can have several host names, also called aliases.

host not responding *n.* An error message issued by an Internet client indicating that the computer to which a request has been sent is refusing the connection or is otherwise unavailable to respond.

host timed out *n.* An error condition that occurs when a remote system fails to respond within a reasonable amount of time (a few minutes) during an exchange of data over a TCP connection. This condition may mean that the remote system has crashed or been disconnected from the network. The error message the user sees may be phrased slightly differently. *See also* TCP. *Compare* host not responding.

host unreachable *n.* An error condition that occurs when the computer to which the user wishes to connect over a TCP/IP network cannot be accessed on its LAN because it is either down or disconnected from the network. The error message the user sees may be phrased slightly differently. *See also* TCP/IP.

hot docking *n.* The process of attaching a laptop computer to a docking station while the computer is running and automatically activating the docking station's video display and other functions. *See also* docking station, laptop.

hot insertion *n.* The insertion of a device or card while there is power to the system. Many newer laptops allow hot insertion of PCMCIA cards. High-end servers may also allow hot insertion to reduce downtime.

hot key[1] *n.* A keystroke or combination of keystrokes that switches the user to a different program, often a TSR program or the operating system user interface. *See also* TSR.

hot key[2] *vb.* To transfer to a different program by pressing a hot key.

hot link *n.* **1.** A connection between two programs that instructs the second program to make changes to data when changes occur in the first program. For example, a word processor could update a document based on information obtained from a database through a hot link. **2.** *See* hyperlink.

hotlist *n.* A list of frequently accessed items, such as Web pages in a Web browser, from which the user can select.

hot plugging *n.* A feature that allows equipment to be connected to an active device, such as a computer, while the device is powered on.

hot spot *n.* The position in a mouse pointer, such as the position at the tip of an arrow or the intersection of the lines in a cross, that marks the exact location that will be affected by a mouse action, such as a button press.

hot swapping *n. See* hot plugging.

housekeeping *n.* Any of various routines, such as updating the clock or performing garbage collection, designed to keep the system, the environment within which a program runs, or the data structures within a program in good working order.

HPC *n. See* handheld PC.

.hqx *n.* A file extension for a file encoded with BinHex. *See also* BinHex[1].

HREF *n.* Short for **h**ypertext **ref**erence. An attribute in an HTML document that defines a link to another document on the Web. *See also* HTML.

HSB *n.* Acronym for **h**ue-**s**aturation-**b**rightness. A color model in which hue is the color itself as placed on a color wheel, where 0° is red, 60° is yellow, 120° is green, 180° is cyan, 240° is blue, and 300° is magenta; saturation is the percentage of the specified hue in the color; and brightness is the percentage of white in the color. *Also called* HLS, HSV, hue. *See also* color model. *Compare* CMY, RGB.

HSV *n.* Acronym for **h**ue-**s**aturation-**v**alue. *See* HSB.

.htm *n.* The MS-DOS/Windows 3.*x* file extension that identifies HTML files, commonly used as Web pages. The .html extension is truncated to three letters because MS-DOS and Windows 3.*x* cannot recognize file extensions longer than three letters. *See also* HTML.

.html *n.* The file extension that identifies HTML files, commonly used as Web pages. *See also* HTML.

HTML *n.* Acronym for **H**yper**t**ext **M**arkup **L**anguage. The markup language used for documents on the World Wide Web. HTML is an application of SGML that uses tags to mark elements such as text and graphics in a document to indicate how Web browsers should display these elements to the user and how browsers should respond to user actions such as activation of a link by means of a key press or mouse click. *See also* .htm, .html, SGML, tag (definition 2), Web browser.

HTML document *n.* **1.** A hypertext document that has been coded with HTML. **2.** *See* Web page.

HTML editor *n.* A software program used to create and modify HTML documents (Web pages). Most HTML editors include a method for inserting HTML tags without having to type out each tag. A number of HTML editors will also automatically reformat a document with HTML tags, based on formatting codes used by the word processing program in which the document was created. *See also* tag (definition 2), Web page.

HTML page *n. See* Web page.

HTML tag *n. See* tag (definition 2).

HTML validation service *n.* A service used to confirm that a Web page uses valid HTML according to the latest standard and/or that its hyperlinks are valid. An HTML validation service can catch small syntactical errors in HTML coding as well as deviations from the HTML standards. *See also* HTML.

HTTP *n.* Acronym for **H**yper**t**ext **T**ransfer **P**rotocol. The client/server protocol used to access information on the World Wide Web. *See also* URL.

HTTP Next Generation *n. See* HTTP-NG.

HTTP-NG *n.* Acronym for **H**yper**t**ext **T**ransfer **P**rotocol **N**ext **G**eneration. A standard under development by the World Wide Web Consortium (W3C) for improving performance and enabling the addition of features such as security. Whereas the current version of HTTP establishes a connection each time a request is made, HTTP-NG will set up one connection (which consists of separate channels for control information and data) for an entire session between a particular client and a particular server.

HTTP server *n.* **1.** Server software that uses HTTP to serve up HTML documents and any associated files and scripts when requested by a client, such as a Web browser. The connection between client and server is usually broken after the requested document or file has been served. HTTP servers are used on Web and intranet sites. *Also called* Web server. *See also* HTML, HTTP, server (definition 2). **2.** Any machine on which an HTTP server program is running.

HTTP status codes *n.* Three-digit codes sent by an HTTP server that indicate the results of a request for data. Codes beginning with 1 respond to requests that the client may not have finished sending; with 2, successful requests; with 3, further action that the client must take; with 4, requests that failed because of client error; and with 5, requests that failed because of server error. *See also* HTTP.

hub *n.* In a network, a device joining communications lines at a central location, providing a common connection to all devices on the network. The term is an analogy to the hub of a wheel. *See also* switching hub.

hue *n.* In the HSB color model, one of the three characteristics used to describe a color. Hue is the attribute that most readily distinguishes one color from other colors. It depends on the frequency of a light wave in the visible spectrum. *See also* color model, HSB. *Compare* brightness, saturation.

human engineering *n.* The designing of machines and associated products to suit the needs of humans. *See also* ergonomics.

human-machine interface *n.* The boundary at which people make contact with and use machines; when applied to programs and operating systems, it is more widely known as the user interface.

hung *adj. See* hang.

HyperCard *n.* An information-management software tool, designed for the Apple Macintosh, that implements many hypertext concepts. A HyperCard document consists of a series of cards, collected into a stack. Each card can contain text, graphical images, sound, buttons that enable travel from card to card, and other controls. Programs and routines can be coded as scripts in an object-oriented language called HyperTalk or developed as external code resources (XCMDs and XFCNs). *See also* hypertext, object-oriented programming, XCMD, XFCN.

hyperlink *n.* A connection between an element in a hypertext document, such as a word, phrase, symbol, or image, and a different element in the document, another hypertext document, a file, or a script. The user activates the link by clicking on the linked element, which is usually underlined or displayed in a different color. Hyperlinks are indicated in a hypertext document through tags in markup languages such as SGML and HTML. These tags are generally not visible to the user. *Also called* hot link, hypertext link. *See also* anchor (definition 2), HTML, hypermedia, hypertext, URL.

hypermedia *n.* The integration of any combination of text, graphics, sound, and video into a primarily associative system of information storage and retrieval in which users jump from subject to related subject in searching for information. Hypermedia attempts to offer an environment that parallels human thinking—that is, one in which the user can make associations between topics, rather than move sequentially from one to the next, as in an alphabetic list. If the information is primarily in text form, it is regarded as hypertext; if video, music, animation, or other elements are included, the information is regarded as hypermedia. *See also* hypertext.

hyperspace *n.* The set of all documents that can be accessed by following hyperlinks in the World Wide Web. *Compare* cyberspace (definition 2).

HyperTalk *n.* The programming language used to manipulate HyperCard stacks. *See also* HyperCard.

hypertext *n.* Text linked together in a complex, nonsequential web of associations in which the user can browse through related topics. Hypertext documents presented by a computer attempt to express the nonlinear structure of ideas as opposed to the linear format of books, film, and speech. *See also* HyperCard, hypermedia.

hypertext link *n.* *See* hyperlink.

Hypertext Markup Language *n.* *See* HTML.

Hypertext Transfer Protocol *n.* *See* HTTP.

Hypertext Transfer Protocol Next Generation *n.* *See* HTTP-NG.

hyphen *n.* A punctuation mark (-) used to break a word between syllables at the end of a line or to separate the parts of a compound word. Word processing programs with sophisticated hyphenation capabilities recognize several types of hyphens. Normal hyphens, also called required or hard hyphens, are part of a word's spelling and are always visible, as in *long-term.* Optional hyphens, also called discretionary or soft hyphens, appear only when a word is broken between syllables at the end of a line; they are usually supplied by the word processing program itself. Nonbreaking hyphens are always visible, like normal hyphens, but they do not allow a line break.

HYTELNET *n.* A menu-driven index of Internet resources that are accessible via telnet, including library catalogs, databases and bibliographies, bulletin boards, and network information services. HYTELNET can operate through a client program on a computer connected to the Internet or through the World Wide Web. *See also* telnet[1].

Hz *n.* Abbreviation for hertz.

I

I2O *n.* Short for **I**ntelligent **I**nput/**O**utput. A specification for I/O device driver architecture that is independent of both the device being controlled and the host operating system. *See also* driver, input/output device.

i486DX *n.* An Intel microprocessor introduced in 1989. In addition to the features of the 80386 (32-bit registers, 32-bit data bus, and 32-bit addressing), the i486DX has a built-in cache controller, a built-in floating-point coprocessor, provisions for multiprocessing, and a pipelined execution scheme, which speeds up execution time. *Also called* 486, 80486.

I-beam *n.* A mouse cursor used by many applications, such as word processors, in text-editing mode. The I-beam cursor, named for its I shape, indicates sections of the document where text can be inserted, deleted, changed, or moved. *Also called* I-beam pointer. *See also* cursor (definition 3), mouse.

I-beam pointer *n.* *See* I-beam.

IBM AT *n.* A class of personal computers introduced in 1984 and conforming to IBM's PC/AT (Advanced Technology) specification. The first AT was based on the Intel 80286 processor and dramatically outperformed its predecessor, the XT, in speed. *See also* 80286.

IBM PC *n.* Short for **IBM P**ersonal **C**omputer. A category of personal computers introduced in 1981 and conforming to IBM's PC specification. The first PC was based on the Intel 8088 processor. For a number of years, the IBM PC was the de facto standard in the computing industry for PCs, and clones (PCs that conform to the IBM specification) have been referred to as PC-compatible. *See also* PC-compatible, Wintel.

IBM PC-compatible *adj.* *See* PC-compatible.

IBM PC/XT *n.* A class of personal computers released by IBM in 1983. XT, short for eXtended Technology, enabled users to add a wider range of peripherals to their machines than was possible with the original IBM PC. Equipped with a 10-MB hard disk drive and one or two 5.25-inch floppy drives, the PC/XT was expandable to 256 KB of RAM on the motherboard and was loaded with MS-DOS 2.1, which supported directories and subdirectories. The popularity of this machine contributed to the production of clones (copies of its design by many manufacturers). *Also called* XT. *See also* IBM AT, IBM PC.

IC *n.* *See* integrated circuit.

ICM *n.* *See* image color matching.

icon *n.* A small image displayed on the screen to represent an object that can be manipulated by the user. By serving as visual mnemonics and allowing the user to control certain computer actions without having to remember commands or type them at the keyboard, icons are a significant factor in the user-friendliness of graphical user interfaces. *See also* graphical user interface, user-friendly.

iconic interface *n.* A user interface based on icons rather than on typed commands. *See also* graphical user interface, icon.

icon parade *n.* The sequence of icons that appears during the boot-up of a Macintosh computer.

IDE *n.* Acronym for **I**ntegrated **D**rive **E**lectronics. A type of disk drive interface in which the controller electronics reside on the drive itself, eliminating the need for a separate adapter card. The IDE interface is compatible with the controller used by IBM in the PC/AT computer but offers advantages such as look-ahead caching.

identifier *n.* Any text string used as a label, such as the name attached to a hard disk or floppy disk. *Compare* descriptor.

idle *adj.* **1.** Operational but not in use. **2.** Waiting for a command.

IDSL *n.* Acronym for **I**nternet **d**igital **s**ubscriber **l**ine. A high-speed digital communications service that provides Internet access as fast as 1.1 Mbps over standard telephone lines. IDSL uses a hybrid of ISDN and digital subscriber line technology. *See also* digital subscriber line, ISDN.

IEEE *n.* Acronym for **I**nstitute of **E**lectrical and **E**lectronics **E**ngineers. An organization of engineering and electronics professionals notable for developing standards for hardware and software.

.iff *n.* The file extension that identifies files in the IFF format. *See also* IFF.

IFF *n.* Acronym for **I**nterchange **F**ile **F**ormat. IFF was most commonly used on the Amiga platform, where it constituted almost any kind of data. On other platforms, IFF is mostly used to store image and sound files.

illegal *adj.* Not allowed, or leading to invalid results. For example, an illegal character in a word processing program would be one that the program cannot recognize; an illegal operation might be impossible for a program or system because of built-in constraints. *Compare* invalid.

illuminance *n.* **1.** The amount of light falling on, or illuminating, a surface area. **2.** A measure of illumination (such as watts per square meter) used in reference to devices such as televisions and computer displays. *Compare* luminance.

.image *n.* A file extension for a Macintosh Disk Image, a storage type often used on Apple's FTP software download sites.

image *n.* **1.** A stored description of a graphic picture, either as a set of brightness and color values of pixels or as a set of instructions for reproducing the picture. *See also* bit map. **2.** A duplicate, copy, or representation of all or part of a hard or floppy disk, a section of memory or hard drive, a file, a program, or data. For example, a RAM disk can hold an image of all or part of a disk in main memory; a virtual RAM program can create an image of some portion of the computer's main memory on disk. *See also* RAM disk.

image color matching *n.* The process of image output correction to match the colors that were scanned or input. *Acronym:* ICM.

| A | B | C | D | E | F | G | H | I | J | K | L | M | N | O | P | Q | R | S | T | U | V | W | X | Y | Z

image compression *n.* The use of a data compression technique on a graphical image. Uncompressed graphics files tend to use up large amounts of storage, so image compression is useful to conserve space. *See also* compressed file, data compression, video compression.

image editing *n.* The process of changing or modifying a bitmapped image, usually with an image editor.

image editor *n.* A program that allows users to modify the appearance of a bitmapped image, such as a scanned photo, by using filters and other functions. Creation of new images is generally accomplished in a paint or drawing program. *See also* bitmapped graphics, filter (definition 4), paint program.

image enhancement *n.* The process of improving the quality of a graphic image, either automatically by software or manually by a user through a paint or drawing program. *See also* anti-aliasing, image processing.

image map *n.* An image that contains more than one hyperlink on a Web page. Clicking on different parts of the image links the user to other resources on another part of the Web page, a different page, or a file. Often an image map, which can be a photograph, a drawing, or a composite of several drawings or photographs, is used as a map to the resources found on a particular Web site. Image maps are created with CGI scripts. *Also called* clickable maps. *See also* CGI script, hyperlink, Web page.

image processing *n.* The analysis, manipulation, storage, and display of graphical images from sources such as photographs, drawings, and video. Image processing can include image capture, digitizing, image enhancement, and data compression. *See also* image enhancement, video digitizer.

imaging *n.* The processes involved in the capture, storage, display, and printing of graphical images.

IMAP4 *n.* Acronym for **I**nternet **M**essage **A**ccess **P**rotocol **4**. The latest version of IMAP, a method that allows an e-mail program to gain access to e-mail and bulletin-board messages stored on a mail server. Unlike POP, IMAP lets a user retrieve messages efficiently from more than one computer. *See also* POP3, Post Office Protocol.

IMHO Acronym for **i**n **m**y **h**umble **o**pinion. IMHO, used in e-mail and in online forums, flags a statement that the writer wants to present as a personal opinion rather than as a statement of fact.

immediate access *n. See* direct access, random access.

immediate printing *n.* A process in which text and printing commands are sent directly to the printer without being stored as a printing file and without the use of an intermediate page-composition procedure or a file containing printer setup commands.

IMO Acronym for **i**n **m**y **o**pinion. A shorthand phrase used often in e-mail and Internet news and discussion groups to indicate an author's admission that a statement he or she has just made is not strictly a fact.

impact printer *n.* A printer, such as a wire-pin dot-matrix printer, that drives an inked ribbon mechanically against the paper to form marks. *See also* dot-matrix printer. *Compare* nonimpact printer.

import *vb.* To bring information from one system or program into another. The system or program receiving the data must somehow support the internal format or structure of the data. Conventions such as the TIFF and PICT formats (for graphics files) make importing easier. *See also* PICT, TIFF. *Compare* export.
inactive window *n.* In an environment capable of displaying multiple onscreen windows, any window other than the one currently being used. An inactive window can be partially or entirely hidden behind another window, and it remains inactive until the user selects it. *Compare* active window.
in-betweening *n. See* tween.
Inbox *n.* In many e-mail applications, the default mailbox where the program stores incoming messages. *See also* e-mail[1], mailbox. *Compare* Outbox.
incident light *n.* The light that strikes a surface in computer graphics. *See also* illuminance.
inclusive OR *n. See* OR.
increment[1] *n.* A scalar or unit amount by which the value of an object such as a number is increased. *Compare* decrement[1].
increment[2] *vb.* To increase a number by a given amount. For example, if an item has a value of 10 and it is incremented successively by 2, it takes the values 12, 14, 16, 18, and so on. *Compare* decrement[2].
indent[1] *n.* **1.** Displacement of the left or right edge of a block of text in relation to the margin or to other blocks of text. **2.** Displacement of the beginning of the first line of a paragraph relative to the other lines in the paragraph. *Compare* hanging indent.
indent[2] *vb.* To displace the left or right edge of a text item, such as a block or a line, relative to the margin or to another text item.
independent content provider *n.* A business or organization that supplies information to an online information service for resale to the information service's customers. *See also* online information service.
independent software vendor *n.* A third-party software developer; an individual or an organization that independently creates computer software. *Acronym:* ISV.
index[1] *n.* A listing of keywords and associated data that point to the location of more comprehensive information, such as files and records on a disk or record keys in a database.
index[2] *vb.* **1.** In data storage and retrieval, to create and use a list or table that contains reference information pointing to stored data. **2.** In a database, to find data by using keys such as words or field names to locate records. **3.** In indexed file storage, to find files stored on disk by using an index of file locations (addresses).
indexed search *n.* A search for an item of data that uses an index to reduce the amount of time required. *See also* index[1].
indicator *n.* A dial or light that displays information about the status of a device, such as a light connected to a disk drive that glows when the disk is being accessed.

Industry Standard Architecture *n. See* ISA.

INET *n.* Short for **Internet.** *See* Internet.

.inf *n.* The file extension for device information files, files containing scripts used to control hardware operations.

infection *n.* The presence of a virus or Trojan horse in a computer system. *See also* Trojan horse, virus, worm.

inference engine *n.* The processing portion of an expert system. It matches input propositions with facts and rules contained in a knowledge base and then derives a conclusion, on which the expert system acts. *See also* expert system.

infobahn *n.* The Internet. The word is a mixture of the terms information and Autobahn (a German highway known for the high speeds at which drivers can legally travel). *Also called* Information Highway, Information Superhighway, the Net.

information *n.* The meaning of data as it is intended to be interpreted by people. Data consists of facts, which become information when they are seen in context and convey meaning to people. Computers process data without any understanding of what the data represents.

information center *n.* **1.** A large computer center and its associated offices; the hub of an information management and dispersal facility in an organization. **2.** A specialized type of computer system dedicated to information retrieval and decision-support functions. The information in such a system is usually read-only and consists of data extracted or downloaded from other production systems.

information explosion *n.* **1.** The current period in human history, in which the possession and dissemination of information has supplanted mechanization or industrialization as a driving force in society. **2.** The rapid growth in the amount of information available today. *Also called* information revolution.

Information Highway or **information highway** *n. See* Information Superhighway.

information kiosk *n. See* kiosk.

information management *n.* The process of defining, evaluating, safeguarding, and distributing data within an organization or a system.

information packet *n. See* packet (definition 1).

information processing *n.* The acquisition, storage, manipulation, and presentation of data, particularly by electronic means.

information resource management *n.* The process of managing the resources for the collection, storage, and manipulation of data within an organization or system.

information retrieval *n.* The process of finding, organizing, and displaying information, particularly by electronic means.

information revolution *n. See* information explosion.

information science *n.* The study of how information is collected, organized, handled, and communicated.
Information Services *n.* The formal name for a company's data processing department. *Acronym:* IS. *Also called* Data Processing, Information Processing, Information Systems, Information Technology, Management Information Services, Management Information Systems.
Information Superhighway *n.* The existing Internet and its general infrastructure, including private networks, online services, and so on. *See also* National Information Infrastructure.
Information Systems *n.* *See* Information Services.
Information Technology *n.* *See* Information Services.
information warehouse *n.* *See* data warehouse[1].
information warfare *n.* Attacks on the computer operations on which an enemy country's economic life or safety depends. Possible examples of information warfare include crashing air traffic control systems or massively corrupting stock exchange records.
infrared *adj.* Having a frequency in the electromagnetic spectrum in the range just below that of red light. Objects radiate infrared in proportion to their temperature. *Acronym:* IR.
infrared port *n.* An optical port on a computer for interfacing with an infrared-capable device. Communication is achieved without physical connection through cables. Currently, the devices must be only a few feet apart, and the ports aligned with one another, for communication to occur. Infrared ports can be found on some laptops, notebooks, and printers. *See also* FIR port, infrared, input/output port.
.ini *n.* In DOS and Windows 3.*x*, the file extension that identifies an initialization file, which contains user preferences and startup information about an application. *See also* ini file.
ini file *n.* Short for **ini**tialization **file**. A text file containing information about the initial configuration of Windows, Windows-based applications, and MS-DOS–based applications, such as default settings for fonts, margins, and line spacing. Two ini files, win.ini and system.ini, are required to run the Windows operating system through version 3.1. In later versions of Windows and Windows NT, ini files are replaced by a database known as the Registry. Because they are composed only of text, ini files can be edited in any text editor or word processor to change information about the application or user preferences. All initialization files bear the extension .ini. *See also* configuration, configuration file, Registry, system.ini, win.ini.
INIT *n.* On older Macintosh computers, a system extension that is loaded into memory at startup time. *See also* extension (definition 3). *Compare* cdev.
initialization file *n.* *See* ini file.
initialization string *n.* A sequence of commands sent to a device, especially a modem, to configure it and prepare it for use. In the case of a modem, the initialization string consists of a string of characters.

A B C D E F G H I J K L M N O P Q R S T U V W X Y Z

initialize *vb.* **1.** To prepare a storage medium, such as a disk or a tape, for use. This may involve testing the medium's surface, writing startup information, and setting up the file system's index to storage locations. **2.** To start up a computer. *See also* cold boot, startup.

initial program load *n.* The process of copying an operating system into memory when a system is booted. *Acronym:* IPL. *See also* boot², startup.

initiator *n.* The device in a SCSI connection that issues commands. The device that receives the commands is the target. *See also* SCSI, target.

ink cartridge *n.* A disposable module that contains ink and is typically used in an ink-jet printer. *See also* ink-jet printer.

ink-jet printer *n.* A nonimpact printer in which liquid ink is vibrated or heated into a mist and sprayed through tiny holes in the print head to form characters or graphics on the paper. Ink-jet printers are competitive with some laser printers in price and print quality if not in speed. However, the highly soluble ink produces fuzzy output on some papers and smears if touched shortly after printing. *See also* nonimpact printer, print head.

inline *adj.* In HTML code, referring to graphics displayed along with HTML-formatted text. Inline images placed in the line of HTML text use the tag <IMG>. Text within an inline image can be aligned to the top, bottom, or middle of a specific image.

inline graphics *n.* Graphics files that are embedded in an HTML document or Web page and are viewable by a Web browser or other program that recognizes HTML. By avoiding the need for separate file opening operations, inline graphics can speed the access and loading of an HTML document. *Also called* inline image.

inline image *n.* An image that is embedded within the text of a document. Inline images are common on Web pages. *See also* inline graphics.

inoculate *vb.* To protect a program against virus infection by recording characteristic information about it. For example, checksums on the code can be recomputed and compared with the stored original checksums each time the program is run; if any have changed, the program file is corrupt and may be infected. *See also* checksum, virus.

input¹ *n.* Information entered into a computer or program for processing, as from a keyboard or from a file stored on a disk drive.

input² *vb.* To enter information into a computer for processing.

input channel *n. See* input/output channel.

input device *n.* A peripheral device whose purpose is to allow the user to give input to a computer system. Examples of input devices are keyboards, mice, joysticks, and styluses. *See also* peripheral.

input driver *n. See* device driver.

input/output *n.* The complementary tasks of gathering data for a computer or a program to work with and of making the results of the computer's activities available to the user or to other computer processes. Data is usually gathered with input devices such as the keyboard and the mouse, as well as disk files. Output is usually made available to the user via the display and the printer or to the computer via disk files or communications ports. *Acronym:* I/O.

input/output bus *n.* A hardware path used inside a computer for transferring information to and from the processor and various input and output devices. *See also* bus.

input/output channel *n.* A hardware path from the CPU to the input/output bus. *See also* bus.

input/output controller *n.* Circuitry that monitors operations and performs tasks related to receiving input and transferring output at an input or output device or port, thus providing the processor with a consistent means of communication (input/output interface) with the device and also freeing the processor's time for other work. *Also called* device controller, I/O controller.

input/output device *n.* A piece of hardware that can be used both for providing data to a computer and for receiving data from it. A disk drive is an example of an input/output device. Most devices require installation of device drivers to enable the computer to communicate with the device. *Also called* I/O device. *See also* device driver.

input/output interface *n.* *See* input/output controller.

input/output port *n.* A channel through which data is transferred between an input or output device and the processor. The port appears to the CPU as one or more memory addresses that it can use to send or receive data. Specialized hardware, such as in an add-on circuit board, places data from the device in the memory addresses and sends data from the memory addresses to the device. Ports may also be dedicated solely to input or to output. *Also called* I/O port.

input/output processor *n.* Hardware designed to handle input and output operations to relieve the burden on the main processing unit. For example, a digital signal processor can perform time-intensive, complicated analysis and synthesis of sound patterns without CPU overhead. *Also called* I/O processor. *See also* front-end processor (definition 1).

input port *n.* *See* input/output port.

insertion point *n.* A blinking vertical bar on the screen, such as in graphical user interfaces, that marks the location at which inserted text will appear. *See also* cursor (definition 1).

insertion sort *n.* A list-sorting algorithm that starts with a list containing one item and builds an ever-larger sorted list by inserting the items to be sorted one at a time into their correct positions on that list. Insertion sorts are ideally suited for sorting linked lists. *See also* sort algorithm. *Compare* bubble sort, quicksort.

Insert key *n.* A key on the keyboard whose usual function is to toggle a program's editing setting between an insert mode and an overwrite mode. This key may perform different functions in different applications. *Also called* Ins key.

A B C D E F G H I J K L M N O P Q R S T U V W X Y Z

insert mode *n.* A mode of operation in which a character typed in a document or at a command line pushes subsequent existing characters farther to the right on the screen rather than overwriting (replacing) them. Insert mode is the opposite of overwrite mode. In many programs, pressing the Insert key lets the user change from one mode to the other. *Compare* overwrite mode.

Ins key *n. See* Insert key.

install *vb.* **1.** To set in place and prepare for operation. Operating systems and applications commonly include a disk-based installation program that does most of the work, such as checking for devices attached to the system and setting up the program to work with them, having the user choose from sets of options, creating a place for the program on the hard disk, and modifying system startup files as necessary. **2.** To transfer one of a limited number of copies of a program to a disk from a copy-protected program disk; a special procedure is needed because the normal method of copying the program has been disabled.

installable device driver *n.* A device driver that can be embedded within an operating system, usually in order to override an existing, less functional service.

installation program *n.* A program whose function is to install another program, either on a storage medium or in memory. An installation program might be used to guide a user through the often complex process of setting up an application for a particular combination of machine, printer, and monitor. Installation programs are necessary for copy-protected applications, which cannot be copied by normal operating system commands. They typically limit the number of copies that can be installed.

instruction *n.* An action statement in any computer language, most often in machine or assembly language. *See also* statement.

instruction set *n.* The set of machine instructions that a processor recognizes and can execute. *See also* assembler.

integer *n.* **1.** A positive or negative "whole" number, such as 37, –50, or 764. **2.** A data type representing whole numbers. Because calculations involving only integers can be performed much faster than other calculations, integers are widely used in programming for counting and numbering purposes. *Also called* integral number.

integral modem *n.* A modem that is built into a computer, as opposed to an internal modem, which is a modem on an expansion card that can be removed. *See also* external modem, internal modem, modem.

integral number *n. See* integer (definition 2).

integrated circuit *n.* A device consisting of a number of connected circuit elements, such as transistors and resistors, fabricated on a single chip of silicon crystal or other semiconductor material. Integrated circuits are categorized by the number of elements they contain; for example, large-scale integration (LSI) involves between 100 and 5,000 components, while very-large-scale integration (VLSI) involves between 5,000 and 50,000 components. *Acronym:* IC. *Also called* chip. *See also* central processing unit.

Integrated Drive Electronics *n. See* IDE.

Integrated Services Digital Network *n. See* ISDN.

integrated software *n.* A program that combines several applications, such as word processing, database management, and spreadsheets, in a single package. Such software is "integrated" in two ways: it can transfer data among its applications, helping users coordinate tasks and merge information created with the different software tools; and it provides users with a consistent interface for choosing commands, managing files, and otherwise interacting with the various programs. Sometimes, however, the applications in such a package do not offer as much capability as single applications, nor does integrated software necessarily include all the applications needed in a particular environment.

integration *n.* **1.** In computing, the combining of different activities, programs, or hardware components into a functional unit. *See also* integrated software, ISDN. **2.** In electronics, the process of packing multiple electronic circuit elements on a single chip. *See also* integrated circuit.

integrity *n.* The completeness and accuracy of data stored in a computer, especially after it has been manipulated in some way. *See also* data integrity.

intellectual property *n.* Content of the human intellect deemed to be unique and original and to have marketplace value—and thus to warrant protection under the law. Intellectual property includes such items as inventions, literary works, computer processes, and product names. Intellectual property protections fall into four categories: copyright, trademarks, patents, and trade secrets. Concern over defining and protecting intellectual property in cyberspace has brought this area of the law under intense scrutiny.

intelligence *n.* **1.** The ability of hardware to process information. A device without intelligence is said to be dumb; for example, a dumb terminal connected to a computer can receive input and display output but cannot process information independently. **2.** The ability of a program to monitor its environment and initiate appropriate actions to achieve a desired state. For example, a program waiting for data to be read from disk might switch to another task in the meantime. **3.** The ability of a program to simulate human thought. *See also* artificial intelligence. **4.** The ability of a machine such as a robot to respond appropriately to changing stimuli (input).

intelligent *adj.* Of, pertaining to, or characteristic of a device partially or totally controlled by one or more processors integral to the device.

intelligent agent *n. See* agent (definition 2).

intelligent cable *n.* A cable that incorporates circuitry to do more than simply pass signals from one end of the cable to the other. For example, it might also determine the characteristics of the connector into which it is plugged. *Also called* smart cable.

A B C D E F G H I J K L M N O P Q R S T U V W X Y Z

intelligent database *n.* A database that manipulates stored information in a way that people find logical, natural, and easy to use. An intelligent database conducts searches relying not only on traditional data-finding routines but also on predetermined rules governing associations, relationships, and even inferences regarding the data. *See also* database.

Intelligent Input/Output *n. See* I2O.

intelligent terminal *n.* A terminal with its own memory, processor, and firmware that can perform certain functions independent of its host computer, most often the rerouting of incoming data to a printer or video screen.

Intensity Red Green Blue *n. See* IRGB.

interactive *adj.* Characterized by conversational exchange of input and output, as when a user enters a question or command and the system immediately responds. The interactivity of microcomputers is a feature that makes them approachable and easy to use.

interactive fiction *n.* A type of computer game in which the user participates in a story by giving commands to the system. These commands determine, to some extent, the events that occur during the story. Typically the story involves a goal that must be achieved, and the puzzle is to determine the correct sequence of actions that will lead to accomplishing that goal.

interactive graphics *n.* A form of user interface in which the user can change and control graphics displays, often with the help of a pointing device such as a mouse or a joystick. Interactive graphics interfaces occur in a range of computer products from games to CAD systems.

interactive processing *n.* Processing that involves the more or less continuous participation of the user. Such a command/response mode is characteristic of microcomputers. *Compare* batch processing (definition 2).

interactive program *n.* A program that exchanges output and input with the user, who typically views a display of some sort and uses an input device, such as a keyboard, mouse, or joystick, to provide responses to the program. For example, a computer game is an interactive program. *Compare* batch program.

interactive session *n.* A processing session in which the user can more or less continuously intervene and control the activities of the computer. *Compare* batch processing (definition 2).

interactive television *n.* A video technology in which a viewer interacts with the television programming. Typical uses of interactive television include Internet access, video on demand, and video conferencing.

interactive video *n.* The use of computer-controlled video, in the form of a CD-ROM or videodisc, for interactive education or entertainment. *See also* interactive, videodisc.

interapplication communication *n.* The process of one program sending messages to another program. For example, some e-mail programs allow users to click on a URL within the message. After the user clicks on the URL, a browser will automatically launch and access the URL.

Interchange File Format *n. See* IFF.

Interchange Format *n. See* Rich Text Format.
interface *n.* **1.** The point at which a connection is made between two elements so that they can work with each other. **2.** Software that enables a program to work with the user (the user interface), with another program such as the operating system, or with the computer's hardware. *See also* user interface. **3.** A card, plug, or other device that connects pieces of hardware with the computer so that information can be moved from place to place. For example, interfaces such as RS-232-C standard and SCSI enable communications between computers and printers or disks. **4.** A networking or communications standard, such as the ISO/OSI model, that defines ways for different systems to connect and communicate.
interface adapter *n. See* network adapter.
interface card *n. See* adapter.
interference *n.* **1.** Noise or other external signals that affect the performance of a communications channel. **2.** Electromagnetic signals that can disturb radio or television reception. The signals can be generated naturally, as by lightning, or by electronic devices such as computers.
interlacing *n.* A technique used in some raster-scan video displays in which the electron beam refreshes (updates) all odd-numbered scan lines in one vertical sweep of the screen and all even-numbered scan lines in the next sweep. The human eye sees a complete display, but the amount of information carried by the display signal and the number of lines that must be displayed per sweep are halved. *Compare* noninterlaced.
interlock *vb.* To prevent a device from acting while the current operation is in progress.
intermediate language *n.* A computer language used as an intermediate step between the original source language, usually a high-level language, and the target language, usually machine code. Some high-level compilers use assembly language as an intermediate language. *See also* compiler, object code.
intermittent *adj.* Pertaining to something, such as a signal or connection, that is not unbroken but occurs at periodic or occasional intervals.
intermittent error *n.* An error that recurs at unpredictable times.
internal clock *n. See* clock/calendar.
internal font *n.* A font that is already loaded in a printer's memory (ROM) when the printer is shipped. *Compare* downloadable font, font cartridge.
internal memory *n. See* primary storage.
internal modem *n.* A modem constructed on an expansion card to be installed in one of the expansion slots inside a computer. *Compare* external modem, integral modem.
internal sort *n.* **1.** A sorting operation that takes place on files completely or largely held in memory rather than on disk during the process. **2.** A sorting procedure that produces sorted subgroups of records that will be subsequently merged into one list.
International Organization for Standardization *n. See* ISO.

#
A
B
C
D
E
F
G
H
I
J
K
L
M
N
O
P
Q
R
S
T
U
V
W
X
Y
Z

International Telecommunications Union *n.* An intergovernmental organization responsible for making recommendations concerning the standardization of telephone and data communications systems for public and private telecommunication organizations. The ITU became an agency of the United Nations in 1947. It was formerly known as CCITT (Comité Consultatif International Télégraphique et Téléphonique). *Acronym:* ITU. *See also* CCITT.

International Telegraph and Telephone Consultative Committee *n.* *See* CCITT.

Internaut *n.* *See* cybernaut.

internet *n.* Short for **internet**work. A set of computer networks that may be dissimilar and are joined together by means of gateways that handle data transfer and conversion of messages from the sending networks' protocols to those of the receiving network.

Internet *n.* The worldwide collection of networks and gateways that use the TCP/IP suite of protocols to communicate with one another. At the heart of the Internet is a backbone of high-speed data communication lines between major nodes or host computers, consisting of thousands of commercial, government, educational, and other computer systems, that route data and messages. One or more Internet nodes can go off line without endangering the Internet as a whole or causing communications on the Internet to stop, because no single computer or network controls it. The genesis of the Internet was a decentralized network called ARPANET created by the Department of Defense in 1969 to facilitate communications in the event of a nuclear attack. Eventually other networks, including BITNET, Usenet, UUCP, and NSFnet, were connected to ARPANET. Currently, the Internet offers a range of services to users, such as FTP, e-mail, the World Wide Web, Usenet news, Gopher, IRC, telnet, and others. *Also called* the Net. *See also* BITNET, FTP[1] (definition 1), Gopher, IRC, telnet[1], Usenet, UUCP, World Wide Web.

Internet access *n.* **1.** The capability of a user to connect to the Internet. A user typically connects to the Internet in one of two ways. The first is by dialing up an Internet service provider or an online information services provider via a modem connected to the user's computer. This method is used by the majority of home computer users. The second way is by going through a dedicated line, such as a T1 carrier, that is connected to a local area network to which, in turn, the user's computer is connected. This latter method is used by larger organizations that either have their own node on the Internet or connect to an ISP that is a node. A third way that is emerging is the use of a set-top box with a TV. Generally, however, this gives users access only to documents on the World Wide Web. *See also* dedicated line (definition 1), ISP, LAN, modem, node (definition 2), set-top box. **2.** The capability of an online information service to exchange data with the Internet, such as e-mail, or to offer Internet services to users, such as newsgroups, FTP, and the World Wide Web. Most online information services offer Internet access. *See also* FTP[1] (definition 1).

Internet access device *n.* A communications and signal-routing mechanism, possibly incorporating usage tracking and billing features, for use in connecting multiple remote users to the Internet.
Internet access provider *n. See* ISP.
Internet account *n.* A generic term for a registered username at an Internet service provider. An Internet account is accessed via username and password. Services such as dial-in PPP Internet access and e-mail are provided by ISPs to Internet account owners. *See also* username.
Internet address *n. See* domain name address, e-mail address, IP address.
Internet appliance *n. See* set-top box.
Internet backbone *n.* One of several high-speed networks connecting many local and regional networks, with at least one connection point where it exchanges packets with other Internet backbones. Different providers have their own backbones so that, for example, the backbone for the National Science Foundation supercomputing centers is independent of backbones for commercial Internet providers such as MCI and Sprint. *See also* backbone.
Internet broadcasting *n.* Broadcasting of audio, or audio plus video, signals across the Internet. Internet broadcasting includes conventional over-the-air broadcast stations that transmit their signals into the Internet as well as Internet-only stations. Listeners use audio Internet software, such as RealAudio. One method of Internet broadcasting is MBONE. *See also* MBONE, RealAudio.
Internet gateway *n.* A device that provides the connection between the Internet backbone and another network, such as a LAN. Usually the device is a computer dedicated to the task or a router. The gateway generally performs protocol conversion between the Internet backbone and the network, data translation or conversion, and message handling. A gateway is considered a node on the Internet. *See also* gateway, Internet backbone, node (definition 2), router.
Internet Protocol *n. See* IP.
Internet Protocol next generation *n. See* IPv6.
Internet Relay Chat *n. See* IRC.
Internet robot *n. See* spider.
Internet security *n.* A broad topic dealing with all aspects of data authentication, privacy, integrity, and verification for transactions over the Internet. For example, credit card purchases made via a World Wide Web browser require attention to ensure that the card number is not intercepted by an intruder or copied from the server where it is stored and to verify that the number is actually sent by the person who claims to be sending it.
Internet service provider *n. See* ISP.
Internet Talk Radio *n.* Audio programs similar to radio broadcasts but distributed over the Internet in the form of files that can be downloaded via FTP. Internet Talk Radio programs are 30 minutes to 1 hour in length; a 30-minute program requires about 15 MB of disk space. *Acronym:* ITR.

Internet telephone *n.* Point-to-point voice communication that uses the Internet instead of the public-switched telecommunications network to connect the calling and called parties. Both the sending and the receiving party need a computer, a modem, an Internet connection, and an Internet telephone software package to make and receive calls.

Internet television *n.* The transmission of television audio and video signals over the Internet.

internetwork *adj.* Of or pertaining to communications between connected networks. Often used to refer to communications between one local area network and another over the Internet or another wide area network. *See also* LAN, wide area network.

Internetwork Packet Exchange *n. See* IPX.

InterNIC *n.* Short for NSFnet (**Inter**net) **N**etwork **I**nformation **C**enter. The organization that is charged with registering domain names and IP addresses as well as distributing information about the Internet. InterNIC was formed in 1993 as a consortium involving the U.S. National Science Foundation, AT&T, General Atomics, and Network Solutions, Inc. (Herndon, Va.). The latter partner administers InterNIC Registration Services, which assigns Internet names and addresses. InterNIC can be reached by e-mail at info@internic.net or on the Web at http://www.internic.net/.

interoperability *n.* Referring to components of computer systems that are able to function in different environments. For example, Microsoft's Windows NT operating system is interoperable on Intel, DEC Alpha, and other CPUs. With software, interoperability occurs when programs are able to share data and resources.

interpolate *vb.* To estimate intermediate values between two known values in a sequence.

interpret *vb.* **1.** To translate a statement or instruction into executable form and then execute it. **2.** To execute a program by translating one statement at a time into executable form and executing it before translating the next statement. *See also* interpreter. *Compare* compile.

interpreted language *n.* A language in which programs are translated into executable form and executed one statement at a time rather than being translated completely (compiled) before execution. *See also* compiler. *Compare* compiled language.

interpreter *n.* A program that translates and then executes each statement in a program written in an interpreted language. *See also* compiler, interpreted language.

interprocess communication *n.* The ability of one task or process to communicate with another in a multitasking operating system. Common methods include shared memory, queues, signals, and mailboxes. *Acronym:* IPC.

interrupt *n.* A request for attention from the processor. When the processor receives an interrupt, it suspends its current operations, saves the status of its work, and transfers control to a special routine known as an interrupt handler, which contains the instructions for dealing with the particular situation that caused the interrupt. Interrupts can be generated by various hardware devices to request service or report problems or by the processor itself in response to program errors or requests for operating system services. A hierarchy of interrupt priorities determines which interrupt request will be handled first if more than one request is made. A program can temporarily disable some interrupts if it needs the full attention of the processor to complete a particular task. *See also* IRQ.

interrupt request *n. See* IRQ.

intranet *n.* A network designed for information processing within a company or organization. Its uses include such services as document distribution, software distribution, access to databases, and training. An intranet is so called because it usually employs applications associated with the Internet, such as Web pages, Web browsers, FTP sites, e-mail, newsgroups, and mailing lists, accessible only to those within the company or organization.

intraware *n.* Groupware or middleware for use on a company's private intranet. Intraware packages typically contain e-mail, database, workflow, and browser applications. *See also* groupware, intranet, middleware.

intrinsic font *n.* A font for which a bit image (an exact pattern) exists that can be used as is, without such modification as scaling. *Compare* derived font.

intruder *n.* An unauthorized user or unauthorized program, generally considered to have malicious intent, on a computer or computer network. *See also* bacterium, cracker, Trojan horse, virus.

invalid *adj.* Erroneous or unrecognizable because of a flaw in reasoning or an error in input. Invalid results, for example, might occur if the logic in a program is faulty. *Compare* illegal.

inverse video *n. See* reverse video.

invert *vb.* **1.** To reverse something or change it to its opposite. For example, to invert the colors on a monochrome display means to change light to dark and dark to light. **2.** In a digital electrical signal, to replace a high level by a low level and vice versa. This type of operation is the electronic equivalent of a Boolean NOT operation.

invoke *vb.* To call or activate; used in reference to commands.

I/O *n. See* input/output.

I/O controller *n. See* input/output controller.

I/O device *n. See* input/output device.

I/O port *n. See* input/output port.

I/O processor *n. See* input/output processor.

IP *n.* Acronym for **I**nternet **P**rotocol. The protocol within TCP/IP that governs the breakup of data messages into packets, the routing of the packets from sender to destination network and station, and the reassembly of the packets into the original data messages at the destination. IP corresponds to the network layer in the ISO/OSI model. *See also* ISO/OSI model, TCP/IP. *Compare* TCP.

#
A
B
C
D
E
F
G
H
I
J
K
L
M
N
O
P
Q
R
S
T
U
V
W
X
Y
Z

IP address *n.* Short for **I**nternet **P**rotocol **address.** A 32-bit (4-byte) binary number that uniquely identifies a host computer connected to the Internet to other Internet hosts, for the purposes of communication through the transfer of packets. An IP address is expressed in "dotted quad" format, consisting of the decimal values of its 4 bytes, separated with periods; for example, 127.0.0.1. The first 1, 2, or 3 bytes of the IP address, assigned by InterNIC Registration Services, identify the network the host is connected to; the remaining bits identify the host itself. *See also* host, InterNIC, IP, packet (definition 2). *Compare* domain name.

IPC *n. See* interprocess communication.

IPL *n. See* initial program load.

IP multicasting *n.* Short for **I**nternet **P**rotocol **multicasting.** The extension of local area network multicasting technology to a TCP/IP network. Hosts send and receive multicast packets of information, the destination fields of which specify IP host group addresses rather than individual IP addresses. *See also* IP, MBONE, multicasting.

IPng *n.* Acronym for **I**nternet **P**rotocol **n**ext **g**eneration. *See* IPv6.

IP spoofing *n.* The act of inserting a false sender IP address into an Internet transmission in order to gain unauthorized access to a computer system. *See also* IP address, spoofing.

IPv6 *n.* Short for **I**nternet **P**rotocol **v**ersion **6**. A proposed next generation for the Internet Protocol, currently version 4, which was introduced in September 1995 and formerly known as IPng. Improvements over the original IP include better security and an increased IP address size of 16 bytes. *See also* IP, IP address.

IPX *n.* Acronym for **I**nternetwork **P**acket E**x**change. The protocol in Novell NetWare that governs addressing and routing of packets within and between LANs. IPX operates at levels 3 and 4 of the ISO/OSI model but does not perform all the functions at those levels. In particular, IPX does not guarantee that a message will be complete (no lost packets); SPX has that job. *See also* packet (definition 1). *Compare* SPX (definition 1).

IPX/SPX *n.* The network and transport level protocols used by Novell NetWare, which together correspond to the combination of TCP and IP in the TCP/IP protocol suite. *See also* IPX, SPX (definition 1).

IR *n. See* infrared.

IRC *n.* Acronym for **I**nternet **R**elay **C**hat. A service that enables an Internet user to participate in a conversation online in real time with other users. An IRC channel, maintained by an IRC server, transmits the text typed by each user who has joined the channel to all other users who have joined the channel. Generally, a channel is dedicated to a particular topic, which may be reflected in the channel's name. An IRC client shows the names of currently active channels, enables the user to join a channel, and then displays the other participants' words on individual lines so that the user can respond. IRC was invented in 1988 by Jarkko Oikarinen of Finland. *See also* channel (definition 2), server (definition 2).

IRGB *n.* Acronym for **I**ntensity **R**ed **G**reen **B**lue. A type of color encoding used in the Video Graphics Array (VGA) video adapters. The standard 3-bit RGB color encoding (specifying eight colors) is supplemented by a fourth bit (called Intensity) that uniformly increases the intensity of the red, green, and blue signals, resulting in a total of 16 colors. *See also* RGB.

IRL Acronym for **i**n **r**eal **l**ife. An expression used by many online users to denote life outside the computer realm, especially in conjunction with virtual worlds such as online talkers, IRC, MUDs, and virtual reality. *See also* IRC, MUD, talker, virtual reality.

IRQ *n.* Short for **i**nterrupt **req**uest. One of a set of possible hardware interrupts, identified by a number, on a Wintel computer. The number of the IRQ determines which interrupt handler will be used. In the AT bus, ISA, and EISA, 15 IRQs are available; each device's IRQ is hardwired or set by a jumper or DIP switch. The VL bus and the PCI local bus have their own interrupt systems, which they translate to IRQ numbers. *See also* AT bus, DIP switch, EISA, interrupt, IRQ conflict, ISA, jumper, PCI local bus, VL bus, Wintel.

IRQ conflict *n.* The condition on a Wintel computer in which two different peripheral devices use the same IRQ to request service from the CPU. An IRQ conflict will prevent the system from working correctly; for example, the CPU may respond to an interrupt from a serial mouse by executing an interrupt handler for interrupts generated by a modem. IRQ conflicts can be prevented by the use of Plug and Play hardware and software. *See also* interrupt, IRQ, Plug and Play, Wintel.

IS *n. See* Information Services.

ISA *n.* Acronym for **I**ndustry **S**tandard **A**rchitecture. A bus design specification that allows components to be added as cards plugged into standard expansion slots in IBM PCs and compatibles. A 16-bit ISA slot actually consists of two separate 8-bit slots mounted end-to-end so that a single 16-bit card plugs into both slots. An 8-bit expansion card can be inserted and used in a 16-bit slot (it occupies only one of the two slots), but a 16-bit expansion card cannot be used in an 8-bit slot. *See also* EISA.

ISA slot *n.* A connection socket for a peripheral designed according to the ISA standard, which applies to the bus developed for use in the 80286 (IBM PC/AT) motherboard. *See also* ISA.

ISDN *n.* Acronym for **I**ntegrated **S**ervices **D**igital **N**etwork. A worldwide digital communications network evolving from existing telephone services. The goal of ISDN is to replace the current telephone network, which requires digital-to-analog conversions, with facilities totally devoted to digital switching and transmission, yet advanced enough to replace traditionally analog forms of data, ranging from voice to computer transmissions, music, and video. ISDN is built on two main types of communications channels: a B channel, which carries data at a rate of 64 Kbps; and a D channel, which carries control information at either 16 or 64 Kbps. Computers and other devices connect to ISDN lines through simple, standardized interfaces.

When fully implemented (possibly around the turn of the century), ISDN is expected to provide users with faster, more extensive communications services. *See also* channel (definition 2).

ISDN terminal adapter *n.* The hardware interface between a computer and an ISDN line. *See also* ISDN.

ISO *n.* Short for **I**nternational **O**rganization for **S**tandardization (often incorrectly identified as an acronym for International Standards Organization). An international association of countries, each of which is represented by its leading standard-setting organization—for example, ANSI for the United States. The ISO works to establish global standards for communications and information exchange. ISO is not an acronym; rather, it is derived from the Greek word *isos,* which means "equal" and is the root of the prefix "iso-." *See also* ISO/OSI model.

isometric view *n.* A display method for three-dimensional objects in which every edge has the correct length for the scale of the drawing and in which all parallel lines appear parallel. An isometric view of a cube, for example, shows the faces in symmetrical relation to one another and the height and width of each face evenly proportioned; the faces do not appear to taper with distance as they do when the cube is drawn in perspective. *Compare* perspective view.

ISO/OSI model *n.* Short for **I**nternational **O**rganization for **S**tandardization/ **O**pen **S**ystems **I**nterconnection **model.** A layered architecture (plan) that standardizes levels of service and types of interaction for computers exchanging information through a communications network. The ISO/OSI model separates computer-to-computer communications into seven layers, or levels, each building upon the standards contained in the levels below it. The lowest of the seven layers deals solely with hardware links; the highest deals with software interactions at the application-program level. See the following table.

ISO/OSI Model

ISO/OSI Layer	***Focus***
Application (highest level)	Program-to-program transfer of information
Presentation	Text formatting and display, code conversion
Session	Establishing, maintaining, and coordinating communication
Transport	Accurate delivery, service quality
Network	Transport routes, message handling and transfer
Data-link	Coding, addressing, and transmitting information
Physical	Hardware connections

ISP *n.* Acronym for **I**nternet **s**ervice **p**rovider. A business that supplies Internet connectivity services to individuals, businesses, and other organizations. Some ISPs are large national or multinational corporations that offer access in many locations, while others are limited to a single city or region. *Also called* access provider, service provider.

ISV *n. See* independent software vendor.

italic *adj.* Describes a type style in which the characters are evenly slanted toward the right. *This sentence is in italics.* Italics are commonly used for emphasis, foreign-language words and phrases, titles of literary and other works, technical terms, and citations. *See also* oblique. *Compare* roman.

ITR *n. See* Internet Talk Radio.

ITU *n. See* International Telecommunications Union.

i-way *n. See* Information Superhighway.

J

jabber *n.* A continuous stream of random data transmitted over a network as the result of some malfunction.

jack *n.* A connector designed to receive a plug. A jack is commonly used in making audio and video connections.

jacket *n. See* disk jacket.

jack in *vb.* **1.** To log on to a computer. **2.** To connect to a network or an online bulletin board system, especially for purposes of entering an IRC or a virtual-reality simulation, such as a MUD. *See also* IRC, MUD.

jack out *vb.* **1.** To log off a computer. **2.** To disconnect from a network or an online bulletin board system.

jaggies *n.* The "stairsteps," or jagged edges, that appear in diagonal lines and curves drawn at low resolutions in computer graphics. *Also called* aliasing.

Janet *n.* Short for the **J**oint **A**cademic **Net**work. A wide area network in the United Kingdom that serves as the principal backbone for the Internet in that country. *See also* backbone (definition 1).

Java *n.* An object-oriented programming language, developed by Sun Microsystems, Inc. Similar to C++, Java is smaller, more portable, and easier to use than C++ because it is more robust and it manages memory on its own. Java was also designed to be secure and platform-neutral (meaning that it can be run on any platform). This makes it a useful language for programming Web applications, since users access the Web from many types of computers. *See also* Java applet, object-oriented programming.

Java applet *n.* A small Java program that can be included in and run from an HTML document. Java applets can be downloaded and run by any Web browser capable of interpreting Java, such as Internet Explorer, Netscape Navigator, and HotJava. Java applets are frequently used to add multimedia effects and interactivity to Web pages, such as background music, real-time video displays, animations, calculators, and interactive games. Applets can be activated automatically when a user views a page, or they may require some action on the part of the user, such as clicking on an icon in the Web page. *See also* applet, Java.

Java-compliant browser *n.* A Web browser with support for the Java programming language built into it. Most current Web browsers are Java-compliant. *See also* Java, Web browser.

JavaScript *n.* A scripting language developed by Netscape Communications and Sun Microsystems, Inc., that is loosely related to Java. JavaScript can be used to add basic online applications and functions to Web pages. JavaScript, however, is not a true object-oriented language, and it is limited in performance compared with Java because it is not compiled. JavaScript code, which is included in a Web page along with the HTML code, is generally considered easier to write than Java, especially for novice programmers. A JavaScript-compliant Web browser, such as Netscape Navigator, is necessary to run JavaScript code. *See also* HTML, scripting language. *Compare* Java.

Java terminal *n.* A type of personal computer with a reduced number of components that is built primarily to provide an access terminal to the Web, including downloadable Java applets. Typically, such machines will not have locally addressable hard disks or installable programs but will obtain any necessary materials, including Java applets, from the network. Centrally obtained software is generally less expensive to administer but usually requires some download delay. Java terminals, currently under development by Sun Microsystems, Inc., are similar in concept to NetPCs. *See also* Java, Java applet, network computer. *Compare* NetPC.

jewel box *n.* A clear plastic container used to package and store a compact disc. *Also called* jewel case.

.jfif *n.* The file extension that identifies graphic image files in the JPEG File Interchange Format. *See also* JPEG (definition 1).

JFIF *n.* Acronym for **J**PEG **F**ile **I**nterchange **F**ormat. A means of saving photographic images stored according to the JPEG image compression technique. JFIF represents a "common language" file format in that it is designed specifically to allow users to transfer JPEG images easily between different computers and applications. *See also* JPEG (definition 1).

jitter *n.* **1.** Small vibrations or fluctuations in a displayed video image caused by irregularities in the display signal. Jitter is often visible in the form of horizontal lines that are of the same thickness as scan lines. **2.** A rough appearance in a fax caused by dots that are incorrectly recorded during the scanning process and thus wrongly positioned in the output. **3.** In digital communications, distortion caused by lack of synchronization of signals.

job *n.* A specified amount of processing performed as a unit by a computer.

job processing *n.* A computing method in which a series of jobs, each consisting of one or more tasks grouped together as a computationally coherent whole, is processed sequentially. *See also* batch processing (definition 2).

job queue *n.* A list of programs or tasks waiting for execution by a computer. Jobs in the queue are often ordered according to a specified priority.

join *n.* **1.** A database table operation that combines information from two or more tables and places it into a new table. The information taken from the tables depends on the criteria given in the statement defining the join. **2.** A multiprocessing command that causes a child process to return control to its parent. *See also* child (definition 1), multiprocessing.

Joint Photographic Experts Group *n. See* JPEG (definition 1).

journal *n.* A computer-based log or record of transactions that take place in a computer or across a network. A journal could be used, for example, to record message transfers on a communications network or to keep track of

#
A
B
C
D
E
F
G
H
I
J
K
L
M
N
O
P
Q
R
S
T
U
V
W
X
Y
Z

system activities that alter the contents of a database. A journal is often kept as a means of reconstructing events or sets of data should they become lost or damaged. *See also* audit trail.

joystick *n.* A pointing device used mainly but not exclusively for computer games. A joystick has a base and a vertical stem, both of which can have control buttons. The user can move the stem in any direction to control the movement of an object on the screen. The control buttons activate various software features, generally producing on-screen events. A joystick is usually used as a relative pointing device, moving a screen object when the stem is moved and stopping the movement when the stem is released. *See also* relative pointing device.

.jpeg *n.* The file extension that identifies graphic image files in the JPEG format. *See also* JPEG (definition 1).

JPEG *n.* **1.** Acronym for **J**oint **P**hotographic **E**xperts **G**roup. An ISO/ITU standard for storing images in compressed form. JPEG trades off compression against loss of image quality; it can achieve a compression ratio of 100:1 with significant loss and possibly 20:1 with little noticeable loss. **2.** A graphic stored as a file in the JPEG format.

JPEG File Interchange Format *n. See* JFIF.

.jpg *n.* The file extension that identifies graphic images encoded in the JPEG File Interchange Format, as originally specified by the Joint Photographic Experts Group. Inline graphics on Web pages are often .jpg files. *See also* JPEG (definition 2).

Jughead *n.* Acronym for **J**onzy's **U**niversal **G**opher **H**ierarchy **E**xcavation **a**nd **D**isplay. An Internet service that enables a user to locate directories in Gopherspace through a keyword search. A Jughead server indexes keywords appearing in directory titles in top-level Gopher menus but does not index the files within the directories. To access Jughead, users must point their Gopher clients to a Jughead server. *See also* Gopher. *Compare* Archie, Veronica.

jukebox *n.* Software designed to play a list of sound files in an order specified by the user, reminiscent of jukeboxes used to play vinyl records. *See also* CD-ROM jukebox.

jumper *n.* A small plug or wire that can be connected between different points in an electronic circuit in order to alter an aspect of a hardware configuration. *Compare* DIP switch.

justify *vb.* **1.** To align vertically. **2.** To align lines of text evenly along both the left and right margins of a column by inserting extra space between the words in each line. If the spacing is excessive, it can be reduced by hyphenating words at the ends of lines. *See also* align (definition 1). *Compare* rag.

K

K[1] *n.* Short for **k**ilobyte.
K[2] *prefix See* kilo-.
.k12.us *n.* On the Internet, the major geographic domain specifying that an address is a U.S. K–12 (kindergarten through high school) educational site.
Kb *n. See* kilobit.
KB *n. See* kilobyte.
Kbit *n. See* kilobit.
Kbps *n. See* kilobits per second.
Kbyte *n. See* kilobyte.
kc *n. See* kilocycle.
Kerberos or **kerberos** *n.* A network authentication protocol developed by MIT. Kerberos authenticates the identity of users attempting to log on to a network and encrypts their communications through secret-key cryptography. *See also* authentication, cryptography.
Kermit *n.* A file transfer protocol used in asynchronous communications between computers. Kermit is a very flexible protocol used in many software packages designed for communications over telephone lines. *Compare* Xmodem, Ymodem, Zmodem.
kern *vb.* To alter selectively the distance between pairs of letters for readability and to make the type spacing more balanced and proportional.
kernel *n.* The core of an operating system—the portion of the system that manages memory, files, and peripheral devices; maintains the time and date; launches applications; and allocates system resources.
key *n.* **1.** On a keyboard, the combination of a plastic keycap, a tension mechanism that suspends the keycap but allows it to be pressed down, and an electronic mechanism that records the key press and key release. **2.** In database management, an identifier for a record or group of records in a datafile. *See also* index, key field. **3.** The code for deciphering encrypted data. **4.** A metal object used with a physical lock to disable a computer system.
keyboard *n.* In computing, a set of switches that resembles a typewriter keyboard and that conveys information from a user to a computer or a data communications circuit. *See also* character code, control character, Dvorak keyboard, enhanced keyboard, ergonomic keyboard, function key, keyboard buffer, keyboard enhancer, keycap, key code, numeric keypad, QWERTY keyboard, scan code, *and names of specific keys.*
keyboard buffer *n.* A small amount of system memory that stores the most recently typed characters, which have not yet been processed. *Also called* type-ahead buffer.

#
A
B
C
D
E
F
G
H
I
J
K
L
M
N
O
P
Q
R
S
T
U
V
W
X
Y
Z

keyboard enhancer *n.* A program that monitors keystrokes as they are typed and that can be used to redefine the meaning of certain keys or key combinations. Keyboard enhancers are used to create and store macros—sets of keystrokes, mouse actions, menu selections, or other instructions—that are then assigned to keys. *Also called* macro program. *See also* macro.

keyboard layout *n.* The key arrangement used for a particular keyboard, including such factors as the number of keys (101 is the current standard) and the configuration of the keys (QWERTY is the U.S. standard). Some proprietary systems use different layouts, and many allow users to map the keys to characters according to preference.

keyboard repeat *n. See* typematic.

keyboard shortcut *n. See* application shortcut key.

keyboard template *n.* A piece of plastic or heavy paper that fits over or around part of the keyboard, such as the function keys, and has information printed on it about the meanings of the keys.

keycap *n.* The plastic piece identifying a key on a keyboard.

key code *n.* A unique code number assigned to a key on a computer keyboard, used to tell the computer which key has been pressed or released. A key code is a special identifier for the key itself and is always the same for a particular key, regardless of the letter, number, or symbol on the key or the character generated by the key. *Compare* character code, scan code.

key escrow *n.* An encryption method in which a key is provided to a third party approved by a government agency so that any encrypted message can be read by the government. *See also* encryption. *Compare* key recovery.

key field *n.* A field in a record structure or an attribute of a relational table that has been designated to be part of a key. Any field can be keyed, or indexed, to improve or simplify the performance of retrieval and/or update operations. *See also* attribute (definition 1), field (definition 1), primary key.

key-frame *adj.* Describing animation in which starting and ending positions of an object are given, and all frames in between are interpolated by a computer to produce smooth automated animation. Most ray-traced computer animation is created using this technique. *See also* ray tracing.

key in *vb.* To enter information into a computer by typing it on the computer's keyboard.

keypad *n. See* numeric keypad.

key recovery *n.* A private key encryption method that enables an authorized party (such as a government agency), using special software, to recover the key from the encrypted data. Under current law, any encryption software exported from the United States after 1998 must implement key recovery. This requirement supplants an earlier proposed requirement that encryption software for export implement key escrow. *See also* encryption, private key. *Compare* key escrow.

key sort *n. See* tag sort.

keystroke *n.* The act of pressing a key on a keyboard to enter a character or initiate a command in a program. The efficiency and ease of use of certain applications are often measured in terms of how many keystrokes it takes to perform common operations.

keyword *n.* **1.** A characteristic word, phrase, or code that is stored in a key field and is used to conduct sorting or searching operations on records. *See also* key field. **2.** Any of the set of words that composes a given programming language or set of operating system routines. *See also* reserved word.

keyword-in-context *n.* An automatic search methodology that creates indexes of document text or titles. Each keyword is stored in the resulting index along with some surrounding text, usually the word or phrase that precedes or follows the keyword in the text or title. *Acronym:* KWIC.

kHz *n. See* kilohertz.

kill *vb.* **1.** To stop or abort a process in a program or an operating system. **2.** In file management, to delete a file, often without hope of reversing the action.

killer app *n.* **1.** An application of such popularity and widespread standardization that it fuels sales of the hardware platform or operating system for which it was written. **2.** An application that supplants its competition.

kill file *n. See* bozo filter.

kilo- *prefix* Abbreviated K or k. **1.** A prefix meaning one thousand (10^3). **2.** In computer-related terms, a prefix meaning 2^{10} (1,024), which is the power of 2 closest to one thousand.

kilobaud *n.* A unit of measure of the transmission capacity of a communications channel, equal to 2^{10} (1,024) baud. *See also* baud.

kilobit *n.* Abbreviated Kb or Kbit. A data unit equal to 1,024 bits.

kilobits per second *n.* Abbreviated Kbps. Data transfer speed, as on a network, measured in multiples of 1,024 bits per second.

kilobyte *n.* Abbreviated K, KB, or Kbyte. A data unit of 1,024 bytes. *See also* kilo-.

kilocycle *n.* Abbreviated kc. A unit of measurement representing 1,000 cycles, generally meaning 1,000 cycles per second. *See also* kilohertz.

kilohertz *n.* Abbreviated kHz. A measure of frequency equivalent to 1,000 hertz, or 1,000 cycles per second. *See also* hertz.

kiosk *n.* A freestanding computer or terminal that provides information to the public, usually through a multimedia display.

kludge *n.* **1.** A short-term or makeshift hardware construction. **2.** A program characterized by a lack of design or forethought, as if written in a hurry to satisfy an immediate need. A kludge basically operates properly, but its construction or design is severely lacking in elegance or logical efficiency. *See also* braindamaged, hack[1].

knockout *n.* **1.** In multicolor printing, the process of removing from one image the overlapping parts of a graphic or text that are to be printed in a different color so that ink colors will not mix. *Compare* overprint. **2.** In hardware, a section of a panel that can be removed to make space for a switch or other component.

knowbot *n.* Short for **know**ledge ro**bot**. An artificial-intelligence program that follows a set of predetermined rules to perform work, such as searching for files or looking for documents that contain specific pieces of information on a network such as the Internet. *See also* bot (definitions 2 and 3).

knowledge base *n.* A form of database used in expert systems that contains the accumulated body of knowledge of human specialists in a particular field. The problem-solving approach that a specialist would use is contained in the inference engine, another crucial part of an expert system. *See also* expert system, inference engine.

knowledge-based system *n.* *See* expert system.

knowledge representation *n.* The methodology that forms the basis for the decision-making structure in an expert system, usually taking the form of if-then rules. *See also* expert system.

KSR terminal *n.* Short for **k**eyboard **s**end/**r**eceive **terminal.** A type of terminal that accepts input from a keyboard only and uses an internal printer rather than a screen to display the keyboard input and the output received from the sending terminal.

KWIC *n.* *See* keyword-in-context.

L

L8R *adv.* Abbreviation for later, as in "See you later." An expression often used in e-mail or Usenet groups as a closing remark.

label *n.* An identifier. A label can be a physical item, such as a stick-on tag used to identify disks and other computer equipment, or an electronic label added to floppy disks or hard disks. It can also be a word, symbol, or other group of characters used to identify a file, a storage medium, an element defined in a computer program, or a specific item in a document such as a spreadsheet or a chart. *See also* identifier.

label prefix *n.* In a spreadsheet, a character at the beginning of a cell entry that identifies the entry to the program as a label.

lag *n.* The time difference between two events. In electronics, a lag is a delay between a change in input and a change in output. On computer displays, a lag is a fading brightness left on the phosphor coating of the screen after an image changes. *See also* persistence.

LAN *n.* Acronym for **l**ocal **a**rea **n**etwork. A group of computers and other devices dispersed over a relatively limited area and connected by a communications link that enables any device to interact with any other on the network. LANs commonly include microcomputers and shared resources such as laser printers and large hard disks. The devices on a LAN are known as nodes, and the nodes are connected by cables through which messages are transmitted. *See also* baseband network, broadband network, bus network, collision detection, communications protocol, contention, network, ring network, star network, token bus network, token passing, token ring network. *Compare* wide area network.

landscape mode *n.* A horizontal print orientation in which text or images are printed "sideways"—that is, the width of the image on the page is greater than the height. *Compare* portrait mode.

landscape monitor *n.* A monitor that is wider than it is high. Landscape monitors are usually about 33 percent wider than they are high—roughly the same proportion as a television screen. *Compare* full-page display, portrait monitor.

LAN Manager *n.* A local area network technology developed by Microsoft Corporation and distributed by Microsoft, IBM (as IBM LAN Server), and others. LAN Manager connects computers running the MS-DOS, OS/2, or UNIX operating system and allows users to share files and system resources and to run distributed applications using a client/server architecture. *See also* client/server architecture, LAN.

#
A
B
C
D
E
F
G
H
I
J
K
M
N
O
P
Q
R
S
T
U
V
W
X
Y
Z

laptop *n.* A small, portable personal computer that runs on either batteries or AC power, designed for use during travel. Laptops have flat LCD or plasma screens and small keyboards. Most can run the same software as their desktop counterparts and can accept similar peripherals, such as sound cards, internal or external modems, and floppy disks and CD-ROM drives. Some laptops are designed to be plugged into a docking station, effectively making them desktop computers. Most have connectors for plugging in external keyboards and full-size monitors. Although ultralight portable computers are generally known as notebook computers, these machines are also commonly referred to as laptops. *See also* portable computer. *Compare* subnotebook computer.

laser or **LASER** *n.* Acronym for **l**ight **a**mplification by **s**timulated **e**mission of **r**adiation. A device that uses certain quantum effects to produce coherent light, which travels with greater efficiency than noncoherent light because the beam diverges only slightly as it travels. Lasers are used in computer technology to transmit data through fiber-optic cables, to read and write data on CD-ROMs, and to place an image on a photosensitive drum in laser printers.

laser engine *n.* *See* printer engine.

laser printer *n.* An electrophotographic printer based on the technology used by photocopiers. A focused laser beam and a rotating mirror are used to draw an image of the page on a photosensitive drum. This image is converted to an electrostatic charge, which attracts and holds toner. Paper is rolled against the drum, and the toner is pulled away from the drum and onto the paper. Heat then fuses the toner to the paper. This process, which results in crisp, clear images, makes laser printers the standard for high-quality printing. The only serious drawback of a laser printer is that it offers less paper-handling flexibility than dot-matrix printers. Both multipart forms and wide-carriage printing, for example, are better handled by line printers or dot-matrix printers. *See also* electrophotographic printers, nonimpact printer, page printer. *Compare* dot-matrix printer, LCD printer, LED printer.

laser storage *n.* The use of optical read/write technology with metallic discs for information storage. *See also* compact disc.

last in, first out *n.* A method of processing a queue in which items are removed in inverse order relative to the order in which they were added—that is, the last in is the first out. *Acronym:* LIFO. *Compare* first in, first out.

latency *n.* The time required for a signal to travel from one point on a network to another.

launch *vb.* To activate a program (especially on the Macintosh) from the operating system's user interface.

layer *n.* **1.** The protocol or protocols operating at a particular level within a protocol suite, such as IP within the TCP/IP suite. Each layer is responsible for providing specific services or functions for computers exchanging information over a communications network (such as the layers outlined in the

ISO/OSI model), and information is passed from one layer to the next. Although different suites have varying numbers of levels, generally the highest layer deals with software interactions at the application level, and the lowest governs hardware-level connections between different computers. *See also* ISO/OSI model, protocol stack, TCP/IP. **2.** In communications and distributed processing, a set of rules and standards that handles a particular class of events.

layering *n.* In computer graphics, the grouping of logically related elements in a drawing. Layering enables a user to view, and work on independently, portions of a graphic instead of the entire drawing.

layout *n.* **1.** The overall plan or design of a document system. *See also* page layout. **2.** In computer design, the arrangement of circuits and other components of the system.

LCD *n. See* liquid crystal display.

LCD printer *n.* Short for **l**iquid **c**rystal **d**isplay **printer**. An electrophotographic printer similar to a laser printer and often incorrectly labeled as one. LCD printers use a bright light source, typically a halogen lamp. *Also called* liquid crystal shutter printer. *See also* electrophotographic printers, nonimpact printer, page printer. *Compare* laser printer, LED printer.

LCD projector *n.* Short for **l**iquid **c**rystal **d**isplay **projector.** A device that casts an image of a computer's video output from a liquid crystal display onto a screen. *See also* liquid crystal display.

lead *n. See* leading.

leader *n.* A row of dots, hyphens, or other such characters used to lead the eye across a printed page to related information.

leading *n.* The vertical space, expressed in points, between lines of type, measured from the baseline (bottom) of one line to the baseline of the next. *Also called* lead, line spacing. *See also* point[1] (definition 1).

leading zero *n.* A zero that precedes the most significant (leftmost) digit of a number. One or more leading zeros may be used as fill characters in a field containing numeric input. Leading zeros have no significance in the value of a number.

lead ion battery *n.* An energy storage device based on the conversion of chemical to electrical energy as ions flow from one terminal to another through an acid medium in which lead and copper are suspended. This type of battery is used in laptop and notebook computers.

leaf *n.* Any node (location) in a tree structure that is at the farthest distance from the root (primary node), no matter which path is followed. Thus, in any tree, a leaf is a node at the end of a branch—one that has no descendants. *See also* root, tree.

leased line *n. See* dedicated line (definition 1).

LED *n. See* light-emitting diode.

LED printer *n.* Short for **l**ight-**e**mitting **d**iode **printer**. An electrophotographic printer similar to LCD and laser printers but using a different light source, an array of light-emitting diodes. *See also* electrophotographic printers, light-emitting diode, nonimpact printer, page printer. *Compare* laser printer, LCD printer.

left justification *n.* The process of aligning text evenly along the left margin of a column or page. The right edge of the text is ragged. *See also* rag. *Compare* full justification, right justification.

legacy *adj.* Of or pertaining to documents or data that existed prior to a certain time. The designation refers particularly to a change in process or technique that requires translating old data files to a new system.

legacy data *n.* Data acquired by one organization that was compiled by another organization. The acquiring organization thus receives the information as a "legacy" from the information's prior owner.

legacy system *n.* A computer, software program, network, or other computer equipment that remains in use after a business or an organization installs new systems. Compatibility with legacy systems is an important consideration when a new version is installed. For example, will new spreadsheet software be able to read existing business records without expensive and time-consuming conversion to a new format? Many legacy systems are based on mainframe computers, which are being slowly replaced in many organizations by client/server architectures. *See also* mainframe computer. *Compare* client/server architecture.

legend *n.* Text that describes or explains a graphic, usually printed below the graphic. On a graph or map, the legend is the key to the patterns or symbols used.

less than *adj. See* relational operator.

less than or equal to *adj. See* relational operator.

letterbomb *n.* An e-mail message that is intended to impair the recipient's computer use. Some sequences of control characters can lock up a terminal, files attached to the message may contain viruses or Trojan horses, and a sufficiently large message can overflow a mailbox or crash a system. *See also* control character, e-mail[1] (definition 1), mailbox, Trojan horse, virus. *Compare* mailbomb[1].

letter quality *adj.* On dot-matrix printers, pertaining to or being a level of print quality that is better than draft quality. As the name implies, letter quality should be crisp and dark enough for use in business letters. *See also* print quality. *Compare* draft quality, near-letter-quality.

letter-quality printer *n.* Any printer that produces output high enough in quality to be acceptable for business letters. *See also* laser printer.

lexicographic sort *n.* A sort that arranges items in the order in which they would appear if listed as words in a dictionary. A lexicographic sort puts numbers, for instance, where they would be if they were spelled out; for example, 567 would fall in the F section. *Compare* alphanumeric sort.

LF *n. See* linefeed.

license agreement *n.* A legal contract between a software provider and a user specifying the rights of the user regarding the software. Usually the license agreement is in effect with retail software once the user opens the software package.

licensing key *n.* A short character string that serves as a password during the installation of licensed commercial software. The use of licensing keys is a security device aimed at reducing illegal duplication of licensed software.

LIFO *n. See* last in, first out.

light-emitting diode *n.* A semiconductor device that converts electrical energy into light, used, for example, for the activity lights on computer disk drives. Light-emitting diodes work on the principle of electroluminescence and are highly efficient, producing little heat for the amount of light output. *Acronym:* LED.

light pen *n.* An input device consisting of a stylus that is connected to a computer's monitor. The user points at the screen with the stylus and selects items or chooses commands either by pressing a clip on the side of the light pen or by pressing the light pen against the surface of the screen (the equivalent of performing a mouse click). *See also* absolute pointing device. *Compare* touch screen.

light source *n.* **1.** The device that provides the luminescence (for example, a bulb or laser) in any technology based on the use and interpretation of light, such as a scanner or a CRT. **2.** In computer graphics, the imaginary location of a source of light, which determines the shading in an image.

LIM EMS *n.* Acronym for **L**otus/**I**ntel/**M**icrosoft **E**xpanded **M**emory **S**pecification. *See* EMS.

line *n.* **1.** Any wire or wires, such as power lines and telephone lines, used to transmit electrical power or signals. **2.** In communications, a connection, usually a physical wire or other cable, between sending and receiving (or calling and called) devices, including telephones, computers, and terminals. **3.** In word processing, a string of characters displayed or printed in a single horizontal row.

line adapter *n.* A device, such as a modem or a network card, that connects a computer to a communications line and converts a signal to an acceptable form for transmission.

linear search *n.* A simple, though inefficient, search algorithm that operates by sequentially examining each element in a list until the target element is found or the last item has been completely processed. Linear searches are primarily used for very short lists. *Also called* sequential search. *See also* search algorithm. *Compare* binary search.

line-based browser *n.* A Web browser whose display is based on text rather than graphics. *See also* Web browser.

line cap *n.* The way in which a line segment is terminated when the segment is printed, especially on a PostScript-compatible printer. *See also* line join, line segment.

line drawing *n.* A drawing made up of solid lines without shading or other features that suggest mass or contouring.

line editor *n.* A text-editing program that numbers each line of text, working with the document on a line-by-line basis rather than on a word-by-word basis. *See also* editor.
linefeed *n.* A control character that tells a computer or printer to advance one line below the current line without moving the position of the cursor or print head. *Acronym:* LF.
line join *n.* The way in which two line segments are connected when they are printed, especially on a PostScript-compatible printer. *See also* line cap.
line noise *n.* Spurious signals in a communications channel that interfere with the exchange of information. In an analog circuit, line noise may take the form of a pure audio tone, static, or signals leaked from another circuit. In a digital circuit, line noise is any signal that makes it difficult or impossible for the device at the receiving end of the circuit to interpret the transmitted signal accurately. *See also* channel.
line number *n.* **1.** A number assigned by a line editor to a line of text and used to refer to that line for purposes of viewing, editing, or printing. The line numbers are sequential. *See also* line editor. **2.** In communications, an identifying number assigned to a communications channel.
line printer *n.* Any printer that prints one line at a time as opposed to one character at a time (as many dot-matrix printers do) or one page at a time (as some dot-matrix and most laser printers do). Line printers typically produce the familiar 11-by-17-inch "computer printouts." They are high-speed devices and are often used with mainframes, minicomputers, or networked machines rather than with single-user systems.
line segment *n.* A portion of a line, defined by its beginning and ending points.
line spacing *n. See* leading.
line speed *n. See* baud rate, data rate.
lines per minute *n.* A measurement of printer speed, the number of lines of characters printed in one minute. *Acronym:* LPM.
line style *n.* The form and quality of a line, such as a dotted line, a double line, or a hairline. *See also* hairline.
line surge *n.* A sudden, transient increase in the voltage or current carried by a line. A lightning strike, for example, can cause a surge in power lines that can damage electrical equipment. Delicate types of equipment such as computers are often protected from line surges by surge suppressors placed in the power lines.
line voltage *n.* The voltage present in a power line. In North America, line voltage is approximately 115 volts alternating current (VAC).
line width *n.* The length of a line of type measured from the left margin to the right margin on a piece of paper or on a computer screen. On a computer monitor or printer, line width is normally measured in inches, centimeters, points, or picas. *See also* pica, point[1] (definition 1).

liquid crystal display *n.* A type of display that uses a liquid compound having a polar molecular structure, sandwiched between two transparent electrodes. When an electrical field is applied, the molecules align with it, forming a crystalline arrangement that polarizes the light passing through. A polarized filter laminated over the electrodes blocks polarized light. In this way, a grid of electrodes can selectively "turn on" a cell, or a pixel, containing the liquid crystal material, turning it dark. In some types of liquid crystal displays, an electroluminescent panel is placed behind the screen to illuminate it. Other types of liquid crystal displays are capable of reproducing color. *Acronym:* LCD.

liquid crystal display printer *n.* *See* LCD printer.

liquid crystal shutter printer *n.* *See* LCD printer.

list box *n.* A control in Windows that enables the user to choose one option from a list of possibilities. The list box appears as a box, displaying the currently selected option, next to a button marked with a down-arrow. When the user clicks on the button, the list drops down, providing a scroll bar if the list of options is long.

LISTSERV *n.* One of the most popular commercial mailing list managers, marketed by L-SOFT International in versions for BITNET, UNIX, and Windows. *See also* mailing list, mailing list manager.

lithium ion battery *n.* An energy storage device based on the conversion of chemical to electrical energy in "dry" chemical cells. Despite the higher cost, the laptop industry is quickly adopting lithium ion batteries because of their increased storage capacity over both nickel cadmium and nickel metal hydride batteries, in response to the demand for greater power brought on by higher processor speeds and the use of devices such as CD-ROM drives. *Compare* nickel cadmium battery, nickel metal hydride battery.

live *adj.* **1.** Of or relating to real-world data or a program working with it, as opposed to test data. **2.** Of or relating to audio or video that is transmitted from one site to another as it is being produced, as opposed to being recorded before broadcast time. *See also* synchronous transmission. **3.** Capable of being manipulated by a user to cause changes in a document or part of a document.

liveware *n.* A slang term for people, to distinguish them from hardware, software, and firmware. *Also called* wetware.

load[1] *n.* **1.** The total computing burden a system carries at one time. **2.** In electronics, the amount of current drawn by a device. **3.** In communications, the amount of traffic on a line.

load[2] *vb.* To place information from storage into memory for processing, if it is data, or for execution, if it is program code.

load sharing *n.* A method of managing one or more tasks, jobs, or processes by scheduling and simultaneously executing portions of them on two or more microprocessors.

local *adj.* Close at hand or restricted to a particular area. More specifically, in communications, a local device is one that can be accessed directly rather than by means of a communications line. In information processing, a local operation is one performed by the computer at hand rather than by a remote computer. *Compare* remote.

local area network *n. See* LAN.

local bus *n.* A PC architecture designed to speed up system performance by allowing some expansion boards to communicate directly with the microprocessor, bypassing the normal system bus entirely. *See also* PCI local bus, VL bus.

localhost *n.* The name used to represent the same computer on which a TCP/IP message originates. An IP packet sent to localhost has the IP address 127.0.0.1 and does not actually go out to the Internet. *See also* IP address, packet (definition 1), TCP/IP.

localization *n.* The process of altering a program so that it is appropriate for the area in which it is used. For example, the developers of a word processing program must localize its sorting tables for different countries or languages because the correct order of characters in one language might be incorrect in another.

local memory *n.* In multiprocessor systems, the memory on the same card or high-speed bus as a particular processor. Typically, memory that is local to one processor cannot be accessed by another without some form of permission.

local newsgroups *n.* Newsgroups that are targeted toward a geographically limited area such as a city or an educational institution. Posts to these newsgroups contain information that is specific to the area, concerning such topics as events, meetings, and sales. *See also* newsgroup.

local reboot *n.* A reboot of the machine that one is directly working on, rather than a remote host. *See also* reboot.

lock *n.* **1.** A software security feature that requires a key or dongle in order to have the application run correctly. *See also* hardware key. **2.** A mechanical device on a removable storage medium (for example, the write-protect notch on a floppy disk) that prevents the contents from being overwritten. *See also* write-protect notch.

locked file *n.* **1.** A file on which one or more of the usual types of manipulative operation cannot be performed—typically, one that cannot be altered by additions or deletions. **2.** A file that cannot be deleted or moved or whose name cannot be changed.

lockout *n.* The act of denying access to a given resource (file, memory location, I/O port), usually to ensure that only one program at a time uses that resource.

lock up *n.* A condition in which processing appears to be completely suspended and in which the program in control of the system will accept no input. *See also* crash[1].

log *n.* A record of transactions or activities that take place on a computer system.

logical *adj.* **1.** Based on true and false alternatives as opposed to arithmetic calculation of numeric values. For example, a logical expression is one that, when evaluated, has a single outcome, either true or false. **2.** Of or pertaining to a conceptual piece of equipment or frame of reference, regardless of how it may be realized physically. *Compare* physical.

logical device *n.* A device named by the logic of a software system, regardless of its physical relationship to the system. For example, a single floppy disk drive can simultaneously be, to the MS-DOS operating system, both logical drive A and drive B.

logical drive *n. See* logical device.

logical network *n.* A way to describe the topology, or layout, of a computer network. Referring to a logical (rather than physical) topology describes the way information moves through the network—for example, in a straight line (bus topology) or in a circle (ring topology). The physical network (the actual layout of hardware and cabling) does not necessarily resemble the logical network (the path followed by transmissions). A logical ring, for example, might include groups of computers cabled octopus-like to hardware "collection points" that, in turn, are cabled to one another. Although this physical layout might not visually resemble a ring, the logical layout followed by network transmissions would indeed be circular. *See also* bus network, ring network, star network, token ring network, topology.

logical operator *n.* An operator that manipulates binary values at the bit level. In some programming languages, logical operators are identical to Boolean operators, which manipulate true and false values. *See also* Boolean operator.

logic board *n.* Another name for motherboard or processor board. The term was used in conjunction with older computers to distinguish the video board (analog board) from the motherboard. *See also* motherboard.

logic chip *n.* An integrated circuit that processes information, as opposed to simply storing it. A logic chip is made up of logic circuits.

logic circuit *n.* An electronic circuit that processes information by performing a logical operation on it. It produces output based on the rules of logic it is designed to follow for the electrical signals it receives as input.

logic diagram *n.* A schematic that shows the connections between computer logic circuits and specifies the expected outputs resulting from a specific set of inputs.

logic operation *n.* An expression that uses logical values and operators; a bit-level manipulation of binary values. *See also* Boolean operator.

logic-seeking printer *n.* Any printer with built-in intelligence that lets it look ahead of the current print position and move the print head directly to the next area to be printed, thus saving time in printing pages that are filled with spaces.

#
A
B
C
D
E
F
G
H
I
J
K
M
N
O
P
Q
R
S
T
U
V
W
X
Y
Z

logic symbol *n.* A symbol that represents a logical operator such as AND or OR.

login *n. See* logon.

log in *vb. See* log on.

logoff *n.* The process of terminating a session with a computer accessed through a communications line. *Also called* logout.

log off *vb.* To terminate a session with a computer accessed through a communications line—usually a computer that is both distant and open to many users. *Also called* log out. *Compare* log on.

logon *n.* The process of identifying oneself to a computer after connecting to it over a communications line. *Also called* login.

log on *vb.* To identify oneself to a computer after connecting to it over a communications line. During the procedure, the computer usually requests the user's name and password. *Also called* log in. *Compare* log off.

logout *n. See* logoff.

log out *vb. See* log off.

LOL Acronym for **l**aughing **o**ut **l**oud. An interjection used in e-mail, online forums, and chat services to express appreciation of a joke or other humorous occurrence.

long filenames *n.* A feature of most current PC operating systems, notably Windows 95, Windows 98, Windows NT, and OS/2, that allows a user to assign a plain-text name to a file, rather than limiting possible names to just a few characters. Names can be over 200 characters long, include upper and lowercase letters, and have spaces between characters. *Compare* 8.3.

long-haul *adj.* Of, pertaining to, or being a type of modem that is able to transmit over long distances. *Compare* short-haul.

look and feel *n.* A general term referring to the appearance and functionality of hardware or software. The phrase is often used comparatively, as in "Windows NT has the same look and feel as Windows 95."

loop[1] *n.* **1.** A set of statements in a program executed repeatedly, either a fixed number of times or until some condition is true or false. **2.** A pair of wires that run between a telephone central office and customer premises.

loop[2] *vb.* To execute a group of statements repeatedly.

loop configuration *n.* A communications link in which multiple stations are joined to a communications line that runs in a closed loop. Generally, data sent by one station is received and retransmitted in turn by each station on the loop. The process continues until the data reaches its final destination. *See also* ring network.

lo-res *adj. See* low resolution.

lossless compression *n.* The process of compressing a file such that, after being compressed and decompressed, it matches its original format bit for bit. Text, code, and numeric data files must be compressed using a lossless method; such methods can typically reduce a file to 40 percent of its original size. *Compare* lossy compression.

A B C D E F G H I J K L M N O P Q R S T U V W X Y Z

lossy compression *n.* The process of compressing a file such that some data is lost after the file is compressed and decompressed. Video and sound files often contain more information than is apparent or necessary to the viewer or listener; a lossy compression method, which does not preserve that excess information, can reduce such data to as little as 5 percent of its original size. *Compare* lossless compression.

lost cluster *n.* A cluster (disk storage unit) marked by the operating system as being in use but not representing part of any chain of stored segments of a file. A lost cluster usually represents debris caused by incomplete data "housekeeping," as might result from the ungraceful exit (messy or abrupt termination) of an application.

lowercase *adj.* In reference to letters, not capital—for example, *a, b, c*. *Compare* uppercase.

low frequency *n.* The portion of the electromagnetic spectrum between 30 kHz and 300 kHz. This range of frequencies is used for several types of radio communication, including the longwave broadcast band in Europe and Asia.

low-level language *n.* A language that is machine-dependent or that offers few control instructions and data types. Each statement in a program written in a low-level language usually corresponds to one machine instruction. *See also* assembly language. *Compare* high-level language.

low memory *n.* Memory locations addressed by the lowest numbers. In the IBM PC, which has an address space of 1 MB, the first 640 KB are referred to as low memory. (This portion of memory is also sometimes called conventional memory.) Low memory is reserved for RAM, which is shared by MS-DOS and applications. *See also* conventional memory. *Compare* high memory.

low resolution *adj.* Appearing in relatively coarse detail, used in reference to text and graphics in raster-oriented computer displays and printing. Low-resolution printing is comparable to draft-quality dot-matrix output printed at 125 dpi or less. *Also called* lo-res. *See also* resolution. *Compare* high resolution.

LPM *n.* *See* lines per minute.

LPT *n.* Logical device name for a line printer, a name reserved by MS-DOS for up to three parallel printer ports designated LPT1, LPT2, and LPT3. The first port, LPT1, is usually the same as the primary MS-DOS hard-copy output device PRN (the logical device name for the printer).

LS-120 *n.* A floppy disk drive capable of storing 120 MB of data on a single 3.5-inch floppy disk. LS-120 drives are also compatible with other floppy disk formats.

luminance *n.* **1.** A measure of the amount of light radiated by a given source, such as a computer display screen. **2.** The perceived brightness component of a given color, as opposed to its hue or its saturation. *See also* HSB. *Compare* illuminance.

luminance decay *n.* *See* persistence.

lurk *vb.* To receive and read articles or messages in a newsgroup or other online forum without contributing anything to the ongoing exchange.

lurker *n.* A person who lurks in a newsgroup or other online forum. *See also* lurk. *Compare* netizen.

LZW compression *n.* A compression algorithm that makes use of repeating strings of data in its compression of character streams into code streams. It is also the basis of GIF compression. *See also* GIF.

M

M *n.* *See* mega-.
Mac *n.* *See* Macintosh.
Mac- *prefix* A prefix used to indicate a software product's applicability for the Apple Macintosh computer, as in MacDraw.
MacBinary *n.* A file transfer protocol used to preserve coding for Macintosh-produced files stored in non-Macintosh computers, containing the file's resource fork, data fork, and Finder information block. *See also* data fork, Finder, resource fork.
machine code *n.* The ultimate result of compiling assembly language or any high-level language such as C: sequences of 1s and 0s that are loaded and executed by a microprocessor. Machine code is the only language computers understand; all other programming languages represent ways of structuring human language so that humans can get computers to perform specific tasks. *Also called* machine language. *See also* compiler.
machine cycle *n.* **1.** The time required for the fastest operation a microprocessor can perform. **2.** The steps taken for each machine instruction. These steps are, typically, fetch the instruction, decode it, execute it, and perform any necessary storing.
machine-dependent *adj.* Of, pertaining to, or being a program or piece of hardware that is linked to a particular type of computer because it makes use of specific or unique features of the equipment and that cannot easily be used with another computer, if at all. *Compare* machine-independent.
machine error *n.* A hardware error. Probably the most common type of machine error involves media, such as an error in reading a hard disk.
machine-independent *adj.* Of, pertaining to, or being a program or piece of hardware that can be used on more than one type of computer with little or no modification. *Compare* machine-dependent.
machine instruction *n.* An instruction (action statement) in machine code that can be directly executed by a processor or microprocessor. *See also* instruction, statement.
machine language *n.* *See* machine code.
machine-readable *adj.* **1.** Presented in a form that a computer can interpret and use as input. For example, bar codes that can be scanned and used directly as computer input contain machine-readable information. **2.** Coded in the binary form used by computers and stored on a suitable medium such as magnetic tape. *See also* optical character recognition.
Macintosh *n.* A popular series of personal computers introduced by the Apple Computer Corporation in January 1984. The Macintosh was one of the

M

earliest personal computers to incorporate a graphical user interface and the first to use 3.5-inch floppy disks. It was also the first to use the 32-bit Motorola 68000 microprocessor. Despite its user-friendly features, the Macintosh has lost market share during the 1990s, losing ground to IBM PC-compatible computers, although it still enjoys widespread use in desktop publishing and graphics-related applications. *Also called* Mac. *See also* graphical user interface, PC-compatible.

Macintosh File System *n.* The early, flat file system used on the Macintosh before the Hierarchical File System was introduced. *Acronym:* MFS. *See also* flat file system. *Compare* Hierarchical File System.

Mac OS *n.* Short for **Mac**intosh **o**perating **s**ystem. The name given to the Macintosh operating system, beginning with version 7.5 in September 1994, when Apple started licensing the software to other computer manufacturers. *See also* Macintosh.

macro *n.* In applications, a set of keystrokes and instructions recorded and saved under a short key code or macro name. When the key code is typed or the macro name is used, the program carries out the instructions of the macro. Users can create a macro to save time by replacing an often-used, sometimes lengthy, series of keystrokes with a shorter version.

macro program *n. See* keyboard enhancer.

macro recorder *n.* A program that records and stores keyboard macros. *See also* macro.

macro virus *n.* A virus that is written in a macro language associated with an application. The macro virus is carried by a document file used with that application and executes when the document is opened.

MacTCP *n.* A Macintosh extension that allows Macintosh computers to use TCP/IP. *See also* TCP/IP.

MAE *n. See* Metropolitan Area Exchange.

magnetic disk *n.* A computer disk enclosed in a protective case (hard disk) or jacket (floppy disk) and coated with a magnetic material that enables data to be stored in the form of changes in magnetic polarity (with one polarity representing a binary 1 and the other a 0) on many small sections of the disk surface. Magnetic disks should be protected from exposure to sources of magnetism, which can damage or destroy the information they hold. *See also* disk, floppy disk, hard disk. *Compare* compact disc, magneto-optic disc.

magnetic head *n. See* head.

magnetic-ink character recognition *n.* A form of character recognition that reads text printed with magnetically charged ink, determining the shapes of characters by sensing the magnetic charge in the ink and then using character recognition methods to translate the shapes into computer text. A familiar use of this form of character recognition is to identify bank checks. *Acronym:* MICR. *See also* character recognition. *Compare* optical character recognition.

magnetic storage *n.* A generic term for non-internal-memory computer data storage involving a magnetic medium, such as disk or tape.

magnetic tape *n.* *See* tape (definition 1).

magneto-optical recording *n.* A type of recording technology used with optical discs in which a laser beam heats a small portion of the magnetic material covering the disc. The heating enables a weak magnetic field to change the orientation of the portion, thus recording onto the disc. This technique can also be used to erase the disc, making the disc rewritable.

magneto-optic disc *n.* An erasable or semi-erasable storage disc, similar to a CD-ROM disc and of very high capacity, in which a laser beam is used to heat the recording surface of the disc to a point at which tiny regions on the surface can be magnetically aligned to store bits of data. *See also* CD-ROM, magneto-optical recording.

mailbomb[1] *n.* An excessively large amount of e-mail data (a very large number of messages or one very large message) sent to a user's e-mail address in an attempt to make the user's mailer program crash or to prevent the user from receiving further legitimate messages. *See also* e-mail[1] (definition 1). *Compare* letterbomb.

mailbomb[2] *vb.* To send a mailbomb to a user. One person might mailbomb a user with a single enormous message; a large number of users might mailbomb an unpopular person by simultaneously sending messages of normal size.

mailbot *n.* A program that automatically responds to e-mail messages or performs actions based on commands within the messages. *See also* mailing list manager.

mailbox *n.* A disk storage area assigned to a network user for receipt of e-mail messages. *See also* e-mail[1] (definition 1).

mail digest *n.* *See* digest (definition 2).

mailer-daemon *n.* A program used to transport e-mail between hosts on a network. *See also* daemon.

mail filter *n.* *See* e-mail filter.

mail header *n.* A block of text at the top of an e-mail message containing such information as the addresses of the sender and recipient(s), the date and time sent, the address to which a reply is to be sent, and the subject. The mail header is used by an e-mail client or program. *See also* e-mail[1] (definition 1).

mailing list *n.* A list of names and e-mail addresses that are grouped under a single name. When a user places the name of the list in a mail client's To: field, the client sends the message to the machine where the mailing list resides, and that machine sends the message to all the addresses on the list (possibly allowing a moderator to edit it first). *See also* LISTSERV, mailing list manager, moderator.

mailing list manager *n.* Software that maintains an Internet or intranet mailing list. The mailing list manager accepts messages posted by subscribers, sends copies of the messages (which may be edited by a moderator) to all the subscribers, and accepts and processes user requests, such as to subscribe or to unsubscribe to the mailing list. *See also* LISTSERV, mailing list, moderator.

mail merge *n.* A mass-mail facility that takes names, addresses, and sometimes pertinent facts about recipients and merges the information into a form letter or another such basic document.

mail reflector *n.* A newsgroup that consists simply of the messages posted to a mailing list translated into newsgroup format.

mailto *n.* A protocol designator used in the HREF of a hyperlink that enables a user to send e-mail to someone. For instance, if Anne E. Oldhacker has the e-mail address aeo@baz.foo.com, the creator of an HTML document could set up the hyperlink *E-mail Anne!* in the document with the code *<A HREF="mailto:aeo@baz.foo.com">E-mail Anne!</A>*. If a user clicks on the hyperlink *E-mail Anne!*, the user's e-mail application is launched and the user can send e-mail to her without knowing her actual e-mail address. *See also* e-mail[1] (definition 1), HREF, HTML, hyperlink.

mainboard *n. See* motherboard.

mainframe computer *n.* A high-level computer designed for the most intensive computational tasks. Mainframe computers are often shared by multiple users connected to the computer by terminals. *See also* computer, supercomputer.

main memory *n. See* primary storage.

major geographic domain *n.* A two-character sequence in an Internet domain name address that indicates the country in which a host is located. The major geographic domain is the last part of the domain name address, following the subdomain and domain codes; for example, uiuc.edu.us indicates a host at the University of Illinois in the United States, whereas cam.ac.uk indicates a host at the University of Cambridge in the United Kingdom. The code .us, which indicates a domain in the United States, is usually omitted. *Also called* country code. *See also* DNS (definition 1), domain name address.

male connector *n.* A type of connector that has pins for insertion into receptacles. Male connector part numbers often include an M (male) or P (plug). For example, a male DB-25 connector might be labeled DB-25M or DB-25P. *Compare* female connector.

MAN *n.* Acronym for **m**etropolitan **a**rea **n**etwork. A high-speed network that can carry voice, data, and images at up to 200 Mbps or faster over distances of up to 75 km. Based on the network architecture, the transmission speed can be higher for shorter distances. A MAN, which can include one or more LANs as well as telecommunications equipment such as microwave and satellite relay stations, is smaller than a wide area network but generally operates at a higher speed. *Compare* LAN, wide area network.

management information service *n.* A department within an organization that functions as a clearinghouse for information. *Acronym:* MIS.

Management Information Services *n.* *See* Information Services.
management information system *n.* A computer-based system for processing and organizing information so as to provide various levels of management within an organization with accurate and timely information needed for supervising activities, tracking progress, making decisions, and isolating and solving problems. *Acronym:* MIS.
Management Information Systems *n.* *See* Information Services.
manager *n.* Any program that is designed to perform a certain set of housekeeping tasks related to computer operation, such as the maintenance of files. On the Apple Macintosh, for example, separate portions of the operating system such as File Manager and Memory Manager handle input, output, and internal functions.
Mandelbrot set *n.* *See* fractal.
man-machine interface *n.* The set of commands, displays, controls, and hardware devices enabling the human user and the computer system to exchange information. *See also* user interface.
map *vb.* To translate one value into another. For example, in computer graphics one might map a three-dimensional image onto a sphere. In reference to virtual memory systems, a computer might map (translate) a virtual address into a physical address. *See also* virtual memory.
mapped drives *n.* **1.** In the Windows environment, network drives that have been assigned local drive letters and are locally accessible. **2.** Under UNIX, disk drives that have been defined to the system and can be made active.
margin *n.* In printing, those portions of a page—top, bottom, and sides—outside the main body of text.
mark *n.* **1.** In applications and data storage, a symbol or other device used to distinguish one item from others like it. **2.** In digital transmission, the state of a communications line (positive or negative) corresponding to a binary 1. In asynchronous serial communications, a mark condition is the continuous transmission of binary 1s to indicate when the line is idle (not carrying information). *See also* parity. **3.** In optical sensing, a pencil line, as on a voting form or an IQ test, that can be recognized by an optical reader.
marker *n.* **1.** Part of a data communications signal that enables the communications equipment to recognize the structure of the message. Examples are the start and stop bits that frame a byte in asynchronous serial communications. **2.** A symbol that indicates a particular location on a display surface.
markup language *n.* A set of codes in a text file that instruct a computer how to format the file on a printer or video display or how to index and link its contents. Examples of markup languages are HTML, which is used for Web pages, and SGML, which is used for typesetting and desktop publishing and in electronic documents. Markup languages of this sort are designed to enable documents and other files to be platform-independent and highly portable between applications. *See also* HTML, SGML.

mass storage *n.* A generic term for disk, tape, or optical disc storage of computer data, so called for the large masses of data that can be stored in comparison with computer memory capacity. *Compare* memory.

master file *n.* In a set of database files, the file containing more or less permanent descriptive information about the principal subjects of the database, summary data, and one or more critical key fields. For example, customers' names, account numbers, addresses, and credit terms might be stored in a master file. *Compare* transaction file.

master key *n.* The server-based component of software or data protection. In some systems, data or applications are stored on a server and must be downloaded to the local machine for use. When a client requests the data, it presents a session key. If the session key supplied matches the master key, the key server sends the requested packet. *See also* client (definition 2), server (definition 2).

master record *n.* A record in a master file; typically, the descriptive and summary data related to the item that is the subject of the record. *See also* master file.

master/slave arrangement *n.* A system in which one device, called the master, controls another device, called the slave. For example, a computer can control devices connected to it.

matching *n.* The process of testing whether two data items are identical or of finding a data item that is identical to a key.

math coprocessor *n.* *See* floating-point processor.

matrix *n.* An arrangement of rows and columns used for organizing related items, such as numbers, dots, spreadsheet cells, or circuit elements. In computing and computer applications, matrices are used to arrange sets of data in table form, as in spreadsheets and lookup tables. In hardware, matrices of dots are used in creating characters on the screen as well as in print (as by dot-matrix printers). *See also* grid.

maximize *vb.* In a graphical user interface, to cause a window to expand to fill all the available space within a larger window or on the screen. *See also* enlarge, graphical user interface, window. *Compare* minimize, reduce.

Mb *n.* *See* megabit.

MB *n.* *See* megabyte.

MBONE or **Mbone** *n.* Short for **m**ulticast back**bone**. A small set of Internet sites, each of which can transmit real-time audio and video simultaneously to all the others. MBONE sites are equipped with special software to send and receive packets at high speed using the IP one-to-many multicasting protocol. The MBONE has been used for video conferencing and even for a Rolling Stones concert in 1994. *See also* RealAudio.

Mbps *n.* *See* megabits per second.

MC *n.* *See* megacycle.

MC68000 *n.* *See* 68000.

MC68020 *n.* *See* 68020.

MC68030 *n.* *See* 68030.

MC68040 *n. See* 68040.
MCF *n. See* Meta-Content Format.
MDI *n.* Acronym for **m**ultiple-**d**ocument **i**nterface. A user interface in an application that allows the user to have more than one document open at the same time. *See also* user interface.
mean time between failures *n. See* MTBF.
mean time to repair *n. See* MTTR.
mechanical mouse *n.* A type of mouse in which the motion of a ball on the bottom of the mouse is translated into directional signals. As the user moves the mouse, the ball rolls, turning a pair of wheels inside the mouse that produce electrical movement signals. The electronics in the mouse translate the electrical movement signals into mouse-movement information that can be used by the computer. *See also* mouse, trackball. *Compare* optical mouse, optomechanical mouse.
media *n.* The physical material, such as paper, disk, or tape, used for storing computer-based information. The term media is plural; the term medium is the singular form.
media eraser *n.* A device that removes or obliterates data from a storage medium on a wholesale basis, usually by writing meaningless data (such as zeros) over it. *See also* bulk eraser.
media filter *n.* **1.** A device used with local area networks as an adapter between two different types of media. For example, an RJ-45 connector might be used between coaxial cable and UTP cables. Media filters are similar in function to transceivers. A LAN expert is needed to decide what media filters are required for a particular LAN. *See also* coaxial cable, connector, LAN, transceiver, UTP. **2.** A device added to data networks to filter out electronic noise from the environment. For example, a media filter might be added to an Ethernet network based on coaxial cabling to prevent data loss caused by interference from nearby electronic equipment. *See also* coaxial cable, Ethernet (definition 1).
medium *n. See* media.
meg *n. See* megabyte.
mega- *prefix* Abbreviated M. **1.** A prefix meaning one million (10^6). **2.** In computer-related terms, a prefix meaning 2^{20} (1,048,576), which is the power of 2 closest to one million.
megabit *n.* Abbreviated Mb or Mbit. A data unit of 1,048,576 (2^{20}) bits; sometimes interpreted as 1 million bits.
megabits per second *n.* Abbreviated Mbps. Data transfer speed, as on a network, measured in multiples of 1 million bits per second.
megabyte *n.* Abbreviated MB. A data unit of 1,048,576 (2^{20}) bytes; sometimes interpreted as 1 million bytes.
megacycle *n.* Abbreviated MC. A unit of measurement representing 1 million cycles, generally meaning 1 million cycles per second. *See also* megahertz.
megahertz *n.* Abbreviated MHz. A measure of frequency equivalent to 1 million hertz, or 1 million cycles per second. *See also* hertz.

megapel display *n. See* megapixel display.
megapixel display *n.* A video display capable of displaying at least 1 million pixels—for example, a display with a screen size of 1,024 horizontal pixels and 1,024 vertical pixels. *Also called* megapel display.
membrane keyboard *n.* A keyboard in which an unbroken plastic or rubber shell (a membrane) covers keys that have little or no travel (movement). Rather than employing normal, full-travel keys, membrane keyboards use pressure-sensitive areas that are sometimes, but not always, defined by small bumps under the membrane.
memo field *n.* A field in a database file that can contain unstructured text.
memory *n.* A device where information can be stored and retrieved. In the most general sense, memory can refer to external storage such as disk drives or tape drives; in common usage, it refers only to the fast semiconductor storage (RAM) directly connected to the processor. *See also* core, EEPROM, EPROM, flash memory, PROM, RAM, ROM. *Compare* bubble memory, mass storage.
memory bank *n.* The physical location on a motherboard where a memory module can be inserted. *See also* bank (definition 1), module (definition 2).
memory cache *n. See* CPU cache.
memory card *n.* A memory module that is used to extend RAM storage capacity or that is used in place of a hard disk in a portable computer, such as a laptop, notebook, or handheld PC. The module is usually the size of a credit card and can be plugged into a PCMCIA-compliant portable computer. The module can be composed of EPROM, RAM, or ROM chips or flash memory. *Also called* RAM card, ROM card. *See also* EPROM, flash memory, handheld PC, hard disk, module (definition 2), PC Card, RAM, ROM.
memory cartridge *n.* A plug-in module containing RAM chips that can be used to store data or programs. Memory cartridges are used primarily in portable computers as smaller, lighter (but more expensive) substitutes for disk drives. Memory cartridges typically use either a nonvolatile form of RAM, which does not lose its contents when power is turned off, or battery-backed RAM, which maintains its contents by drawing current from a rechargeable battery within the cartridge. *Also called* RAM cartridge. *See also* memory card, RAM. *Compare* ROM cartridge.
memory chip *n.* An integrated circuit devoted to memory storage. The memory storage can be volatile and hold data temporarily, such as RAM, or nonvolatile and hold data permanently, such as ROM, EPROM, EEPROM, or PROM. *See also* EEPROM, EPROM, integrated circuit, nonvolatile memory, PROM, RAM, volatile memory.
memory management *n.* In operating systems for personal computers, procedures for optimizing the use of random access memory. These procedures include selectively storing data, monitoring it carefully, and freeing memory when the data is no longer needed. Most current operating systems optimize RAM usage on their own; some older operating systems, such as

early versions of MS-DOS, required third-party utilities to optimize RAM usage and required the user to be knowledgeable about how the operating system and applications used memory. *See also* RAM.

memory management program *n.* **1.** A program used to store data and programs in system memory, monitor their use, and reassign the freed space following their execution. **2.** A program that uses hard disk space as an extension of random access memory.

memory-resident *adj.* Permanently located in a computer's memory, rather than swapped in and out of memory as needed. *See also* memory, TSR.

memory size *n.* The memory capacity of a computer, usually measured in megabytes. *See also* megabyte, memory.

menu *n.* A list of options from which a user can choose in order to perform a desired action, such as executing a command or applying a format to text. Many applications, especially those with a graphical interface, offer menus as a means of providing the user with an easy-to-use alternative to memorizing program commands.

menu bar *n.* A rectangular bar displayed in an application's on-screen window, often at the top, from which the user can choose menus. Names of available menus are displayed in the menu bar; choosing one with the keyboard or with a mouse causes the list of options on that menu to be displayed.

menu-driven *adj.* Using menus to present choices of commands and available options. Menu-driven programs are usually considered friendlier and easier to learn than programs that have a command-line interface. *Compare* command-line interface.

menu item *n.* A choice on a menu, selectable with either the keyboard or a mouse. In some instances, a menu item that is not available (that is, not appropriate) for a given situation is "grayed" (dimmed in comparison to the valid menu choices).

merge *vb.* To combine two or more items, such as lists, in an ordered way and without changing the basic structure of either. *Compare* concatenate.

merge sort *n.* A sorting technique that combines several sorted (input) lists into a single sorted (output) list. *See also* bubble sort, insertion sort, quicksort, sort algorithm.

mesh network *n.* A communications network having two or more paths to any node.

message *n.* **1.** In communications, a unit of information transmitted electronically from one device to another. A message can contain one or more blocks of text as well as beginning and ending characters, control characters, a software-generated header (destination address, type of message, and other such information), and error-checking or synchronizing information. A message can be routed directly from sender to receiver through a physical link, or it can be passed, either whole or in parts, through a switching system that routes it from one intermediate station to another. *See also* asynchronous transmission, control character (definition 1), frame (definitions 1

A B C D E F G H I J K L M N O P Q R S T U V W X Y Z

and 2), header (definition 2), message switching, network, packet (definition 1), packet switching, synchronous transmission. **2.** In software, a piece of information passed from the application or operating system to the user to suggest an action, indicate a condition, or inform the user that an event has occurred. **3.** In message-based operating environments, such as Windows, a unit of information passed among running programs, certain devices in the system, and the operating environment itself.

message header *n.* A sequence of bits or bytes at the beginning of a message that usually provides a timing sequence and specifies such aspects of the message structure as its length, data format, and block identification number. *See also* header (definition 2).

message of the day *n.* A daily bulletin for users of a network, multi-user computer, or other shared system. In most cases, users are shown the message of the day when they log on to the system. *Acronym:* MOTD.

message queue *n.* An ordered list of messages awaiting transmission, from which they are taken on a first in, first out (FIFO) basis.

Message Security Protocol *n.* A protocol for Internet messages that is based on the use of encryption and verification to ensure security. It also allows for permissions at the server level for delivery or rejection of e-mail. *Acronym:* MSP.

message switching *n.* A technique used on some communications networks in which a message, with appropriate address information, is routed through one or more intermediate switching stations before being sent to its destination. On a typical message-switching network, a central computer receives messages, stores them (usually briefly), determines their destination addresses, and then delivers them. Message switching enables a network both to regulate traffic and to use communications lines efficiently. *Compare* circuit switching, packet switching.

messaging *n.* The use of computers and data communications equipment to convey messages from one person to another, as by e-mail, voice mail, or fax.

messaging application *n.* An application that enables users to send messages (such as e-mail or fax) to each other.

messaging client *n.* A program that enables its user to send and receive messages (such as e-mail or fax) to and from other users with the help of a remote server.

Meta-Content Format *n.* An open format for describing information about the content of a structured body of data such as a Web page, a set of files on a Windows desktop, or a relational database. Meta-Content Format might be used for indexes, data dictionaries, or price lists. *Acronym:* MCF.

meta data or **metadata** *n.* Data about data. For example, the title, subject, author, and size of a file constitute meta data about the file. *See also* data dictionary.

metafile *n.* A file that contains or defines other files. Many operating systems use metafiles to contain directory information about other files on a given storage device.

Metropolitan Area Exchange *n.* An interconnection point for Internet access providers within a metropolitan area. Data sent between participants in a Metropolitan Area Exchange can pass directly from one network to another without passing through a major backbone. *Acronym:* MAE. *See also* backbone (definition 1), ISP.

metropolitan area network *n. See* MAN.

MFS *n. See* Macintosh File System.

mget *n.* Short for **m**ultiple **get.** A command in most FTP clients with which a user can request the transfer of several files at once. *See also* FTP[1] (definition 1).

MHz *n. See* megahertz.

MICR *n. See* magnetic-ink character recognition.

microchip *n. See* integrated circuit.

microcomputer *n.* A computer built around a single-chip microprocessor. Less powerful than minicomputers and mainframes, microcomputers have nevertheless evolved into very powerful machines capable of complex tasks. State-of-the-art microcomputers are now as powerful as the mainframe computers of only a few years ago, at a fraction of the cost. *See also* computer.

microfloppy disk *n.* A 3.5-inch floppy disk of the type used with the Apple Macintosh and with IBM and compatible microcomputers. A microfloppy disk is a round piece of polyester film coated with ferric oxide and encased in a rigid plastic shell equipped with a sliding metal cover. On the Macintosh, a single-sided microfloppy disk can hold 400 KB; a double-sided (standard) disk can hold 800 KB; and a double-sided high-density disk can hold 1.44 MB. On IBM and compatible machines, a microfloppy can hold either 720 KB or 1.44 MB. *See also* floppy disk.

microprocessor *n.* A central processing unit on a single chip. A modern microprocessor can have over 1 million transistors in an integrated-circuit package roughly 1 inch square. Microprocessors are at the heart of all personal computers. When memory and power are added to a microprocessor, all the pieces, excluding peripherals, required for a computer are present. The most popular lines of microprocessors today are the 680x0 family from Motorola, which powers the Apple Macintosh line, and the 80x86 family from Intel, which is at the core of all IBM PC-compatible and PS/2 computers. *See also* 68000, 68020, 68030, 68040, 80286, 80386, central processing unit, i486DX, Pentium, Pentium Pro, PowerPC.

microsecond *n.* Abbreviated µs. One millionth (10^{-6}) of a second.

Microsoft DOS *n. See* MS-DOS.

Microsoft Windows *n. See* Windows.

microtransaction *n.* A business transaction that involves a very small amount of money, typically under $5. *See also* millicent technology.

middleware *n.* **1.** Software that sits between two or more types of software (generally between an application and an operating system, a network operating system, or a database management system) and translates information

A B C D E F G H I J K L M N O P Q R S T U V W X Y Z

between them. Middleware can cover a broad spectrum of software. **2.** Software that provides a common application programming interface. Applications written using that API will run in the same computer systems as the middleware. *See also* application programming interface. **3.** Software development tools that enable users to create simple programs by selecting existing services and linking them with a scripting language. *See also* scripting language.

MIDI *n.* Acronym for **M**usical **I**nstrument **D**igital **I**nterface. A serial interface standard that allows for the connection of music synthesizers, musical instruments, and computers. The MIDI standard is based partly on hardware and partly on a description of how music and sound are encoded and communicated between MIDI devices. The information transmitted between MIDI devices is in a form called a MIDI message, which encodes aspects of sound such as pitch and volume as 8-bit bytes of digital information. MIDI devices can be used for creating, recording, and playing back music. Using MIDI, computers, synthesizers, and sequencers can communicate with each other, either keeping time or actually controlling the music created by other connected equipment. *See also* synthesizer.

midrange computer *n.* A medium-size computer. The term is used interchangeably with the term minicomputer, except that midrange computers do not include single-user workstations. *See also* minicomputer.

migration *n.* The process of making existing applications and data work on a different computer or operating system.

.mil *n.* In the Internet's Domain Name System, the top-level domain that identifies addresses operated by U.S. military organizations. The designation .mil appears as a suffix at the end of the address. *See also* DNS (definition 1), domain (definition 3). *Compare* .com, .edu, .gov, .net, .org.

Military Network *n.* *See* MILNET.

millicent technology *n.* A set of protocols for small-scale commercial transactions over the Internet, developed by Digital Equipment Corporation. Millicent technology is intended to handle purchases of items of information at prices less than a cent.

millions of instructions per second *n.* *See* MIPS.

millisecond *n.* Abbreviated ms or msec. One thousandth of a second.

MILNET *n.* Short for **Mil**itary **Net**work. A wide area network that represents the military side of the original ARPANET. MILNET carries nonclassified U.S. military traffic. *See also* ARPANET.

MIME *n.* Acronym for **M**ultipurpose **I**nternet **M**ail **E**xtensions. A standard that extends the Simple Mail Transfer Protocol to permit data such as video, sound, and binary files to be transmitted by Internet e-mail without having to be translated into ASCII format first. This is done by using MIME types, which describe the contents of a document. A MIME-compliant application sending a file, such as some e-mail programs, assigns a MIME type to the file. The receiving application, which must also be MIME-compliant, refers to a standardized list of documents that are organized into MIME types and subtypes to interpret the content of the file. MIME is part of HTTP, and both Web browsers and HTTP servers use MIME to interpret e-mail files they send and receive. *See also* HTTP, HTTP server, Simple Mail Transfer Protocol, Web browser. *Compare* BinHex[1] (definition 1).

miniaturization *n.* In the development of integrated circuits, the process of reducing the size and increasing the density of transistors and other elements on a semiconductor chip. Besides providing the benefits of small size, miniaturization of electronic circuits lowers power requirements, reduces heat, and shortens delays in the propagation of signals from one circuit element to the next. *See also* integrated circuit, integration (definition 2).

minicomputer *n.* A mid-level computer manufactured to perform complex computations while dealing efficiently with a high level of input and output from users connected via terminals. Minicomputers also frequently connect to other minicomputers on a network and distribute processing among all the attached machines. Minicomputers are used heavily in transaction-processing applications and as interfaces between mainframe computer systems and wide area networks. *See also* computer, mainframe computer, microcomputer, supercomputer, wide area network. *Compare* midrange computer, workstation (definition 2).

minifloppy *n.* A 5.25-inch floppy disk. *See also* floppy disk.

minimize *vb.* In a graphical user interface, to hide a window without shutting down the program responsible for the window. Usually an icon, button, or name for the window is placed on the desktop; when the user clicks on the icon, button, or name, the window is restored to its previous size. *See also* graphical user interface, window. *Compare* maximize.

miniport drivers *n.* Drivers containing device-specific information that communicate with non-device-specific port drivers, which in turn communicate with the system. *See also* driver.

minitower *n.* A vertical floor-standing computer cabinet that is about half the height (13 inches) of a tower case (24 inches). *See also* tower.

MIPS *n.* Acronym for **m**illions of **i**nstructions **p**er **s**econd. A common measure of processor speed. *See also* central processing unit.

mirror image *n.* An image that is an exact duplicate of an original except that one dimension is reversed. For example, < and > (left and right angle brackets) are mirror images.

mirroring *n.* In computer graphics, the ability to display a mirror image of a graphic—a duplicate rotated or reflected relative to some reference such as an axis of symmetry.

mirror site *n.* A file server that contains a duplicate set of files matching the set on a popular server. Mirror sites exist to spread the distribution burden over more than one server or to eliminate the need to use high-demand international circuits.

MIS *n.* *See* management information service, management information system.

misc. newsgroups *n.* Usenet newsgroups that are part of the misc. hierarchy and use the misc. prefix in their names. These newsgroups cover topics

A B C D E F G H I J K L M N O P Q R S T U V W X Y Z

that do not fit into the other standard Usenet hierarchies (comp., news., rec., sci., soc., talk.). *See also* newsgroup, traditional newsgroup hierarchy, Usenet.

mixed cell reference *n.* In spreadsheets, a cell reference (the address of a cell needed to solve a formula) in which either the row or the column is relative (automatically changed when the formula is copied or moved to another cell) while the other is absolute (not changed when the formula is copied or moved). *See also* cell.

MMX *n.* Short for **M**ulti**m**edia E**x**tensions. An enhancement to the architecture of Intel Pentium processors that improves the performance of multimedia and communications applications.

mnemonic *n.* A word, rhyme, or other memory aid used to associate a complex or lengthy set of information with something that is simple and easy to remember. Operating systems and applications based on typed commands use mnemonics to represent instructions to the program. In MS-DOS, for example, the dir command (short for **dir**ectory) is used to request a list of files.

mobile computing *n.* The process of using a computer while traveling. Mobile computing usually requires a battery-powered portable computer rather than a desktop system.

mode *n.* The operational state of a computer or a program. For example, edit mode is the state in which a program accepts changes to a file. *See also* compatibility mode, safe mode, video mode, virtual real mode.

modec *n.* In telecommunications, a device that generates analog modem signals digitally. The term is a combination of the terms modem and codec. *See also* codec (definition 1), modem.

model *n.* A mathematical or graphical representation of a real-world situation or object—for example, a spreadsheet model of business operations or a graphical model of a molecule. Models can generally be changed or manipulated to see how the real version might be affected by modifications or varying conditions. *See also* modeling, simulation.

modeling *n.* **1.** The use of computers to describe the behavior of a system. Spreadsheet programs, for example, can be used to manipulate financial data, representing the activity of a company; to develop business projections; or to evaluate the impact of proposed changes on the company's operations. *See also* simulation, spreadsheet program. **2.** The use of computers to describe physical objects and the spatial relationships among them mathematically. CAD programs, for example, which create on-screen representations of physical objects, use equations to create lines and shapes and to place them accurately in relation to each other and to the two-dimensional or three-dimensional space in which they are drawn. *See also* CAD, rendering, solid model, surface modeling, three-dimensional model, two-dimensional model, wire-frame model.

modem *n.* Short for **mo**dulator/**dem**odulator. A communications device that enables a computer to transmit information over a standard telephone line. Because a computer is digital and a telephone line is analog, modems are needed to convert digital to analog and vice versa. In addition to transmitting and receiving, sophisticated modems are also capable of such functions as automatic dialing, answering, and redialing. Without communications software, however, modems cannot perform any useful work. *See also* analog, baud rate, digital.

modem bank *n.* A collection of modems connected to a server maintained by an ISP or the operator of a BBS or remote-access LAN. Most modem banks are configured to allow a remote user to dial a single phone number that routes calls to an available phone number on the bank. *See also* BBS (definition 1), ISP, LAN.

modem eliminator *n.* A device that enables two computers to communicate without modems. *See also* null modem.

modem port *n.* A serial port used for connecting an external modem to a personal computer. *See also* modem, serial port.

modem ready *n.* *See* MR.

moderated discussion *n.* Communication taking place on a mailing list, newsgroup, or other online forum that is edited by a moderator. When one submits a message to a moderated discussion, the moderator decides whether the message is relevant to the discussion topic. If it is, it is forwarded to the discussion group. The content of a moderated discussion is often perceived as more valuable than that of an unmoderated one because the information has been read and approved by a "gatekeeper," who has (presumably) filtered out irrelevant submissions. Some moderators also filter submissions for obscene or pornographic material or material that is potentially offensive. *See also* mailing list, moderator, newsgroup.

moderator *n.* In some Internet newsgroups and mailing lists, a person through whom all messages are filtered before they are distributed to the members of the newsgroup or list. The moderator discards or edits any messages that are not considered appropriate. *See also* mailing list, newsgroup.

modifier key *n.* A key on the keyboard that, when held down while another key is pressed, changes the meaning of the keystroke. *See also* Alt key, Command key, Control key, Shift key.

MO disk *n.* *See* magneto-optic disc.

MO disk drive *n.* *See* magneto-optic disc.

modular design *n.* An approach to designing hardware or software. In modular design, a project is broken into smaller units, or modules, each of which can be developed, tested, and finished independently before being combined with the others in the final product. Each unit performs a particular task or function and thus can often be reused in other products having similar requirements.

modular jack *n.* *See* phone connector.

modular programming *n.* An approach to programming in which the program is broken into several independently compiled modules, or units. Each module exports specified elements, which other modules can use. The use of modules facilitates group programming efforts and promotes reliable programming practices. Modular programming is a predecessor of object-oriented programming. *See also* modular design, module (definition 1), object-oriented programming.

modular software *n.* A program created from multiple stand-alone software components. Modular components can work together to perform the work for which the larger program is designed while still remaining individually usable—and reusable—in other programs. A programmer can change or modify one component without adversely affecting other components in the same program. *See also* component software, modular design. *Compare* integrated software.

modulation *n.* In computer communications, the means by which a modem converts digital information sent by a computer to the analog form that it sends over a telephone line.

module *n.* **1.** In programming, a collection of routines and data structures that performs a particular task or implements a particular tool for use in the rest of the program. *See also* modular design, modular programming. **2.** In hardware, a self-contained component that can provide a complete function to a system and can be interchanged with other modules that provide similar functions. *See also* memory card, SIMM.

moiré *n.* A visible wavy distortion or flickering in an image that is displayed or printed with an inappropriate resolution. Several factors affect moiré patterns, including the size and resolution of the image, the resolution of the output device, and the halftone screen angle.

monitor *n.* The device on which images generated by the computer's video adapter are displayed. The term usually refers to a video display and its housing. The monitor is attached to the video adapter by a cable. *See also* CRT, video adapter.

monochrome *adj.* Of, pertaining to, or being a monitor that displays images in only one color—black on white (as on early monochrome Macintosh screens) or amber or green on black (as on early IBM and other monochrome monitors). The term is also applied to a monitor that displays only variable levels of a single color, such as a gray-scale monitor.

monochrome adapter *n.* A video adapter capable of generating a video signal for one foreground color or sometimes for a range of intensities in a single color, as for a gray-scale monitor.

monochrome display *n.* **1.** A video display capable of rendering only one color. The color displayed depends on the phosphor of the display (often green or amber). **2.** A display capable of rendering a range of intensities in only one color, as in a gray-scale monitor.

monochrome monitor *n.* *See* monochrome display.

monospace font *n.* A font in which each character occupies the same amount of horizontal space regardless of the character's width—an *i,* for example, taking as much room as an *m.* `This is a sentence in a monospace font.` *Also called* fixed-width font. *See also* font, monospacing. *Compare* proportional font.

monospacing *n.* A form of print and display spacing in which each character occupies the same amount of horizontal space on the line, regardless of whether the character itself is wide or narrow. *Also called* fixed-pitch spacing, fixed spacing, fixed-width spacing. *See also* monospace font. *Compare* proportional spacing.

MOO *n.* Short for **M**UD, **O**bject-**O**riented. A form of multi-user dungeon (MUD) that contains an object-oriented language with which users can create areas and objects within the MOO. In comparison to MUDs, MOOs are generally focused more on communications and programming and less on games. *See also* MUD.

Moore's Law *n.* A prediction by Intel cofounder Gordon Moore regarding the growth of semiconductor technology. Moore predicted that chip capacity would double every two years. Capacity has actually doubled every 18 months since then, and this rate of doubling capacity is popularly referred to as a "law."

.moov *n.* A file extension indicating a QuickTime MooV video file for a Macintosh computer. *See also* MooV.

MooV *n.* The file format for QuickTime movies that stores synchronized tracks for control, video, audio, and text. *See also* QuickTime.

morphing *n.* Short for meta**morph**os**ing.** A process by which one image is gradually transformed into another, creating the illusion of a metamorphosis occurring in a short time. A common motion picture special-effects technique, morphing is available in many advanced computer animation packages. *See also* tween.

Mosaic *n.* The first popular graphical Web browser. Released on the Internet in early 1993 by NCSA at the University of Illinois at Urbana-Champaign, Mosaic is available as freeware and shareware for Windows, Macintosh, and X Window systems. Mosaic is distinguished from other early Web browsers by its ease of use and its addition of inline images to Web documents. *Also called* NCSA Mosaic.

MOTD *n. See* message of the day.

motherboard *n.* The main circuit board containing the primary components of a computer system: the processor, main memory, support circuitry, and bus controller and connector. Other boards, including expansion memory and input/output boards, may attach to the motherboard via the bus connector. *See also* expansion slot. *Compare* daughterboard.

Motion JPEG *n.* A standard for storing motion video, proposed by the Joint Photographic Experts Group, that uses JPEG image compression for each frame. *See also* JPEG (definition 1). *Compare* MPEG (definition 1).

mount *vb.* To make a physical disk or tape accessible to a computer's file system. The term is most commonly used to describe accessing disks in Apple Macintosh and UNIX-based computers.

mouse *n.* A common pointing device. The basic features of a mouse are a flat-bottomed casing designed to be gripped by one hand; one or more buttons on the top; a multidirectional detection device (usually a ball) on the

A B C D E F G H I J K L M N O P Q R S T U V W X Y Z

A B C D E F G H I J K L M N O P Q R S T U V W X Y Z

bottom; and a cable connecting the mouse to the computer. By moving the mouse on a surface (such as a desktop), the user typically controls an on-screen cursor. A mouse is a relative pointing device because there are no defined limits to the mouse's movement and because its placement on a surface does not map directly to a specific screen location. To select items or choose commands on the screen, the user presses one of the mouse's buttons, producing a "mouse click." *See also* bus mouse, mechanical mouse, optical mouse, optomechanical mouse, relative pointing device, serial mouse. *Compare* trackball.

mouse pad *n.* A surface on which a mouse can be moved, typically a rectangular rubber pad covered with fabric, providing more traction than a wooden or glass desktop or tabletop. *See also* mouse.

mouse pointer *n.* An on-screen element whose location changes as the user moves the mouse. Depending on the location of the mouse pointer and the operation of the program with which it is working, the area of the screen where the mouse pointer appears serves as the target for an action when the user presses a mouse button. *See also* block cursor, cursor (definition 3).

mouse port *n.* **1.** In many PC-compatible computers, a dedicated connector where a mouse or other pointing device plugs into the computer. If a mouse port is not available, a serial port can be used to connect the mouse to the computer. *See also* connector, mouse, pointing device, serial port. **2.** In a Macintosh, the Apple Desktop Bus port. *See also* Apple Desktop Bus.

mouse scaling *n.* *See* mouse sensitivity.

mouse sensitivity *n.* The relationship of mouse movement to screen cursor movement. Increasing the sensitivity can result in smaller cursor moves for a given mouse move, making it easier for the user to position the cursor precisely. High sensitivity is good for exacting work, such as CAD and graphic art; low sensitivity is good for tasks in which getting around the screen quickly is important and for applications such as Web browsers, word processors, and spreadsheets, in which the cursor is used mostly to select buttons or text. *Also called* mouse scaling, mouse tracking.

mouse tracking *n.* *See* mouse sensitivity.

mouse trails *n.* The creation of a shadowlike trail following the mouse pointer on screen in order to make it easier to see. Mouse trails are useful for laptops and notebook computers, particularly ones with passive-matrix displays or older models with monochrome screens. The relatively low resolution and contrast of these screens make it easy to lose sight of a small mouse pointer. *See also* mouse pointer, submarining.

.mov *n.* A filename extension for a movie file in Apple's QuickTime format. *See also* QuickTime.

move *n.* A command or instruction to transfer information from one location to another. Depending on the operation involved, a move can affect data in a computer's memory, or it can affect text or a graphical image in a data file. In applications, for example, a move command might relocate a paragraph of text or a graphic in a document. Unlike a copy procedure, which duplicates information, a move indicates that information can be deleted from its original location. *Compare* copy.

.movie *n. See* .mov.

Moving Pictures Experts Group *n. See* MPEG (definition 1).

MPC *n. See* Multimedia PC.

.mpeg *n.* The file extension that identifies graphic image files in the MPEG format specified by the Moving Pictures Experts Group. *See also* MPEG (definition 1).

MPEG *n.* **1.** Acronym for **M**oving **P**ictures **E**xperts **G**roup. A set of standards for audio and video compression established by the Joint ISO/IEC Technical Committee on Information Technology. The MPEG standard has different types that are designed to work in different situations. *Compare* Motion JPEG. **2.** A video/audio file in the MPEG format. Such files generally have the extension .mpg. *See also* JPEG (definition 1). *Compare* Motion JPEG.

.mpg *n.* A file extension that identifies encoded data streams that contain compressed audio and video information, using the format specified by the Moving Pictures Experts Group. *See also* MPEG (definition 1).

MPPP *n. See* Multilink Point-to-Point Protocol.

MPR II *n.* A standard for limiting magnetic and electric field emissions from video monitors, including VLF radiation. *See also* VLF radiation.

mput *n.* In many FTP clients, the command that instructs the local client to transmit multiple files to the remote server.

MR *n.* Acronym for **m**odem **r**eady. A light on the front panel of a modem indicating that the modem is ready.

ms *n. See* millisecond.

MS-DOS *n.* Short for **Micros**oft **D**isk **O**perating **S**ystem. A single-tasking, single-user operating system with a command-line interface, released in 1981, for IBM PCs and compatibles. MS-DOS, like other operating systems, oversees operations such as disk input and output, video support, keyboard control, and many internal functions related to program execution and file maintenance.

MS-DOS mode *n.* A shell in which the MS-DOS environment is emulated in 32-bit systems such as Windows 95. *See also* MS-DOS, shell.

msec *n. See* millisecond.

MSP *n. See* Message Security Protocol.

MS-Windows *n. See* Windows.

MTBF *n.* Acronym for **m**ean **t**ime **b**etween **f**ailures. The average time interval, usually expressed in thousands or tens of thousands of hours (sometimes called power-on hours, or POH), that will elapse before a hardware component fails and requires service.

MTTR *n.* Acronym for **m**ean **t**ime **t**o **r**epair. The average time interval, usually expressed in hours, that it takes to repair a failed component.

MUD *n.* Acronym for **m**ulti-**u**ser **d**ungeon. A virtual environment on the Internet in which multiple users simultaneously participate in a role-playing game and interact with each other in real time. *Also called* multi-user simulation environment.

MUD, Object-Oriented *n. See* MOO.

multiboot *n.* The startup capability of some operating systems, such as Windows NT, OS/2, UNIX, and some Power Macs, that allows users to choose which of two or more installed operating systems—for example, Windows NT or UNIX—they want to use for the current session. *See also* boot[1].

multicast backbone *n. See* MBONE.

multicasting *n.* The process of sending a message simultaneously to more than one destination on a network.

multifile sorting *n.* The process of sorting a body of data that resides in more than one file.

MultiFinder *n.* A version of the Apple Macintosh Finder that provides support for multitasking. The primary use of MultiFinder is to allow multiple applications to be simultaneously resident in memory. A single mouse click switches between applications, and information from one application can be copied to another. If the active application allows true multitasking, background tasks can be processed. *See also* Finder.

multifunction board *n.* A computer add-in board that provides more than one function. Multifunction boards for personal computers frequently offer additional memory, serial/parallel ports, and a clock/calendar.

multilayer *adj.* **1.** In board design, of or pertaining to a printed circuit board consisting of two or more layers of board material. Multilayer design allows many more discrete paths between components than single-layer boards do. **2.** In CAD programs, of or pertaining to drawings that are built up using multiple layers, each with a different level of detail or a different object, so that distinct parts of the drawing can easily be manipulated, overlaid, or peeled off.

Multilink Point-to-Point Protocol *n.* An Internet protocol that allows computers to establish multiple physical links to combine their bandwidths. This technology creates a virtual link with more capacity than a single physical link. *Acronym:* MPPP. *See also* PPP.

multimedia *n.* The combination of sound, graphics, animation, and video. In the world of computers, multimedia is a subset of hypermedia, which combines the aforementioned elements with hypertext. *See also* hypermedia, hypertext.

Multimedia Extensions *n. See* MMX.

Multimedia PC *n.* Software and hardware standards set forth by the Multimedia PC Marketing Council, which sets minimum standards for a PC's sound, video, and CD-ROM playing capabilities. *Acronym:* MPC.

Multimedia Personal Computer *n. See* Multimedia PC.

multinode computer *n.* A computer that uses multiple processors to share in the computation of a complex task. *See also* central processing unit, parallel processing.

multipass sort *n.* A sorting operation that, usually because of the sorting algorithm being used, requires two or more passes through the data before completion. *See also* bubble sort, insertion sort, sort algorithm.

multiple-document interface *n. See* MDI.

multiple recipients *n.* **1.** The ability to send e-mail to more than one user at a time by listing more than one e-mail address on a line. Delimiters such as commas or semicolons are used to separate the e-mail addresses. *See also* e-mail[1] (definition 1), mailing list. **2.** The subscribers on a mailing list. A message sent to the list is addressed to the "multiple recipients of" the list.

multiple-user system *n. See* multi-user system.

multiplexer *n.* **1.** A hardware circuit for selecting a single output from multiple inputs. **2.** A device for funneling several different streams of data over a common communications line. Multiplexers are used either to attach many communications lines to a smaller number of communications ports or to attach a large number of communications ports to a smaller number of communications lines. *Acronym:* MUX.

multiplexing *n.* A technique used in communications and input/output operations for transmitting a number of separate signals simultaneously over a single channel or line. The device used to combine the signals is a multiplexer.

multiprocessing *n.* A mode of operation in which two or more connected and roughly equal processing units each carry out one or more processes (programs or sets of instructions) in tandem. In multiprocessing, each processing unit works on a different set of instructions or on different parts of the same process. The objective is increased speed or computing power. *Compare* coprocessor, parallel processing.

Multipurpose Internet Mail Extensions *n. See* MIME.

multiscan monitor *n.* A computer monitor capable of operating at different scanning frequencies to accommodate different screen resolutions.

multisystem network *n.* A communications network in which two or more host computers can be accessed by network users.

multitasking *n.* A mode of operation offered by an operating system in which a computer works on more than one task at a time. *See also* background[1], context switching, cooperative multitasking, foreground[1].

multi-user dungeon *n. See* MUD.

multi-user simulation environment *n. See* MUD.

multi-user system *n.* Any computer system that can be used by more than one person. Although a microcomputer shared by several people can be considered a multi-user system, the term is generally reserved for machines that can be accessed simultaneously by several people through communications facilities or via network terminals. *Compare* single-user computer.

MUSE *n.* Short for **m**ulti-**u**ser **s**imulation **e**nvironment. *See* MUD.

Musical Instrument Digital Interface *n. See* MIDI.

MUX *n. See* multiplexer (definition 2).

A B C D E F G H I J K L M N O P Q R S T U V W X Y Z

MYOB Acronym for **M**ind **y**our **o**wn **b**usiness. An expression used in e-mail and newsgroups.

my two cents *n.* An expression used informally in newsgroup articles and, less frequently, in e-mail messages or mailing lists to indicate that the message is the writer's contribution t o an ongoing discussion. *Also called* $0.02. *See also* mailing list, newsgroup.

N

NAK *n.* Acronym for **n**egative **ack**nowledgment. A control code, ASCII character 21 (hexadecimal 15), transmitted to a sending station or computer by the receiving unit as a signal that transmitted information has arrived incorrectly. *Compare* ACK.

named anchor *n.* In HTML, a tag within a document that can act as a destination for a hyperlink. Named anchors are useful because they allow a link to a specific location within a document. *Also called* named target. *See also* anchor (definition 2), HTML, hyperlink.

named target *n. See* named anchor.

name server *n. See* CSO name server, DNS server.

nanosecond *n.* Abbreviated ns. One billionth of a second. A nanosecond is a time measure used to represent computing speed, particularly the speed at which electrical signals travel through circuits within the computer.

NAP *n. See* National Attachment Point.

narrowband *n.* A bandwidth set aside by the Federal Communications Commission for mobile or portable radio services, such as advanced two-way paging systems, including transmission rates between 50 bps and 64 Kbps. Narrowband formerly referred to the bandwidth from 50 to 150 bps. *See also* bandwidth. *Compare* broadband.

NAT *n.* Acronym for **n**etwork **a**ddress **t**ranslation. The process of converting between IP addresses used within an intranet or other private network (called a stub domain) and Internet IP addresses. This approach makes it possible to use a large number of addresses within the stub domain without depleting the limited number of available numeric Internet IP addresses. *See also* intranet, IP address.

National Attachment Point *n.* One of the four exchange points for Internet traffic sponsored by the National Science Foundation. Internet service providers connect with one of the National Attachment Points in order to exchange data with other providers. The four National Attachment Points are located in the San Francisco Bay area, Chicago, New York, and Washington, D.C. *Acronym:* NAP.

National Center for Supercomputing Applications *n. See* NCSA.

National Information Infrastructure *n.* A future high-bandwidth wide area network proposed by the U.S. government to carry data, fax, video, and voice transmissions to users throughout the United States. The network is to be developed mostly by private carriers; the government anticipates that the principal motive will be to deliver movies to homes on demand.

A B C D E F G H I J K L M N O P Q R S T U V W X Y Z

Many of the proposed services are or will soon become available on the Internet itself. *Acronym:* NII. *See also* Information Superhighway. *Compare* Internet.

National Television System Committee *n. See* NTSC.

native application *n.* A program designed specifically for a particular type of microprocessor—that is, a program that is binary-compatible with a processor. A native application generally will run much faster than a non-native application, which must be run with the help of an emulator program. *See also* binary compatibility, emulator.

native file format *n.* The format an application uses internally to process data. The application must convert files in other formats to the native format before it can work with them. For example, a word processor might recognize text files in ASCII text format, but it will convert them to its own native format before it displays them.

natural language *n.* A language spoken or written by humans, as opposed to a programming language or a machine language. Approximating natural language in a computer environment is one goal of research in artificial intelligence.

natural-language processing *n.* A field of computer science and linguistics that studies computer systems that can recognize and react to human language, either spoken or written. *See also* artificial intelligence. *Compare* voice recognition.

natural language query *n.* A query to a database system composed in a subset of a natural language, such as English or Japanese. The query must often conform to some restrictive syntax rules so that the system can parse it. *See also* parse.

natural-language recognition *n. See* voice recognition.

natural language support *n.* A voice recognition system that allows the user to issue verbal commands in his or her own language to direct a computer's actions. *Acronym:* NLS.

navigation bar *n.* On a Web page, a grouping of hyperlinks that help the user get around in that particular Web site. *See also* hyperlink.

navigation keys *n.* The keys on a keyboard controlling cursor movement, including the four arrow keys and the Backspace, End, Home, Page Down, and Page Up keys. *See also* arrow key, Backspace key, End key, Home key, Page Down key, Page Up key.

NC *n. See* network computer.

NCSA *n.* Acronym for **N**ational **C**enter for **S**upercomputing **A**pplications. A research center located at the University of Illinois at Urbana-Champaign. NCSA, founded in 1985 as a part of the National Science Foundation, is best known as the home of NCSA Mosaic (the first graphical Web browser) and of NCSA Telnet. *See also* Mosaic.

NCSA Mosaic *n. See* Mosaic.

near-letter-quality *adj.* A print mode on high-end dot-matrix printers that produces clearer, darker characters than normal (draft-quality) printing.

Near-letter-quality printing is not as legible as output from a fully-formed-character printer. *Acronym:* NLQ. *See also* print quality. *Compare* draft quality, letter quality.

negative acknowledgment *n. See* NAK.

.net *n.* In the Internet's Domain Name System, the top-level domain that identifies addresses of network providers. The designation .net appears as a suffix at the end of the address. *See also* DNS (definition 1), domain (definition 3). *Compare* .com, .edu, .gov, .mil, .org.

net. *prefix* A prefix used to describe people and institutions on the Internet. For example, a very well respected person might be described as a net.god.

Net *n.* **1.** Short for Inter**net**. **2.** Short for Use**net**. *See also* Usenet.

net address *n.* **1.** A World Wide Web address (URL). *See also* URL. **2.** An e-mail address. **3.** The DNS name or IP address of a machine. *See also* DNS (definition 1), IP address.

net.god *n.* A highly respected person within the Internet community.

nethead *n.* **1.** A person who uses the Internet as if addicted to it. **2.** A Grateful Dead fan who participates in the rec.music.gdead newsgroup or some other forum dedicated to that band.

netiquette *n.* Short for **net**work et**iquette**. Principles of courtesy observed in sending electronic messages, such as e-mail and Usenet postings. The consequences of violating netiquette include being flamed and having one's name placed in the bozo filter of one's intended audience. Disapproved behavior includes gratuitous personal insults; posting large amounts of irrelevant material; giving away the plot of a movie, television show, or novel without warning; posting offensive material without encrypting it; and excessive cross-posting of a message to multiple groups without regard to whether the group members are likely to find it interesting. *See also* bozo filter, flame[2].

netizen *n.* A person who participates in online communication through the Internet and other networks, especially conference and chat services, such as Internet news or Fidonet. *Compare* lurker.

NetPC *n.* A computer platform specification created by Microsoft and Intel in 1996 for systems that use Windows NT server–based applications rather than applications located on the client computer.

net.personality *n.* A slang term for a person who has attained some degree of celebrity on the Internet.

net.police *n.* Persons (usually self-appointed) who try to enforce their understanding of the "rules" that apply to conduct on the Internet. Their activities may be directed toward users who violate the rules of netiquette, spammers who send unsolicited advertising as e-mail or to newsgroups, or even people who post "politically incorrect" comments to newsgroups or mailing lists. *See also* netiquette, spam[1].

Netspeak *n.* The set of conventions for writing English in e-mail, IRCs, and newsgroups. Netspeak is characterized by acronyms (such as IMHO or ROFL) and clarifying devices such as emotags and emoticons. Use of

Netspeak should be governed by netiquette. *See also* emotag, emoticon, IMHO, IRC, netiquette, ROFL.
Net surfing *n.* The practice of exploring the Internet without a specific goal in mind. The concept of Net surfing is similar to "channel surfing" by individuals watching television.
net-top box *n.* A type of personal computer with a reduced number of components, built primarily to provide a low-cost access terminal for the various services available on the Internet, such as e-mail, Web access, and telnet connectivity. These machines, which are under development, will not have locally addressable hard disks or installable programs; instead, a net-top box will obtain any necessary materials for the user from a network to which it is connected. *Compare* Java terminal, NetPC.
Net TV *n. See* Internet television.
network *n.* A group of computers and associated devices that are connected by communications facilities. A network can involve permanent connections, such as cables, or temporary connections made through telephone or other communications links. A network can be as small as a local area network consisting of a few computers, printers, and other devices, or it can consist of many small and large computers distributed over a vast geographic area.
network adapter *n.* An expansion card or other device used to connect a computer to a LAN. *Also called* network card, network interface card.
network address translation *n. See* NAT.
network administrator *n.* The person in charge of operations on a computer network. The duties of a network administrator might include such tasks as installing new workstations and devices, maintaining the list of authorized users, archiving files, overseeing password protection and other security measures, monitoring usage of shared resources, and handling malfunctioning equipment. *See also* system administrator.
network architecture *n.* The underlying structure of a computer network, including hardware, functional layers, interfaces, and protocols, used to establish communications and ensure the reliable transfer of information. Network architectures are designed to provide both philosophical and physical standards for the complexities of establishing communications links and transferring information without conflict. Various network architectures exist, including the internationally accepted seven-layer ISO/OSI model. *See also* ISO/OSI model.
network card *n. See* network adapter.
network computer *n.* A computer having the hardware and software necessary to be connected to a network. *Acronym:* NC.
network database *n.* **1.** A database that runs in a network. **2.** A database containing the address of other users in the network. **3.** In information management, a type of database in which data records can be related to one another in more than one way. A network database is similar to a hierarchical database in the sense that it contains a progression from one record to

another. It differs in being less rigidly structured: any single record can point to more than one other record and, conversely, can be pointed to by one or more records. In effect, a network database allows more than one path between any two records, whereas a hierarchical database allows only one, from parent (higher-level record) to child (lower-level record). *Compare* hierarchical database, relational database.

network device driver *n.* Software that coordinates communication between the network adapter and the computer's hardware and other software, controlling the physical function of the network adapter.

network directory *n.* On a local area network, a directory on a disk that is located on a computer other than the one the user is operating. A network directory differs from a network drive in that the user has access to only that directory. The rest of the disk is accessible to the user only if the network administrator has granted access rights to the user. On the Apple Macintosh, a network directory is referred to as a shared folder. *Also called* networked directory, shared directory. *See also* network drive, shared folder.

network drive *n.* On a local area network, a disk drive whose disk is available to other computers on the network. Access to a network drive might not be allowed to all users of the network, however; many operating systems contain security provisions that enable a network administrator to grant or deny access to part or all of a network drive. *Also called* networked drive. *See also* network directory.

network information center *n. See* NIC (definition 2).

Network Information Service *n. See* Yellow Pages (definition 1).

network interface card *n. See* network adapter.

network latency *n.* The time it takes for information to be transferred between computers in a network.

network layer *n.* The third of the seven layers in the ISO/OSI model for standardizing computer-to-computer communications. The network layer is one level above the data-link layer and ensures that information arrives at its intended destination. It is the middle of the three layers (data-link, network, and transport) concerned with the actual movement of information from one device to another. *See also* ISO/OSI model.

network meltdown *n. See* broadcast storm.

network model *n.* A database structure, or layout, similar to a hierarchical model, except that records can have multiple parent records as well as multiple child records. A database management system that supports a network model can be used to simulate a hierarchical model. *See also* network database (definition 3). *Compare* hierarchical model.

network modem *n.* A modem that is shared by users of a network, for calling an online information service, an ISP, or other online source. *See also* ISP, modem, online information service.

network news *n.* The newsgroups on the Internet, especially those in the Usenet hierarchy. *See also* Usenet.

A B C D E F G H I J K L M N O P Q R S T U V W X Y Z

Network News Transfer Protocol *n. See* NNTP.

network operating system *n.* An operating system installed on a server in a local area network that coordinates the activities of providing services to the computers and other devices attached to the network. Unlike a single-user operating system, a network operating system must acknowledge and respond to requests from many workstations, managing such details as network access and communications, resource allocation and sharing, data protection, and error control. *Acronym:* NOS.

network operation center *n.* The office in an enterprise that is responsible for maintaining network integrity and improving network efficiency while reducing system downtime. *Acronym:* NOC.

network OS *n. See* network operating system.

network protocol *n.* A set of rules and procedures that define and enable communications through a network.

network server *n. See* server.

network services *n.* **1.** In a corporate environment, the division that maintains the network and the computers. **2.** In a Windows environment, extensions to the operating system that allow it to perform network functions such as network printing and file sharing.

network software *n.* Software including a component that facilitates connection to or participation in a network.

network structure *n.* The record organization used in a particular network model.

Network Time Protocol *n. See* NTP.

network topology *n. See* topology.

neural network *n.* A type of artificial-intelligence system modeled after the neurons (nerve cells) in a biological nervous system and intended to simulate the way a brain processes information, learns, and remembers. A neural network is designed as an interconnected system of processing elements, each with a limited number of inputs and an output. These processing elements are able to "learn" by receiving weighted inputs that, with adjustment, time, and repetition, can be made to produce appropriate outputs. Neural networks are used in areas such as speech analysis and speech synthesis. *See also* artificial intelligence, speech synthesis.

newbie *n.* **1.** An inexperienced user on the Internet. **2.** In a particularly derogatory sense, an inexperienced Usenet user who asks for information that is readily available in the FAQ. *See also* FAQ.

newline character *n.* A control character that causes the cursor on a display or the printing mechanism on a printer to move to the beginning of the next line. It is functionally equivalent to a combination of the carriage return and linefeed characters. *Acronym:* NL. *See also* carriage return, linefeed.

news.announce.newusers *n.* A newsgroup that contains general information for new users about using Internet newsgroups.

news feed or **newsfeed** *n.* Deliveries, exchanges, or distributions of newsgroup articles to and from news servers. News feeds are accomplished through cooperating news servers, which communicate via NNTP through network connections. *Also called* feed. *See also* newsgroup, news server, NNTP.

newsgroup *n.* A forum on the Internet for threaded discussions on a specified range of subjects. A newsgroup consists of articles and follow-up posts. An article with all its follow-up posts—all of which should be related to the subject specified in the original article's subject line—constitutes a thread. Each newsgroup has a name that consists of a series of words, separated by periods, indicating the newsgroup's subject in terms of increasingly narrow categories, such as rec.crafts.textiles.needlework. Some newsgroups can be read and posted to only on one site; others, such as those in the seven Usenet hierarchies, circulate throughout the Internet. *See also* article, bit. newsgroups, follow-up, local newsgroups, mail reflector, threaded discussion, traditional newsgroup hierarchy, Usenet. *Compare* mailing list.

newsmaster *n.* The person in charge of maintaining the Internet news server at a particular host. To reach a given newsmaster, a user can send e-mail to the address newsmaster@*domain.name*.

news. newsgroups *n.* Usenet newsgroups that are part of the news. hierarchy and use the prefix news. in their names. These newsgroups cover topics that deal with Usenet itself, such as Usenet policy and the creation of new Usenet newsgroups. *See also* newsgroup, traditional newsgroup hierarchy, Usenet.

.newsrc *n.* The file extension that identifies a setup file for UNIX-based newsreaders. The setup file typically contains a current list of newsgroups that the user subscribes to and the articles in each newsgroup that the user has already read. *See also* newsreader, setup (definition 2).

newsreader *n.* A Usenet client program that enables a user to subscribe to Usenet newsgroups, read and post articles, post follow-ups, and reply by e-mail. Many Web browsers also provide these functions. *See also* follow-up, newsgroup, Usenet, Web browser.

news server *n.* A computer or program that exchanges Internet newsgroups with newsreader clients and other servers. *See also* newsgroup, newsreader.

nibble or **nybble** *n.* Half a byte (4 bits). *Compare* quadbit.

NIC *n.* **1.** Acronym for **n**etwork **i**nterface **c**ard. *See* network adapter. **2.** Acronym for **n**etwork **i**nformation **c**enter. An organization that provides information about a network and other support to users of the network. The principal NIC for the Internet is InterNIC. Intranets and other private networks may have their own NICs. *See also* InterNIC.

NiCad battery *n.* *See* nickel cadmium battery.

nickel cadmium battery *n.* A rechargeable battery that uses an alkaline electrolyte. Nickel cadmium batteries typically have a longer operating life and storage life than similar lead-acid batteries. *Also called* NiCad battery. *Compare* lead ion battery, lithium ion battery, nickel metal hydride battery.

A B C D E F G H I J K L M N O P Q R S T U V W X Y Z

nickel metal hydride battery *n.* A rechargeable battery that offers longer life and superior performance compared with similar nickel cadmium or other alkaline batteries. *Also called* NiMH battery. *Compare* lead ion battery, lithium ion battery, nickel cadmium battery.

nickname *n.* A name used in the destination field of an e-mail editor in place of one or more complete network addresses. For example, "Fred" might be a nickname for fred@history.washington.edu. If the nickname has been established within the program, a user need only type *Fred* instead of the entire address, or perhaps *history faculty* instead of all the individual faculty addresses. *See also* alias (definition 2).

NII *n. See* National Information Infrastructure.

NiMH battery *n. See* nickel metal hydride battery.

NIS *n.* Acronym for **N**etwork **I**nformation **S**ervice. *See* Yellow Pages (definition 1).

nixpub *n.* A list of ISPs, available in the newsgroups comp.bbs.misc and alt.bbs and at ftp://VFL.Paramax.COM:/pub/pubnetc/nixpub.long. *See also* ISP.

NL *n. See* newline character.

NLQ *n. See* near-letter-quality.

NLS *n. See* natural language support.

NNTP *n.* Acronym for **N**etwork **N**ews **T**ransfer **P**rotocol. The Internet protocol that governs the transmissions of newsgroups.

NOC *n. See* network operation center.

node *n.* **1.** A junction of some type. **2.** In LANs, a device that is connected to the network and is capable of communicating with other network devices. **3.** In tree structures, a location on the tree that can have links to one or more nodes below it. *See also* tree.

noise *n.* **1.** Any interference that affects the operation of a device. **2.** Unwanted electrical signals, produced either naturally or by the circuitry, that degrade the quality or performance of a communications channel. *See also* distortion.

nonbreaking space *n.* A character that replaces the standard space character in order to keep two words together on one line rather than allowing a line to break between them.

nonimpact printer *n.* Any printer that makes marks on the paper without striking it mechanically. The most common types are ink-jet, thermal, and laser printers. *See also* ink-jet printer, laser printer, thermal printer. *Compare* impact printer.

noninterlaced *adj.* A display method on raster-scan monitors in which the electron beam scans each line of the screen once during each refresh cycle. *Compare* interlacing.

nonvolatile memory *n.* A storage system that does not lose data when power is removed from it. Intended to refer to core memory, ROM, EPROM, flash memory, bubble memory, or battery-backed CMOS RAM, the term is occasionally used in reference to disk subsystems as well. *See also* bubble memory, CMOS RAM, core, EPROM, flash memory, ROM.

normal form *n.* In a relational database, an approach to structuring information in order to avoid redundancy and inconsistency and to promote efficient maintenance, storage, and updating. Several "rules" or levels of normalization are accepted; of these, three forms are commonly used: first normal (1NF), second normal (2NF), and third normal (3NF). First normal forms, the least structured, are groups of records (such as employee lists) in which each field contains unique and nonrepeating information. Second and third normal forms break down first normal forms, separating them into different tables by defining successively finer interrelationships between fields. Second normal forms do not include fields that are subsets of fields other than the primary (key) field; for example, a second normal form keyed to employee name would not include both job grade and hourly rate if pay were dependent on job grade. Third normal forms do not include fields that provide information about fields other than the key field; for example, a third normal form keyed to employee name would not include project name, crew number, and supervisor unless the crew number and supervisor were assigned only to the project the employee was working on. Further normalization refinements, less commonly used, include fourth normal form (4NF) and projection-join (or fifth) normal form (PJ/NF or 5NF).

normal hyphen *n. See* hyphen.

NOS *n. See* network operating system.

NOT *n.* An operator that performs Boolean or logical negation. *See also* Boolean operator, logical operator.

notebook computer *n. See* portable computer.

ns *n. See* nanosecond.

NT *n. See* Windows NT.

NTP *n.* Acronym for **N**etwork **T**ime **P**rotocol. A protocol used for synchronizing the system time on a computer to that of a server or other reference source such as a radio, satellite receiver, or modem. NTP provides a high level of time accuracy and reliability. *See also* communications protocol.

NTSC *n.* Acronym for **N**ational **T**elevision **S**ystem (later changed to Standards) **C**ommittee. The standards-setting body for television and video in the United States. It is the sponsor of the NTSC standard for encoding color, a coding system compatible with black-and-white signals and the system used for color broadcasting in the United States.

nuke *vb.* **1.** To erase a file, a directory, or an entire hard disk. **2.** To stop a process in an operating system or a program. *Also called* kill.

NUL *n.* **1.** A character code with a null value; literally, a character meaning "nothing." Although it is real in the sense of being recognizable, occupying space internally in the computer, and being sent or received as a character, a NUL character displays nothing, takes no space on the screen or on paper, and causes no specific action when sent to a printer. In ASCII, NUL is represented by the character code 0. *See also* ASCII. **2.** A "device," recognized by the operating system, that can be addressed like a physical output device (such as a printer) but that discards any information sent to it.

null character *n. See* NUL (definition 1).

null modem *n.* A way of connecting two computers via a cable that enables them to communicate without the use of modems. A null modem cable accomplishes this by crossing the sending and receiving wires so that the wire used for transmitting by one device is used for receiving by the other and vice versa.

null modem cable *n.* A serial data cable used to connect two personal computers, without a modem or other DCE device in between, through the computers' serial ports. Because both computers use the same pins to send data, a null modem cable connects the output pins in one computer's serial port to the input pins in the other. A null modem cable is used to transfer data between two personal computers that are in close proximity. *See also* DCE, serial port.

number cruncher *n.* **1.** A computer that is able to quickly perform large amounts of mathematical computation. **2.** A powerful workstation. **3.** A program whose main task is to perform mathematical computations; for example, a statistical program. **4.** A person who uses a computer to analyze numbers.

numeric coprocessor *n. See* floating-point processor.

numeric keypad *n.* A calculator-style block of keys, usually at the right side of a keyboard, that can be used to enter numbers. In addition to keys for the digits 0 through 9 and keys for indicating addition, subtraction, multiplication, and division, a numeric keypad often includes an Enter key (usually not the same as the Enter or Return key on the main part of the keyboard). On Apple keyboards, the numeric keypad also includes a Clear key that usually functions like the Backspace key for deleting characters. In addition, many of the keys can serve dual purposes, such as cursor movement, scrolling, or editing tasks, depending on the status of the Num Lock key. *See also* Num Lock key.

Num Lock key *n.* Short for **Num**eric **Lock key**. A toggle key that, when turned on, activates the numeric keypad so that its keys can be used for calculator-style data entry. When the Num Lock key is toggled off, most of the numeric keypad keys are used for cursor movement and on-screen scrolling. *See also* numeric keypad.

nybble *n. See* nibble.

O

object *n.* **1.** Short for object code (machine-readable code). **2.** In object-oriented programming, a variable including both routines and data that is treated as a discrete entity. *See also* module (definition 1), object-oriented programming. **3.** In graphics, a distinct entity. For example, a bouncing ball might be an object in a graphics program.

object code *n.* The code, generated by a compiler or an assembler, that was translated from the source code of a program. The term most commonly refers to machine code that can be directly executed by the system's CPU. *See also* central processing unit.

object database *n.* *See* object-oriented database.

object linking and embedding *n.* *See* OLE.

Object Management Architecture *n.* *See* OMA.

object-oriented *adj.* Of, pertaining to, or being a system or language that supports the use of objects. *See also* object (definition 2).

object-oriented database *n.* A flexible database that supports the use of object-oriented programming constructs and that can store a wide range of data, often including sound, video, and graphics in addition to text and numbers. Some object-oriented databases allow data retrieval procedures and rules for processing data to be stored along with the data or in place of it. This allows the data to be stored in areas other than in the physical database, which is often desirable when the data files are large, such as those for video files. *Acronym:* OODB. *Also called* object database. *See also* object (definition 2), object-oriented programming. *Compare* relational database.

object-oriented design *n.* A modular approach to creating a software product or computer system, in which the modules (objects) can be easily and affordably adapted to meet new needs. *See also* object (definition 2).

object-oriented graphics *n.* Computer graphics that are based on the use of graphics primitives, such as lines, curves, circles, and squares. In contrast to bitmapped graphics, object-oriented graphics, which are used in applications such as CAD and drawing programs, describe an image mathematically as a set of instructions for creating the objects in the image. Object-oriented graphics enable the user to manipulate objects as units. Because the objects are described mathematically, object-oriented graphics can be layered, rotated, and magnified relatively easily. *Also called* structured graphics. *See also* graphics primitive. *Compare* bitmapped graphics, paint program.

object-oriented interface *n.* A user interface in which elements of the system are represented by visible screen entities, such as icons, that are used to

A B C D E F G H I J K L M N O P Q R S T U V W X Y Z

manipulate the system elements. An object-oriented display interface does not necessarily imply any relation to object-oriented programming. *See also* object-oriented graphics.

object-oriented operating system *n.* An operating system based on objects and designed in a manner that facilitates software development by third parties, using an object-oriented design. *See also* object (definition 2), object-oriented design.

object-oriented programming *n.* A programming paradigm in which a program is viewed as a collection of discrete objects that are self-contained collections of data structures and routines that interact with other objects. *Acronym:* OOP. *See also* C++, object (definition 2).

object-relational server *n.* A database server that supports object-oriented management of complex data types in a relational database. *See also* database server, relational database.

oblique *adj.* Describing a style of text created by slanting a roman typeface to simulate italics when a true italic typeface isn't available on the computer or printer. *See also* italic, roman, typeface.

OCR *n. See* optical character recognition.

octal *adj.* Of or pertaining to the base-8 number system. The octal system uses the eight digits 0 through 7. This system is used in programming as a compact means of representing binary numbers.

OCX *n.* Short for **O**LE **c**ustom control. A software module based on OLE and COM technologies that, when called by an application, produces a control that attaches a desired feature to the application. OCX technology is portable across platforms, works on both 16-bit and 32-bit operating systems, and can be used with many applications. It is the basis for ActiveX controls. *See also* ActiveX controls, COM (definition 2), control (definition 2), OLE.

ODBC *n.* Acronym for **o**pen **d**ata**b**ase **c**onnectivity. In the Microsoft WOSA structure, an interface providing a common language for Windows-based applications to gain access to a database on a network. *See also* WOSA.

odd parity *n. See* parity.

OEM *n. See* original equipment manufacturer.

offline *adj.* **1.** In reference to a computing device or a program, unable to communicate with or be controlled by a computer. *Compare* online (definition 1). **2.** In reference to one or more computers, being disconnected from a network. *Compare* online (definition 2).

offline navigator *n.* Software designed to download e-mail, Web pages, or newsgroup articles or postings from other online forums and save them locally to a disk, where they can be browsed without the user paying the cost of idle time while being connected to the Internet or an online information service. *Also called* offline reader.

offline reader *n. See* offline navigator.

offline storage *n.* A storage resource, such as a disk, that is not currently available to the system.

offload *vb.* To assume part of the processing demand from another device. For example, some LAN-attached gateways can offload TCP/IP processing from the host machine, thereby freeing up significant processing capacity in the CPU. *See also* gateway, host, TCP/IP.
off-the-shelf *adj.* Ready-to-use; packaged. The term can refer to hardware or software.
OLE *n.* Acronym for **o**bject **l**inking and **e**mbedding. A technology for transferring and sharing information among applications. When an object, such as an image file created with a paint program, is linked to a compound document, such as a document created with a word processing program, the document contains only a reference to the object; any changes made to the contents of the linked object will be seen in the compound document. When an object is embedded in a compound document, the document contains a copy of the object; any changes made to the contents of the original object will not be seen in the compound document unless the embedded object is updated.
OLTP *n.* Acronym for **onl**ine **t**ransaction **p**rocessing. A system for processing transactions as soon as the computer receives them and updating master files immediately in a database management system. OLTP is useful in financial record keeping and inventory tracking. *See also* database management system, transaction processing. *Compare* batch processing (definition 3).
OMA *n.* Acronym for **O**bject **M**anagement **A**rchitecture. A definition for object-oriented distributed processing. OMA includes the Common Object Request Broker Architecture (CORBA). *See also* CORBA.
on-board computer *n.* A computer that resides within another device.
one-off *n.* **1.** A product that is produced one at a time, instead of being mass-produced. **2.** A CD-ROM created on a CD-R machine, which can create only one copy of a CD-ROM at a time.
online *adj.* **1.** In reference to a computing device or a program, activated and ready for operation; capable of communicating with or being controlled by a computer. *Compare* offline (definition 1). **2.** In reference to one or more computers, connected to a network. *Compare* offline (definition 2). **3.** In reference to a user, currently connected to the Internet, an online service, or a BBS or using a modem to connect to another modem. **4.** In reference to a user, being able to connect to the Internet, an online service, or a BBS by virtue of having an account that gives the user access.
online community *n.* **1.** All users of the Internet and World Wide Web collectively. **2.** A local community that places political forums online for the discussion of local government or issues of public concern. **3.** Members of a specific newsgroup, mailing list, MUD, BBS, or other online forum or group. *See also* BBS (definition 1), mailing list, MUD, newsgroup.
online help *n. See* help.
online information service *n.* A business that provides access to databases, file archives, conferences, chat groups, and other forms of information through dial-up or dedicated communications links or through the

A B C D E F G H I J K L M N O P Q R S T U V W X Y Z

Internet. Most online information services also offer access to Internet connections along with their own proprietary services.

online service *n. See* online information service.

online state *n.* The state of a modem when it is communicating with another modem. *Compare* command state.

online transaction processing *n. See* OLTP.

on the fly *adv.* Doing a task or process as needed without suspending or disturbing normal operations. For example, it is often said that an HTML document can be edited on the fly because its content can be revised without the need to completely shut down or re-create the Web site on which it resides. *See also* HTML document, Web site.

OO *adj. See* object-oriented.

OOP *n. See* object-oriented programming.

open¹ *adj.* Of, pertaining to, or providing accessibility. For example, an open file is one that can be used.

open² *vb.* To make an object, such as a file, accessible. For example, a program can make a file accessible to a user by issuing a command to the operating system to open the file.

open architecture *n.* **1.** Any computer or peripheral design that has published specifications. A published specification lets third parties develop add-on hardware for a computer or device. *Compare* closed architecture (definition 1). **2.** A design that provides for expansion slots on the motherboard, thereby allowing the addition of boards to enhance or customize a system. *Compare* closed architecture (definition 2).

OpenDoc *n.* An object-oriented application programming interface (API) that enables multiple independent programs on several platforms to work together on a single document (compound document). Similar to OLE, OpenDoc allows images, sound, video, other documents, and other files to be embedded in or linked to the document. *See also* application programming interface. *Compare* ActiveX, OLE.

open file *n.* A file that can be read from, written to, or both. A program must first open a file before the file's contents can be used, and it must close the file when done. *See also* open².

Open Group *n.* An international, nonprofit consortium of firms that promotes the development of multivendor technologies such as the Distributed Computing Environment (DCE), which makes it possible to create applications that run on multiple platforms at one time. The Open Group was formed in 1996 with the merger of two groups: the Open Software Foundation (OSF) and X/Open Company Ltd.

Open Software Foundation *n. See* Open Group.

open standard *n.* A publicly available set of specifications describing the characteristics of a hardware device or software program. Open standards are published to encourage interoperability and thereby help popularize new technologies. *See also* standard (definition 2).

open system *n.* **1.** In communications, a computer network designed to incorporate all devices—regardless of the manufacturer or model—that can use the same communications facilities and protocols. **2.** In reference to computer hardware or software, a system that can accept add-ons produced by third-party suppliers. *See also* open architecture (definition 1).

Open Systems Interconnection model *n. See* ISO/OSI model.

operand *n.* The object of a mathematical operation or a computer instruction.

operating system *n.* The software that controls the allocation and usage of hardware resources such as memory, CPU time, disk space, and peripheral devices. The operating system is the foundation on which applications are built. Popular operating systems include Windows 95, Windows NT, the Mac OS, and UNIX. *Acronym:* OS. *Also called* executive.

operation *n.* **1.** A specific action carried out by a computer in the process of executing a program. **2.** In mathematics, an action performed on a set of entities that produces a new entity. Examples of mathematical operations are addition and subtraction.

operator *n.* **1.** In mathematics and in programming and computer applications, a symbol or other character indicating an operation that acts on one or more elements. *See also* operation (definition 2). **2.** A person who controls a machine or system, such as a computer or a telephone switchboard.

operator precedence *n.* The priority of the various operators when more than one is used in an expression. In the absence of parentheses, operations with higher precedence are performed first. *See also* operator (definition 1).

optical character recognition *n.* The process in which an electronic device such as a scanner or reader examines printed characters on paper, determines their shapes by detecting patterns of dark and light, and then uses character recognition methods to translate the shapes into computer text. *Acronym:* OCR. *See also* character recognition. *Compare* magnetic-ink character recognition.

optical communications *n.* The use of light and of light-transmitting technology, such as optical fibers and lasers, in sending and receiving data, images, or sound.

optical disc *n. See* compact disc.

optical drive *n.* A disk drive that reads and often can write data on optical (compact) discs. Examples of optical drives include CD-ROM drives and WORM disc drives. *See also* CD-ROM drive, compact disc, WORM.

optical fiber *n.* A thin strand of transparent material used to carry optical signals. Optical fibers are inexpensive, compact, and lightweight and are often packaged many hundred to a single cable. *See also* fiber optics.

optical mouse *n.* A type of mouse that uses a pair of light-emitting diodes (LEDs) and a special reflective mouse pad to detect motion. The two lights are of different colors, and the mouse pad has a grid of lines in the same colors, one color for vertical lines and another for horizontal. Light detectors paired with the LEDs sense when a colored light passes over a line of the

A B C D E F G H I J K L M N O P Q R S T U V W X Y Z

same color, indicating the direction of movement. *See also* mouse. *Compare* mechanical mouse, optomechanical mouse.

optical reader *n.* A device that reads text from printed paper by detecting the pattern of light and dark on a page and then applying optical character recognition methods to identify the characters. *See also* optical character recognition.

optical recognition *n. See* optical character recognition.

optical scanner *n.* An input device that uses light-sensing equipment to scan paper or another medium, translating the pattern of light and dark or color into a digital signal that can be manipulated by either optical character recognition software or graphics software. *See also* flatbed scanner, handheld scanner, sheet-fed scanner. *Compare* magnetic-ink character recognition.

optimizer *n.* A program or device that improves the performance of a computer, network, or other device or system. For example, a disk optimizer program reduces file access time.

optional hyphen *n. See* hyphen.

Option key *n.* A key on Apple Macintosh keyboards that, when pressed in combination with another key, produces special characters: graphics, such as boxes; international characters, such as currency symbols; and special punctuation marks, such as en dashes and em dashes. The Option key serves a purpose similar to that of the Control key or the Alt key on IBM and compatible keyboards in that it changes the meaning of the key with which it is used.

Options *n. See* Preferences.

optomechanical mouse *n.* A type of mouse in which motion is translated into directional signals through a combination of optical means (pairs of light-emitting diodes and matching sensors) and mechanical means (rotating wheels with cutout slits). When the mouse is moved, the wheels turn and the light from the LEDs either passes through the slits and strikes a light sensor or is blocked by the solid portions of the wheels. These changes in light contact are detected by the sensors and interpreted as indications of movement. An optomechanical mouse does not need as much wear-related repair and maintenance as a purely mechanical mouse, nor does it require the special operating surfaces associated with optical mice. *See also* mouse. *Compare* mechanical mouse, optical mouse.

OR *n.* A logical operation for combining two bits (0 or 1) or two Boolean values (false or true). If one or both values are 1 (true), it returns the value 1 (true); otherwise it returns the value 0 (false).

order[1] *n.* **1.** In computing, the relative significance of a digit or byte. The term high-order refers to the most significant (usually leftmost) digit or byte; the term low-order refers to the least significant (usually rightmost) digit or byte. **2.** The magnitude of a database in terms of the number of fields it contains. **3.** The sequence in which arithmetic operations are performed.

order[2] *vb.* To arrange in a sequence, such as alphabetic or numeric.

.org *n.* In the Internet's Domain Name System, the top-level domain that identifies addresses operated by organizations that do not fit in any of the other standard domains. The designation .org appears as a suffix at the end of the address. *See also* DNS (definition 1), domain (definition 3). *Compare* .com, .edu, .gov, .mil, .net.

orientation *n. See* landscape mode, portrait mode.

original equipment manufacturer *n.* The maker of a piece of equipment. In making computers and related equipment, manufacturers of original equipment typically purchase components from other manufacturers of original equipment, integrate them into their own products, and then sell the products to the public. *Acronym:* OEM. *Compare* value-added reseller.

orphan *n.* The first line of a paragraph printed alone at the bottom of a page or column of text, or the last line of a paragraph printed alone at the top of a page or column. Orphans are visually unattractive and thus undesirable in printed materials. *Compare* widow.

orphan file *n.* A file that remains on a system after it has ceased to be of use. For example, a file may be created to support a particular application but may remain after the application has been removed.

OS *n. See* operating system.

OS/2 *n.* A protected-mode, virtual-memory, multitasking operating system for personal computers based on the Intel 80286, 80386, i486, and Pentium processors. OS/2 can run most MS-DOS applications and can read all MS-DOS disks. Important OS/2 subsystems include Presentation Manager, which provides a graphical user interface, and LAN Manager, which provides networking facilities. OS/2 was initially developed as a joint project of Microsoft and IBM but is now an IBM product. *See also* protected mode, virtual memory.

OSF *n. See* Open Group.

OSI *n. See* ISO/OSI model.

OTOH Acronym for **o**n **t**he **o**ther **h**and. A shorthand expression often used in e-mail, Internet newsgroups, and discussion groups.

Outbox *n.* In many e-mail applications, the default mailbox where the program stores outgoing messages. *See also* e-mail[1] (definition 1), mailbox. *Compare* Inbox.

outdent *n. See* hanging indent.

outline font *n.* A font stored in a computer or printer as a set of outlines for drawing each of the alphabetic and other characters in a character set. Outline fonts are templates rather than actual patterns of dots, and they are scaled up or down to match a particular type size. Such fonts are most often used for printing, as is the case with most PostScript fonts on a PostScript-compatible laser printer and TrueType fonts. *Compare* bitmapped font, screen font, stroke font.

out-of-band signaling *n.* Transmission of some signals, such as control information, on frequencies outside the bandwidth available for voice or data transfer on a communications channel.

output[1] *n.* The results of processing, whether sent to the screen or printer, stored on disk as a file, or sent to another computer in a network.

output² *vb.* To send out data by a computer or sound by a speaker.
output channel *n. See* channel (definition 1), input/output channel.
overhead *n.* Work or information that provides support—possibly critical support—for a computing process but is not an intrinsic part of the operation or data. Overhead often adds to processing time but is generally necessary.
overlaid windows *n. See* cascading windows.
overlay¹ *n.* **1.** A section of a program designed to reside on a designated storage device, such as a disk, and to be loaded into memory when needed, usually overwriting one or more overlays already in memory. Use of overlays allows large programs to fit into a limited amount of memory, but at the cost of speed. **2.** A printed form positioned over a screen, tablet, or keyboard for identification of particular features. *See also* keyboard template.
overlay² *vb.* **1.** In computer graphics, to superimpose one graphic image over another. **2.** In video, to superimpose a graphic image generated on a computer over video signals, either live or recorded.
overprint *vb.* To print an element of one color over an element of another color without removing, or knocking out, the material underneath. *Compare* knockout (definition 1).
override *vb.* To prevent something from happening in a program or in an operating system or to initiate another response. For example, a user can often override and thus abort a lengthy sorting procedure in a database program by pressing the Escape key.
overrun *n.* In information transfer, an error that occurs when a device receiving data cannot handle or make use of the information as rapidly as it arrives.
overscan *n.* The part of a video signal sent to a raster display that controls the area outside the rectangle containing visual information. The overscan area is sometimes colored to form a border around the screen.
overstrike *vb.* To type or print one character directly over another so that the two occupy the same space on the page or screen.
overtype mode *n. See* overwrite mode.
overwrite mode *n.* A text-entry mode in which newly typed characters replace existing characters under or to the left of the cursor or insertion point. *Also called* overtype mode, typeover mode. *Compare* insert mode.

P

P5 *n.* Intel Corporation's internal working name for the Pentium microprocessor. Although it was not intended to be used publicly, the name P5 leaked out to the computer-industry trade press and was commonly used to reference the microprocessor before it was released. *See also* 586, Pentium.

pack *vb.* To store information in a more compact form. Packing eliminates unnecessary spaces and other such characters and may also use other special methods of compressing data. Some programs use packing to minimize storage requirements.

package *n.* **1.** A computer application consisting of one or more programs created to perform a particular type of work—for example, an accounting package. **2.** In electronics, the housing in which an electronic component is packaged. *See also* DIP.

packaged software *n.* A software program sold through a retail distributor, as opposed to custom software. *Compare* canned software.

packet *n.* **1.** A unit of information transmitted as a whole from one device to another on a network. **2.** In packet-switching networks, a transmission unit of fixed maximum size that consists of binary digits representing both data and a header containing an identification number, source and destination addresses, and sometimes error-control data. *See also* packet switching.

packet filtering *n.* The process of controlling network access based on IP addresses. Firewalls often incorporate filters that allow or deny users the ability to enter or leave a LAN. Packet filtering is also used to accept or reject packets such as e-mail, based on the origin of the packet, to ensure security on a private network. *See also* firewall, IP address, packet (definition 1).

Packet Internet Groper *n. See* ping[1] (definition 1).

packet switching *n.* A message-delivery technique in which small units of information (packets) are relayed through stations in a computer network along the best route available between the source and the destination. A packet-switching network (for example, the Internet) usually breaks long messages into multiple packets before routing; when the packets arrive at their destination, the receiving computer reassembles the original message correctly. Packet-switching networks are considered fast and efficient.

paddle *n.* An early type of input device often used with computer games, especially for side-to-side or up-and-down movements of an on-screen object. A paddle is less sophisticated than a joystick because it permits the user, by turning a dial, to specify movement only along a single axis.

paddle switch *n.* Any switch that has a wide handle. The large on/off switch on many IBM personal computers is one type of paddle switch.

page *n.* **1.** In word processing, the text and display elements to be printed on one side of a sheet of paper, subject to formatting specifications such as depth, margin size, and number of columns. **2.** A fixed-size block of memory. When used in the context of a paging memory system, a page is a block of memory whose physical address can be changed via mapping hardware. *See also* EMS, virtual memory. **3.** In computer graphics, a portion of display memory that contains one complete full-screen image; the internal representation of a screenful of information.

page break *n.* The point at which the flow of text in a document moves to the top of a new page. Most word processors automatically place a page break when the material on the page reaches a specified maximum. By contrast, a "hard" or "manual" page break is a command or code inserted by the user to force a page break at a specific place in the text. *See also* form feed.

page-description language *n.* A programming language, such as PostScript, that is used to describe output to a printer or a display device, which then uses the instructions from the language to construct text and graphics that create the required page image. A page-description language, like a blueprint, sets out specifications (such as for fonts) but leaves the detail work of drawing characters and graphics to the output device itself. Page-description languages are machine-independent, but they require printers with processing power and memory comparable to, and often exceeding, that of personal computers. *Acronym:* PDL. *See also* PostScript.

Page Down key *n.* A standard key (often labeled PgDn) on most computer keyboards that typically moves the cursor down to the top of the next page or down a specific number of lines. The specific meaning of this key can vary in different programs.

page frame *n.* A physical address to which a page of virtual memory may be mapped. In a system with 4,096-byte pages, page frame 0 corresponds to physical addresses 0 through 4,095. *See also* paging, virtual memory.

page layout *n.* In desktop publishing, the process of arranging text and graphics on the pages of a document. Although page-layout programs are generally slower than word processing programs, they can perform such advanced tasks as flowing text into complex multicolumn page designs, applying special effects to text, printing documents in signatures, managing color separations, and supporting sophisticated kerning and hyphenation.

page makeup *n.* The assembling of graphics and text on a page in preparation for printing.

page orientation *n.* *See* landscape mode, portrait mode.

page printer *n.* Any printer, such as a laser printer, that prints an entire page at once. Because page printers must store the entire page in memory before printing, they require relatively large amounts of memory. *Compare* line printer.

page reader *n. See* document reader.
page setup *n.* A set of choices that affect how a file is printed on the page. Page setup might reflect the size of paper, the page margins, the specific document pages to be printed, and whether the image is to be reduced or enlarged when printed.
pages per minute *n.* Abbreviated PPM or ppm. A rating of a printer's output capacity—that is, the number of printed pages the printer can produce in one minute. A printer's PPM rating is usually provided by the manufacturer and is based on a "normal" page. Pages with excessive graphics or fonts may reduce a printer's PPM rate dramatically.
Page Up key *n.* A standard key (often labeled PgUp) on most computer keyboards that typically moves the cursor up to the top of the previous page or up a specific number of lines. The specific meaning of this key can vary in different programs.
pagination *n.* **1.** The process of dividing a document into pages for printing. **2.** The process of adding page numbers, as in a running head.
paging *n.* A technique for implementing virtual memory. The virtual address space is divided into a number of fixed-size blocks called pages, each of which can be mapped onto any of the physical addresses available on the system. Special memory management hardware performs the address translation from virtual addresses to physical addresses. *See also* virtual memory.
paint[1] *n.* A color and pattern used with graphics programs to fill areas of a drawing, applied with tools such as a paintbrush or a spraycan.
paint[2] *vb.* To fill a portion of a drawing with paint.
paintbrush *n.* An artist's tool in a paint program or another graphics application for applying a streak of solid color to an image. The user can usually select the width of the streak. *See also* paint program. *Compare* spraycan.
paint program *n.* An application that creates graphics as bit maps. A paint program is particularly appropriate for freehand drawing because it treats a drawing as a group of dots. Such a program commonly provides tools for images requiring lines, curves, and geometric shapes but does not treat any shape as an entity that can be moved or modified as a discrete object without losing its identity. *Compare* drawing program.
palette *n.* **1.** In paint programs, a collection of drawing tools, such as patterns, colors, brush shapes, and line widths, from which the user can choose. **2.** A subset of the color look-up table that establishes the colors that can be displayed on the screen at a particular time. The number of colors in a palette is determined by the number of bits used to represent a pixel. *See also* color bits, color look-up table, pixel.
palmtop *n.* A portable personal computer whose size enables it to be held in one hand while it is operated. Unlike laptop computers, palmtops are usually powered by off-the-shelf batteries such as AA cells. Palmtops typically do not have disk drives; rather, their programs are stored in ROM and are loaded into RAM when they are switched on. More recent palmtop computers are equipped with PCMCIA slots to provide wider flexibility and

greater capability. *See also* handheld PC, PCMCIA slot, PDA, portable computer. *Compare* laptop.

panning *n.* In computer graphics, a display method in which a viewing window on the screen scans horizontally or vertically, like a camera, to bring offscreen extensions of the current image smoothly into view.

Pantone Matching System *n.* In graphic arts and printing, a standard system of ink color specification consisting of a swatch book in which each of about 500 colors is assigned a number. *Acronym:* PMS. *See also* color model.

PAP *n.* **1.** Acronym for **P**assword **A**uthentication **P**rotocol. A method for verifying the identity of a user attempting to log on to a Point-to-Point Protocol server. **2.** Acronym for **P**rinter **A**ccess **P**rotocol. The protocol in AppleTalk networks that governs communication between computers and printers.

paper feed *n.* A mechanism that moves paper through a printer. In laser printers and other page printers, the paper feed is usually a series of rollers that firmly grip and align the paper. *See also* friction feed, pin feed, sheet feeder, tractor feed.

paper-white *adj.* Of, pertaining to, or being a type of monochrome computer monitor whose default operating colors are black text on a white background. Paper-white monitors are popular in desktop publishing and word processing environments because the monitor resembles a white sheet of paper printed with black characters.

paradigm *n.* An archetypical example or pattern that provides a model for a process or system.

paragraph *n.* In word processing, any part of a document preceded by one paragraph mark and ending with another. To the program, a paragraph represents a unit of information that can be selected as a whole or given formatting distinct from the surrounding paragraphs.

parallel *adj.* **1.** In data communications, of, relating to, or being information that is sent in groups of bits over multiple wires, one wire for each bit in a group. *See also* parallel interface. *Compare* serial. **2.** In data handling, of or relating to handling more than one event at a time, with each event having its own portion of the system's resources. *See also* parallel processing.

parallel access *n.* The ability to store or retrieve all of the bits composing a single unit of information, such as a byte, at the same time. *Also called* simultaneous access.

parallel computer *n.* A computer that uses several processors that work concurrently. Software written for parallel computers can increase the amount of work done in a specific amount of time by dividing a computing task among several simultaneously functioning processors. *See also* parallel processing.

parallel computing *n.* The use of multiple computers or processors to solve a problem or perform a function. *See also* SMP.

parallel database *n.* A database system involving the concurrent use of two or more processors or operating system processes to service database management requests such as SQL queries and updates, transaction logging, and I/O handling. A parallel database can perform many simultaneous tasks across multiple processors and storage devices, providing quick access to databases containing many gigabytes of data.

parallel interface *n.* The specification of a data transmission scheme that sends multiple data and control bits simultaneously over wires connected in parallel. *Compare* serial interface.

parallel port *n.* The input/output connector for a parallel interface device. *See also* input/output port.

parallel printer *n.* A printer that is connected to the computer via a parallel interface. In general, a parallel connection can move data between devices faster than a serial connection can. The parallel interface is preferred in the IBM PC world because its cabling is more standardized than that of the serial interface and because the MS-DOS operating system assumes that the system printer is attached to the parallel port. *See also* parallel interface. *Compare* serial printer.

parallel processing *n.* A method of processing that can run only on a computer that contains two or more processors running simultaneously. Parallel processing differs from multiprocessing in the way a program's work is distributed over the available processors. In multiprocessing, the work might be separated into distinct tasks that are divided among the processors. In parallel processing, the work of each distinct task can be split among several processors, which makes it possible to distribute all the work more or less evenly among the processors. *Compare* coprocessor, multiprocessing.

parallel transmission *n.* The simultaneous transmission of a group of bits over separate wires. With microcomputers, parallel transmission refers to the transmission of 1 byte (8 bits). *Compare* serial transmission.

parameter RAM *n. See* PRAM.

parent/child *adj.* **1.** Pertaining to or constituting a relationship between processes in a multitasking environment in which the parent process calls the child process and most often suspends its own operation until the child process aborts or is completed. **2.** Pertaining to or constituting a relationship between nodes in a tree data structure in which the parent is one step closer to the root (that is, one level higher) than the child.

parity *n.* The quality of sameness or equivalence; in the case of computers, usually referring to an error-checking procedure in which the number of 1s must always be the same—either even or odd—for each group of bits transmitted without error. In typical modem-to-modem communications, parity is one of the settings that must be agreed upon by sending and receiving parties before transmission can take place. When an even parity setting is used, the number of 1s in each successfully transmitted set of bits must be an even number. When odd parity is used, the number of 1s in each successfully transmitted set of bits must be an odd number. Other types of parity include space parity (a parity bit is used and is always set to 0), mark parity (a parity bit is used and is always set to 1), and no parity (no parity bit is used). *See also* parity bit, parity check, parity error.

A B C D E F G H I J K L M N O P Q R S T U V W X Y Z

parity bit *n.* An extra bit used in checking for errors in groups of data bits transferred within or between computer systems. With microcomputers, a parity bit is often used in modem-to-modem communications to check the accuracy with which each character is transmitted. A parity bit is also often used to check the accuracy with which each byte is stored in RAM.

parity check *n.* The use of parity to check the accuracy of transmitted data. *See also* parity, parity bit.

parity error *n.* An error in parity that indicates an error in transmitted data or in data stored in memory. If a parity error occurs in communications, all or part of a message must be retransmitted; if a parity error occurs in RAM, the computer usually halts. *See also* parity, parity bit.

park *vb.* To position the read/write head over a portion of a disk that stores no data (and therefore can never be damaged) or beyond the surface of the disk, prior to shutting down the drive, especially in preparation for moving it. Parking can be performed manually, automatically, or, most typically, by a disk utility program.

parse *vb.* To break input into smaller chunks so that a program can act upon the information.

partition *n.* **1.** A logically distinct portion of memory or a storage device that functions as though it were a physically separate unit. **2.** In database programming, a subset of a database table or file.

passive-matrix display *n.* An inexpensive, low-resolution LCD made from a large array of liquid crystal cells that are controlled by transistors outside the display screen. One transistor controls an entire row or column of pixels. Passive-matrix displays are common in portable computers, such as laptops and notebooks, because of their thin width. While these displays have good contrast for monochrome screens, the resolution is weaker for color screens. Passive-matrix displays are also difficult to view from any angle other than straight on, unlike more expensive active-matrix displays. *Also called* dual-scan display. *See also* liquid crystal display, transistor. *Compare* active-matrix display.

password *n.* A security measure used to restrict access to computer systems and sensitive files. A password is a unique string of characters that a user types in as an identification code. The system compares the code against a stored list of authorized passwords and users. If the code is legitimate, the system allows the user access at whatever security level has been approved for the owner of the password.

Password Authentication Protocol *n. See* PAP (definition 1).

password protection *n.* The use of passwords as a means of allowing only authorized users access to a computer system or its files.

paste *vb.* To insert text or a graphic that has been cut or copied from one document into a different location in the same or a different document. *See also* cut, cut and paste.

patch[1] *n.* A piece of object code inserted in an executable program as a temporary fix of a bug.

patch² *vb.* In programming, to repair a deficiency in the functionality of an existing routine or program, generally in response to an unforeseen need or set of operating circumstances. Patching is a common means of adding a feature or a function to a program until the next version of the software is released. *Compare* hack¹ (definition 2), kludge (definition 2).

path *n.* **1.** In communications, a link between two nodes in a network. **2.** A route through a structured collection of information, as in a database, a program, or files stored on disk. **3.** In file storage, the route followed by the operating system through the directories in finding, sorting, and retrieving files on a disk. **4.** In graphics, an accumulation of line segments or curves to be filled or drawn.

pathname *n.* In a hierarchical filing system, a listing of the directories or folders that lead from the current directory to a file. *Also called* directory path.

Pause key *n.* **1.** A key on a keyboard that temporarily stops the operation of a program or a command. The Pause key is used, for example, to halt scrolling so that a multiscreen document can be read. **2.** Any key that creates a pause in an operation. For example, many game programs have a Pause key, often simply the P key, that temporarily suspends the game.

PC *n.* **1.** A microcomputer that conforms to the standard developed by IBM for personal computers, which uses a microprocessor in the Intel 80x86 family (or compatible) and can execute the BIOS. *See also* BIOS, clone, IBM PC. **2.** A computer in IBM's Personal Computer line. *Also called* IBM PC. *See also* PC-compatible (definition 1). **3.** *See* personal computer.

PCB *n.* *See* printed circuit board.

PC board *n.* *See* printed circuit board.

PC Card *n.* A trademark of the Personal Computer Memory Card International Association (PCMCIA) that is used to describe add-in cards that conform to the PCMCIA specification. A PC Card is a removable device, approximately the same size as a credit card, that is designed to plug into a PCMCIA slot. A Type I card is intended to be used primarily as a memory-related peripheral. Type II cards accommodate devices such as modem, fax, and network cards. Type III cards accommodate devices that require more space, such as wireless communications devices and rotating storage media (such as hard disks). *See also* PCMCIA slot.

PC Card slot *n.* *See* PCMCIA slot.

PC-compatible *adj.* **1.** Conforming to IBM PC/XT and PC/AT hardware and software specifications, which have been the de facto standard in the computing industry for personal computers that use the Intel 80x86 family or compatible chips. Most PC-compatible computers today are developed outside IBM; they are still sometimes referred to as clones. *Also called* IBM PC-compatible. *See also* clone, IBM AT, IBM PC. **2.** *See* Wintel.

PC-DOS *n.* Acronym for **P**ersonal **C**omputer **D**isk **O**perating **S**ystem. The version of MS-DOS sold by IBM. MS-DOS and PC-DOS are virtually identical, although filenames of utility programs sometimes differ in the two versions. *See also* MS-DOS.

PCI *n. See* PCI local bus.

PCI local bus *n.* Short for **P**eripheral **C**omponent **I**nterconnect **local bus.** A specification introduced by Intel that defines a local bus system allowing up to 10 PCI-compliant expansion cards to be installed in the computer. A PCI local bus system requires the presence of a PCI controller card, which must be installed in a PCI-compliant slot. The PCI controller can exchange data with the system's CPU either 32 bits or 64 bits at a time, depending on the implementation, and it allows intelligent, PCI-compliant adapters to perform tasks concurrently with the CPU using a technique called bus mastering. The PCI specification allows for multiplexing. *See also* local bus, multiplexing. *Compare* VL bus.

PCL *n. See* Printer Control Language.

PCMCIA card *n. See* PC Card.

PCMCIA connector *n.* The 68-pin female connector inside a PCMCIA slot designed to hold the 68-pin male connector on a PC Card. *See also* PC Card, PCMCIA slot.

PCMCIA slot *n.* An opening in the housing of a computer, peripheral, or other intelligent electronic device designed to hold a PC Card. *Also called* PC Card slot. *See also* PC Card, PCMCIA connector.

PC memory card *n.* **1.** An add-in circuit card that increases the amount of RAM in a system. *See also* memory card. **2.** A Type I PC Card as specified by PCMCIA. In this context, such a card consists of conventional static RAM chips powered by a small battery and is designed to provide additional RAM to the system. *See also* PC Card. *Compare* flash memory.

.pcx *n.* The file extension that identifies bitmapped images in the PC Paintbrush file format.

PC/XT *n. See* IBM PC/XT.

PDA *n.* Acronym for **P**ersonal **D**igital **A**ssistant. A lightweight palmtop computer designed to provide functions such as personal organization (calendar, note taking, database, calculator, and so on) as well as communications. More advanced models also offer multimedia features. Many PDA devices rely on a pen or other pointing device for input instead of a standard keyboard or mouse. For data storage, a PDA relies on flash memory instead of power-hungry disk drives. *See also* firmware, flash memory, PC Card, pen computer.

PDD *n.* Acronym for **P**ortable **D**igital **D**ocument. A graphics file created from a document by QuickDraw GX under the Mac OS. PDDs are stored in a form independent of printer resolution; they print at the highest resolution available; and they can contain the original fonts used in the document. Therefore, a PDD can be printed by a computer other than the one on which it was created.

.pdf *n.* The file extension that identifies documents encoded in the Portable Document Format developed by Adobe Systems. In order to display or print a .pdf file, the user should obtain the freeware Adobe Acrobat Reader. *See also* Acrobat, Portable Document Format.

PDF *n. See* Portable Document Format.
PDL *n. See* page-description language.
PDS *n.* Acronym for **P**rocessor **D**irect **S**lot. An expansion slot in Macintosh computers that is connected directly to the CPU signals. There are several kinds of PDS slots with different numbers of pins and different sets of signals, depending on which CPU is used in a particular computer.
peer *n.* Any of the devices on a layered communications network that operate on the same protocol level. *See also* network architecture.
peer-to-peer architecture *n.* A network of two or more computers that use the same program or type of program to communicate and share data. Each computer, or peer, is considered equal in terms of responsibilities, and each acts as a server to the others in the network. In contrast to a client/server architecture, a dedicated file server is not required. Network performance is generally not as good as under client/server, especially under heavy loads. *Also called* peer-to-peer network. *See also* peer, peer-to-peer communications, server. *Compare* client/server architecture.
peer-to-peer communications *n.* Interaction between devices that operate on the same communications level on a network based on a layered architecture. *See also* network architecture.
peer-to-peer network *n. See* peer-to-peer architecture.
pel *n.* Short for **p**icture **el**ement. *See* pixel.
PEM *n. See* Privacy Enhanced Mail.
pen *n. See* light pen, stylus.
pen-based computing *n.* The process of entering handwritten symbols into a computer via a stylus and pressure-sensitive pad. *See also* pen computer.
pen computer *n.* Any of a class of computers whose primary input device is a pen (stylus) instead of a keyboard. A pen computer is usually a small, handheld device and has a flat semiconductor-based display such as an LCD display. It requires either a special operating system designed to work with the pen input device or a proprietary operating system designed to work with a specific-purpose device. The pen computer is the primary model for an emerging class of computers known as personal digital assistants (PDAs). *See also* clipboard computer, PC Card, PDA.
pen plotter *n.* A traditional graphics plotter that uses one or more colored pens to draw on paper. *See also* plotter. *Compare* electrostatic plotter.
Pentium *n.* A superscalar, CISC-based microprocessor containing 3.3 million transistors, introduced by Intel Corporation in March 1993 as the successor to the i486. The Pentium has a 32-bit address bus, a 64-bit data bus, a built-in floating-point unit and memory management unit, and a System Management Mode, which allows the microprocessor to slow or halt some system components when the system is idle or performing non-CPU-intensive tasks, thereby lessening power consumption. The Pentium also provides faster system performance and has some built-in features to ensure data integrity. *See also* CISC, i486DX, microprocessor, P5, superscalar. *Compare* Pentium Pro (definition 1).

Pentium Pro *n.* **1.** Intel's 150–200 MHz family of 32-bit processors, released in 1995. The Pentium Pro is considered the next generation of processors in the 80x86 family, following the Pentium, and is designed for running 32-bit operating systems and applications. *See also* 32-bit application, 32-bit operating system, microprocessor, Pentium. **2.** A PC that has a Pentium Pro processor.

Pentium upgradable *n.* **1.** An i486 motherboard capable of being adapted to run a Pentium-class processor. *See also* i486DX, microprocessor, motherboard, Pentium. **2.** A 486 PC that can be upgraded to Pentium class by adding a Pentium processor. *See also* i486DX.

performance monitor *n.* A process or program that appraises and records status information about various system devices and other processes.

peripheral *n.* In computing, a device, such as a disk drive, printer, modem, or joystick, that is connected to a computer and is controlled by the computer's microprocessor. *Also called* peripheral device. *See also* console.

Peripheral Component Interconnect *n.* *See* PCI local bus.

peripheral device *n.* *See* peripheral.

peripheral power supply *n.* An auxiliary source of electricity used by a computer or a device as a backup in case of a power failure. *Acronym:* PPS.

Perl *n.* Acronym for **P**ractical **E**xtraction and **R**eport **L**anguage. An interpreted language, based on C and several UNIX utilities, that was devised by Larry Wall at NASA's Jet Propulsion Laboratory. Perl has powerful features for extracting information from text files. A program in Perl is known as a script.

permanent storage *n.* A recording medium that retains the data recorded on it for long periods of time without power. Magnetic media, such as floppy disks or tape, are generally accepted as permanent, even though the magnetic fields that encode data in the media tend to fade eventually (in five years or more). *See also* nonvolatile memory.

permission *n.* In a networked or multi-user computer environment, the ability of a user to access a particular resource by means of his or her user account. Permissions are granted by the system administrator or other authorized person; these permissions are stored in the system (often in a file called a permissions log) and are checked when a user attempts to access a resource.

persistence *n.* A characteristic of some light-emitting materials, such as the phosphors used in CRTs, that causes an image to be retained for a short while after being irradiated, as by an electron beam in a CRT. The decay in persistence is sometimes called luminance decay.

persistent data *n.* Data stored in a database or on tape so that it is retained by the computer between sessions.

persistent link *n.* *See* hot link (definition 1).

persistent storage *n.* Memory that remains intact when the power to a device is turned off, such as ROM. *See also* memory.

personal computer *n.* A computer designed for use by one person at a time. Personal computers do not need to share the processing, disk, and printer resources of another computer. IBM PC-compatible computers and Apple Macintoshes are both examples of personal computers. *Acronym:* PC.

Personal Computer *n. See* IBM PC.

personal digital assistant *n. See* PDA.

personal finance manager *n.* A software application designed to assist the user in performing simple financial accounting tasks, such as balancing checkbooks and paying bills.

personal information manager *n. See* PIM.

perspective view *n.* In computer graphics, a display method that shows objects in three dimensions (height, width, and depth), with the depth aspect rendered according to the desired perspective. An advantage of perspective view is that it presents a more accurate representation of what the human eye perceives. *Compare* isometric view.

petabyte *n.* Abbreviated PB. A data unit of 1,125,899,906,842,624 (2^{50}) bytes, sometimes interpreted as 1 quadrillion bytes.

PgDn key *n. See* Page Down key.

PGP *n.* Acronym for **P**retty **G**ood **P**rivacy. A program for public key encryption, using the RSA algorithm, developed by Philip Zimmermann. PGP software is available in unsupported free versions and supported commercial versions. *See also* privacy, public key encryption, RSA encryption.

PgUp key *n. See* Page Up key.

phone connector *n.* An attachment, usually an RJ-11 connector, used to join a telephone line to a device such as a modem.

phoneme *n.* In linguistics, the smallest unit of speech that distinguishes one word sound from another. Phonemes are the elements on which computer speech is based.

phono connector *n.* An attachment used to connect a device, such as a microphone or headphones, to audio equipment or to a computer peripheral or adapter with audio capability.

phosphor *n.* Any substance capable of emitting light when struck by radiation. The inside surface of a CRT screen is coated with a phosphor that, when excited by an electron beam, displays an image on the screen. *See also* persistence.

PhotoCD *n.* A digitizing system from Kodak that allows 35mm film pictures, negatives, slides, and scanned images to be stored on a compact disc. Images are stored in a file format called Kodak PhotoCD IMAGE PAC File Format, or PCD. Many photography or film development businesses offer this service. Images stored on a PhotoCD can usually be viewed by any computer with CD-ROM capabilities and the software required to read PCD as well as by a variety of players designed to display images stored on CDs.

photo editor *n.* A graphics application used to manipulate an image, such as a scanned photograph, digitally.

#
A
B
C
D
E
F
G
H
I
J
K
L
M
N
O
P
Q
R
S
T
U
V
W
X
Y
Z

photorealism *n.* The process of creating images that are as close to photographic or "real-life" quality as possible. In computer graphics, photorealism requires powerful computers and highly sophisticated software and is heavily mathematical. *See also* ray tracing.

phreak¹ *n.* A person who breaks into, or cracks, telephone networks or other secured systems. In the 1970s, the telephone system used audible tones as switching signals, and phone phreaks used homebrew hardware to match the tones and steal long-distance service. *See also* homebrew. *Compare* cracker, hacker (definition 2).

phreak² *vb.* To break into, or crack, telephone networks or computer systems. *Compare* hack².

physical *adj.* In computing, of, pertaining to, or characteristic of a real, as opposed to a conceptual, piece of equipment or frame of reference. *Compare* logical (definition 2).

physical layer *n.* The first, or lowest, of the seven layers in the ISO/OSI model for standardizing computer-to-computer communications. The physical layer is totally hardware-oriented and deals with all aspects of establishing and maintaining a physical link between communicating computers. Among the specifications covered on the physical layer are cabling, electrical signals, and mechanical connections. *See also* ISO/OSI model.

physical memory *n.* Memory actually present in the system, as opposed to virtual memory. A computer might have only 4 MB of physical RAM but support a virtual memory capacity of 20 MB. *Compare* virtual memory.

physical network *n.* One of two ways of describing the topology, or layout, of a computer network. In contrast to a logical network, a physical network refers to the actual configuration of the hardware forming a network—that is, to the computers, the connecting hardware, and, especially, the cabling patterns that give the network its shape. Basic physical layouts include the bus, ring, and star topologies. *See also* bus network, ring network, star network. *Compare* logical network.

physical storage *n.* *See* real storage.

pica *n.* As used by typographers, a unit of measure equal to 12 points or approximately ⅙ inch. *See also* point¹ (definition 1).

picosecond *n.* Abbreviated psec. One trillionth of a second.

PICS *n.* Acronym for **P**latform for **I**nternet **C**ontent **S**election. A standard that enables users to filter their Web access automatically using software that detects codes for ratings in the HTML files of Web sites. In addition to filtering out undesirable material, PICS can be used to screen sites according to whether they contain material of interest. Several rating systems, emphasizing different sets of criteria, are in use.

.pict *n.* The file extension that identifies graphical images in the Macintosh PICT format. *See also* PICT.

PICT *n.* A file format standard for encoding graphical images, both object-oriented and bitmapped. The PICT file format was first used in Apple

Macintosh applications, but many IBM PC-compatible applications can read the format too. *See also* bitmapped graphics, object-oriented graphics.

picture element *n. See* pixel.

piggyback board *n.* A printed circuit board that plugs into another circuit board to enhance its capabilities. A piggyback board is sometimes used to replace a single chip, in which case the chip is removed and the piggyback board is inserted into the empty socket. *See also* daughterboard.

PIM *n.* Acronym for **p**ersonal **i**nformation **m**anager. An application that usually includes an address book and organizes information such as notes, appointments, and names.

pin *n.* A slender prong; for example, one of the contacts protruding from a male connector. Connectors are often identified by the number of pins they have. Other types of pins are the spidery, leglike metal appendages that connect computer chips to sockets on a circuit board or directly to the circuit board.

pinch-roller plotter *n.* A type of plotter, intermediate between drum and flatbed types, that uses hard rubber or metal wheels to hold the paper against the main roller. *See also* plotter. *Compare* drum plotter, flatbed plotter.

pin-compatible *adj.* Having pins that are equivalent to the pins on another chip or device. A chip, for example, might have internal circuitry different from that used in another chip, but if the two chips use the same pins for input and output of identical signals, they are pin-compatible. *Compare* plug-compatible.

pin feed *n.* A method of feeding paper through a printer in which small pins, mounted on rollers on the ends of the platen, engage holes near the edges of continuous-form paper. *See also* continuous-form paper, paper feed. *Compare* tractor feed.

ping[1] *n.* **1.** Acronym for **P**acket **In**ternet **G**roper. A protocol for testing whether a particular computer is connected to the Internet by sending a packet to its IP address and waiting for a response. **2.** A UNIX utility that implements the ping protocol.

ping[2] *vb.* **1.** To test whether a computer is connected to the Internet using the ping utility. **2.** To test which users on a mailing list are current by sending e-mail to the list asking for a response.

Ping of Death *n.* A form of Internet vandalism that entails sending a packet substantially larger than the usual 64 bytes over the Internet via the ping protocol to a remote computer. The size of the packet causes the computer to crash or reboot. *See also* packet (definition 2), ping[1] (definition 1).

ping pong *n.* **1.** In communications, a technique that changes the direction of transmission so that the sender becomes the receiver and vice versa. **2.** In information processing and transfer, the technique of using two temporary storage areas (buffers) rather than one to hold both input and output.

pinout *n.* A description or diagram of the pins of a chip or connector. *See also* pin.

pipe *n.* **1.** A portion of memory that can be used by one process to pass information along to another. Essentially, a pipe works like its namesake: it connects two processes so that the output of one can be used as the input to the other. **2.** The vertical line character (|) that appears on a PC keyboard as the shift character on the backslash (\) key.
piracy *n.* **1.** The theft of a computer design or program. **2.** Unauthorized distribution and use of a computer program.
pitch *n.* **1.** A measure, generally used with monospace fonts, that describes the number of characters that fit in a horizontal inch. *See also* characters per inch. *Compare* point[1] (definition 1). **2.** *See* screen pitch.
pixel *n.* Short for picture (**pix**) **el**ement. One spot in a rectilinear grid of thousands of such spots that are individually "painted" to form an image produced on the screen by a computer or on paper by a printer. A pixel is the smallest element that display or print hardware and software can manipulate in creating letters, numbers, or graphics. *Also called* pel.
pixel image *n.* The representation of a color graphic in a computer's memory. A pixel image is similar to a bit image, which also describes a screen graphic, but a pixel image has an added dimension, sometimes called depth, that describes the number of bits in memory assigned to each on-screen pixel.
PJ/NF *n.* Acronym for **p**rojection-**j**oin **n**ormal **f**orm. *See* normal form.
Plain Old Telephone Service *n.* *See* POTS.
plaintext *n.* **1.** Nonencrypted or decrypted text. *See also* decryption, encryption. **2.** A file that is stored as plain ASCII data.
plain vanilla *adj.* Ordinary; the standard version of hardware or software without any enhancements. For example, a plain vanilla modem might have data transfer capability but no fax or voice features.
.plan *n.* A file in a UNIX user's home directory that is displayed when other users finger that account. Users can enter information into .plan files at their discretion to provide information in addition to that normally displayed by the finger command. *See also* finger.
plasma display *n.* *See* gas-discharge display.
platen *n.* The cylinder in most impact printers and typewriters, around which the paper wraps and against which the print mechanism strikes the paper. The paper bail, a spring-loaded bar with small rollers, holds the paper smoothly against the platen just above the print mechanism.
platform *n.* **1.** The foundation technology of a computer system. Because computers are layered devices composed of a chip-level hardware layer, a firmware and operating system layer, and an applications program layer, the bottommost layer of a machine is often called a platform. **2.** In everyday usage, the type of computer or operating system being used.
Platform for Internet Content Selection *n.* *See* PICS.
plot *vb.* To create a graphic or a diagram by connecting points representing values that are defined by their positions in relation to a horizontal (*x*) axis and a vertical (*y*) axis (and sometimes a depth, or *z*, axis).

plotter *n.* Any device used to draw charts, diagrams, and other line-based graphics. Plotters use either pens or electrostatic charges and toner, and they use three basic types of paper handling: flatbed, drum, and pinch roller. *See also* drum plotter, electrostatic plotter, flatbed plotter, pen plotter, pinch-roller plotter.

Plug and Play *n.* A set of specifications developed by Intel that allow a PC to configure itself automatically to work with peripherals such as monitors, modems, and printers. A user can "plug" in a peripheral and "play" it without manually configuring the system. A Plug and Play PC requires both a BIOS that supports Plug and Play and a Plug and Play expansion card. *See also* BIOS, expansion board, peripheral.

plugboard *n.* A board that permits users to control the operation of a device by plugging cables into sockets.

plug-compatible *adj.* Equipped with connectors that are equivalent both in structure and in usage. For example, most modems having DB-25 connectors on their rear panels are plug-compatible; that is, one can be replaced by another without rewiring the cable. *Compare* pin-compatible.

plug-in *n.* **1.** A small software program that plugs into a larger application to provide added functionality. **2.** A software component that plugs into Netscape Navigator. Plug-ins permit the Web browser to access and execute files embedded in HTML documents that are in formats the browser normally would not recognize, such as many animation, video, and audio files. Most plug-ins are developed by software companies who have proprietary software in which the embedded files have been created. *Compare* helper application.

PMS *n. See* Pantone Matching System.

PNG *n. See* Portable Network Graphics.

PNP *n. See* Plug and Play.

point[1] *n.* **1.** A unit of measure used in typography, equal to approximately $^1/_{72}$ of an inch. Character height and the amount of space (leading) between lines of text are usually specified in points. **2.** A single pixel on the screen, identified by its row and column numbers. **3.** A location in a geometric form, represented by two or more numbers that constitute its coordinates.

point[2] *vb.* To move an arrow or other such indicator to a particular item or position on the screen by using direction keys or by maneuvering a pointing device such as a mouse.

point-and-click *adj.* Enabling a user to select data and activate programs by using a mouse or other pointing device to move a cursor to a desired location ("point") and pressing a button on the mouse or other pointing device ("click").

pointer *n. See* mouse pointer.

pointing device *n.* An input device used to control an on-screen cursor for such actions as "pressing" on-screen buttons in dialog boxes, choosing menu items, and selecting ranges of cells in spreadsheets or groups of words in a document. A pointing device is often used to create drawings or graphical shapes. The most common pointing device is the mouse. Other pointing devices include styluses (typically used with graphics tablets), light pens, joysticks, pucks, and trackballs. *See also* graphics tablet, joystick, light pen, mouse, puck, stylus, trackball.

point listing *n.* A database of popular Web sites categorized by topics of interest and often rated by design and content.

point of presence *n.* **1.** A point in a wide area network to which a user can connect with a local telephone call. **2.** A point at which a long-distance telephone carrier connects to a local telephone exchange or to an individual user. *Acronym:* POP.

Point-to-Point Protocol *n. See* PPP.

Point-to-Point Tunneling Protocol *n.* A specification for virtual private networks in which some nodes of a LAN are connected through the Internet. *Acronym:* PPTP. *See also* virtual network.

polarizing filter *n.* A transparent piece of glass or plastic that polarizes the light passing through it; that is, it allows only waves vibrating in a certain direction to pass through. Polarizing filters are often used to reduce glare on monitor screens. *See also* glare filter.

polygon *n.* Any two-dimensional closed shape composed of three or more line segments, such as a hexagon, an octagon, or a triangle. Computer users encounter polygons in graphics programs.

polyline *n.* An open shape consisting of multiple connected segments. Polylines are used in CAD and other graphics programs.

POP *n. See* point of presence, Post Office Protocol.

POP3 *n.* Acronym for **P**ost **O**ffice **P**rotocol **3**. This is the current version of the Post Office Protocol standard in common use on TCP/IP networks. *See also* Post Office Protocol, TCP/IP.

populate *vb.* **1.** To put chips in the sockets of a circuit board. **2.** To import prepared data into a database from a file using a software procedure rather than by having a human operator enter individual records.

pop-up menu or **popup menu** *n.* In a graphical user interface, a menu that appears when a user selects a certain item. Pop-up menus can appear anywhere on the screen and generally disappear when the user selects an item on the menu. *Also called* popup. *Compare* drop-down menu, pull-down menu.

pop-up window *n.* A window that appears when an option is selected. Typically, the window remains visible until the mouse button is released.

port[1] *n. See* input/output port, port number.

port[2] *vb.* **1.** To change a program in order to be able to run it on a different computer. **2.** To move documents, graphics, and other files from one computer to another.

portable *adj.* **1.** Capable of running on more than one computer system or under more than one operating system. For example, highly portable software can be moved to other systems with little effort. **2.** Light enough, rugged enough, and free enough of encumbering external connections to be carried by a user.

portable computer *n.* Any computer designed to be transported easily. Portable computers can be characterized by size and weight. Transportable computers (15–30 lbs.; sometimes called luggable) are the largest type of portable computer. Their power source is house current, and they usually have floppy and hard drives and a standard CRT screen. Laptop computers (8–15 lbs.) run on house current or batteries. They typically have a floppy drive and use a flat LCD or plasma screen. Ultralight computers (2–8 lbs.) run on batteries or a transformer pack and are easy to carry in a briefcase. They sometimes use a RAM drive or EPROM instead of a floppy or hard drive. (Thinner models are known as notebook computers.) Handheld computers weigh less than 2 lbs. and can be held in one hand. Also called palmtops, they run on batteries or a transformer pack. Most portable computers now include PCMCIA slots, which make it possible to expand the functionality of the computer. *See also* handheld computer, laptop computer, PCMCIA slot, PDA.
Portable Digital Document *n. See* PDD.
Portable Document Format *n.* The Adobe specification for electronic documents that use the Adobe Acrobat family of servers and readers. *Acronym:* PDF. *See also* Acrobat, .pdf.
Portable Network Graphics *n.* A file format for bitmapped graphic images, designed to be a replacement for the GIF format, without the legal restrictions associated with GIF. *Acronym:* PNG. *See also* GIF.
port enumerator *n.* In Windows, part of the Plug and Play system that detects I/O ports and reports them to the configuration manager. *See also* Plug and Play.
port expander *n.* A hardware mechanism used for connecting several devices to a single port. Although several devices might be connected, only one can use the port at any given moment.
port number *n.* A number that enables IP packets to be sent to a particular process on a computer connected to the Internet. Some port numbers, called "well-known" port numbers, are permanently assigned; for example, e-mail data under SMTP goes to port number 25. *See also* IP, Simple Mail Transfer Protocol, socket (definition 1). *Compare* IP address.
portrait mode *n.* A vertical print orientation in which a document is printed across the narrower dimension of a rectangular sheet of paper. This is the print mode typical of most letters, reports, and other such documents. *Compare* landscape mode.
portrait monitor *n.* A monitor with a screen shape higher than it is wide. The proportions (but not necessarily the size) of the screen are usually the same as for a sheet of $8\frac{1}{2}$-by-11-inch paper. *Compare* landscape monitor.
post *vb.* To submit an article in a newsgroup or other online conference. The term is derived from the "posting" of a notice on a physical bulletin board. *See also* newsgroup.
POST *n. See* power-on self test.

A B C D E F G H I J K L M N O P Q R S T U V W X Y Z

posterization *n. See* contouring.
postmaster *n.* The logon name (and therefore the e-mail address) of an account that is responsible for maintaining e-mail services on a mail server. When an account holder is having trouble with e-mail, a message addressed to postmaster or postmaster@*machine.org.domain.name* will usually reach a human who can solve the problem.
Post Office Protocol *n.* A protocol for servers on the Internet that receive, store, and transmit e-mail and for clients on computers that connect to the servers to download and upload e-mail. *Acronym:* POP.
PostScript *n.* A page-description language from Adobe Systems that offers flexible font capability and high-quality graphics. The most well-known page-description language, PostScript uses English-like commands to control page layout and to load and scale outline fonts. *See also* Display PostScript, outline font, page-description language.
PostScript font *n.* A font that is defined in terms of the PostScript page-description language rules and intended to be printed on a PostScript-compatible printer. PostScript fonts are distinguished from bitmapped fonts by their smoothness, detail, and faithfulness to standards of quality established in the typographic industry. *See also* PostScript. *Compare* screen font.
POTS *n.* Acronym for **P**lain **O**ld **T**elephone **S**ervice. Basic dial telephone connections to the public switched network, without any added features or functions. A POTS line is nothing but a phone line connected to a simple desktop telephone instrument.
power *n.* **1.** In mathematics, the number of times a value is multiplied by itself—for example, 10 to the third power means 10 × 10 × 10. **2.** In computing, the electricity used to run a computer. **3.** The speed at which a computer performs and the availability of various features. *See also* computer power.
PowerBook *n.* Any of several computers in the family of portable Macintosh computers made by Apple.
power down *vb.* To shut down (a computer); to turn off the power.
power failure *n.* Loss of electricity, which causes a loss of unsaved data in a computer's random access memory if no backup power supply is connected to the machine. *Compare* surge.
Power Mac *n. See* Power Macintosh.
Power Macintosh *n.* An Apple Macintosh computer based on the PowerPC processor. The first Power Macintoshes, 6100/60, 7100/66, and 8100/80, were unveiled in 1994. *Also called* Power Mac. *See also* PowerPC.
Power-on key *n.* A special key on the Apple ADB and Extended keyboards used for turning on a Macintosh II. The Power-on key is marked with a left-pointing triangle and is used in lieu of the on/off switch. There is no Power-off key; the system is shut down by choosing the Shut Down command from the Special menu.
power-on self test *n.* A set of routines stored in a computer's ROM that test various system components such as RAM, the disk drives, and the key-

board to see if they are properly connected and operating. If problems are found, these routines alert the user. If the power-on self test is successful, it passes control to the system's bootstrap loader. *Acronym:* POST. *See also* bootstrap loader.

PowerPC *n.* A microprocessor architecture developed in 1992 by Motorola and IBM, with some participation by Apple. A PowerPC microprocessor is RISC-based and superscalar, with a 64-bit data bus and a 32-bit address bus. It also has separate data and instruction caches. All PowerPC microprocessors have multiple integer and floating-point units. The operating speed and the number of instructions executed per clock cycle vary with the implementation; depending on the version, the microprocessor operates at either three or four instructions per clock cycle and ranges in speed from 80 MHz to 200 MHz. *See also* microprocessor, RISC, superscalar.

PowerPC Platform *n.* A platform developed by IBM, Apple, and Motorola based on the 601 and later chips. This platform supports the use of multiple operating systems such as the Mac OS, Windows NT, and AIX as well as software designed for those operating systems. *Acronym:* PPCP.

power supply *n.* An electrical device that transforms standard wall outlet electricity (115–120 VAC in the United States) into the lower voltages (typically 5–12 volts DC) required by computer systems. Personal computer power supplies are rated by wattage; they usually range from about 90 watts at the low end to 250 watts at the high end.

power surge *n. See* surge.

power up *vb.* To start up a computer; to begin a cold boot procedure; to turn on the power.

power user *n.* A person adept with computers, particularly on an applications level rather than on a programming level. A power user is someone who is comfortable enough with applications to be able to work with their most sophisticated features.

PPCP *n. See* PowerPC Platform.

PPM or **ppm** *n. See* pages per minute.

PPP *n.* Acronym for **P**oint-to-**P**oint **P**rotocol. A data-link protocol for dial-up telephone connections, such as between a computer and the Internet. PPP provides greater protection for data integrity and security than does SLIP, at a cost of greater overhead. *Compare* SLIP.

PPS *n. See* peripheral power supply.

PPTP *n. See* Point-to-Point Tunneling Protocol.

PRAM *n.* Short for **p**arameter **RAM.** A few bytes of battery-backed CMOS RAM on the motherboard of an Apple Macintosh computer that contain configuration information such as the date and time, desktop pattern, and other control panel settings. *See also* CMOS RAM, RAM. *Compare* CMOS (definition 2).

P-rating *n.* Short for **p**erformance **rating**. A microprocessor rating system by IBM, Cyrix, and others, based on throughput in realistic applications. Formerly, microprocessor clock speed was widely used as a method of

A B C D E F G H I J K L M N O P Q R S T U V W X Y Z

rating, but it does not account for differing chip architectures or different types of work people do with computers. *See also* central processing unit, clock (definition 1), microprocessor.

precedence *n.* In applications, the order in which values in a mathematical expression are calculated. In general, applications perform multiplication and division first, followed by addition and subtraction. Sets of parentheses can be placed around expressions to control the order in which they are calculated. *See also* operator precedence.

preemptive multitasking *n.* A form of multitasking in which the operating system periodically interrupts the execution of a program and passes control of the system to another waiting program. Preemptive multitasking prevents any one program from monopolizing the system. *See also* multitasking.

Preferences *n.* A menu choice in many graphical user interface applications that allows the user to specify how the application will act each time it is used. For example, in a word processing application the user might specify whether the ruler will appear or whether the document will appear in the same way as it will print (including margins). *Also called* Options, Prefs.

Prefs *n. See* Preferences.

preprocessor *n.* A device or routine that performs preliminary operations on input before passing it on for further processing. *See also* front-end processor (definition 1).

presentation graphics *n.* The representation of business information, such as sales figures and stock prices, in chart form rather than as lists of numbers. Presentation graphics can give viewers an immediate grasp of business statistics and their significance. *Also called* business graphics.

presentation layer *n.* The sixth of the seven layers in the ISO/OSI model for standardizing computer-to-computer communications. The presentation layer is responsible for formatting information so that it can be displayed or printed. This task generally includes interpreting codes (such as tabs) related to presentation, but it can also include converting encryption and other codes and translating different character sets. *See also* ISO/OSI model.

pressure-sensitive *adj.* Of or pertaining to a device in which pressing on a thin surface produces an electrical connection and causes an event to be registered by the computer. Pressure-sensitive devices include membrane keyboards, touch-sensitive drawing pens, and some touch screens. *See also* touch screen.

Pretty Good Privacy *n. See* PGP.

preview *n.* In word processors and other applications, the feature that formats a document for printing but displays it on the video monitor rather than sending it directly to the printer.

PRI *n.* Acronym for **P**rimary **R**ate **I**nterface. An ISDN service, which has two variations. One variation of PRI, which operates at 1.536 Mbps, transmits data over 23 B channels and sends signaling information at 64 Kbps over one D channel in the United States, Canada, and Japan. The second variation, which operates at 1.984 Mbps, transmits data over 30 B channels and sends signaling information at 64 Kbps over one D channel in Europe and Australia. *See also* BRI, ISDN.

primary channel *n.* The data transmission channel in a communications device, such as a modem. *Compare* secondary channel.

primary key *n.* In databases, the key field that serves as the unique identifier of a specific tuple (row) in a relation (database table). *Also called* major key. *Compare* secondary key.

Primary Rate Interface *n. See* PRI.

primary storage *n.* Random access memory (RAM); the primary general-purpose storage region to which the microprocessor has direct access. *Compare* secondary storage.

primitive *n.* In computer graphics, a shape, such as a line, circle, curve, or polygon, that can be drawn, stored, and manipulated as a discrete entity by a graphics program. A primitive is one of the elements from which a large graphic design is created.

print *vb.* In computing, to send information to a printer. The word is also sometimes used in the sense of "show me" or "copy this." For example, the PRINT statement in Basic causes output to be displayed (printed) on the screen. Similarly, an application that can be told to "print" a file to disk interprets the command as an instruction to route output to a disk file instead of to a printer.

print buffer *n.* A section of memory to which print output can be sent for temporary storage until the printer is ready to handle it. A print buffer can exist in a computer's RAM, in the printer, in a separate unit between the computer and the printer, or on disk. It frees the computer for other tasks by taking print output at high speed from the computer and passing it along at the much slower rate required by the printer. Some print buffers simply hold the next few characters to be printed, whereas others can queue, reprint, or delete documents sent for printing.

printed circuit board *n.* A flat board made of nonconducting material, such as plastic or fiberglass, on which chips and other electronic components are mounted, usually in predrilled holes designed to hold them. The component holes are connected electrically by predefined conductive metal pathways that are printed on the surface of the board. The metal leads protruding from the electronic components are soldered to the conductive metal pathways to form a connection. A printed circuit board should be held by the edges and protected from dirt and static electricity to avoid damage. *Acronym:* PCB.

printer *n.* A computer peripheral that puts text or a computer-generated image on paper or on another medium, such as a transparency film. Printers are commonly categorized as impact or nonimpact. Impact printers, such as dot-matrix printers, physically strike the paper; nonimpact printers include every other type of print mechanism, including laser, ink-jet, and thermal

A B C D E F G H I J K L M N O P Q R S T U V W X Y Z

printers. Other possible methods of categorizing printers include (but are not limited to) the type of print technology and the print quality, as well as the following distinctions:

- Character formation: Fully formed characters made of continuous lines versus dot-matrix characters composed of patterns of dots (such as those produced by standard dot-matrix, ink-jet, and thermal printers). Laser printers, while technically dot-matrix, are generally considered to produce fully formed characters because their output is very clear and the dots are extremely small and closely spaced.
- Method of transmission: Parallel (byte-by-byte transmission) versus serial (bit-by-bit transmission). These categories refer to the means by which output is sent to the printer rather than to any mechanical distinctions. Many printers are available in either parallel or serial versions, and still other printers offer both choices.
- Method of printing: Character by character, line by line, or page by page. Character printers include standard dot-matrix, ink-jet, and thermal printers. Line printers include the band, chain, and drum printers that are commonly associated with large computer installations or networks. Page printers include the electrophotographic printers, such as laser printers.
- Print capability: Text-only versus text-and-graphics. Text-only printers, including many older printers and some dot-matrix and laser printers, can reproduce only characters for which they have matching patterns, such as embossed type, or internal character maps. Text-and-graphics printers—dot-matrix, ink-jet, laser, and others—can reproduce all manner of images by "drawing" each as a pattern of dots.

See also character printer, color printer, dot-matrix printer, draft quality, electrophotographic printers, graphics printer, impact printer, ink-jet printer, laser printer, LCD printer, LED printer, letter-quality printer, line printer, logic-seeking printer, near-letter-quality, nonimpact printer, page printer, parallel printer, print quality, serial printer, thermal printer.

Printer Access Protocol *n. See* PAP (definition 2).

Printer Control Language *n.* A printer control language from Hewlett-Packard, used in its LaserJet, DeskJet, and RuggedWriter printer lines. Because of the LaserJet's dominance in the laser printer market, Printer Control Language has become a de facto standard. *Acronym:* PCL. *Also called* Hewlett-Packard Printer Control Language.

printer controller *n.* The processing hardware in a printer, especially in a page printer. It includes the raster image processor, the memory, and any general-purpose microprocessors. A printer controller can also reside in a personal computer, attached via a high-speed cable to a printer that simply carries out its instructions. *Compare* printer engine.

printer driver *n.* A software program designed to enable other programs to work with a particular printer without concerning themselves with the specifics of the printer's hardware and internal "language." Applications can communicate properly with a variety of printers by using printer drivers, which handle all the subtleties of each printer on behalf of the application. Today, because graphical user interfaces offer their own printer drivers, an application that runs under the interface does not need to have its own printer driver.

printer engine *n.* The part of a page printer, such as a laser printer, that actually performs the printing. Most printer engines are self-contained, replaceable cartridges. The engine is distinct from the printer controller, which includes all the processing hardware in the printer. *Compare* printer controller.

printer file *n.* Output that would normally be destined for the printer but has been diverted to a computer file instead. A printer file might be created to allow output to be transferred to another program or to another computer or to allow additional copies to be made at any time by simply copying the print image to the printer. Occasionally, the term printer file is used, incorrectly, to refer to the printer driver.

printer font *n.* A font residing in or intended for a printer. A printer font can be internal, downloaded, or on a font cartridge. *Compare* screen font.

printer port *n.* A port through which a printer can be connected to a personal computer. On PC-compatible machines, printer ports are usually parallel ports and are identified in the operating system by the logical device name LPT. On many newer PCs, the parallel port on the case of the CPU has a printer icon beside it to identify it as a printer port. Serial ports can also be used for some printers (logical device name COM), although configuration is generally required. On Macintoshes, printer ports are usually serial ports and are also used to connect Macs to an AppleTalk network. *See also* AppleTalk, central processing unit, logical device, parallel port, serial port.

print head *n.* The part of a printer that mechanically controls the imprinting of characters on paper.

print job *n.* A single batch of characters printed as a unit. A print job usually consists of a single document, which can be one page or hundreds of pages long. Some software can group multiple documents into a single print job. *See also* print spooler.

print mode *n.* A general term for the format of print output by a printer. Print modes range from portrait or landscape orientation of the paper to letter quality and size of the print. Dot-matrix printers support two print modes: draft and letter quality (LQ) or near-letter-quality (NLQ). Some printers can interpret both plain text (ASCII) and a page-description language such as PostScript. *See also* PostScript, printer.

printout *n.* *See* hard copy.

print quality *n.* The quality and clarity of characters produced by a printer. Print quality varies with the type of printer; in general, dot-matrix

A B C D E F G H I J K L M N O P Q R S T U V W X Y Z

printers produce lower-quality output than laser printers. The print mode can also affect quality. *See also* draft quality, letter quality, near-letter-quality, resolution (definition 1).

print queue *n.* A buffer for documents and images waiting to be printed. When an application places a document in a print queue, it is held in a special part of the computer's memory, where it waits until the printer is ready to receive it.

Print Screen key *n.* A key on IBM PC and compatible keyboards that normally causes the computer to send a character-based "picture" of the screen contents to the printer. The print screen feature works only when the display is in text mode or CGA graphics mode (the lowest-resolution color and graphics mode available on IBM compatibles); it will not work properly in other graphics modes. Some programs use the Print Screen key to capture a screen image and record it as a file on disk. These programs can typically work in any graphics mode and record the file as a graphics image. In MS-DOS and in some programs, pressing the combination Ctrl-Print Screen toggles the printer on or off. With printing turned on, the system sends every character to the printer as well as to the screen. The Print Screen key on the Apple Extended Keyboard is included for compatibility with operating systems such as MS-DOS. *Also called* PrtSc key.

print server *n.* A workstation dedicated to managing printers on a network. The print server can be any station on the network.

print spooler *n.* Computer software that intercepts a print job on its way to the printer and sends it to disk or memory instead, where the print job is held until the printer is ready for it.

print to file *n.* A command in many applications that instructs the program to format a document for printing and store the formatted document as a file rather than sending it to a printer.

priority *n.* Precedence in receiving the attention of the microprocessor and the use of system resources. Within a computer, levels of priority are the means by which many types of potential clashes and disruptions are avoided. On networks, stations can be assigned priorities that determine when and how often they can control the communications line, and messages can be assigned priorities that indicate how soon they must be transmitted. *See also* interrupt.

privacy *n.* The concept that a user's data, such as stored files and e-mail, is not to be examined by anyone else without that user's permission. A right to privacy is not generally recognized on the Internet. Federal law protects only e-mail in transit or in temporary storage, and only against access by federal agencies. Employers often claim a right to inspect any data on their systems. To obtain privacy, the user must take active measures such as encryption. *See also* encryption, PGP, Privacy Enhanced Mail. *Compare* security.

Privacy Enhanced Mail *n.* An Internet standard for e-mail systems that use encryption techniques to ensure the privacy and security of messages. *Acronym:* PEM. *See also* encryption, standard. *Compare* PGP.

private channel *n.* In Internet Relay Chat, a channel reserved for the use of a certain group of people. Private channel names cannot be viewed by the public at large. *Also called* secret channel. *See also* IRC.

private folders *n.* In a shared network environment, those folders on a user's computer that are not currently accessible by other users on the network. *Compare* public folders.

private key *n.* One of two keys in public key encryption. The user keeps the private key secret and uses it to encrypt digital signatures and to decrypt received messages. *See also* public key encryption. *Compare* public key.

private line *n. See* dedicated line (definition 1).

privileges *n. See* access privileges.

PRN *n.* The logical device name for *printer.* A name reserved by MS-DOS for the standard print device. PRN usually refers to a system's first parallel port, also known as LPT1.

procedure *n.* In a program, a named sequence of statements, often with associated data types and variables, that usually performs a single task. A procedure can usually be called (executed) by other procedures, as well as by the main body of the program. *See also* function, routine.

process *vb.* To manipulate data with a program.

process color *n.* A method of handling color in a document in which each block of color is separated into its subtractive primary color components for printing: cyan, magenta, and yellow (as well as black). All other colors are created by blending layers of various sizes of halftone spots printed in cyan, magenta, and yellow to create the image. *See also* color model.

processing *n.* The manipulation of data within a computer system. Processing is the vital step between receiving data (input) and producing results (output)—the task for which computers are designed.

processor *n. See* central processing unit, microprocessor.

Processor Direct Slot *n. See* PDS.

profile *n. See* user profile.

program *n.* A sequence of instructions that can be executed by a computer. The term can refer to the original source code or to the executable (machine language) version. *Also called* software. *See also* routine, statement.

program card *n. See* PC Card, ROM card.

program cartridge *n. See* ROM cartridge.

program file *n.* A disk file that contains the executable portion(s) of a computer program. Depending on its size and complexity, an application or other program, such as an operating system, can be stored in several different files, each containing the instructions necessary for some part of the program's overall functioning. *Compare* document file.

programmable *adj.* Capable of accepting instructions for performing a task or an operation. Being programmable is a characteristic of computers.

programmable function key *n.* Any of several, sometimes unlabeled, keys on some third-party keyboards that allow the user to "play back" previously stored key combinations or sequences of keystrokes called macros.

A B C D E F G H I J K L M N O P Q R S T U V W X Y Z

The same effect can be achieved with a standard keyboard and a keyboard enhancer, the latter of which intercepts the keyboard codes and substitutes modified values; but programmable function keys accomplish this without requiring RAM-resident software. *Compare* keyboard enhancer.

programmable read-only memory *n. See* PROM.

program maintenance *n.* The process of supporting, debugging, and upgrading a program in response to feedback from individual or corporate users or the marketplace in general.

programmatic interface *n.* **1.** A user interface dependent on user commands or on a special programming language, as contrasted with a graphical user interface. UNIX and MS-DOS have programmatic interfaces; the Apple Macintosh and Microsoft Windows have graphical user interfaces. *See also* command-line interface, graphical user interface, iconic interface. **2.** The set of functions any operating system makes available to a programmer developing an application. *See also* application programming interface.

programmer *n.* **1.** An individual who writes and debugs computer programs. Depending on the size of the project and the work environment, a programmer might work alone or as part of a team, be involved in part or all of the process from design through completion, or write all or a portion of the program. *See also* program. **2.** In hardware, a device used to program read-only memory chips. *See also* PROM, ROM (definition 2).

programmer's switch *n.* A pair of buttons on Macintosh computers that enable the user to reboot the system or to enter a command-line interface at a low level of the operating system. In many later models of the Macintosh, the buttons are built into the cabinet; the button to reboot the system is marked with a triangle pointing leftward, and the other button is marked with a circle.

programming *n.* The art and science of creating computer programs. Programming begins with knowledge of one or more programming languages, such as Basic, C, or assembly language. Creating a good program can also require expertise in the theory of algorithms, in user interface design, and in the characteristics of hardware devices as well as a logical approach to designing, writing (coding), testing, and debugging a program. Low-level languages, such as assembly language, also require familiarity with the capabilities of a microprocessor and the basic instructions built into it. *See also* algorithm, modular design, object-oriented programming, structured programming.

programming language *n.* Any artificial language that can be used to define a sequence of instructions that can ultimately be processed and executed by the computer. Defining what is or is not a programming language can be tricky, but general usage implies that the translation process—from the source code expressed using the programming language to the machine code that the computer needs to work with—be automated by means of another program, such as a compiler. *See also* compiler, program.

Project Gutenberg *n.* A project that makes the texts of books in the public domain available over the Internet. The files for the books are in plain

ASCII, to make them accessible to as many people as possible. Project Gutenberg is based at the University of Illinois at Urbana-Champaign *See also* ASCII.

projection-join normal form *n. See* normal form.

PROM *n.* Acronym for **p**rogrammable **r**ead-**o**nly **m**emory. A type of ROM that allows data to be written into the device with hardware called a PROM programmer. After a PROM has been programmed, it is dedicated to that data, and it cannot be reprogrammed. *See also* EEPROM, EPROM, ROM (definition 2).

PROM blaster *n. See* PROM programmer.

PROM blower *n. See* PROM programmer.

promiscuous-mode transfer *n.* In network communications, a transfer of data in which a node accepts all packets regardless of their destination addresses.

PROM programmer *n.* A hardware device that records instructions or data on a PROM chip or an EPROM chip. *Also called* PROM blaster, PROM blower. *See also* EPROM, PROM.

prompt *n.* **1.** In command-driven systems, one or more symbols that indicate where users are to enter commands. For instance, in MS-DOS, the prompt is generally a drive letter followed by a greater than symbol (C>). In UNIX, it is usually %. *See also* command-driven system, DOS prompt. **2.** Displayed text indicating that a computer program is waiting for input from the user.

propagation *n.* Travel of a signal, such as an Internet packet, from its source to one or more destinations. Propagation of messages over different paths with different lengths can cause messages to appear at a user's computer with varying delivery times. *See also* propagation delay.

propagation delay *n.* The time needed by a communications signal to travel between two points; in satellite links, a noticeable delay of between one-quarter second and one-half second, caused by the signal traveling through space.

proportional font *n.* A font in which a variable amount of horizontal space is allotted to each letter or number. In a proportional font, the letter *i,* for example, is allowed less space than the letter *m. Compare* monospace font.

proportional spacing *n.* A form of character spacing in which the horizontal space each character occupies is proportional to the width of the character. The letter *w,* for example, takes up more space than the letter *i. Compare* monospacing.

proprietary *adj.* Of, pertaining to, or characteristic of something that is privately owned. Generally, the term refers to technology that has been developed by a particular corporation or entity, with specifications that are considered by the owner to be trade secrets. Proprietary technology may be legally used only by a person or entity purchasing an explicit license. Also, other companies are unable to duplicate the technology, both legally and because its specifications have not been divulged by the owner. *Compare* public domain.

proprietary software *n.* A program owned or copyrighted by an individual or a business and available for use only through purchase or by permission of the owner. *Compare* public-domain software.
protected mode *n.* An operating mode of the Intel 80286 and higher microprocessors that supports larger address spaces and more advanced features than real mode. When started in protected mode, these CPUs provide hardware support for multitasking, data security, and virtual memory. The Windows NT and OS/2 operating systems run in protected mode, as do most versions of UNIX for these microprocessors. *Compare* real mode.
protocol *n. See* communications protocol.
protocol layer *n. See* layer (definition 1).
protocol stack *n.* The set of protocols that work together on different levels to enable communication on a network. For example, TCP/IP, the protocol stack on the Internet, incorporates more than 100 standards including FTP, IP, SMTP, TCP, and Telnet. *Also called* protocol suite. *See also* ISO/OSI model.
protocol suite *n. See* protocol stack.
prototyping *n.* The creation of a working model of a new computer system or program for testing and refinement. Prototyping is used in the development of both new hardware and software systems and new systems of information management.
proxy *n. See* proxy server.
proxy server *n.* A firewall component that manages Internet traffic to and from a LAN and can provide other features, such as document caching and access control. A proxy server can improve performance by supplying frequently requested data, such as a popular Web page, and can filter and discard requests that the owner does not consider appropriate, such as requests for unauthorized access to proprietary files. *See also* firewall.
PrtSc key *n. See* Print Screen key.
.ps *n.* The file extension that identifies PostScript printer files. *See also* PostScript.
psec *n. See* picosecond.
PSN *n.* Acronym for **p**acket-**s**witching **n**etwork. *See* packet switching.
/pub *n.* Short for **pub**lic. A directory in an anonymous FTP archive that is accessible by the public and that generally contains files available for free download. *See also* anonymous FTP.
pub *n. See* /pub.
public directory *n.* A directory on an FTP server that is accessible by anonymous users for the purpose of retrieving or storing files. Often the directory is called /pub. *See also* anonymous FTP, FTP[1] (definition 1), FTP server, /pub.
public domain *n.* The set of all creative works, such as books, music, or software, that are not covered by copyright or other property protection. Works in the public domain can be freely copied, modified, and otherwise

used in any manner for any purpose. Much of the information, text, and software on the Internet is in the public domain, but putting a copyrighted work on the Internet does not put it in the public domain. *Compare* proprietary.

public-domain software *n.* A program donated for public use by its owner or developer and freely available for copying and distribution. *Compare* free software, freeware, proprietary software, shareware.

public files *n.* Files with no access restrictions.

public folders *n.* The folders that are made accessible on a particular machine or by a particular user in a shared networking environment. *Compare* private folders.

public key *n.* One of two keys in public key encryption. The user releases this key to the public, who can use it for encrypting messages to be sent to the user and for decrypting the user's digital signature. *See also* public key encryption. *Compare* private key.

public key cryptography *n. See* public key encryption.

public key encryption *n.* An asymmetric scheme that uses a pair of keys for encryption: the public key encrypts data, and a corresponding secret key decrypts it. For digital signatures, the process is reversed: the sender uses the secret key to create a unique electronic number that can be read by anyone possessing the corresponding public key, which verifies that the message is truly from the sender. *See also* private key, public key.

public rights *n.* In the context of the Internet, the extent to which members of the public are permitted to use (and to place) information on the Internet under intellectual property law. *See also* fair use, intellectual property, public domain, public-domain software.

puck *n.* A pointing device used with a graphics tablet. A puck, which is often used in engineering applications, is a mouselike device with buttons for selecting items or choosing commands and a clear plastic section extending from one end with cross hairs printed on it. The intersection of the cross hairs on the puck points to a location on the graphics tablet, which in turn is mapped to a specific location on the screen. Because the puck's cross hairs are on a transparent surface, a user can easily trace a drawing by placing it between the graphics tablet and the puck and moving the cross hairs over the lines of the drawing. *See also* graphics tablet, stylus.

pull *vb.* In networks and the Internet, the process of retrieving data from a server. *Compare* push.

pull-down menu *n.* A menu that is pulled down from the menu bar and that remains available as long as the user holds it open. *Compare* drop-down menu.

purge *vb.* To eliminate old or unneeded information systematically; to clean up, as files.

push *vb.* In networks and the Internet, to send data or a program from a server to a client at the instigation of the server. *Compare* pull.

Q

QBE *n.* *See* query by example.
QoS *n.* *See* quality of service.
.qt *n.* A file extension used to identify multimedia files that use the QuickTime format. *See also* QuickTime.
quadbit *n.* A set of 4 bits representing one of 16 possible combinations. In communications, quadbits are a means of increasing transmission rates by encoding 4 bits at a time, instead of 1 or 2. *Compare* nibble.
quality assurance *n.* A system of procedures carried out to ensure that a product or a system adheres or conforms to established standards. *Also called* quality control.
quality of service *n.* **1.** Generally, the handling capacity of a system or service; the time interval between request and delivery of a product or service to the client or customer. **2.** In computer technology, the guaranteed throughput (data transfer rate) level. *Acronym:* QoS.
query *n.* **1.** The process of extracting data from a database and presenting it for use. **2.** A specific set of instructions for extracting particular data repetitively.
query by example *n.* A simple-to-use query language implemented on several relational database management systems. Using query by example, the user specifies fields to be displayed, intertable linkages, and retrieval criteria directly onto forms displayed on the screen. These forms are a direct pictorial representation of the table and row structures that make up the database. Thus, the construction of a query becomes a simple "checkoff" procedure from the viewpoint of the user. *Acronym:* QBE.
query language *n.* A subset of the data manipulation language; specifically, that portion relating to the retrieval and display of data from a database. The term is sometimes used loosely to refer to the entire data manipulation language. *See also* data manipulation language.
question mark *n.* In some operating systems and applications, a wildcard character often used to represent any other single character. The question mark is one of two wildcard characters supported by the MS-DOS, Windows NT, and OS/2 operating systems. *See also* asterisk (definition 2).
QuickDraw *n.* On the Apple Macintosh, the built-in group of routines within the operating system that control the display of graphics and text. Applications call QuickDraw for on-screen displays.
QuickDraw 3-D *n.* A version of the Macintosh QuickDraw library that includes routines for doing 3-D graphics calculations. *See also* QuickDraw.

quicksort *n.* An efficient sort algorithm in which the essential strategy is to "divide and conquer." A quicksort begins by scanning the list to be sorted for a median value. This value, called the pivot, is then moved to its final position in the list. Next, all items in the list whose values are less than the pivot value are moved to one side of the list, and the items with values greater than the pivot value are moved to the other side. Each resulting side is sorted the same way, until a fully sorted list results. *See also* sort algorithm. *Compare* bubble sort, insertion sort, merge sort.

QuickTime *n.* The multimedia extensions to the Apple Macintosh System 7 software, also available for Windows. QuickTime can synchronize up to 32 tracks of sounds, video images, or MIDI or other control output.

quit¹ *n.* **1.** An FTP command that instructs the server to drop the current connection with the client from which it received the command. **2.** A command in many applications for exiting the program.

quit² *vb.* **1.** To stop in an orderly manner. **2.** To execute the normal shutdown of a program and return control to the operating system. *Compare* abort, bomb², crash² (definition 1), hang.

QWERTY keyboard *n.* A keyboard layout named for the six leftmost characters in the top row of alphabetic characters on most keyboards—the standard layout of most typewriters and computer keyboards. *Compare* Dvorak keyboard, ergonomic keyboard.

#
A
B
C
D
E
F
G
H
I
J
K
L
M
N
O
P
Q
R
S
T
U
V
W
X
Y
Z

R&D *n.* Acronym for **r**esearch and **d**evelopment.

radio *n.* **1.** Electromagnetic waves longer than about 0.3 mm. Radio is used to transmit a wide variety of signals, using various frequency ranges and types of modulation, such as AM and FM broadcasts, microwave relays, and television broadcasts. *See also* hertz, radio frequency. **2.** Audio signals transmitted over the Internet of quality comparable to those broadcast by commercial radio stations. *See also* Internet Talk Radio, MBONE, RealAudio.

radio button *n.* In graphical user interfaces, a means of selecting one of several options in a set, usually in a dialog box. A radio button appears as a small circle that, when selected, has a smaller, filled circle inside it. Radio buttons act like the station selector buttons on a car radio. Selecting one button in a set deselects the previously selected button, so only one of the options in the set can be selected at any given time. *Compare* check box.

radio clock *n.* A device that receives a broadcast containing a standard time signal. Radio clocks are used in network communications to synchronize the host's hardware clock to the Universal Time Coordinate format in accordance with the Network Time Protocol. *See also* NTP, Universal Time Coordinate.

radio frequency *n.* Abbreviated RF. The portion of the electromagnetic spectrum with frequencies between 3 kHz and 300 GHz (wavelengths between 30 km and 0.3 mm). *See also* radio (definition 1).

radio frequency interference *n. See* RFI.

rag *n.* Irregularity along the left or right edge of a set of lines of text on a printed page. Rag complements justification, in which one or both edges of the text form a straight vertical line. *See also* justify, ragged left, ragged right.

ragged left *adj.* Of, relating to, or being lines of text whose left ends are not vertically aligned but form an irregular edge. Text may be right-justified and have a ragged left margin. Ragged left text is used infrequently—typically, for visual effect in advertisements. *See also* rag, right justification.

ragged right *adj.* Of, relating to, or being lines of text whose right ends are not vertically aligned but form an irregular edge. Letters and other word-processed documents are commonly left-justified, with ragged right margins. *See also* left justification, rag.

RAID *n.* Acronym for **r**edundant **a**rray of **i**ndependent **d**isks (formerly called **r**edundant **a**rray of **i**nexpensive **d**isks). A data storage method in which data, along with information used for error correction, is distributed among two or more hard disk drives in order to improve performance and reliability. The hard disk array is governed by array management software and a disk controller, which handles the error correction. RAID is generally used on network servers. *See also* disk controller, hard disk, server (definition 1).

RAID array *n. See* RAID.

RAM *n.* Acronym for **r**andom **a**ccess **m**emory. Semiconductor-based memory that can be read and written to by the CPU or other hardware devices. The storage locations can be accessed in any order. Note that the various types of ROM memory are capable of random access but cannot be written to. The term RAM, however, is generally understood to refer to volatile memory that can be written to as well as read. *Compare* core, EPROM, flash memory, PROM, ROM (definition 2).

RAM cache *n.* Cache memory that is used by the system to store and retrieve data from RAM. Frequently accessed segments of data may be stored in the cache for quicker access than that afforded by secondary storage devices such as disks. *See also* cache, RAM.

RAM card *n.* An add-in circuit board containing RAM memory and the interface logic necessary to decode memory addresses.

RAM cartridge *n. See* memory cartridge.

RAM chip *n.* A semiconductor storage device. RAM chips can be either dynamic or static memory. *See also* dynamic RAM, RAM, static RAM.

RAM compression *n.* A technology developed to solve the problem of running out of global memory under Windows 3.*x*. Compressing the usual contents of RAM may lessen the system's need to read or write to virtual (hard disk–based) memory and may thus speed up the system, as virtual memory is much slower than physical RAM. Because of the falling prices of RAM and the introduction of Windows 95 and Windows NT, which handle RAM more effectively, RAM compression is generally used only on older PCs. *See also* compression, RAM, Windows.

RAMDAC *n.* Acronym for **r**andom **a**ccess **m**emory **d**igital-to-**a**nalog **c**onverter. A chip built into some VGA and SVGA video adapters that translates the digital representation of a pixel into the analog information the monitor needs to display it. A RAMDAC chip generally enhances overall video performance. *See also* SVGA, VGA.

RAM disk *n.* A simulated disk drive whose data is actually stored in RAM memory. A special program allows the operating system to read from and write to the simulated device as if it were a disk drive. RAM disks are extremely fast, but they require that system memory be given up for their use. Also, RAM disks typically use volatile memory, so the data stored on them disappears when power is turned off. Many portables offer RAM disks that use battery-backed CMOS RAM to avoid this problem. *See also* CMOS RAM.

RAM refresh *n. See* refresh (definition 2).

RAM-resident *adj. See* memory-resident.

RAM-resident program *n. See* TSR.

A B C D E F G H I J K L M N O P Q R S T U V W X Y Z

random access *n.* The ability of a computer to find and go directly to a particular storage location without having to search sequentially from the beginning location. A human equivalent would be the ability to find a particular address in an address book without having to proceed sequentially through all the addresses. A computer's semiconductor memory (both RAM and ROM) provides random access. Certain types of files stored on disk under some operating systems also allow random access. Such files are best used for data in which each record has no intrinsic relationship to what comes physically before or after it, as in a client list or an inventory. *Also called* direct access. *See also* RAM, ROM. *Compare* sequential access.

random access memory *n. See* RAM.

random noise *n.* A signal in which there is no relationship between amplitude and time and in which many frequencies occur randomly, without pattern or predictability.

range *n.* A block of cells selected for similar treatment in a spreadsheet. A range of cells can extend across a row, down a column, or over a combination of the two, but all cells in the range must be contiguous, sharing at least one common border. Ranges allow the user to affect many cells with a single command—for example, to format them similarly, enter the same data into all of them, or select and incorporate them into a formula.

RARP *n.* Acronym for **R**everse **A**ddress **R**esolution **P**rotocol. A TCP/IP protocol for determining the IP address of a node on a local area network connected to the Internet, when only the hardware address is known. Although RARP refers only to finding the IP address, and ARP technically refers to the reverse procedure, ARP is commonly used for both senses. *See also* ARP, IP address, TCP/IP.

RAS *n. See* remote access server, Remote Access Service.

raster *n.* A rectangular pattern of lines; on a video display, the horizontal scan lines from which the term raster scan is derived.

raster display *n.* A video monitor (typically a CRT) that displays an image on the screen as a series of horizontal scan lines from top to bottom. Each scan line consists of pixels that can be illuminated and colored individually. TV screens and most computer monitors are raster displays. *See also* CRT, pixel. *Compare* vector display.

raster graphics *n.* A method of generating graphics that treats an image as a collection of small, independently controlled dots (pixels) arranged in rows and columns. *Compare* vector graphics.

raster image *n.* A display image formed by patterns of light and dark or differently colored pixels in a rectangular array. *See also* raster graphics.

raster image processor *n.* A device, consisting of hardware and software, that converts vector graphics or text into a raster (bitmapped) image. Raster image processors, used in page printers and electrostatic plotters, compute the brightness and color value of each pixel so that the resulting pattern of pixels recreates the vector graphics and text originally described. *Acronym:* RIP.

rasterization *n.* The conversion of vector graphics to equivalent images composed of pixel patterns that can be stored and manipulated as sets of bits. *See also* pixel, vector graphics.
raster-scan display *n. See* raster display.
raw data *n.* **1.** Unprocessed, typically unformatted, data, such as a stream of bits that has not been filtered for commands or special characters. **2.** Information that has been collected but not evaluated.
ray tracing *n.* A sophisticated method of producing high-quality computer graphics. Ray tracing calculates the color and intensity of each pixel in an image by tracing single rays of light backward and determining how they were affected on their way from a defined source of light illuminating the objects in the image. Ray tracing is demanding in terms of processing capability because the computer must account for reflection, refraction, and absorption of individual rays as well as for the brightness, transparency level, and reflectivity of each object and the positions of the viewer and the light source.
RCA connector *n.* A connector used for attaching audio and video devices, such as stereo equipment or a composite video monitor, to a computer's video adapter. *Compare* phono connector.
RDBMS *n.* Acronym for **r**elational **d**ata**b**ase **m**anagement **s**ystem. *See* relational database.
read[1] *n.* The action of transferring data from an input source into a computer's memory or from memory into the CPU. *Compare* write[1].
read[2] *vb.* To transfer data from an external source, such as from a disk or the keyboard, into memory or from memory into the CPU. *Compare* write[2].
read error *n.* An error encountered while a computer is in the process of obtaining information from storage or from another source of input. *Compare* write error.
README *n.* A file containing information that the user either needs or will find informative and that might not have been included in the documentation. README files are placed on disk in plain-text form (without extraneous or program-specific characters) so that they can be read easily by a variety of word processing programs.
read notification *n.* An e-mail feature providing feedback to the sender that a message has been read by the recipient.
read-only *adj.* Capable of being retrieved (read) but not changed (written). A read-only file or document can be displayed or printed but cannot be altered in any way; read-only memory (ROM) holds programs that cannot be changed; a read-only storage medium, such as CD-ROM, can be played back but cannot be used for recording information. *Compare* read/write.
read-only attribute *n.* In Windows and OS/2, a file attribute, stored with a file's directory, indicating whether or not a file may be changed or erased. When the read-only attribute is off, the file can be modified or deleted; when it is on, the file can only be displayed.

A B C D E F G H I J K L M N O P Q R S T U V W X Y Z

read-only memory *n. See* ROM.
read-only terminal *n. See* RO terminal.
read/write *adj.* Abbreviated R/W. Able to be both read from and written to. *Compare* read-only.
read/write channel *n. See* input/output channel.
read/write head *n. See* head.
read/write memory *n.* Memory that can be both read from and written to (modified). Semiconductor RAM and core memory are typical read/write memory systems. *Compare* ROM (definition 2).
RealAudio *n.* Web software that streams prerecorded or live audio to a client, such as a Web browser, by decompressing it on the fly so that it can be played back to the browser user in real time.
real mode *n.* An operating mode in the Intel 80x86 family of microprocessors. In real mode, the processor can execute only one program at a time. It can access no more than about 1 MB of memory, but it can freely access system memory and input/output devices. Real mode is the only mode possible in the 8086 processor and is the only operating mode supported by MS-DOS. In contrast, the protected mode offered in the 80286 and higher microprocessors provides the memory management and memory protection needed for multitasking environments such as Windows. *Compare* protected mode, virtual real mode.
Real Soon Now *adv.* Soon, but not really expected to be as soon as claimed. One might say, for example, that a commercial program will have some desired feature Real Soon Now if the vendor knew of the need for the feature several versions ago and has done nothing. *Acronym:* RSN.
real storage *n.* The amount of RAM memory in a system, as distinguished from virtual memory. *Also called* physical memory, physical storage. *See also* virtual memory.
real-time *adj.* Of or relating to a time frame imposed by external constraints. Real-time operations are those in which the machine's activities match the human perception of time or those in which computer operations proceed at the same rate as a physical or external process. Real-time operations are characteristic of aircraft guidance systems, transaction-processing systems, and other areas in which a computer must respond to situations as they occur.
real-time animation *n.* Computer animation in which images are computed and updated on the screen at the same rate at which the objects simulated might move in the real world. Real-time animation allows dynamic involvement by the user because the computer can accept and incorporate keystrokes or controller movements as it is drawing the next image in the animation sequence. Arcade-style animation uses real-time animation in translating game plays into on-screen actions. In contrast, in animation done in virtual time, image frames are first calculated and stored and later replayed at a higher rate to achieve smoother movement. *See also* animation.

real-time clock *n. See* clock (definition 2).
real-time conferencing *n. See* teleconferencing.
real-time system *n.* A computer and/or software system that reacts to events before the events become obsolete. For example, airline collision avoidance systems must process radar input, detect a possible collision, and warn air traffic controllers or pilots while there is still time to react.
reboot *vb.* To restart a computer by reloading the operating system. *See also* boot[2], cold boot, warm boot.
receipt notification *n.* An e-mail feature providing feedback to the sender that a message has been received by the recipient.
receive *vb.* To accept data from an external communications system, such as a LAN or a telephone line, and store the data as a file.
Receive Data *n. See* RXD.
rec. newsgroups *n.* Usenet newsgroups that are part of the rec. hierarchy, use the prefix rec. in their names, and are devoted to discussions of recreational activities, hobbies, and the arts. *See also* newsgroup, traditional newsgroup hierarchy, Usenet.
record[1] *n.* A data structure that is a collection of fields (elements), each with its own name and type. The elements of a record represent different types of information and are accessed by name. A record can be accessed as a collective unit of elements, or the elements can be accessed individually. *See also* data structure, type[1] (definition 1).
record[2] *vb.* To retain information, usually in a file.
record format *n. See* record structure.
record layout *n.* The organization of data fields within a record.
record length *n.* The amount of storage space required to contain a record, typically given in bytes.
record locking *n.* A strategy employed in distributed processing and other multi-user situations to prevent more than one user at a time from writing data to a record.
record number *n.* A unique identifying number assigned to a record in a database. A record number can identify an existing record by its position, or it can be assigned to the record to serve as a key.
record structure *n.* An ordered list of the fields that compose a record, together with a definition of the domain (acceptable values) of each field.
recover *vb.* **1.** To return to a stable condition after some error has occurred. A program recovers from an error by stabilizing itself and resuming execution of instructions without user intervention. **2.** To restore to a stable condition. A computer user may be able to recover lost or damaged data by using a program to search for and salvage whatever information remains in storage.
recoverable error *n.* An error that can be successfully managed by software. For example, if the user enters a number when a letter is required, the program can simply display an error message and prompt the user again.

#
A
B
C
D
E
F
G
H
I
J
K
L
M
N
O
P
Q
R
S
T
U
V
W
X
Y
Z

recovery *n.* The restoration of lost data or the reconciliation of conflicting or erroneous data, after a system failure. Recovery is often achieved using a disk or tape backup and system logs. *See also* backup.

red-green-blue *n.* *See* RGB.

redirection *n.* The process of writing to or reading from a file or device different from the one that would normally be the target or the source. For example, the MS-DOS or OS/2 command dir >prn redirects a directory listing from the screen to the printer.

redlining *n.* A feature of a word processing application that marks changes, additions, or deletions made to a document by a coauthor or an editor. The purpose of redlining is to produce a record of the changes made to a document during the course of its development.

redraw *n.* *See* refresh (definition 1).

reduce *vb.* In a graphical user interface, to decrease the size of a window. A user can reduce a window either by clicking on the appropriate button in the title bar or by clicking the mouse on the border of the window and dragging the border toward the middle of the window. *See also* maximize, minimize.

reduced instruction set computing *n.* *See* RISC.

redundancy check *n.* *See* CRC.

reflective liquid-crystal display *n.* A liquid crystal display that is not equipped with edge or back lighting to enhance readability but instead depends on reflecting ambient light, making it difficult to read in brightly lit environments such as the outdoors. *Also called* reflective LCD.

reformat *vb.* **1.** In applications, to change the look of a document by altering stylistic details, such as font, layout, indention, and alignment. **2.** In data storage, to prepare for reuse a disk that already contains programs or data, effectively destroying the existing contents.

refresh *vb.* **1.** To retrace a video screen at frequent intervals, even if the image does not change, in order to keep the phosphors irradiated. **2.** To recharge dynamic RAM chips (DRAMs) so that they continue to retain the information stored in them. Circuitry on the memory board automatically performs this function.

refresh rate *n.* In reference to video hardware, the frequency with which the entire screen is redrawn to maintain a constant, flicker-free image. On TV screens and raster-scan monitors, the refresh rate is typically about 60 times per second.

regenerate *vb.* *See* rewrite.

register *n.* A set of bits of high-speed memory within a microprocessor or other electronic device, used to hold data for a particular purpose. For example, the AX register in an Intel 80x86 processor is the register that contains the results of arithmetic operations.

registration *n.* The process of precisely aligning elements or superimposing layers in a document or a graphic so that everything will print in the correct relative position. *See also* registration marks.

registration marks *n.* Marks placed on a page so that, in printing, the elements or layers in a document can be arranged correctly with respect to each other. Each element contains its own registration marks; when the marks are precisely superimposed, the elements are assembled correctly.

Registry or **registry** *n.* A central hierarchical database in Windows 95 and Windows NT used to store information necessary to configure the system for one or more users, applications, and hardware devices. The Registry contains information that the operating system continually references, such as profiles for each user, which applications are installed and what types of documents each can create, what hardware exists on the system, and which ports are in use. The Registry replaces most of the text-based .ini files used in Windows 3.*x* and the MS-DOS configuration files, such as AUTOEXEC.BAT and CONFIG.SYS. *Also called* System Registry. *See also* hierarchical database, .ini, input/output port.

relation *n.* A database table composed of attributes (individual characteristics, such as name or address, corresponding to the columns in a table) and tuples (sets of attribute values describing particular entities, such as customers, corresponding to the rows in a table). Within a relation, each tuple must be unique, nonrepeating, and unordered. If relational theory is to be applicable, each attribute must be a simple value, rather than a structure such as an array or a record. A relation in which all attributes can be only simple values is said to be normalized or in first normal form. *See also* normal form, table (definition 1), tuple.

relational database *n.* A database or database management system that stores information in tables—rows and columns of data—and conducts searches by utilizing data in specified columns of one table to find additional data in another table. In a relational database, the rows of a table represent records (collections of data about separate items) and the columns represent fields. In conducting searches, the database matches data from a field in one table with data in a corresponding field of another table to produce a third table that combines requested data from both tables. For example, if one table contains the fields EMPLOYEE-ID, LAST-NAME, FIRST-NAME, and HIRE-DATE, and another contains the fields DEPT, EMPLOYEE-ID, and SALARY, a relational database can match the EMPLOYEE-ID fields in the two tables to find such information as the names of all employees earning a certain salary. Microcomputer database products typically are relational databases. *Compare* flat-file database.

relational database management system *n.* *See* relational database.

relational expression *n.* An expression that uses a relational operator such as less than (<) or greater than (>) to compare two or more expressions. A relational expression resolves to a Boolean (true or false) value. *See also* Boolean, relational operator.

relational model *n.* A data model in which the data is organized in relations (tables). This is the model implemented in most modern database management systems. *See also* relation.

relational operator *n.* An operator used to compare two (or more) values or expressions. Typical relational operators are greater than (>), equal to (=), less than (<), not equal to (<>), greater than or equal to (>=), and less than or equal to (<=). *See also* relational expression.

relational structure *n.* The record organization used in the implementation of a relational model.

relative path *n.* A path that is implied by the current working directory. When a user enters a command that refers to a file and does not enter the full pathname, the current working directory becomes the relative path of the file referred to. *Compare* full path.

relative pointing device *n.* A cursor-control device, such as a mouse or a trackball, in which the movement of an on-screen cursor is linked to the movement of the device but not to the position of the device. For example, if a user picks up a mouse and puts it down in a different location on a desk, the position of the on-screen cursor does not change, because no movement (rolling) is detected. When the user rolls the mouse again, the cursor moves to reflect the mouse movement against the surface of the desk. *Compare* absolute pointing device.

relative URL *n.* Short for **relative u**niform **r**esource **l**ocator. A form of URL in which the domain and some or all directory names are omitted, leaving only the document name and extension (and perhaps a partial list of directory names). The indicated file is found in a location relative to the pathname of the current document. *Acronym:* RELURL. *See also* extension (definition 1), URL.

relay *n.* A switch activated by an electrical signal. A relay allows another signal to be controlled without the need for human action to route the other signal to the control point, and it also allows a relatively low-power signal to control a high-power signal.

release[1] *n.* **1.** A particular version of a piece of software, often associated with the most recent version (as in "the latest release"). Some companies use the term as an integral part of the product name (as in Lotus 1-2-3 Release 2.2). **2.** A version of a product that is available in general distribution. *Compare* beta[2].

release[2] *vb.* **1.** To relinquish control of a block of memory, a device, or another system resource to the operating system. **2.** To formally make a product available to the marketplace.

reliability *n.* The likelihood of a computer system or device continuing to function over a given period of time and under specified conditions. Reliability is measured by different performance indexes. For example, the reliability of a hard disk is often given as mean time between failures (MTBF), the average length of time the disk can be expected to function without failing. *See also* MTBF, MTTR.

reload *vb.* **1.** To load a program into memory from a storage device again in order to run it, because the system has crashed or the program's operation was otherwise interrupted. **2.** To retrieve a new copy of the Web page currently visible in a Web browser.

RELURL *n. See* relative URL.

remote *adj.* Not in the immediate vicinity, as a computer or other device located in another place (room, building, or city) and accessible through some type of cable or communications link.

remote access *n.* The use of a remote computer.

remote access server *n.* A host on a LAN that is equipped with modems to enable users to connect to the network over telephone lines. *Acronym:* RAS.

Remote Access Service *n.* Windows-based software that allows a user to gain remote access to the network server via a modem. *Acronym:* RAS. *See also* remote access.

remote administration *n.* The performance of tasks related to system administration via access from another machine in a network.

remote communications *n.* Interaction with a remote computer through a telephone connection or another communications line.

remote computer system *n. See* remote system.

remote login *n.* The action of logging in to a computer at a distant location by means of a data communications connection between the distant computer and the user's own computer. After remote login, the user's computer behaves like a terminal connected to the remote system. On the Internet, remote login is done primarily through rlogin and telnet. *See also* logon, rlogin[1], telnet[1].

remote system *n.* The computer or network that a remote user is accessing via a modem. *Compare* remote terminal.

remote terminal *n.* A terminal located at a site that is removed from the computer to which the terminal is attached. Remote terminals rely on modems and telephone lines to communicate with the host computer. *Compare* remote system.

removable disk *n.* A disk that can be removed from a disk drive. Floppy disks are removable; hard disks usually are not. *Also called* exchangeable disk. *See also* floppy disk.

rename *n.* A command in most FTP clients and in many other systems that allows the user to assign a new name to a file or files.

render *vb.* To produce a graphic image from a data file on an output device such as a video display or printer.

rendering *n.* The creation of an image containing geometric models, using color and shading to give the image a realistic look. Usually part of a geometric modeling package such as a CAD program, rendering uses mathematics to calculate how a light source would create highlights, shading, and color variations on the object. *See also* ray tracing.

repaginate *vb.* To recalculate the page breaks in a document.

repeat key *n.* On some keyboards, a key that must be held down at the same time as a character key to cause the character key's key code to be

A B C D E F G H I J K L M N O P Q R S T U V W X Y Z

sent repeatedly. On most computer keyboards, however, a repeat key is not needed because a key automatically repeats if held down for longer than a brief delay. *Compare* typematic.

repetitive strain injury *n.* An occupational disorder of the tendons, ligaments, and nerves caused by the cumulative effects of prolonged repetitious movements. Repetitive strain injuries are appearing with increasing frequency among office workers who spend long hours typing at computerized workstations that are not equipped with safeguards such as wrist supports. *Acronym:* RSI. *See also* carpal tunnel syndrome, wrist support.

replace *vb.* To put new data in the place of other data, usually after conducting a search for the data to be replaced. Text-based applications such as word processors typically include search-and-replace commands. *See also* search[1], search and replace.

replication *n.* In a distributed database management system, the process of copying the database (or parts of it) to the other parts of the network. Replication allows distributed database systems to remain synchronized. *See also* distributed database, distributed database management system.

report generator *n.* An application, commonly part of a database management program, that uses a report "form" created by the user to lay out and print the contents of a database. A report generator is used to select specific record fields or ranges of records, to make the output attractive, and to specify such features as headings, running heads, page numbers, and fonts.

report writer *n. See* report generator.

reprogrammable PROM *n. See* EPROM.

reprogrammable read-only memory *n. See* EPROM.

Request for Comments *n. See* RFC.

Request for Discussion *n.* A formal proposal for a discussion concerning the addition of a newsgroup to the Usenet hierarchy, the first step in a process that ends with a call for votes. *Acronym:* RFD. *See also* traditional newsgroup hierarchy, Usenet.

Request to Send *n. See* RTS.

required hyphen *n. See* hyphen.

reserved character *n.* A keyboard character that has a special meaning to a program and, as a result, normally cannot be used in assigning names to files, documents, and other user-generated tools such as macros. Characters commonly reserved for special uses include the asterisk (*), forward slash (/), backslash (\), question mark (?), and pipe, or vertical bar (|).

reserved memory *n. See* UMA.

reserved word *n.* A word that has special meaning to a program or in a programming language. A reserved word can be used only in certain predefined circumstances; it cannot be used in naming documents, files, labels, variables, or user-generated tools such as macros.

reset button *n.* A device that restarts a computer without turning off its power. *Compare* big red switch.

resident font *n. See* internal font.
resident program *n. See* TSR.
resize *vb.* To make an object or space larger or smaller. *Also called* scale.
resolution *n.* **1.** The fineness of detail attained by a printer or a monitor in producing an image. For printers that form characters from small, closely spaced dots, resolution is measured in dots per inch (dpi) and ranges from about 125 dpi for low-quality dot-matrix printers to about 600 dpi for some laser and ink-jet printers. (Typesetting equipment can print at resolutions of over 1,000 dpi.) For a video display, the number of pixels is determined by the graphics mode and video adapter, but the size of the display depends on the size and adjustment of the monitor; hence the resolution of a video display is taken as the total number of pixels displayed horizontally and vertically. For example, an SVGA adapter in a PC can provide a resolution of 1,024 pixels across by 768 pixels down, while Apple Computer offers a display system that provides resolutions up to 1,600 pixels across by 1,200 pixels down. *See also* high resolution, low resolution. **2.** The process of translation between a domain name address and an IP address. *See also* DNS (definition 1).
resolve *vb.* **1.** To match one piece of information to another in a database or lookup table. **2.** To find a setting in which no hardware conflicts occur.
resource *n.* **1.** Any part of a computer system or a network, such as a disk drive, printer, or memory, that can be allotted to a program or a process while it is running. **2.** An item of data or code that can be used by more than one program or in more than one place in a program, such as a dialog box, a sound effect, or a font in a windowing environment.
resource allocation *n.* The process of distributing a computer system's facilities to different components of a job in order to perform the job.
resource fork *n.* One of the two forks of a Macintosh file (the other being the data fork). The resource fork contains reusable items of information that a program can use during the course of execution, such as fonts, icons, digitized sound, dialog boxes, menus, and the program code itself. A user-created document typically stores its user-supplied data in the data fork, but it can also use its resource fork for storing items that might be used again in the document. *See also* resource (definition 2). *Compare* data fork.
response time *n.* **1.** The time, often an average, that elapses between the issuance of a request and the provision of the data requested (or notification of inability to provide it). **2.** The time required for a memory circuit or storage device to furnish data requested by the CPU.
restart *vb. See* reboot.
restore¹ *n.* The act of restoring a file or files. *See also* backup, recovery.
restore² *vb.* To copy files from a backup storage device to their normal location, especially if the files are being copied to replace files that were accidentally lost or deleted.

A B C D E F G H I J K L M N O P Q R S T U V W X Y Z

retrace *n.* The path followed by the electron beam in a raster-scan computer monitor as it returns either from the right to the left edge of the screen or from the bottom to the top of the screen. The retrace positions the electron beam for its next sweep across or down the screen; during this interval, the beam is briefly turned off to avoid drawing an unwanted line on the screen. Retracing occurs many times each second and uses tightly synchronized signals to ensure that the electron beam is turned off and on during the retrace. *See also* blanking, raster display.

retrieve *vb.* To obtain a specific requested item or set of data by locating it and returning it to a program or to the user. Computers can retrieve information from any source of storage—disks, tapes, or memory.

return from the dead *vb.* To regain access to the Internet after having been disconnected.

Return key *n.* A key on a keyboard used to terminate input of a field or record or to execute the default action of a dialog box. On IBM PCs and compatibles, this key is called Enter. *See also* Enter key.

Reverse Address Recognition Protocol *n. See* RARP.

Reverse ARP *n. See* RARP.

reverse video *n.* The reversal of light and dark in the display of selected characters on a video screen. For example, if text is normally displayed as black characters on a white background, reverse video presents text as white letters on a black background. Reverse video is commonly used as a means of highlighting text or special items (such as menu choices or the cursor) on the screen.

revert *vb.* To return to the last saved version of a document. Choosing this command tells the application to abandon all changes made in a document since the last time it was saved.

rewritable digital video disc *n.* Technology for recording data on discs that have the same storage capacity as digital video discs (DVDs) but can be rewritten like the compact disc–rewritable (CD-RW) devices. *See also* digital video disc.

rewrite *vb.* To write again, especially in situations where information is not permanently recorded, such as RAM or a video display. *Also called* refresh, regenerate. *See also* dynamic RAM.

RF *n. See* radio frequency.

RFC *n.* Acronym for **R**equest **f**or **C**omments. A document in which a standard, a protocol, or other information pertaining to the operation of the Internet is published. The RFC is actually issued after discussion and serves as the standard. RFCs can be obtained from sources such as InterNIC. *See also* InterNIC.

RFD *n. See* Request for Discussion.

RFI *n.* Acronym for **r**adio **f**requency **i**nterference. Noise introduced into an electronic circuit, such as a radio or television, by electromagnetic radiation produced by another circuit, such as a computer.

RF shielding *n.* A structure, generally sheet metal or metallic foil, designed to prevent the passage of radio frequency (RF) electromagnetic radiation. RF shielding is intended to keep RF radiation either inside a device or out of a device. Without proper RF shielding, devices that use or emit RF radiation can interfere with each other. Computers generate RF radiation and, to meet Federal Communications Commission standards, must be properly shielded to prevent this RF radiation from leaking out. A personal computer's metal case provides most of the needed RF shielding. Devices meeting FCC type A standards are suitable for business use. Devices meeting the more stringent FCC type B standards are suitable for home use. *See also* radio frequency, RFI.

RGB *n.* Acronym for **r**ed-**g**reen-**b**lue. A model for describing colors produced by emitting light, as on a video monitor, rather than by absorbing it, as with ink on paper. The three kinds of cone cells in the eye respond to red, green, and blue light, respectively, so percentages of these additive primary colors can be mixed to get the appearance of any desired color. Adding no color produces black; adding 100 percent of all three colors results in white. *See also* CMYK, RGB monitor. *Compare* CMY.

RGB display *n. See* RGB monitor.

RGB monitor *n.* A color monitor that receives its signals for red, green, and blue levels over separate lines. An RGB monitor generally produces sharper and cleaner images than those produced by a composite monitor, which receives levels for all three colors over a single line. *See also* RGB.

ribbon cable *n.* A flat cable containing up to 100 parallel wires for data and control lines. For example, ribbon cables are used inside a computer's case to connect the disk drives to their controllers.

Rich Text Format *n.* An adaptation of Document Content Architecture used for transferring formatted text documents between applications, even those applications running on different platforms, such as an IBM PC and an Apple Macintosh. *Acronym:* RTF.

right click *vb.* To make a selection using the button on the right side of a mouse or other pointing device. Right-clicking in the Windows 95 environment, for example, typically brings up a pop-up menu with options applicable to the object over which the pointer is positioned. *See also* click, mouse, pointing device.

right justification *n.* The process of aligning text evenly along the right margins of a column or page. The left edge of the text is ragged. *See also* ragged left. *Compare* full justification, left justification.

rigid disk *n. See* hard disk.

ring network *n.* A LAN in which devices (nodes) are connected in a closed loop, or ring. Messages pass around the ring from node to node in one direction. When a node receives a message, it examines the destination address. If the address matches the node's, the node accepts the message; otherwise, it regenerates the signal and passes the message along to the next node. Such regeneration allows a ring network to cover larger distances than star

A B C D E F G H I J K L M N O P Q R S T U V W X Y Z

and bus networks. The ring can also be designed to bypass any malfunctioning or failed node. Because of the closed loop, however, adding new nodes can be difficult. *See also* token passing, token ring network. *Compare* bus network, star network.

RIP *n. See* raster image processor.

RISC *n.* Acronym for **r**educed **i**nstruction **s**et **c**omputing. A microprocessor design that focuses on rapid and efficient processing of a relatively small set of simple instructions that includes most of the instructions a computer decodes and executes. RISC architecture optimizes each instruction so that it can be carried out very rapidly. RISC chips thus execute simple instructions more quickly than general-purpose CISC microprocessors, which are designed to handle a much wider array of instructions. They are, however, slower than CISC chips at executing complex instructions, which must be broken down into many machine instructions that RISC microprocessors can perform. Families of RISC chips include Sun Microsystems' SPARC, Motorola's 88000, Intel's i860, and the PowerPC developed by Apple, IBM, and Motorola. *See also* architecture. *Compare* CISC.

Rivest-Shamir-Adleman encryption *n. See* RSA encryption.

RJ-11 connector *n. See* phone connector.

RJ-11 jack *n. See* phone connector.

RJ-45 connector *n.* Abbreviation for **R**egistered **J**ack **45**. An eight-wire connector used to attach devices to category 5 cables. The wires are encased in a plastic sheath and color-coded to match corresponding slots in jacks. RJ-45 jacks are used to connect computers to LANs and to link ISDN devices to Network Terminator 1 devices. *See also* ISDN. *Compare* phone connector.

RJ-45 jack *n. See* RJ-45 connector.

rlogin[1] *n.* A protocol used to log in to a networked computer, in which the local system automatically supplies the user's login name. *See also* communications protocol, logon. *Compare* telnet[1].

rlogin[2] *vb.* To connect to a networked computer using the rlogin protocol.

RLSD *n.* Acronym for **R**eceived **L**ine **S**ignal **D**etect. *See* DCD.

robopost *vb.* To post articles to newsgroups automatically, usually by means of a bot. *See also* bot (definition 3), newsgroup, post.

robot *n.* **1.** A machine that can sense and react to input and cause changes in its surroundings with some degree of intelligence, ideally without human supervision. Although robots are often designed to mimic human movements in carrying out their work, they are seldom humanlike in appearance. Robots are commonly used in manufacturing products such as automobiles and computers. **2.** *See* bot, spider.

ROFL Acronym for **r**olling **o**n the **f**loor, **l**aughing. An expression, used mostly in newsgroups and online discussions, to indicate one's appreciation of a joke or other humorous circumstance. *Also called* ROTFL.

role-playing game *n.* A game that is played online, such as a MUD, in which participants take on the identities of characters that interact with each other. Often these games have a fantasy or science fiction setting and have a set of rules that all players need to follow. *See also* MUD.

ROM *n.* **1.** Acronym for **r**ead-**o**nly **m**emory. A semiconductor circuit into which code or data is permanently installed by the manufacturing process. The use of this technology is economically viable only if the chips are produced in large quantities; experimental designs or small volumes are best handled using PROM or EPROM. **2.** Acronym for **r**ead-**o**nly **m**emory. Any semiconductor circuit serving as memory that contains instructions or data that can be read but not modified (whether placed there by manufacturing or by a programming process, as in PROM and EPROM). *See also* EEPROM, EPROM, PROM.

roman *adj.* Describes a type style in which the characters are upright rather than slanted. *Compare* italic.

ROM BIOS *n.* Acronym for **r**ead-**o**nly **m**emory **b**asic **i**nput/**o**utput **s**ystem. *See* BIOS.

ROM card *n.* A plug-in module that contains one or more printer fonts, programs, games, or other information stored in ROM. A typical ROM card is about the size of a credit card and several times thicker. It stores information directly in integrated circuit boards. *Also called* font card, game card. *See also* ROM (definition 1), ROM cartridge.

ROM cartridge *n.* A plug-in module that contains one or more printer fonts, programs, games, or other information stored in ROM chips on a board enclosed in a plastic case with a connector exposed at one end so that it can easily plug into a printer, computer, game system, or other device. *Also called* game cartridge. *See also* ROM (definition 1), ROM card.

root *n.* The main or uppermost level in a hierarchically organized set of information. The root is the point from which subsets branch in a logical sequence that moves from a broad focus to narrower perspectives. *See also* leaf, tree.

root directory *n.* The point of entry into the directory tree in a disk-based hierarchical directory structure. Branching from this root are various directories and subdirectories, each of which can contain one or more files and subdirectories of its own. In MS-DOS, the root directory is identified by a name consisting of a single backslash character (\).

root name *n.* In MS-DOS and Windows, the first part of a filename. In MS-DOS and earlier versions of Windows, the maximum length of the root name was 8 characters; in Windows NT and later versions of Windows, the root name may be as long as 255 characters. *See also* 8.3, extension (definition 1), filename, long filenames.

ROT13 encryption *n.* A simple encryption method in which each letter is replaced with the letter of the alphabet 13 letters after the original letter, so that A is replaced by N, and so forth; N, in turn, is replaced by A, and Z is replaced by M. ROT13 encryption is not used to protect messages against unauthorized readers; rather, it is used in newsgroups to encode messages that a user may not want to read, such as sexual jokes or spoilers. Some newsreaders can automatically perform ROT13 encryption and decryption at the touch of a key.

RO terminal *n.* Short for **r**ead-**o**nly **terminal.** A terminal that is able to receive data but cannot send data. Nearly all printers can be classified as RO terminals.

ROTFL *See* ROFL.

router *n.* An intermediary device on a communications network that expedites message delivery. On a single network linking many computers through a mesh of possible connections, a router receives transmitted messages and forwards them to their correct destinations over the most efficient available route. On an interconnected set of local area networks (LANs) using the same communications protocols, a router serves the somewhat different function of acting as a link between LANs, enabling messages to be sent from one to another. *See also* bridge, gateway.

routine *n.* Any section of code that can be invoked (executed) within a program. A routine usually has a name (identifier) associated with it and is executed by referencing that name. Related terms (which may or may not be exact synonyms, depending on the context) are function, procedure, and subroutine. *See also* function (definition 3), procedure.

row *n.* A series of items arranged horizontally within some type of framework—for example, a continuous series of cells running from left to right in a spreadsheet; a horizontal line of pixels on a video screen; or a set of data values aligned horizontally in a table. *Compare* column.

RPROM *n.* Short for **r**eprogrammable **PROM.** *See* EPROM.

RS-232-C standard *n.* An accepted industry standard for serial communications connections. Adopted by the Electrical Industries Association, this Recommended Standard (RS) defines the specific lines and signal characteristics used by serial communications controllers to standardize the transmission of serial data between devices. The letter C denotes that the current version of the standard is the third in a series.

RS-422/423/449 *n.* Standards for serial communications with transmission distances over 50 feet. RS-449 incorporates RS-422 and RS-423. Macintosh serial ports are RS-422 ports. *See also* RS-232-C standard.

RSA encryption *n.* Short for **R**ivest-**S**hamir-**A**dleman **encryption.** The patented public key encryption algorithm, introduced by Ronald Rivest, Adi Shamir, and Leonard Adleman in 1978, on which the PGP (Pretty Good Privacy) encryption program is based. *See also* PGP, public key encryption.

RSI *n. See* repetitive strain injury.

RSN *See* Real Soon Now.

RTF *n. See* Rich Text Format.

RTFM Acronym for **r**ead **t**he **f**laming (or **f**riendly) **m**anual. In an Internet newsgroup or product support conference, a common answer to a question that is adequately explained in the instruction manual. *Also called* RTM.
RTM Acronym for **r**ead **t**he **m**anual. *See* RTFM.
RTS *n.* Acronym for **R**equest **t**o **S**end. A signal sent, as from a computer to its modem, to request permission to transmit; the signal is often used in serial communications. *Compare* CTS.
rubber banding *n.* In computer graphics, changing the shape of an object made up of connected lines by "grabbing" a point on an anchored line and "pulling" it to the new location.
rudder control *n.* A device, consisting of a pair of pedals, that enables a user to input rudder movements in a flight simulation program. The rudder control is used along with a joystick and possibly a throttle control.
rule *n.* **1.** A line printed above, below, or to the side of some element, either to set that item off from the rest of the page or to improve the look of the page. The thickness of a rule is typically measured in points. *See also* point[1] (definition 1). **2.** In expert systems, a statement that can be used to verify premises and to enable a conclusion to be drawn. *See also* expert system.
ruler *n.* In some applications, such as word processors, an on-screen scale marked off in inches or other units of measure and used to show line widths, tab settings, paragraph indents, and so on. In programs in which the ruler is "live," the on-screen ruler can be used with the mouse or the keyboard to set, adjust, or remove tab stops and other settings.
run *vb.* To execute a program.
run around *vb.* In page composition, to position text so that it flows around an illustration or other display.
running foot *n.* One or more lines of text in the bottom margin area of a page, composed of one or more elements such as the page number, the name of the chapter, the date, and so on. *Also called* footer.
running head *n.* One or more lines of text in the top margin area of a page, composed of one or more elements such as the page number, the name of the chapter, the date, and so on. *Also called* header.
run time *n.* **1.** The time period during which a program is running. **2.** The amount of time needed to execute a given program.
run-time version *n.* A special release that provides the computer user with some, but not all, of the capabilities available in the full-fledged software package.
R/W *adj.* *See* read/write.
RXD *n.* Short for Receive (**rx**) **D**ata. A line used to carry received serial data from one device to another, as from a modem to a computer. *Compare* TXD.

S

Sad Mac *n.* An error indication that occurs on Apple Macintosh computers when the system fails the initial diagnostic test. A Sad Mac is a picture of a Macintosh with a frowning face and Xs for eyes, with an error code beneath the picture.
safe mode *n.* In some versions of Windows, such as Windows 95, a boot mode in which most drivers and peripherals are disconnected to allow the user to correct some problem with the system. This will occur if the system was not shut down properly or if the system failed to complete a boot-up. *See also* boot[1].
sans serif *adj.* Literally, "without stroke"; describes any typeface in which the characters have no serifs. In contrast to typefaces with serifs, sans serif typefaces usually possess a more straightforward, geometric appearance. They are used more frequently in display type, such as headlines, than in blocks of text. This sentence appears in a sans serif typeface. *See also* serif[2]. *Compare* serif[1].
satellite *n. See* communications satellite.
satellite computer *n.* A computer that is connected to another computer, with which it interacts over a communications link. As its name indicates, a satellite computer is of lesser "stature" than the main, or host, computer; the host controls either the satellite itself or the tasks the satellite performs. *See also* remote communications.
saturation *n.* In color graphics and printing, the amount of color in a specified hue, often specified as a percentage. *See also* HSB.
save *vb.* To write data (typically a file) to a storage medium, such as a disk or tape.
scalable *adj.* Of or relating to the characteristic of a piece of hardware or software that makes it possible for it to expand to meet future needs. For example, a scalable network allows the network administrator to add many nodes without needing to redesign the basic system.
scalable font *n.* Any font that can be scaled to produce characters in varying sizes. Examples of scalable fonts are screen fonts in a graphical user interface, stroke fonts and outline fonts common to most PostScript printers, TrueType fonts, and the method for screen font definition used in Macintosh System 7. In contrast, most text-based interfaces and printing devices offer text in only one size. *See also* outline font, PostScript font, screen font, stroke font, TrueType.
scale[1] *n.* A horizontal or vertical line on a graph that shows minimum, maximum, and interval values for the data plotted.

scale[2] *vb.* To enlarge or reduce a graphics display, such as a drawing or a proportional character font, by adjusting its size proportionally.
scaling *n.* In computer graphics, the process of enlarging or reducing a graphical image—scaling a font to a desired size or scaling a model created with a CAD program, for example.
scan *vb.* **1.** In television and computer display technologies, to move an electron beam across the inner surface of the screen, one line at a time, to light the phosphors that create a displayed image. **2.** In facsimile and other optical technologies, to transport a light-sensitive device across an image-bearing surface such as a page of text, converting the light and dark areas on the surface to binary digits that can be interpreted by a computer.
scan code *n.* A code number transmitted to an IBM or compatible computer whenever a key is pressed or released. Each key on the keyboard has a unique scan code. This code is not the same as the ASCII code for the letter, number, or symbol shown on the key; it is a special identifier for the key itself and is always the same for a particular key. When a key is pressed, the ROM BIOS translates the scan code into its ASCII equivalent. Because a single key can generate more than one character (lowercase *a* and uppercase *A,* for example), the ROM BIOS also takes into account the status of keys that change the keyboard state, such as the Shift key, when it performs the translation. *Compare* key code.
scan head *n.* An optical device found in scanners and fax machines that moves across the subject being scanned, converts light and dark areas to electrical signals, and sends those signals to the scanning system for processing.
scan line *n.* **1.** One of many horizontal lines of a graphics display screen, such as a raster-scan monitor or a television. **2.** A single row of pixels read by a scanning device.
scanner *n.* An optical input device that uses light-sensing equipment to capture an image on paper or some other subject. The image is translated into a digital signal that can then be manipulated by optical character recognition software or graphics software. *See also* drum scanner, flatbed scanner, handheld scanner, sheet-fed scanner.
scan rate *n. See* refresh rate.
schema *n.* A description of a database to a database management system in the language provided by the DBMS. A schema defines aspects of the database, such as its attributes (fields) and the accepted values of the attributes.
sci. newsgroups *n.* Usenet newsgroups that are part of the sci. hierarchy and use the prefix .sci in their names. These newsgroups are devoted to discussions of scientific research and applications, except computer science, which is discussed in the comp. newsgroups. *See also* newsgroup, traditional newsgroup hierarchy, Usenet.
scissoring *n. See* clip.
scrambler *n.* A device or program that reorders a signal sequence so as to render it indecipherable. *See also* encryption.

A B C D E F G H I J K L M N O P Q R S T U V W X Y Z

A B C D E F G H I J K L M N O P Q R S T U V W X Y Z

scrap *n.* An application or a system file maintained for storing data that has been marked for movement, copying, or deletion. *See also* clipboard (definition 1).
scrapbook *n.* **1.** A file in which a series of text and graphical images can be saved for subsequent use. **2.** A Macintosh system file that can hold text and graphical images for later use. *Compare* clipboard (definition 1).
scratch *vb.* To erase or discard data.
scratchpad *n.* **1.** A temporary storage area used by a program or an operating system for calculations, data, and other work in progress. *See also* temporary file. **2.** A high-speed memory circuit used to hold small items of data for rapid retrieval. *See also* cache.
screen angle *n.* The angle at which the dots in a halftone screen are printed. A correct angle will minimize blur and other undesirable effects, such as moiré patterns. *See also* halftone, moiré.
screen dump *n.* A duplicate of a screen image; essentially, a "snapshot" of the screen that is either sent to a printer or saved as a file.
screen flicker *n. See* flicker.
screen font *n.* A typeface designed for display on a computer monitor screen. Screen fonts often have accompanying PostScript fonts for printing to PostScript-compatible printers. *See also* derived font, intrinsic font. *Compare* PostScript font, printer font.
screen grabber *n. See* grabber (definition 3).
screen phone *n.* A type of Internet appliance combining a telephone with an LCD display screen, a digital fax modem, and a computer keyboard, with ports for a mouse, printer, and other peripheral devices. Screen phones can be used as regular telephones for voice communications and can also be used as terminals to gain access to the Internet and other online services.
screen pitch *n.* A measurement of a computer monitor's screen density, representing the distance between phosphors on the display. The lower the number, the more detail can be displayed clearly. For example, a .28-dot-pitch screen has better resolution than one with .32. *See also* phosphor.
screen saver *n.* A utility that causes a monitor to blank out or display a certain image after a specified amount of time passes without the keyboard being touched or the mouse being moved. Touching a key or moving the mouse deactivates the screen saver. Screen savers were originally used to prevent images from becoming permanently etched on a monitor's screen. Although modern monitors are not susceptible to this problem, screen savers remain popular for their decorative and entertainment value.
screen shot *n.* An image that shows all or part of a computer display.
script *n.* A program consisting of a series of instructions to an application or a utility program. For example, a script can be used with a word processor to open all documents and italicize every instance of a particular word. *See also* macro.

scripting language *n.* A simple programming language designed to perform special or limited tasks, sometimes associated with a particular application or function. An example of a scripting language is Perl. *See also* Perl, script.

scroll *vb.* To move a document or other data in a window in order to view a particular portion of the document. Scrolling may be controlled by the mouse, arrow keys, or other keys on the keyboard. *See also* scroll bar.

scroll arrow *n.* *See* scroll bar.

scroll bar *n.* In some graphical user interfaces, a vertical or horizontal bar at the side or bottom of a display area that can be used with a mouse for moving around in that area. Scroll bars often have four active areas: two scroll arrows for moving line by line, a sliding scroll box (elevator) for moving to an arbitrary location in the display area, and gray areas for moving in increments of one window at a time.

scroll box *n.* *See* elevator, scroll bar.

Scroll Lock key *n.* On the IBM PC/XT and AT and compatible keyboards, a key on the top row of the numeric keypad that controls the effect of the cursor control keys and sometimes prevents the screen from scrolling. On the enhanced and Macintosh keyboards, this key is to the right of the function keys on the top row. Many modern applications ignore the Scroll Lock setting.

SCSI *n.* Acronym for **S**mall **C**omputer **S**ystem **I**nterface. A standard high-speed parallel interface defined by ANSI. A SCSI interface is used to connect microcomputers to SCSI peripheral devices, such as many hard disks and printers, and to other computers and LANs. The term SCSI is commonly pronounced "scuzzy." *Compare* ESDI, IDE.

SCSI connector *n.* A cable connector used to connect a SCSI device to a SCSI bus. *See also* bus, connector, SCSI device.

SCSI device *n.* A peripheral device that uses the SCSI standard to exchange data and control signals with a computer's CPU. *See also* peripheral, SCSI.

SCSI ID *n.* The unique identity of a SCSI device. Each device connected to a SCSI bus must have a different SCSI ID. A maximum of eight SCSI IDs can be used on the same SCSI bus. *See also* bus, SCSI device.

SCSI network *n.* A set of devices on a SCSI bus, which acts like a local area network. *See also* SCSI.

SCSI port *n.* **1.** A SCSI host adapter within a computer, which provides a logical connection between the computer and all the devices on the SCSI bus. *See also* host adapter, SCSI. **2.** A connector on a device for a SCSI bus cable. *See also* SCSI.

scuzzy *n.* *See* SCSI.

SDRAM *n.* *See* synchronous DRAM.

SDSL *n.* *See* symmetric digital subscriber line.

#
A
B
C
D
E
F
G
H
I
J
K
L
M
N
O
P
Q
R
S
T
U
V
W
X
Y
Z

.sea *n.* A file extension for a self-extracting Macintosh archive compressed with StuffIt. *See also* self-extracting file, StuffIt.

seamless integration *n.* The favorable result that occurs when a new hardware component or program blends smoothly into the overall operation of the system.

search[1] *n.* The process of seeking a particular file or specific data. A search is carried out by a program through comparison or calculation to determine whether a match to some pattern exists or whether some other criteria have been met. *See also* binary search, linear search, search and replace, wildcard character.

search[2] *vb.* **1.** To look for the location of a file. **2.** To seek specific data within a file or data structure. *See also* replace.

search algorithm *n.* An algorithm designed to locate a certain element, called the target, in a data structure. *See also* algorithm, binary search, linear search.

search and replace *n.* A common process in applications such as word processors in which the user specifies two strings of characters. The process searches for instances of the first string in a document and replaces them with the second string. This operation may or may not be sensitive to uppercase and lowercase, depending on the application.

search criteria *n.* The terms or conditions that a search engine uses to find items. *See also* search engine.

search engine *n.* **1.** A program that searches for keywords in documents or in a database. **2.** On the Internet, a program that searches for keywords in files and documents found on the Web, in newsgroups, on Gopher menus, and in FTP archives. Some search engines are used only for a single Internet or Web site; others search across many sites, using such agents as spiders to gather lists of available files and documents and to store these lists in databases that users can search by keyword. Most search engines reside on a server. *See also* agent (definition 2), FTP[1] (definition 1), Gopher, newsgroup, spider, World Wide Web.

search key *n.* **1.** The particular field (or column) of the records to be searched in a database. *See also* primary key, secondary key. **2.** The value that is to be searched for in a document or any collection of data.

search string *n.* The string of characters to be matched in a search—typically (but not necessarily) a text string.

seat[1] *n.* One workstation or computer, in the context of software licensing on a per-seat basis. *See also* license agreement, workstation (definition 1).

seat[2] *vb.* To insert a piece of hardware fully and position it correctly in a computer or affiliated equipment, as in seating a single inline memory module (SIMM) in its socket.

secondary channel *n.* A transmission channel in a communications system that carries testing and diagnostic information rather than actual data. *Compare* primary channel.

secondary key *n.* A field that is to be sorted or searched within a subset of the records having identical primary key values. *Compare* primary key.
secondary service provider *n.* An ISP that provides a Web presence but not direct connectivity. *See also* ISP.
secondary storage *n.* Any data storage medium other than a computer's random access memory—typically tape or disk. *Compare* primary storage.
second-generation computer *n.* *See* computer.
second normal form *n.* Abbreviated 2NF. *See* normal form.
secret channel *n.* *See* private channel.
sector *n.* A portion of the data storage area on a disk. A disk is divided into sides (top and bottom), tracks (rings on each surface), and sectors (sections of each ring). Sectors are the smallest physical storage units on a disk and are of fixed size; typically, they are each capable of holding 512 bytes of information.
secure channel *n.* A communications link that has been protected against unauthorized access, operation, or use by means of isolation from the public network, encryption, or other forms of control. *See also* encryption.
Secure Electronics Transactions protocol *n.* A protocol for conducting secure transactions on the Internet, the result of a joint effort by GTE, IBM, MasterCard, Microsoft, Netscape, SAIC, Terisa Systems, VeriSign, and Visa. *Acronym:* SET.
Secure HTTP *n.* *See* S-HTTP.
Secure Hypertext Transfer Protocol *n.* *See* S-HTTP.
Secure/Multipurpose Internet Mail Extensions *n.* *See* S/MIME.
secure site *n.* A Web site capable of providing secure transactions, ensuring that credit card numbers and other personal information will not be accessible to unauthorized parties.
Secure Sockets Layer *n.* A proposed open standard developed by Netscape Communications for establishing a secure communications channel to prevent the interception of critical information, such as credit card numbers. The primary purpose of the Secure Sockets Layer is to enable secure electronic financial transactions on the World Wide Web, although it is designed to work with other Internet services as well. This technology, which uses public key encryption, is incorporated into the Netscape Navigator Web browser and Netscape's commerce servers. *Acronym:* SSL. *See also* commerce server, open standard, public key encryption. *Compare* S-HTTP.
Secure Transaction Technology *n.* The use of the Secure Sockets Layer, Secure HTTP, or both in online transactions, such as form transmission or credit card purchases. *Acronym:* STT. *See also* Secure Sockets Layer, S-HTTP.
secure wide area network *n.* A set of computers that communicate over a public network, such as the Internet, but use security measures such as encryption, authentication, and authorization to prevent their communications from being intercepted and understood by unauthorized users. *Acronym:* S/WAN. *See also* authentication, authorization, encryption, virtual private network.

#
A
B
C
D
E
F
G
H
I
J
K
L
M
N
O
P
Q
R
S
T
U
V
W
X
Y
Z

security *n.* Protection of a computer system and its data from harm or loss. A major focus of computer security, especially on systems accessed by many people or through communications lines, is preventing system access by unauthorized individuals.

security log *n.* A log, generated by a firewall or other security device, that lists events that could affect security, such as access attempts or commands, and the names of the users involved. *See also* firewall, log.

seek *n.* The process of moving the read/write head in a disk drive to the proper site, typically for a read or write operation.

seek time *n.* The time required to move a disk drive's read/write head to a specific location on a disk. *See also* access time (definition 2).

select *vb.* **1.** In general computer use, to specify a block of data or text on screen by highlighting it or otherwise marking it, with the intent of performing some operation on it. **2.** In database management, to choose records according to a specified set of criteria. *See also* sort. **3.** In information processing, to choose from a number of options or alternatives, such as input/output channels.

selection *n.* **1.** In applications, the highlighted portion of an on-screen document. **2.** In communications, the initial contact made between a computer and a remote station receiving a message.

selector pen *n.* *See* light pen.

self-checking digit *n.* A digit, appended to a number during its encoding, whose function is to confirm the accuracy of the encoding. *See also* checksum, parity bit.

self-extracting archive *n.* *See* self-extracting file.

self-extracting file *n.* An executable program file that contains one or more compressed text or data files. When a user runs the program, it uncompresses the compressed files and stores them on the user's hard drive.

self-test *n.* A set of one or more diagnostic tests that a computer or peripheral device (such as a printer) performs on itself. *See also* power-on self test.

semiconductor *n.* A substance, commonly silicon or germanium, whose ability to conduct electricity falls between that of a conductor and that of a nonconductor (insulator). The term is used loosely to refer to electronic components made from semiconductor materials.

send *vb.* To transmit a message or file through a communications channel.

sensor *n.* A device that detects or measures something by converting nonelectrical energy to electrical energy. A photocell, for example, detects or measures light by converting it to electrical energy.

sensor glove *n.* A hand-worn computer input device for virtual-reality environments. The glove translates finger movements by the user into commands for manipulating objects in the environment. *Also called* data glove. *See also* virtual reality.

sequence check *n.* A process that verifies that data or records conform to a particular order.

Sequenced Packet Exchange *n.* *See* SPX (definition 1).

sequential access *n.* A method of storing or retrieving information that requires the program to start reading at the beginning and continue until it finds the desired data. Sequential access is best used for files in which each piece of information is related to the information that comes before it, such as mailing list files and word processing documents. *Also called* serial access. *Compare* random access.

sequential processing *n.* **1.** The processing of items of information in the order in which they are stored or input. **2.** The execution of one instruction, routine, or task followed by the execution of the next in line. *Compare* multiprocessing, parallel processing.

sequential search *n.* *See* linear search.

serial *adj.* One by one. For example, in serial transmission, information is transferred one bit at a time. *Compare* parallel (definition 1).

serial access *n.* *See* sequential access.

serial communications *n.* The exchange of information between computers or between computers and peripheral devices one bit at a time over a single channel. Serial communications can be synchronous or asynchronous. Both sender and receiver must use the same baud rate, parity, and control information. *See also* baud rate, parity, start bit, stop bit.

Serial Infrared *n.* A system developed by Hewlett-Packard for transmitting data between two devices up to 1 meter apart using an infrared light beam. Infrared ports on the receiving and the sending devices must be aligned. Generally, Serial Infrared is used with laptops and many notebook computers, as well as with peripherals such as printers. *Acronym:* SIR. *See also* infrared port.

serial interface *n.* A data transmission scheme in which data and control bits are sent sequentially over a single channel. In reference to a serial input/output connection, the term usually implies the use of an RS-232 or RS-422 interface. *See also* RS-232-C standard, RS-422/423/449. *Compare* parallel interface.

serialize *vb.* To change from parallel transmission (byte by byte) to serial transmission (bit by bit).

Serial Line Internet Protocol *n.* *See* SLIP.

serial mouse *n.* A pointing device that attaches to the computer through a standard serial port. *See also* mouse. *Compare* bus mouse.

serial port *n.* An input/output location (channel) that sends and receives data to and from a computer's CPU or a communications device one bit at a time. Serial ports are used for serial data communication and as interfaces with some peripheral devices, such as mice and printers.

serial port adapter *n.* An interface card or device that either provides a serial port or converts a serial port to another use. *See also* adapter, serial port.

serial printer *n.* A printer connected to the computer via a serial interface (commonly RS-232-C or compatible). Connectors for serial printers vary widely, which is one reason they are less popular than parallel printers

#
A
B
C
D
E
F
G
H
I
J
K
L
M
N
O
P
Q
R
S
T
U
V
W
X
Y
Z

among those who use IBM PCs and compatibles. Serial printers are standard for Apple computers. *See also* DB connector, serial, serial transmission. *Compare* parallel printer.

serial processing *n.* *See* sequential processing (definition 2).

serial transmission *n.* The transfer of discrete signals one after another. In communications and data transfer, serial transmission involves sending information over a single line one bit at a time, as in modem-to-modem connections. *Compare* parallel transmission.

serif^1 *adj.* Describes a typeface characterized by the use of serifs. For example, the typeface used in this dictionary is a serif typeface. *See also* serif^2. *Compare* sans serif.

serif^2 *n.* Any of the short lines or ornaments at the ends of the strokes that form a typeface character.

server *n.* **1.** On a local area network, a computer running administrative software that controls access to the network and its resources, such as printers and disk drives, and provides resources to computers functioning as workstations on the network. **2.** On the Internet or other network, a computer or program that responds to commands from a client. For example, a file server may contain an archive of data or program files; when a client submits a request for a file, the server transfers a copy of the file to the client. *See also* client/server architecture. *Compare* client (definition 2).

server-based application *n.* A program that is shared over a network. The program is stored on the network server and can be used at more than one client machine at a time.

server cluster *n.* A group of independent computers that work together as a single system. A server cluster presents the appearance of a single server to a client.

server error *n.* A failure to complete a request for information through HTTP that results from an error at the server rather than an error by the client or the user. Server errors are indicated by HTTP status codes beginning with 5. *See also* HTTP, HTTP status codes.

server push-pull *n.* A combination of Web client/server techniques individually called server push and client pull. In server push, the server loads data to the client; the data connection stays open, allowing the server to continue sending data to the browser as necessary. In client pull, the server loads data to the client, but the data connection does not stay open. The server sends an HTML directive to the browser telling it to reopen the connection after a certain interval to get more data or possibly to open a new URL. *See also* HTML, server (definition 2), URL.

server-side includes *n.* A mechanism for including dynamic text in Web documents. Server-side includes are special command codes recognized and interpreted by the server; their output is placed in the document body before the document is sent to the browser. Server-side includes can be used, for example, to include the date/time stamp in the text of the file. *See also* server (definition 2), SHTML.

service *n.* **1.** A customer-based or user-oriented function, such as technical support or network provision. **2.** In reference to programming and software, a program or routine that provides support to other programs, particularly at a low (close to the hardware) level. *See also* utility.

service provider *n. See* ISP.

servlet or **servelet** or **serverlet** *n.* A small Java program that runs on a server. Servlets perform lightweight Web services, such as redirecting a user from an outdated address to the correct page—tasks traditionally handled by CGI applications. Servlets execute quickly, thereby reducing system overhead. *See also* applet, CGI (definition 1).

session *n.* **1.** The time during which a program is running. In most interactive programs, a session is the time during which the program accepts input and processes information. **2.** In communications, the time during which two computers maintain a connection. **3.** *See* session layer.

session layer *n.* The fifth of the seven layers in the ISO/OSI model for standardizing computer-to-computer communications. The session layer manages the communications between remote users or processes. It establishes, maintains, and coordinates the communications, handling the many details that must be agreed on by the two communicating devices. *See also* ISO/OSI model.

SET protocol *n. See* Secure Electronics Transactions protocol.

set-top box *n.* A device that converts a cable TV signal to an input signal to the TV set. Set-top boxes can be used to access the World Wide Web.

setup *n.* **1.** A computer along with all its devices. **2.** The procedures involved in preparing a software program or application to operate within a computer.

setup program *n.* **1.** A built-in BIOS program for reconfiguring system settings to accommodate a new disk drive. *See also* BIOS. **2.** *See* installation program.

setup string *n. See* control code.

seven-segment display *n.* An LED or LCD display that can show any of the 10 decimal digits. The seven segments are the seven bars that form a numeral 8, as in a calculator display.

sex changer *n. See* gender changer.

sfil *n.* The file type of a Macintosh System 7 sound file.

.sgm *n.* The MS-DOS/Windows 3.*x* file extension that identifies files encoded in SGML. The .sgml extension is truncated to three letters because MS-DOS and Windows 3.*x* cannot recognize file extensions longer than three letters. *See also* SGML.

.sgml *n.* The file extension that identifies files encoded in SGML. *See also* SGML.

SGML *n.* Acronym for **S**tandard **G**eneralized **M**arkup **L**anguage. An information management standard adopted by the ISO in 1986 as a means of providing platform- and application-independent documents that retain formatting, indexing, and linked information. SGML provides a grammarlike mechanism for users to define the structure of their documents and the tags they will use to denote the structure in individual documents. *See also* ISO.

shade¹ *n.* A particular color variation produced by mixing black with a pure color. *See also* brightness, IRGB.

shade² *vb.* To give added dimension to an image by including changes in appearance caused by light and shadow. *See also* color model.

shadow memory *n.* A technique employed by the BIOS in some 80x86-based computers to copy the system's ROM BIOS routines into an unused section of RAM during the computer's startup process. This helps boost system performance by diverting system requests for the BIOS routines to their "shadow" copies. *Also called* shadow RAM, shadow ROM.

shadow print *n.* A style applied to text in which a duplicate of each character is shifted, typically down and to the right, to create a shadow effect.

shadow RAM *n. See* shadow memory.

shadow ROM *n. See* shadow memory.

share *vb.* To make files, directories, or folders accessible to other users over a network.

shared directory *n. See* network directory.

shared folder *n.* On a Macintosh computer connected to a network and running System 6.0 or higher, a folder that a user has made available to others on the network. A shared folder is analogous to a network directory on a PC. *See also* network directory.

shared memory *n.* **1.** Memory accessed by more than one program in a multitasking environment. **2.** A portion of memory that parallel-processor computer systems use to exchange information. *See also* parallel processing.

shared network directory *n. See* network directory.

shared printer *n.* A printer that receives input from more than one computer.

shared resource *n.* **1.** Any device, data, or program used by more than one device or program. **2.** In Windows NT, any resource made available to network users, such as directories, files, and printers.

shareware *n.* Copyrighted software that is distributed on a try-before-you-buy basis. Users who want to continue using the program after the trial period are encouraged to send a payment to the program's author. *Compare* free software, freeware, public-domain software.

sharpness *n. See* resolution (definition 1).

sheet-fed scanner *n.* A scanner with a single-sheet feed mechanism, in which sheets of paper are pulled in by the scanner and scanned as they pass over a stationary scanning mechanism. Sheet-fed scanners allow for automatic scanning of multiple-sheet documents. *Also called* feed scanner. *See also* scanner. *Compare* drum scanner, flatbed scanner, handheld scanner.

sheet feeder *n.* A device that accepts a stack of paper and feeds it to a printer one page at a time.

shelfware *n.* Software that has been unsold or unused for a long time and so has remained on a retailer's or user's shelf.

shell *n.* A piece of software, usually a separate program, that provides direct communication between the user and the operating system. Examples of shells are the Macintosh Finder and the MS-DOS command interface program COMMAND.COM. *See also* Finder. *Compare* kernel.
shell account *n.* A computer service that permits a user to enter operating system commands on the ISP's system through a command-line interface (usually one of the UNIX shells) rather than having to access the Internet through a graphical user interface. *See also* ISP, shell.
Shift+click or **Shift click** *vb.* To click the mouse button while holding down the Shift key. Shift+clicking performs different operations in different applications, but its most common use in Windows is to allow users to select multiple items in a list—for example, to select a number of files for deletion or copying.
Shift key *n.* A key that, when pressed in combination with another key, gives the other key an alternative meaning; for example, producing an uppercase character when a letter key is pressed. The Shift key is also used in various key combinations to create nonstandard characters and to perform special operations. *See also* Caps Lock key.
Shift-PrtSc *n.* *See* Print Screen key.
short card *n.* A printed circuit board that is half as long as a standard-size circuit board. *Also called* half-card. *See also* printed circuit board.
shortcut *n.* In Windows 95, an icon on the desktop on which a user can double-click to immediately access a program, a text or data file, or a Web page. *See also* symbolic link.
shortcut key *n.* *See* accelerator.
short-haul *adj.* Of or pertaining to a communications device that transmits a signal over a communications line for a distance less than approximately 20 miles. *Compare* long-haul.
shout *vb.* To use ALL CAPITAL LETTERS for emphasis in e-mail or a newsgroup article. Excessive shouting is considered a violation of netiquette. A word can be more acceptably emphasized by placing it between *asterisks* or _underscores_. *See also* netiquette.
shovelware *n.* A commercially sold CD-ROM containing a miscellaneous assortment of software, graphic images, text, or other data that could otherwise be obtained at little or no cost, such as freeware or shareware from the Internet and BBSs or public-domain clip art. *See also* BBS (definition 1), freeware, shareware.
shrink-wrapped *adj.* Boxed and sealed in clear plastic film for commercial distribution. Use of the term implies a final version of a product as opposed to a beta version. *See also* beta[2].
SHTML *n.* Acronym for **s**erver-parsed **HTML**. HTML text that contains embedded server-side include commands. SHTML documents are fully read, parsed, and modified by the server before being passed to the browser. *See also* HTML, server-side includes.

S-HTTP *n.* Acronym for **S**ecure **H**yper**t**ext **T**ransfer **P**rotocol. A proposed extension to HTTP that supports various encryption and authentication measures to keep all transactions secure from end to end.

shut down *vb.* To close a program or an operating system in a manner ensuring that no data is lost.

sidebar *n.* A block of text placed to the side of the main body of text in a document, often set off by a border or other graphic element.

side head *n.* A heading placed in the margin of a printed document and top-aligned with the body text, rather than being vertically aligned with text, as is a normal head.

.sig *n.* A file extension for a signature file for e-mail or Internet newsgroup use. The contents of this file are automatically appended to e-mail correspondence or newsgroup articles by their respective client software.

SIG *n.* Acronym for **s**pecial **i**nterest **g**roup. An e-mail online discussion group or a group of users who meet and share information on a specific topic, such as SIGGRAPH for computer graphics.

signal *n.* **1.** Any electrical quantity, such as voltage, current, or frequency, that can be used to transmit information. **2.** A beep or tone from a computer's speaker or a prompt displayed on screen that tells a user that the computer is ready to receive input.

signal converter *n.* A device or circuit that converts a signal from one form to another, such as analog to digital.

signal-to-noise ratio *n.* Abbreviated S/N. The amount of power, measured in decibels, by which the signal exceeds the amount of channel noise at the same point in transmission. *See also* noise (definition 2).

signature *n.* **1.** A sequence of data used for identification, such as text appended to an e-mail message or fax. **2.** A unique number built into hardware or software for authentication purposes.

signature block *n.* A block of text that an e-mail client or a newsreader automatically places at the end of all messages or articles before they are transmitted. Signature blocks typically contain the name, e-mail address, and affiliation of the person who created the message or article.

signature file *n. See* .sig.

sign off *vb. See* log off.

sign on *vb. See* log on.

silica gel *n.* A desiccant (moisture-absorbent substance) often packaged with optical or electronic equipment.

silicon *n.* A semiconductor used in many devices, especially microchips.

silicon chip *n.* An integrated circuit that uses silicon as its semiconductor material.

Silicon Valley *n.* The region of California south of San Francisco Bay, otherwise known as the Santa Clara Valley, roughly extending from Palo Alto to San Jose. Silicon Valley is a major center of electronics and computer research, development, and manufacturing.

SIMM *n.* Acronym for **s**ingle **i**nline **m**emory **m**odule. A small circuit board designed to accommodate surface-mount memory chips.
Simple Mail Transfer Protocol *n.* A TCP/IP protocol for sending messages from one computer to another on a network. This protocol is used on the Internet to route e-mail. *Acronym:* SMTP. *See also* communications protocol, TCP/IP. *Compare* CCITT X series, Post Office Protocol.
Simple Network Management Protocol *n. See* SNMP.
simplex transmission *n.* Communication that takes place only from sender to receiver. *Compare* duplex[2] (definition 1), half-duplex transmission.
simulation *n.* The imitation of a physical process or object by a program that causes a computer to respond mathematically to data and changing conditions as though it were the process or object itself. *See also* emulator, modeling (definition 1).
simultaneous access *n. See* parallel access.
simultaneous processing *n.* **1.** True multiple-processor operation in which more than one task can be processed at a time. *See also* multiprocessing, parallel processing. **2.** Loosely, concurrent operation in which more than one task is processed by dividing processor time among the tasks. *See also* concurrent, multitasking.
single-board *adj.* Of or pertaining to a computer that occupies only one circuit board, usually with no capacity for additional boards.
single-density disk *n.* An early generation of floppy disks that, by current standards, didn't hold much data. For example, IBM PC single-density floppy disks held only 180 KB of data. *Compare* double-density disk.
single inline memory module *n. See* SIMM.
single inline package *n. See* SIP.
single inline pinned package *n. See* SIP.
single-sided *adj.* Of or pertaining to a floppy disk in which data can be stored on only one side.
single-user computer *n.* A computer designed for use by a single individual; a personal computer. *Compare* multi-user system.
sink *n.* A device or part of a device that receives something from another device. *See also* data sink, heat sink.
SIP *n.* Acronym for **s**ingle **i**nline **p**ackage. A type of housing for an electronic component in which all leads (connections) protrude from one side of the package. *Also called* single inline pinned package. *Compare* DIP.
SIPP *n.* Acronym for **s**ingle **i**nline **p**inned **p**ackage. *See* SIP.
SIR *n. See* Serial Infrared.
.sit *n.* The file extension for a Macintosh file compressed with StuffIt. *See also* StuffIt.
site *n. See* Web site.
site license *n.* A purchase agreement for using multiple copies of the same software at a business or an institution, usually at a volume discount.
slave *n.* Any device, including a computer, that is controlled by another computer, referred to as the master. *See also* master/slave arrangement.

sleep¹ *n.* In a multiprocessing environment, a temporary state of suspension during which a process remains in memory so that some event, such as an interrupt or a call from another process, can "awaken" it.
sleep² *vb.* To suspend operation without terminating.
sleep mode *n.* A power management mode that shuts down all unnecessary computer operations to save energy. Many battery-powered devices, including portable computers, support sleep mode. *Also called* suspend mode. *See also* green PC, sleep¹, Suspend command.
sleeve *n. See* disk envelope.
SLIP *n.* Acronym for **S**erial **L**ine **I**nternet **P**rotocol. A data link protocol that allows transmission of IP data packets over dial-up telephone connections, thus enabling a computer or a local area network to be connected to the Internet or some other network. *See also* data link, IP. *Compare* PPP.
SLIP emulator *n.* Software that mimics a SLIP connection in UNIX shell accounts that do not offer a direct SLIP connection. Many ISPs are UNIX-based and offer shell accounts to users for Internet access. Like a SLIP connection, the SLIP emulator allows the user to avoid dealing with the ISP's UNIX environment directly when accessing the Internet and to use Internet applications such as graphical Web browsers. *See also* emulator, ISP, shell account, SLIP.
slot *n. See* expansion slot.
slotted-ring network *n.* A ring network allowing data to be transmitted between data stations in one direction. A slotted-ring network transfers data in predefined time slots in the transmission stream over one transmission medium. *See also* ring network. *Compare* token ring network.
SlowKeys *n.* An accessibility feature built into Macintosh computers and available for DOS and Windows that allows the user to add a delay to the keyboard so that a key must be held down for a certain amount of time before it is accepted. This feature facilitates the use of the keyboard by individuals with poor motor control who might accidentally bump keys when moving around the keyboard.
small caps *n.* A font of capital letters that are smaller than the standard capital letters in that typeface. THIS TEXT IS IN SMALL CAPS.
Small Computer System Interface *n. See* SCSI.
smart cable *n. See* intelligent cable.
smart card *n.* **1.** In computers and electronics, a circuit board with built-in logic or firmware that gives it some kind of independent decision-making ability. **2.** In banking and finance, a credit card containing an integrated circuit that gives it a limited amount of "intelligence" and memory.
smart quotes *n.* In word processors, a function that automatically converts the ditto marks (") produced by most computer keyboards to the inverted commas (“ and ”) used in typeset text.
smart terminal *n.* A terminal that contains a microprocessor and RAM and that does some rudimentary processing without intervention from the host computer. *Compare* dumb terminal.

smiley *n. See* emoticon.
S/MIME *n.* Acronym for **S**ecure/**M**ultipurpose **I**nternet **M**ail **E**xtensions. An Internet e-mail security standard that makes use of public key encryption. *See also* public key encryption.
SMP *n.* Acronym for **s**ymmetric **m**ulti**p**rocessing. A computer architecture in which multiple processors share the same memory, which contains one copy of the operating system, one copy of any applications that are in use, and one copy of the data. Because the operating system divides the workload into tasks and assigns those tasks to whatever processors are free, SMP reduces transaction time. *See also* architecture, multiprocessing.
SMP server *n.* Short for **s**ymmetric **m**ulti**p**rocessing **server**. A computer designed with the SMP architecture to improve its performance as a server in client/server applications. *See also* SMP.
SMT *n. See* surface-mount technology.
SMTP *n. See* Simple Mail Transfer Protocol.
snail mail *n.* A popular phrase on the Internet for referring to mail services provided by the U.S. Postal Service and similar agencies in other countries. The term has its origins in the fact that regular postal mail is slow compared with e-mail.
snap-in *n. See* plug-in.
snapshot *n.* A copy of main memory or video memory at a given instant, sent either to the printer or to a hard disk. *Also called* snapshot dump. *See also* screen dump.
.snd *n.* A file extension for a type of interchangeable sound file format used on Sun, NeXT, and Silicon Graphics computers, consisting of raw audio data preceded by a text identifier.
sneakernet *n.* Transfer of data between computers that are not networked together. The files must be written to floppy disks on the source machine, and a person must physically transport the disks to the destination machine.
SNMP *n.* Acronym for **S**imple **N**etwork **M**anagement **P**rotocol. The network management protocol of TCP/IP. In SNMP, agents, which can be hardware as well as software, monitor the activity in the various devices on the network and report to the network console workstation. Control information about each device is maintained in a structure known as a management information block. *See also* agent (definition 4), TCP/IP.
snow *n.* In computer displays, a specific type of distortion characterized by the blinking on and off of random pixels that occurs when the microprocessor and the display hardware interfere with each other by attempting to use the computer's video memory at the same time.
socket *n.* **1.** An identifier for a particular service on a particular node on a network. The socket consists of a node address and a port number, which identifies the service. For example, port 80 on an Internet node indicates a Web server. *See also* port number. **2.** The receptacle part of a connector, which receives a plug. *See also* female connector.

soc. newsgroups *n.* Usenet newsgroups that are part of the soc. hierarchy, use the soc. prefix in their names, and are devoted to discussions of current events and social issues. *See also* newsgroup, traditional newsgroup hierarchy, Usenet.
soft *adj.* In computing, temporary or changeable. For example, a soft error is a problem from which a program or a system can recover, and a soft patch is a temporary program fix that holds only while the program is running. *Compare* hard.
soft boot *n. See* warm boot.
soft copy *n.* The temporary images presented on a computer display screen. *Compare* hard copy.
soft error *n.* An error from which a program or an operating system is able to recover. *Compare* hard error.
soft font *n. See* downloadable font.
soft hyphen *n. See* hyphen.
soft link *n. See* symbolic link.
softmodem *n. See* software-based modem.
soft return *n.* A line break inserted in a document by a word processor when the next word in the current line of text would cause the line to overflow into the margin; a movable line break. *See also* wordwrap. *Compare* hard return.
software *n.* Computer programs; instructions that make hardware work. Two main types of software are system software (operating systems), which controls the workings of the computer; and applications, such as word processors, spreadsheets, and databases, which perform the tasks for which people use computers. Two additional categories, which are neither system nor application software but contain elements of both, are network software, which enables groups of computers to communicate; and language software, which provides programmers with the tools they need to write programs. In addition to these task-based categories, several types of software are described based on their method of distribution, such as canned (packaged) software, freeware, and shareware. *See also* application, canned software, freeware, network software, operating system, public-domain software, shareware, system software, vaporware. *Compare* firmware, hardware, liveware.
software-based modem *n.* A modem that uses a general-purpose, reprogrammable digital signal processor chip and RAM-based program memory rather than a dedicated chip with the modem functions burned into the silicon. A software-based modem can be reconfigured to update and change the modem's features and functions.
software-dependent *adj.* Of, pertaining to, or being a computer or device that is tied to a particular program or set of programs developed for it.
software engineering *n.* The design and development of software. *See also* programming.
software handshake *n. See* handshake.

software house *n.* An organization that develops and supports software for its customers.
software package *n.* A program sold to the public, ready to run and containing all necessary components and documentation.
software piracy *n. See* piracy.
software portability *n. See* portable (definition 1).
software program *n. See* application.
software protection *n. See* copy protection.
software publisher *n.* A business engaged in the development and distribution of computer software.
software publishing *n.* The design, development, and distribution of noncustom software packages.
software suite *n. See* suite.
SOHO *n.* Acronym for **S**mall **O**ffice/**H**ome **O**ffice, a term used for home-based and small businesses. The fast-growing SOHO market has sparked a concomitant expansion in computer software and hardware products designed specifically to meet the needs of self-employed individuals or small businesses. *See also* distributed workplace, telecommuter.
Solaris *n.* A distributed UNIX-based computing environment created by Sun Microsystems, Inc., widely used as a server operating system. Versions of Solaris exist for SPARC computers, 386 and higher Intel platforms, and the PowerPC.
solid-ink printer *n.* A computer printer using solid ink sticks. The ink sticks are heated until they melt, and the molten ink is sprayed onto the page, where it cools and solidifies.
solid model *n.* A geometric shape or construction that has continuity in length, width, and depth and is treated by a program as if it had both surface and internal substance. *Compare* surface modeling, wire-frame model.
solid-state device *n.* A circuit component whose properties depend on the electrical or magnetic characteristics of a solid substance (as opposed to a gas or vacuum). Transistors, diodes, and integrated circuits are solid-state devices.
solid-state disk drive *n.* A mass storage device that holds data in RAM rather than in magnetic storage. *See also* magnetic storage, RAM.
solid-state memory *n.* Computer memory that stores information in solid-state devices.
solid-state relay *n.* A relay that depends on solid-state components, rather than mechanical components, to open and close a circuit.
SOM *n.* Acronym for **S**ystem **O**bject **M**odel. A language-independent architecture from IBM that implements the Common Object Request Broker Architecture (CORBA) standard. *See also* CORBA, OMA.
sort *vb.* To organize data, typically a set of records, in a particular order. Programs and programming algorithms for sorting vary in performance and application. *See also* bubble sort, distributive sort, insertion sort, merge sort, quicksort.

A B C D E F G H I J K L M N O P Q R S T U V W X Y Z

sort algorithm *n.* An algorithm that puts a collection of data elements into some sequenced order, sometimes based on one or more key values in each element. *See also* algorithm, bubble sort, distributive sort, insertion sort, merge sort, quicksort.

sort field *n. See* sort key.

sort key *n.* A field (commonly called a key) whose entries are sorted to produce a desired arrangement of the records containing the field. *See also* field (definition 1), primary key, secondary key.

sound board *n. See* sound card.

sound buffer *n.* A region of memory used to store the bit image of a sequence of sounds to be sent to a computer's speaker(s).

sound card *n.* A type of expansion board on PC-compatible computers that allows the playback and recording of sound, such as from a WAV or MIDI file or a music CD-ROM. Most PCs sold at retail include a sound card. *Also called* sound board. *See also* expansion board, MIDI, WAV.

sound clip *n.* A file that contains a short audio item, usually an excerpt from a longer recording.

sound editor *n.* A program that allows the user to create and manipulate sound files.

sound generator *n.* A chip or chip-level circuit that can produce electronic signals that can drive a speaker and synthesize sound.

sound hood *n.* A five-sided box, lined with soundproofing material, that is placed over a loud printer to muffle its noise.

source *n.* In information processing, a disk, file, document, or other collection of information from which data is taken or moved. *Compare* destination.

source code *n.* Human-readable program statements, written in a high-level or assembly language, that are not directly readable by a computer. *Compare* object code.

source directory *n.* During a file copy operation, the directory in which the original versions of the files are located.

source disk *n.* Any disk from which data will be read, as during a copy operation or when an application is loaded from a disk into memory. *Compare* target disk.

source document *n.* The original document from which data is taken.

source drive *n.* The disk drive from which files are being copied during a copy operation.

source file *n.* In MS-DOS and Windows commands that involve the copying of data or program instructions, the file containing the data or instructions being copied.

Spacebar *n.* A long key occupying much of the bottom row of most keyboards that sends a space character to the computer.

space character *n.* A character that is entered by pressing the Spacebar on the keyboard and that typically appears on the screen as a blank space.

spam[1] *n.* An unsolicited e-mail message sent to many recipients at one time, or a news article posted simultaneously to many newsgroups. Spam is the electronic equivalent of junk mail. In most cases, the content of a spam message or article is not relevant to the topic of the newsgroup or the interests of the recipient; spam is an abuse of the Internet in order to distribute a message (usually commercial or religious) to a huge number of people at minimal cost.

spam² *vb.* To distribute unwanted, unrequested mail widely on the Internet by posting a message to too many recipients or too many newsgroups. The act of distributing such mail, known as spamming, angers most Internet users and has been known to invite retaliation, often in the form of return spamming that can flood and possibly disable the electronic mailbox of the original spammer.

spambot *n.* A program or device that automatically posts large amounts of repetitive or otherwise inappropriate material to newsgroups on the Internet. *See also* bot (definition 3), robopost, spam¹, spam².

span *n. See* range.

spec *n. See* specification.

special character *n.* Any character that is not alphabetic, numeric, or the space character (for example, a punctuation character). *See also* reserved character, wildcard character.

special interest group *n. See* SIG.

specification *n.* **1.** A detailed description of something. **2.** In relation to computer hardware, an item of information about the computer's components, capabilities, and features. **3.** In relation to software, a description of the operating environment and proposed features of a new program. **4.** In information processing, a description of the data records, programs, and procedures involved in a particular task.

speech recognition *n. See* voice recognition.

speech synthesis *n.* The ability of a computer to produce "spoken" words either by splicing together prerecorded words or by programming the computer to produce the sounds that make up spoken words. *See also* artificial intelligence, neural network.

spelling checker *n.* An application that employs a disk-based dictionary to check for misspellings in a document. *Also called* spell checker.

spew *vb.* On the Internet, to post an excessive number of e-mail messages or newsgroup articles.

spider *n.* An automated program that searches the Internet for new Web documents and places their addresses and content-related information in a database, which can be accessed with a search engine. Spiders are generally considered to be a type of bot, or Internet robot. *See also* bot (definition 3), search engine (definition 2).

spike *n.* A transient electrical signal of very short duration and, usually, high amplitude. *Compare* surge.

split screen *n.* A display method in which a program can divide the display area into two or more sections, which can contain different files or show different parts of the same file.

spoiler *n.* A post to a newsgroup or mailing list that reveals what is intended to be a surprise, such as a plot twist in a film or TV episode or the solution to a game. The subject line should contain the word Spoiler, but netiquette also requires that the sender further protect readers by encrypting the post, putting one or more screenfuls of white space above the text, or both. *See also* netiquette.
spoofing *n.* The practice of making a transmission appear to come from an authorized user. For example, in IP spoofing, a transmission is given the IP address of an authorized user in order to obtain access to a computer or network. *See also* IP address.
spool *vb.* To store a data document in a queue, where it awaits its turn to be printed. *See also* print spooler.
spot *n.* A "composite dot" produced through the halftone creation process on a PostScript printer that consists of a group of dots arranged in a pattern reflecting the gray level of a particular pixel. *See also* gray scale, halftone. *Compare* dot (definition 2).
spraycan *n.* An artist's tool in Paintbrush or another graphics application, for applying a pattern of dots to an image.
spreadsheet program *n.* An application commonly used for budgets, forecasting, and other finance-related tasks that organizes data values using cells, where the relationships between cells are defined by formulas. A change to one cell produces changes to related cells. Spreadsheet programs usually provide graphing capabilities for output and a variety of formatting options for text, numeric values, and graph features. *See also* cell.
sprite *n.* In computer graphics, a small image that can be moved on the screen independently of other images in the background. Sprites are widely used in animation sequences and video games. *See also* object (definition 3).
sprocket feed *n.* A paper feed in which pins engage holes in the paper to move it through a printer. Pin feed and tractor feed are both sprocket feeds. *See also* paper feed, pin feed, tractor feed.
SPX *n.* **1.** Acronym for **S**equenced **P**acket E**x**change. The transport level (ISO/OSI level 4) protocol used by Novell NetWare. SPX uses IPX to transfer the packets, but SPX ensures that messages are complete. *See also* ISO/OSI model. *Compare* IPX. **2.** Acronym for **s**im**p**le**x**. *See* simplex transmission.
SQL *n.* *See* structured query language.
SRAM *n.* *See* static RAM.
SSD *n.* Acronym for **s**olid-**s**tate **d**isk. *See* solid-state disk drive.
SSL *n.* *See* Secure Sockets Layer.
stackware *n.* A HyperCard application consisting of a HyperCard data stack and HyperCard programming. *See also* HyperCard.
stairstepping *n.* A rough outline like stairsteps in a graphics line or curve that should be smooth. *Also called* aliasing, jaggies.
stale link *n.* A hyperlink to an HTML document that has been deleted or moved, rendering the hyperlink useless. *See also* HTML document, hyperlink.

stand-alone *adj.* Of, pertaining to, or being a device that does not require support from another device or system; for example, a computer that is not connected to a network.

standard *n.* **1.** A de jure technical guideline, advocated by a recognized noncommercial or government organization, that is used to establish uniformity in an area of hardware or software development. The standard is the result of a formal process, based on specifications drafted after intensive study of existing methods, approaches, and technological developments. Such standards include the ASCII character set, the RS-232-C standard, the SCSI interface, and ANSI-standard programming languages such as C. *See also* ANSI, RS-232-C standard, SCSI. **2.** A de facto technical guideline for hardware development or software development that occurs when a product or philosophy is developed by a single company and then, through success and imitation, becomes so widely used that deviation from the norm causes compatibility problems or limits marketability. This type of informal standard setting is exemplified by Hayes-compatible modems and IBM PC-compatible computers. *See also* compatibility (definition 3).

standard disclaimer *n.* A phrase placed in an e-mail message or a news article that is intended to replace the statement required by some businesses and institutions that the contents of the message or article do not necessarily represent the opinions or policies of the organization from whose e-mail system the message originated.

Standard Generalized Markup Language *n. See* SGML.

star-dot-star *n.* A file specification (*.*) using the asterisk wildcard, which means "any combination of filename and extension" in operating systems such as MS-DOS. *See also* asterisk (definition 2), wildcard character.

star network *n.* A LAN in which each device (node) is connected to a central computer in a star-shaped configuration; commonly, a network consisting of a central computer (the hub) surrounded by terminals. *Compare* bus network, ring network.

start bit *n.* In asynchronous transmission, the bit that signals the beginning of a character. *See also* asynchronous transmission.

starting point *n.* A World Wide Web document designed to help users begin navigating the Web. A starting point often contains tools such as search engines and hyperlinks to selected Web sites. *See also* hyperlink, search engine (definition 2), World Wide Web.

start page *n. See* home page (definition 2).

start/stop transmission *n. See* asynchronous transmission.

startup *n. See* boot[1].

startup application *n.* On the Macintosh, the application that takes control of the system when the computer is turned on.

startup disk *n. See* system disk.

startup ROM *n.* The bootstrap instructions coded into a computer's ROM and executed at startup. The startup ROM routines enable a computer to check itself and its devices (such as the keyboard and disk drives), prepare itself for operation, and run a short program to load an operating system loader program. *See also* boot[1], power-on self test.

startup screen *n.* A text or graphics display that appears on the screen when a program is started (run). Startup screens usually contain information about the software's version and often contain a product or corporate logo.

state *n.* *See* status.

statement *n.* The smallest executable entity within a programming language.

state-of-the-art *adj.* Up-to-date; at the forefront of current hardware or software technology.

static[1] *adj.* In information processing, fixed or predetermined. For example, a static memory buffer remains invariant in size throughout program execution. The opposite condition is described by the term dynamic, or ever-changing.

static[2] *n.* In communications, a crackling noise caused by electrical interference with a transmitted signal. *See also* noise (definition 2).

static electricity *n.* An electrical charge accumulated in an object. Although generally harmless to humans, the discharge of static electricity through an electronic circuit can cause severe damage to the circuit.

static RAM *n.* A form of semiconductor memory (RAM) based on the logic circuit known as a flip-flop, which retains information as long as there is enough power to run the device. Static RAMs are usually reserved for use in caches. *Acronym:* SRAM. *See also* cache, RAM. *Compare* dynamic RAM.

stationery *adj.* Describing a type of document that, when opened by the user, is duplicated by the system; the copy is opened for the user's modification while the original document remains intact. Stationery documents can be used as document templates or boilerplates. *See also* boilerplate, template (definition 5).

status *n.* The condition at a particular time of any of numerous elements of computing—a device, a communications channel, a network station, a program, a bit, or other element—used to report on or to control computer operations.

status bar *n.* In Windows, a space at the bottom of many program windows that contains a short text message about the current condition of the program. Some programs also display an explanation of the currently selected menu command in the status bar.

status codes *n.* Strings of digits or other characters that indicate the success or failure of some attempted action. Status codes were commonly used to report the results of early computer programs, but most software today uses words or graphics. Internet users, especially those with UNIX shell accounts, are likely to encounter status codes while using the Web or FTP. *See also* HTTP status codes.

step-frame *n.* The process of capturing video images one frame at a time. This process is used by computers that are too slow to capture analog video images in real time.

StickyKeys *n.* An accessibility feature built into Macintosh computers and available for Windows and DOS that causes modifier keys such as Shift, Control, or Alt to "stay on" after they are pressed. This feature facilitates the use of modifier keys by users who are unable to press multiple keys simultaneously.

stop bit *n.* In asynchronous transmission, a bit that signals the end of a character. *See also* asynchronous transmission.

storage *n.* In computing, any device in or on which information can be kept. Microcomputers have two main types of storage: random access memory, and disk drives and other external storage media. Other types of storage include read-only memory and buffers.

storage device *n.* An apparatus for recording computer data in permanent or semipermanent form. When a distinction is made between primary (main) storage devices and secondary (auxiliary) storage devices, the former refers to RAM and the latter refers to disk drives and other external devices.

storage media *n.* The various types of physical material on which data bits are written and stored, such as floppy disks, hard disks, tape, and optical discs.

store-and-forward *n.* A message-passing technique used on communications networks in which a message is held temporarily at a collecting station before being forwarded to its destination.

storefront *n.* *See* virtual storefront.

STP *n.* Acronym for **s**hielded **t**wisted **p**air. A cable consisting of one or more twisted pairs of wires and a sheath of foil and copper braid. The twists protect the pairs from interference from each other, and the shielding protects the pairs from interference from outside. Therefore, STP cable can be used for high-speed transmission over long distances. *See also* twisted-pair cable. *Compare* UTP.

stream¹ *n.* Any data transmission, such as the movement of a file between disk and memory, that occurs in a continuous flow. Manipulating a data stream is a programming task. Consumers, however, can encounter references to streams and streaming in connection with the Internet, which has increased reliance on stream techniques to enable users (even those with slower equipment) to access large multimedia files—especially those containing audio and video—and to begin to display or play them before all the data has been transferred.

stream² *vb.* To transfer data continuously, beginning to end, in a steady flow. Many aspects of computing rely on the ability to stream data: file input and output, for example, and communications. If necessary, an application receiving a stream must be able to save the information to a buffer in order to prevent loss of data. On the Internet, streaming enables users to begin accessing and using a file before it has been transmitted in its entirety.

streaming *n.* In magnetic tape storage devices, a low-cost technique to control the motion of the tape by removing tape buffers. Although streaming tape compromises start/stop performance, it allows highly reliable storage and retrieval of data and is useful when an application or a computer requires a steady supply of data. *See also* stream[1], stream[2].

streaming tape *n.* *See* streaming, tape (definition 1).

street price *n.* The actual retail or mail-order price of a consumer hardware or software product. In most cases, the street price is somewhat lower than the "suggested retail price."

strikethrough *n.* One or more lines drawn through a selected range of text, usually to show deletion or the intent to delete, as in ~~strikethrough~~.

string *n.* A data structure composed of a sequence of characters usually representing human-readable text.

strobe *n.* A timing signal that initiates and coordinates the passage of data, typically through an I/O device interface, such as a keyboard or printer.

stroke *n.* **1.** In data entry, a keystroke; a signal to the computer that a key has been pressed. **2.** In typography, a line representing part of a letter. **3.** In paint programs, a "swipe" of the brush made with the mouse or keyboard in creating a graphic. **4.** In display technology, a line created as a vector (a path between two coordinates) on a vector graphics display (as opposed to a line of pixels drawn dot by dot on a raster graphics display).

stroke font *n.* A font printed by drawing a combination of lines rather than by filling a shape, as with an outline font. *Compare* outline font.

stroke weight *n.* The width, or thickness, of the lines (strokes) that make up a character. *See also* typeface.

stroke writer *n.* In video, a display unit that draws characters and graphic images as sets of strokes—lines or curves connecting points—rather than as sets of dots, as on a typical raster-scan monitor. *See also* vector graphics.

structured graphics *n.* *See* object-oriented graphics.

structured programming *n.* Programming that produces programs with clean flow, clear design, and a degree of modularity or hierarchical structure. *See also* modular programming, object-oriented programming.

structured query language *n.* A database sublanguage used in querying, updating, and managing relational databases—the de facto standard for database products. *Acronym:* SQL.

STT *n.* *See* Secure Transaction Technology.

StuffIt *n.* A file compression program originally written for the Apple Macintosh, used for storing a file on one or more disks. Originally shareware, StuffIt is now a commercial product for Macs and PCs that supports multiple compression techniques and allows file viewing. StuffIt files can be uncompressed using a freeware program, StuffIt Expander.

style sheet *n.* **1.** A file of instructions used to apply character, paragraph, and page-layout formats in word processing and desktop publishing. **2.** A text file containing code to apply certain rules such as page-layout specifications to an HTML document. *See also* HTML document.

stylus *n.* A pointing device used with a graphics tablet, usually attached to the tablet with a cord. *Also called* pen. *See also* graphics tablet, puck.

A B C D E F G H I J K L M N O P Q R S T U V W X Y Z

subcommand *n.* A command on a submenu. *See also* submenu.
subdirectory *n.* A directory (logical grouping of related files) within another directory.
subject drift *n. See* topic drift.
subject tree *n.* A type of World Wide Web index organized by subject categories, many of which are broken down into subcategories, or "branches." The lowest level of the tree consists of links to specific Web pages.
submarining *n.* A phenomenon that occurs when some part of a screen display moves more quickly than the screen can show. The object (such as the mouse pointer) disappears from the screen and reappears where it comes to rest, just as a submarine resurfaces after a dive. Submarining is especially a problem with the slow-response passive-matrix LCD displays on many laptop computers.
submenu *n.* A menu that appears as the result of the user choosing an option on another, higher-level menu.
subnet *n.* A network that is a component of a larger network.
subnotebook computer *n.* A portable computer that is smaller and lighter than a conventional laptop computer.
subportable *n. See* subnotebook computer.
subscribe *vb.* **1.** To add a newsgroup to the list of such groups from which a user receives all new articles. **2.** To add a name to a LISTSERV distribution list. *See also* LISTSERV.
subscript *n.* One or more characters printed slightly below the baseline of surrounding text. *Compare* superscript.
suite *n.* A set of applications sold as a package, usually at a lower price than that of the individual applications sold separately. A suite for office work, for example, might contain a word processor, a spreadsheet, a database management program, and a communications program.
summarize *vb.* To post the results of a survey or vote in short form to a newsgroup or mailing list after collecting the results by e-mail.
supercomputer *n.* A large, extremely fast, and expensive computer used for complex or sophisticated calculations. *See also* computer.
superminicomputer *n. See* computer.
superscalar *adj.* Of, pertaining to, or being a microprocessor architecture that enables the microprocessor to execute multiple instructions per clock cycle. *See also* CISC, RISC.
superscript *n.* A character printed slightly above the surrounding text, usually in smaller type. *Compare* subscript.
superserver *n.* A network server with especially high capabilities for speed and data storage. *See also* server.
superuser *n.* A UNIX user account with root (unrestricted) access privileges, usually that of a system administrator. *See also* system administrator, user account.
super VAR *n.* Short for **super v**alue-**a**dded **r**eseller. A large value-added reseller. *See also* value-added reseller.

A B C D E F G H I J K L M N O P Q R S T U V W X Y Z

super VGA *n. See* SVGA.
supervisor state *n.* The most privileged of the modes in which a Motorola 680x0 microprocessor can operate. Every operation of which the microprocessor is capable can be executed in the supervisor state.
support¹ *n.* Assistance, such as technical advice provided to customers.
support² *vb.* To work with another program or product; for example, an application might support file transfers from another program.
surf *vb.* To browse collections of information on the Internet, in newsgroups, in Gopherspace, and especially on the World Wide Web. As in channel surfing while watching TV, users ride the wave of what interests them, jumping from topic to topic or from one Internet site to another. *Also called* cruise.
surface modeling *n.* A display method used by some CAD programs that gives on-screen constructions the appearance of solidity. *See also* CAD. *Compare* solid model, wire-frame model.
surface-mount technology *n.* A method of manufacturing printed circuit boards in which chips are fixed directly to the surface of the board instead of being soldered into holes predrilled to hold them. Its advantages are compactness, resistance to vibration, and the capacity for dense interconnections on both sides of the board. *Acronym:* SMT. *Compare* DIP.
surge *n.* A sudden—and possibly damaging—increase in line voltage. *See also* surge protector. *Compare* power failure.
surge protector *n.* A device that prevents surges from reaching a computer or other kinds of electronic equipment. *Also called* surge suppressor. *See also* surge.
surge suppressor *n. See* surge protector.
suspend *vb.* To halt a process temporarily. *See also* sleep².
Suspend command *n.* A power management feature of Windows 95 for portable computers. Choosing the Suspend command on the Start menu allows the user to temporarily suspend operations of the machine (enter "suspend mode") without turning the power off, thus saving battery power without the need to restart applications or reload data.
suspend mode *n. See* sleep mode.
sustained transfer rate *n.* A measure of the speed at which data can be transferred to a storage device such as a disk or a tape. The sustained transfer rate is the data transfer speed that can be kept up by the device for an extended period of time.
SVGA *n.* Acronym for **S**uper **V**ideo **G**raphics **A**rray. A video standard established by VESA in 1989 to provide high-resolution color display on IBM PC-compatible computers. Although SVGA is a standard, compatibility problems can occur with the video BIOS. *See also* BIOS, video adapter.
S-video connector *n.* A hardware interface for video devices that handles chrominance (color) and luminance (black and white) separately. An S-video connector is capable of providing a sharper image than those achieved with systems using RCA-type, or composite, connectors.

S/WAN *n. See* secure wide area network.
swap *vb.* **1.** To exchange one item for another, as in swapping floppy disks in and out of a single drive. **2.** To move segments of programs or data between memory and disk storage. *See also* virtual memory.
swap file *n.* A hidden file on the hard drive that Windows uses to hold parts of programs and data files that do not fit in memory. The operating system moves data from the swap file to memory as needed and moves data out of memory to the swap file to make room for new data. The swap file is a form of virtual memory. *See also* memory, virtual memory.
swim *n.* A condition in which images slowly move about the positions they are supposed to occupy on screen.
switch *n.* **1.** A circuit element that has two states: on and off. **2.** A control device that allows the user to choose one of two or more possible states. **3.** In communications, a computer or an electromechanical device that controls routing and operation of a signal path. **4.** In operating systems such as MS-DOS, an argument used to control the execution of a command or an application, typically starting with a slash character (/).
switched Ethernet *n.* An Ethernet network run through a high-speed switch instead of an Ethernet hub. A switched Ethernet involves dedicated bandwidth of 10 Mbps between stations rather than a shared medium. *See also* Ethernet (definition 1), switch (definition 3).
switched line *n.* A standard dial-up telephone connection; the type of line established when a call is routed through a switching station. *Compare* leased line.
switched network *n.* A communications network that uses switching to establish a connection between parties, such as the dial-up telephone system. *See also* switching.
switching *n.* A communications method that uses temporary rather than permanent connections to establish a link or to route information between two parties. In computer networks, message switching and packet switching allow any two parties to exchange information; messages are routed (switched) through intermediary stations that together serve to connect the sender and the receiver.
switching hub *n.* A central device (switch) that connects separate communication lines in a network and routes messages and packets among the computers on the network. The switch functions as a hub for the network. *See also* hub, packet (definition 1), switch (definition 3), switched Ethernet, switched network.
switching speed *n.* In a packet-switching telecommunications technology, such as ATM, the speed at which data packets are sent through the network. Switching speed is generally measured in kilobits or megabits per second. *See also* ATM, packet switching.
symbol font *n.* A special font or typeface that replaces the characters normally accessible from the keyboard with alternative characters used as symbols, such as scientific, linguistic, or foreign-alphabet characters.

A B C D E F G H I J K L M N O P Q R S T U V W X Y Z

symbolic link *n.* A reference to an item that, when accessed, takes the user directly to that item. For example, a symbolic link in one folder on a disk could, when double-clicked, open a file that is in a completely different folder. *Also called* alias, shortcut, soft link, symlink.
symbol set *n.* Any collection of symbols legitimized by a data-coding system, such as extended ASCII, or a programming language.
symlink *n. See* symbolic link.
symmetric digital subscriber line *n.* A digital telecommunications technology that allows data transmission at speeds up to 384 Kbps in both directions through copper wire. *Acronym:* SDSL. *Compare* asymmetric digital subscriber line.
symmetric multiprocessing *n. See* SMP.
symmetric multiprocessing server *n. See* SMP server.
synchronization *n.* **1.** In networking, a communications transmission in which multibyte packets of data are sent and received at a fixed rate. **2.** In networking, the matching of timing between computers on the network, to facilitate and coordinate communications. **3.** In a computer, the matching of timing between components of the computer so that all are coordinated. For instance, operations performed by the operating system are generally synchronized with the signals of the machine's internal clock. **4.** In application or database files, version comparisons of copies of the files to ensure they contain the same data. **5.** In multimedia, precise real-time processing. Audio and video are transmitted over a network in synchronization so that they can be played back together without delayed responses. *See also* real-time.
synchronize *vb.* To cause to occur at the same time.
synchronous DRAM *n.* A form of dynamic RAM that can run at higher clock speeds than conventional DRAM by employing a bursting technique in which the DRAM predicts the address of the next memory location to be accessed. *Acronym:* SDRAM. *See also* dynamic RAM.
synchronous operation *n.* **1.** Any procedure under the control of a clock or timing mechanism. *Compare* asynchronous operation. **2.** In communications and bus operation, data transfer accompanied by clock pulses either embedded in the data stream or provided simultaneously on a separate line.
synchronous transmission *n.* Data transfer in which information is transmitted in blocks (frames) of bits separated by equal time intervals. *Compare* asynchronous transmission.
synchronous UART *n.* A universal asynchronous receiver/transmitter (UART) that supports synchronous serial transmission, where the sender and receiver share a timing signal. *See also* UART.
synthesizer *n.* A computer peripheral, chip, or stand-alone system that generates sound from digital instructions rather than through manipulation of physical equipment or recorded sound. *See also* MIDI.
.sys *n.* A file extension for system configuration files.
sysadmin *n.* The usual logon name or e-mail address for the system administrator of a UNIX-based system. *See also* system administrator.

sysgen *n.* *See* system generation.
sysop *n.* Short for **sys**tem **op**erator. The overseer of a BBS or a small multi-user computer system. *See also* BBS (definition 1).
system *n.* Any collection of component elements that work together to perform a task. Examples are a hardware system consisting of a microprocessor, its allied chips and circuitry, input and output devices, and peripheral devices; an operating system consisting of a set of programs and data files; and a database management system that is used to process specific kinds of information.
system administrator *n.* The person responsible for administering use of a multi-user computer system, a communications system, or both. A system administrator performs such duties as assigning user accounts and passwords, establishing security access levels, allocating storage space, and watching for unauthorized access to prevent virus or Trojan horse programs from entering the system. *Also called* sysadmin. *See also* Trojan horse, virus. *Compare* sysop.
system board *n.* *See* motherboard.
system clock *n.* *See* clock (definition 1).
system console *n.* The control center of a computer system, primarily with reference to mainframe and minicomputers. In networked or distributed systems, one workstation is designated as the system administrator's; this workstation is analogous to the LAN system console. *See also* console, LAN.
system disk *n.* A disk that contains an operating system and can be used to boot a computer. *Also called* startup disk. *See also* boot², operating system.
system error *n.* A software condition that renders the operating system incapable of continuing to function normally. This type of error usually requires rebooting the system.
system failure *n.* The inability of a computer to continue functioning, usually caused by software rather than hardware.
System file *n.* A resource file on the Macintosh that contains the resources needed by the operating system, such as fonts, icons, and default dialog boxes.
System folder *n.* The Macintosh file folder (directory) that contains the System file and other vital files such as Finder, device drivers, INIT files, and control panel files. *See also* control panel, Finder, INIT, System file.
system font *n.* On the Macintosh and in some PC-based applications, the font used by the computer for on-screen text such as menu titles and items (but not on-screen text within a word processor or other application). *See also* font.
system generation *n.* The process of configuring and installing system software for a particular set of hardware components. *Also called* sysgen.
system.ini *n.* In Windows 3.*x,* the initialization file used to store the hardware configuration information necessary to run the Windows operating environment. The system.ini file was replaced by the Registry database in Windows 95 and in Windows NT. *See also* ini file.

A B C D E F G H I J K L M N O P Q R S T U V W X Y Z

system life cycle *n.* An information system's useful life. At the end of a system's life cycle it is not feasible to repair or expand it, so it must be replaced.
System Object Model *n.* *See* SOM.
system operator *n.* *See* sysop.
system prompt *n.* *See* prompt (definition 1).
system recovery *n.* Processing that takes place after a system failure in order to restore a system to normal operation. System recovery sometimes requires that tasks in process during the failure be backed out of and that structures in memory during the failure be reconstructed.
System Registry *n.* *See* Registry.
system resource *n.* On the Macintosh, any of numerous routines, definitions, and data fragments that are stored in the Macintosh System file, such as font definitions and peripheral drivers. *See also* resource (definition 2).
system software *n.* The collection of programs and data that make up and relate to the operating system. *See also* software. *Compare* application.
system support *n.* The provision of services and material resources for the use, maintenance, and improvement of an implemented system.
system timer *n.* *See* clock (definition 1).
system unit *n.* *See* console.

T

T1 or **T-1** *n.* A T-carrier that can handle 1.544 Mbps or 24 voice channels. Although originally designed by AT&T to carry voice calls, this high-bandwidth telephone line can also transmit text and images. T1 lines are commonly used by larger organizations for Internet connectivity. *See also* T-carrier. *Compare* fractional T1, T2, T3, T4.

T2 or **T-2** *n.* A T-carrier that can handle 6.312 Mbps or 96 voice channels. *See also* T-carrier. *Compare* T1, T3, T4.

T3 or **T-3** *n.* A T-carrier that can handle 44.736 Mbps or 672 voice channels. *See also* T-carrier. *Compare* T1, T2, T4.

T4 or **T-4** *n.* A T-carrier that can handle 274.176 Mbps or 4,032 voice channels. *See also* T-carrier. *Compare* T1, T2, T3.

tab character *n.* A character used to align lines and columns on screen and in print. Although a tab is visually indistinguishable from a series of blank spaces in most programs, the tab character and the space character are different to a computer. A tab is a single character and therefore can be added, deleted, or overtyped with a single keystroke. *See also* Tab key.

Tab key *n.* A key, often labeled with both a left-pointing arrow and a right-pointing arrow, that traditionally is used to insert tab characters into a document, as in word processing. In other applications, such as menu-driven programs, the Tab key is often used to move the on-screen highlight from place to place. In many database and spreadsheet programs, the user can press the Tab key to move around within a record or between cells. *See also* tab character.

table *n.* **1.** In relational databases, a data structure characterized by rows and columns, with data occupying or potentially occupying each cell formed by a row-column intersection. The table is the underlying structure of a relation. *See also* relation, relational database. **2.** In word processing, desktop publishing, and HTML documents, a block of text formatted in aligned rows and columns.

table lookup *n.* The process of using a known value to search for data in a previously constructed table of values—for example, using a purchase price to search a tax table for the appropriate sales tax.

tablet *n. See* graphics tablet.

tabulate *vb.* **1.** To total a row or column of numbers. **2.** To arrange information in table form.

tag *n.* **1.** In certain types of data files, a key or an address that identifies a record and its storage location in another file. *See also* tag sort. **2.** In markup languages such as SGML and HTML, a code that identifies an element in a document, such as a heading, for the purposes of formatting, indexing, and linking information in the document. In both SGML and HTML, a tag is generally a pair of angle brackets containing one or more letters and numbers. Usually an element is both preceded and followed by a pair of angle brackets, to indicate where the element begins and ends. For example, in HTML, the code <I>hello world</I> indicates that the phrase *hello world* should be italicized. *See also* <>, element (definition 2), emotag, HTML, SGML.

Tagged Image File Format *n. See* TIFF.

tag sort *n.* A sort performed on one or several key fields for the purpose of establishing the order of their associated records. *Also called* key sort.

talk[1] *n.* The UNIX command that, when followed by another user's name and address, is used to generate a request for a synchronous chat session on the Internet. *See also* chat[1] (definition 1).

talk[2] *vb. See* chat[2].

talker *n.* An Internet-based synchronous communications mechanism that supports multi-user chat functions. Such systems typically provide commands for moving through separate rooms, or chat areas, and allow users to communicate in real time through text messages, to use a BBS for posting comments, and to send internal e-mail. *See also* BBS (definition 1), chat room.

talk. newsgroups *n.* Usenet newsgroups that are part of the talk. hierarchy and use the prefix talk. in their names. These newsgroups are devoted to debate and discussion of controversial topics. *See also* newsgroup, traditional newsgroup hierarchy, Usenet.

TANSTAAFL *n.* Acronym for **T**here **a**in't **n**o **s**uch **t**hing **as** **a** **f**ree **l**unch. An expression used on the Internet in e-mail, chat sessions, mailing lists, newsgroups, and other online forums.

tap *n.* A device that can be attached to an Ethernet bus to enable a computer to be connected.

tape *n.* **1.** A thin strip of polyester film coated with magnetic material that permits the recording of data. Tape must be read or written sequentially, not randomly (as can be done on a floppy disk or a hard disk). **2.** A storage medium consisting of a thin strip of paper used to store information in the form of sequences of punched holes, chemical impregnation, or magnetic ink imprinting.

tape cartridge *n.* A module that resembles an audio cassette and contains magnetic tape that can be written on and read from by a tape drive. Tape cartridges are primarily used to back up hard disks. *See also* tape (definition 1).

tape drive *n.* A device for reading and writing on tapes. *See also* tape (definition 1).

tape dump *n.* The process of simply printing the data contained on a tape cartridge without performing any report formatting. *See also* tape cartridge.

tape tree *n.* A means of audiotape distribution, used in Usenet music newsgroups and mailing lists, in which a recording is copied and sent to a number of branch participants, who in turn send copies to their children, or leaves. *See also* branch (definition 1), child (definition 2), leaf, tree structure.

.tar *n.* The file extension that identifies uncompressed UNIX archives in the format produced by the tar utility.
tar¹ *n.* Acronym for **t**ape **ar**chive. A UNIX utility for making a single file out of a set of files that a user wishes to store together. The resulting file, which is not compressed, has the extension .tar. *Compare* untar¹.
tar² *vb.* To make a single file out of a set of files using the tar utility. *Compare* untar².
target *n.* Loosely, the objective of a computer command or operation. In terms of the SCSI connection, for example, the target is the device that receives commands. *See also* SCSI, target computer, target disk.
target computer *n.* The computer that receives data from a communications device, a hardware add-in, or a software package.
target disk *n.* The disk to which data is to be written, as in a copy operation. *Compare* source disk.
task *n.* A stand-alone application or a subprogram run as an independent entity.
task management *n.* An operating system process that tracks the progress of and provides necessary resources for separate tasks running on a computer, especially in a multitasking environment.
task swapping *n.* The process of switching from one application to another by saving the data for the application currently running in the foreground to a storage device and loading the other application. *See also* foreground² (definition 2), task.
task switching *n.* The act of moving from one program to another without shutting down the first program. Task switching is a single act, as compared to multitasking, in which the CPU rapidly switches back and forth between two or more programs. *See also* task, task swapping. *Compare* multitasking.
TB *n. See* terabyte.
T-carrier *n.* A long-distance, digital communications line provided by a common carrier. Multiplexers at either end merge several voice channels and digital data streams for transmission and separate them when received. T-carrier service, introduced by AT&T in 1993, is defined at several capacity levels: T1, T2, T3, T4. In addition to voice communication, T-carriers are used for Internet connectivity. *See also* T1, T2, T3, T4.
TCO *n. See* total cost of ownership.
TCP *n.* Acronym for **T**ransmission **C**ontrol **P**rotocol. The protocol within TCP/IP that governs the breakup of data messages into packets to be sent via IP and the reassembly and verification of the complete messages from packets received by IP. TCP corresponds to the transport layer in the ISO/OSI model. *See also* ISO/OSI model, packet (definition 2), TCP/IP. *Compare* IP.
TCP/IP *n.* Acronym for **T**ransmission **C**ontrol **P**rotocol/**I**nternet **P**rotocol. A protocol developed by the Department of Defense for communications between computers. It is built into the UNIX system and has become the de facto standard for data transmission over networks, including the Internet.

tear-off *adj.* Capable of being dragged from an original position in a graphical user interface and placed where the user desires. For example, many graphics applications feature tear-off menus of tool palettes that can be dragged to locations other than the menu bar.
techie *n.* A technically oriented person. Typically, a techie is the person on whom a user calls when something breaks or the user cannot understand a technical problem. A techie may be an engineer or a technician, but not all engineers are techies. *See also* guru.
technology *n.* The application of science and engineering to the development of machines and procedures in order to enhance or improve human conditions, or at least to improve human efficiency in some respect. *See also* high tech.
technophile *n.* Someone who is enthusiastic about emerging technology. *Compare* technophobe.
technophobe *n.* A person who is afraid of or dislikes technological advances, especially computers. *Compare* technophile.
telco *n.* Short for **tel**ephone **co**mpany. A term generally used in reference to a telephone company's provision of Internet services.
telecommunications *n.* The transmission and reception of information of any type, including data, television pictures, sound, and facsimiles, using electrical or optical signals sent over wires or fibers or through the air.
telecommute *vb.* To work in one location (often at home) and communicate with a main office at a different location through a personal computer equipped with a modem and communications software.
telecommuter *n.* A member of the workforce who conducts business outside the traditional office setting, collaborating with business associates through communications and computer technologies. The ranks of telecommuters include self-employed home workers, small-business entrepreneurs, and employees of large organizations. *See also* distributed workplace, SOHO. *Compare* teleworker.
teleconferencing *n.* The use of audio, video, or computer equipment linked through a communications system to enable geographically separated individuals to participate in a meeting or discussion. *See also* video conferencing.
telecopy *vb. See* fax.
telephony *n.* Telephone technology; the conversion of sound into electrical signals, its transmission to another location, and its reconversion to sound, with or without the use of connecting wires.
teleprocess *vb.* To use a terminal or computer and communications equipment to access computers and computer files located elsewhere. *See also* distributed processing, remote access.
teleworker *n.* A businessperson who substitutes information technologies for work-related travel. Teleworkers include home-based and small businesses that use computer and communications technologies to interact with customers and/or colleagues. *See also* distributed workplace, SOHO. *Compare* telecommuter.

telnet¹ *n.* A client program that implements the Telnet protocol.
telnet² *vb.* To access a remote computer over the Internet using the Telnet protocol. *See also* telnet¹.
Telnet *n.* A protocol that enables an Internet user to log on to and enter commands on a remote computer linked to the Internet, as if the user were using a text-based terminal directly attached to that computer. Telnet is part of the TCP/IP suite of protocols. *See also* TCP/IP.
template *n.* **1.** In an application package, an overlay for the keyboard that identifies special keys and key combinations. **2.** In image processing, a pattern that is used to identify or match a scanned image. **3.** In spreadsheet programs, a predesigned spreadsheet that contains formulas, labels, and other elements. **4.** In MS-DOS, a small portion of memory that holds the most recently typed MS-DOS command. **5.** In word processing and desktop publishing, a predesigned document that contains formatting and, in many cases, generic text.
temporary file *n.* A file created either in memory or on disk, by the operating system or some other program, to be used during a session and then discarded. *Also called* temp file.
temporary storage *n.* A region in memory or on a storage device that is temporarily allocated for storing intermediate data in a computational, sorting, or transfer operation.
terabyte *n.* Abbreviated TB. A data unit of 1,099,511,627,776 (2^{40}) bytes; sometimes interpreted as 1 trillion bytes. This measurement is used in high-capacity data storage.
terminal *n.* A device consisting of a video adapter, a monitor, and a keyboard. A terminal does little or no computer processing on its own; instead, it is connected to a computer with a communications link over a cable. Terminals are used primarily in multi-user systems and today are not often found on single-user personal computers. *See also* dumb terminal, smart terminal, terminal emulation.
terminal emulation *n.* The imitation of a terminal by using software that conforms to a standard such as the ANSI standard for terminal emulation. Terminal-emulation software is used to make a microcomputer act as if it were a particular type of terminal while it is communicating with another computer, such as a mainframe.
terminal server *n.* In a LAN, a computer or a controller that allows terminals, microcomputers, and other devices to connect to a network or host computer or to devices attached to that particular computer. *See also* controller, LAN, microcomputer, terminal.
terminate *vb.* **1.** With reference to software, to end a process or program. Abnormal termination occurs in response to user intervention or because of a hardware or software error. **2.** With reference to hardware, to install a plug, jack, or other connector at the end of a wire or cable.
terminate-and-stay-resident program *n.* *See* TSR.

A B C D E F G H I J K L M N O P Q R S T U V W X Y Z

terminator *n.* **1.** A character that indicates the end of a string. **2.** An item of hardware that must be installed in the last device in a daisy chain or bus network, such as Ethernet or SCSI. *See also* terminator cap.
terminator cap *n.* A special connector that must be attached to each end of an Ethernet bus. If one or both terminator caps are missing, the Ethernet network will not work. *See also* Ethernet (definition 1).
test post *n.* A newsgroup article that contains no actual message but is used simply as a means of checking the connection. *See also* article, newsgroup.
text *n.* **1.** Data that consists of characters representing the words and symbols of human speech; usually, characters coded according to the ASCII standard. *See also* ASCII. **2.** In word processing and desktop publishing, the main portion of a document, as opposed to headlines, illustrations, and other elements.
text box *n.* In a dialog box or an HTML form, a box in which the user may enter text.
text editor *n. See* editor.
text entry *n.* The inputting of text characters by means of a keyboard.
text file *n.* A file composed of text characters. A text file can be a word processing file or a "plain" ASCII file encoded in a format practically all computers can use. *See also* ASCII file, text (definition 1).
text mode *n.* A display mode in which the monitor can display letters, numbers, and other text characters but no graphical images or WYSIWYG character formatting (italics, superscripts, and so on). *Also called* alphanumeric mode, character mode. *See also* WYSIWYG. *Compare* graphics mode.
text-only file *n. See* ASCII file.
text-to-speech *n.* The conversion of text-based data into voice output by speech synthesis devices, to allow users to gain access to information by telephone or to allow blind people or those who cannot read to use computers. *See also* speech synthesis.
texture *n.* In computer graphics, shading or other attributes added to the "surface" of a graphical image to give it the illusion of a physical substance. For example, a surface could be made to appear reflective to simulate metal or glass.
TFT display *n. See* active-matrix display.
TFT LCD *n. See* active-matrix display.
thermal printer *n.* A nonimpact printer that uses heat to generate an image on specially treated paper. The printer uses pins to produce an image by heating the pins and bringing them into gentle contact with the paper. The special coating on the paper discolors when it is heated.
thesaurus *n.* **1.** A book of words and their synonyms. **2.** In microcomputer applications, both a file of synonyms stored on disk and the program used to search the file.

thick Ethernet *n. See* 10Base5, Ethernet (definition 1).
ThickNet *n. See* 10Base5.
ThickWire *n. See* 10Base5.
thin client *n.* In a client/server architecture, a client computer that performs little or no data processing. The processing is instead performed by the server. *See also* client/server architecture, fat server, thin server. *Compare* fat client.
thin Ethernet *n. See* 10Base2, Ethernet (definition 1).
ThinNet *n. See* 10Base2.
thin server *n.* A client/server architecture in which most of an application is run on the client machine (called a fat client), with occasional data operations on a remote server. Such a configuration yields good client performance but complicates administrative tasks, such as software upgrades. *Also called* thin system. *See also* client/server architecture, fat client, thin client. *Compare* fat server.
thin system *n. See* thin server.
ThinWire *n. See* 10Base2.
third-generation computer *n. See* computer.
third normal form *n.* Abbreviated 3NF. *See* normal form.
third party *n.* A company that manufactures and sells accessories or peripherals for use with a major manufacturer's computer or peripheral, usually without any involvement from the major manufacturer.
thread *n.* In e-mail and Internet newsgroups, a series of messages and replies related to a specific topic.
threaded discussion *n.* In a newsgroup or other online forum, a series of messages or articles in which replies to an article are nested directly under it, instead of the articles being arranged in chronological or alphabetical order. *See also* newsgroup, thread.
threaded newsreader *n.* A newsreader that displays posts in newsgroups as threads. Replies to a post appear directly after the original post, rather than in chronological or any other order. *See also* newsreader, post, thread.
three-dimensional model *n.* A computer simulation of a physical object in which length, width, and depth are real attributes—a model, with *x*-, *y*-, and *z*-axes, that can be rotated for viewing from different angles. *Compare* two-dimensional model.
three-tier client/server *n.* A client/server architecture in which software systems are structured into three tiers, or layers: the user interface layer, the business logic layer, and the database layer. Layers may have one or more components. For example, the top tier may have more than one user interface, and applications in the middle tier may use more than one database at a time. Components in one tier may run on a separate computer from the other tiers, communicating with the other components over a network. *See also* client/server architecture. *Compare* two-tier client/server.

#
A
B
C
D
E
F
G
H
I
J
K
L
M
N
O
P
Q
R
S
T
U
V
W
X
Y
Z

throttle control *n.* A device that enables the user of a flight simulator or game to control simulated engine power. The throttle control is used along with a joystick and possibly a rudder control.

throughput *n.* A measure of the data transfer rate through a typically complex communications system or of the data processing rate in a computer system.

thumb *n. See* elevator.

thumbnail *n.* A miniature version of an image or of the electronic version of a page, generally used to allow quick browsing through multiple images or pages. For example, Web pages often contain thumbnails of images (which can be loaded much more quickly by the Web browser than the full-size images). The user can sometimes click on these thumbnails to load the complete versions of the images.

thumbwheel *n.* A wheel embedded in a case so that only a portion of the outside rim is revealed. When rolled with the thumb, the wheel can control an on-screen element such as a pointer or a cursor. Thumbwheels are used with three-dimensional joysticks and trackballs to control the depth aspect of the pointer or cursor. *See also* joystick, relative pointing device, trackball.

TIA *n.* Acronym for **t**hanks **i**n **a**dvance. On the Internet, a popular sign-off to a request of some sort. *Also called* aTdHvAaNnKcSe.

tie line *n.* A private line leased from a communications carrier and often used to link two or more points in an organization.

.tif *n.* The file extension that identifies bitmap images in Tagged Image File Format. *See also* TIFF.

TIFF or **TIF** *n.* Acronym for **T**agged (or **T**ag) **I**mage **F**ile **F**ormat. A standard file format commonly used for scanning, storage, and interchange of gray-scale graphic images. TIFF may be the only format available for older programs (such as older versions of MacPaint), but most modern programs are able to save images in a variety of other formats, such as GIF or JPEG. *See also* gray scale. *Compare* GIF, JPEG.

tile *vb.* **1.** In computer-graphics programming, to fill adjacent blocks of pixels on the screen with a design or pattern without allowing any blocks to overlap. **2.** To fill the space on a monitor or within a smaller area with multiple copies of the same graphic image. **3.** In an environment with multiple windows, to rearrange and resize all open windows so that they appear fully on the screen without any overlap.

time and date *n.* In computing, the timekeeping and datekeeping functions maintained by the computer's operating system, used most visibly as a means of "stamping" files with the time and date of creation or last revision.

time out or **timeout** or **time-out** *n.* An event indicating that a predetermined amount of time has elapsed without some other expected event taking place. The time-out event is used to interrupt the process that had been waiting for the other expected event. For example, a dial-up remote system might allow the user 60 seconds to log in after making a connection. If the user fails to enter a valid login name and password within this time, the computer breaks the connection, thus protecting itself against crackers as well as freeing a phone line that may have gone dead.

time-sharing *n.* The use of a computer system by more than one individual at the same time. Time-sharing runs separate programs concurrently by interleaving portions of processing time allotted to each program (user).

Time to Live *n.* A header field for a packet sent over the Internet indicating how long the packet should be held. *Acronym:* TTL. *See also* header (definition 2), packet (definition 1).

title bar *n.* In a graphical user interface, a horizontal space at the top of a window that contains the name of the window. Most title bars also contain boxes or buttons for closing and resizing the window. By dragging the title bar, the user can move the entire window.

TLA *n.* Acronym for **t**hree-**l**etter **a**cronym. An ironic term, usually used in jest on the Internet in e-mail, newsgroups, and other online forums, referring to the large number of acronyms in computer terminology, particularly those consisting of three letters.

toggle[1] *n.* An electronic device with two states or a program option that can be turned on or off using the same action, such as a mouse click.

toggle[2] *vb.* To switch back and forth between two states. For example, the Num Lock key on an IBM-style keyboard toggles the numeric keypad between numbers and cursor movement.

token *n.* A unique structured data object or message that circulates continuously among the nodes of a token ring and describes the current state of the network. Before any node can send a message, it must first wait to control the token. *See also* token bus network, token passing, token ring network.

token bus network *n.* A LAN formed in a bus topology (stations connected to a single, shared data highway) that uses token passing to regulate traffic on the line. On a token bus network, a token governing the right to transmit is passed from one station to another, and each station holds the token for a brief time, during which it alone can transmit information. In essence, the token "circles" through the network in a logical ring rather than a physical one. *See also* bus network, LAN, token passing. *Compare* token ring network.

token passing *n.* A method of controlling access on LANs by using a special signal (a token) that determines which station is allowed to transmit. The token is passed from station to station around the network, and only the station with the token can transmit information. *See also* token, token bus network, token ring network. *Compare* collision detection, contention.

token ring network *n.* A LAN formed in a ring (closed loop) topology that uses token passing to regulate traffic on the line. On a token ring network, a token governing the right to transmit is passed from one station to the next in a physical circle. A station with information to transmit "seizes" the token, marks it as being in use, and inserts the information. The "busy" token, plus message, is then passed around the circle, copied at its destination, and eventually returned to the sender. The sender removes the attached message and then passes the freed token to the next station in line. *See also* LAN, ring network, token passing. *Compare* token bus network.

Token Ring network *n.* A token-passing, ring-shaped LAN developed by IBM that operates at 4 Mbps. With standard telephone wiring, the Token Ring network can connect up to 72 devices; with STP wiring, the network supports up to 260 devices. Although it is based on a ring (closed loop) topology, the Token Ring network uses star-shaped clusters of up to eight workstations connected to a wiring concentrator, which, in turn, is connected to the main ring. The Token Ring network is designed to accommodate microcomputers, minicomputers, and mainframes; it follows standards for token ring networks. *See also* LAN, ring network, STP, token passing.

tone *n.* **1.** A particular tint of a color. *Also called* shade, value. *See also* brightness, color model. **2.** One sound or signal of a particular frequency.

toner *n.* Powdered pigment used in office copiers and in laser, LED, and LCD printers. *See also* electrophotographic printers.

toner cartridge *n.* A disposable container that holds toner for a laser printer or other page printer. Some types of toner cartridge contain toner only; however, the most popular printer engines pack all expendables, including toner and the photosensitive drum, in a single cartridge. Toner cartridges are interchangeable among printers that use the same engine.

toolbar *n.* In an application in a graphical user interface, a row, column, or block of on-screen buttons or icons. When the user clicks on these buttons or icons, macros or certain functions of the application are activated. For example, word processors often feature toolbars with buttons for changing text to italic, boldface, and other styles. The user can sometimes customize toolbars and move them around on the screen according to preference. *See also* graphical user interface. *Compare* menu bar, palette (definition 1), title bar.

topic drift *n.* The tendency of an online discussion to move from its original subject to other related or unrelated subjects. For example, someone in a newsgroup devoted to TV might ask about a news program; then someone else might comment about a story on that program about food poisoning, which leads someone else to start a general discussion on the advantages of organic food.

topic group *n.* An online discussion area for participants with a common interest in a particular subject.

top-level domain *n.* In the domain name system of Internet addresses, any of the broadest category of names, under which all domain names fit. Top-level domains for sites in the United States include .com, .edu, .gov, .mil, .net, and .org. *See also* DNS (definition 1), major geographic domain.

topology *n.* The configuration formed by the connections between devices on a LAN or between two or more LANs. *See also* bus network, LAN, ring network, star network, token ring network, tree network.

total bypass *n.* A communications network that uses satellite transmission to bypass both local and long-distance telephone links.

total cost of ownership *n.* Specifically, the cost of owning, operating, and maintaining a single personal computer; more generally, the cost to businesses and organizations of setting up and maintaining complex and far-reaching networked computer systems. Total cost of ownership includes the up-front costs of hardware and software added to later costs of installation, personnel training, technical support, upgrades, and repairs. *Acronym:* TCO. *Also called* cost of ownership (CO).

touch pad *n.* A variety of graphics tablet that uses pressure sensors, rather than the electromagnetics used in more expensive high-resolution tablets, to track the position of a device on its surface. *See also* absolute pointing device, graphics tablet.

touch screen *n.* A computer screen designed or modified to recognize the location of a touch on its surface. By touching the screen, the user can make a selection or move a cursor. *Compare* light pen.

touch-sensitive display *n. See* touch screen.

touch-sensitive tablet *n. See* touch pad.

tower *n.* A microcomputer system in which the cabinet for the CPU is tall, narrow, and deep rather than short, wide, and deep. The motherboard is usually vertical, and the disk drives are often perpendicular to the motherboard. A tower cabinet is at least 24 inches tall. *See also* cabinet, microcomputer, motherboard. *Compare* minitower.

TP *n. See* transaction processing.

track[1] *n.* One of numerous circular data storage areas on a floppy disk or a hard drive. Tracks, composed of sectors, are recorded on a disk by an operating system during a disk format operation. On other storage media, such as tape, a track runs parallel to the edge of the medium.

track[2] *vb.* **1.** To follow a path. **2.** In data management, to follow the flow of information through a manual or an automated system. **3.** In data storage and retrieval, to follow and read from a recording channel on a disk or a magnetic tape. **4.** In computer graphics, to cause a displayed symbol, such as a pointer, to match on the screen the movements of a mouse or another pointing device.

trackball *n.* A pointing device that consists of a ball resting on two rollers at right angles to each other, which translate the ball's motion into vertical and horizontal movement on the screen. A trackball also typically has one or more buttons to initiate other actions. A trackball's housing is stationary; its ball is rolled with the hand. *Compare* mechanical mouse.

trackpad *n.* A pointing device consisting of a small, flat pad that is sensitive to touch. Users move the mouse cursor on screen by touching the trackpad and moving their fingers across the trackpad's surface. Such devices are most commonly installed on laptop computers. *See also* pointing device.

tractor feed *n.* A method of feeding paper through a printer using pins that are mounted on rotating belts. The pins engage holes near the edges of continuous-form paper and either push or pull the paper through. *See also* continuous-form paper. *Compare* pin feed.

A B C D E F G H I J K L M N O P Q R S T U V W X Y Z

traditional newsgroup hierarchy *n.* The seven standard newsgroup categories in Usenet: comp., misc., news., rec., sci., soc., and talk. Newsgroups can be added within the traditional hierarchy only following a formal voting process. *See also* comp. newsgroups, misc. newsgroups, newsgroup, news. newsgroups, rec. newsgroups, Request for Discussion, sci. newsgroups, soc. newsgroups, talk. newsgroups, Usenet. *Compare* alt. newsgroups.
traffic *n.* The load carried by a communications link or channel.
trailer *n.* Information, typically occupying several bytes, at the tail end of a block (section) of transmitted data, often containing a checksum or other error-checking data for confirming the accuracy and status of the transmission. *See also* checksum. *Compare* header (definition 2).
transaction *n.* A discrete activity within a computer system, such as an entry of a customer order or an update of an inventory item. Transactions are usually associated with database management, order entry, and other online systems.
transaction file *n.* A file that contains the details of transactions, such as items and prices on invoices. It is used to update a master database file. *See also* transaction. *Compare* master file.
transaction log *n.* *See* change file.
transaction processing *n.* A processing method in which transactions are executed immediately after they are received by the system. *Acronym:* TP. *See also* transaction. *Compare* batch processing (definition 3).
transceiver *n.* Short for **trans**mitter/re**ceiver.** A device that can both transmit and receive signals. On LANs, a transceiver is the device that connects a computer to the network.
transceiver cable *n.* A cable used to connect a host adapter within a computer to a LAN. *See also* LAN.
transfer rate *n.* The rate at which a circuit or a communications channel transfers information from source to destination, as over a network or to and from a disk drive. Transfer rate is measured in units of information per unit of time—for example, bits per second or characters per second—and can be measured either as a raw rate, which is the maximum transfer speed, or as an average rate, which includes gaps between blocks of data as part of the transmission time.
transfer time *n.* The time elapsed between the start of a data transfer operation and its completion.
transform *vb.* **1.** To change the appearance or format of data without altering its content; that is, to encode information according to predefined rules. **2.** In computer graphics, to alter the position, size, or nature of an object by moving it to another location, making it larger or smaller (scaling), turning it (rotation), changing its description from one type of coordinate system to another, and so on.
transient *adj.* **1.** Fleeting, temporary, or unpredictable. **2.** Of or pertaining to the region of memory used for programs, such as applications, that are read from disk storage and that reside in memory temporarily until they are

replaced by other programs. In this context, the term can also refer to the programs themselves.

transistor *n.* Short for **tran**sfer re**sistor.** A solid-state circuit component, usually with three leads, in which a voltage or a current controls the flow of another current. The transistor can serve many functions, including those of amplifier, switch, and oscillator, and is a fundamental component of almost all modern electronics.

translated file *n.* A file containing data that has been changed from binary (8-bit) format to ASCII (7-bit) format. BinHex and uuencode both translate binary files into ASCII. Such translation is necessary to transmit data through systems (such as e-mail) that may not preserve the eighth bit of each byte. A translated file must be decoded to its binary form before being used. *See also* BinHex[1], uuencode[1].

translator *n.* A program that translates one language or data format into another.

transmission channel *n.* *See* channel.

Transmission Control Protocol/Internet Protocol *n.* *See* TCP/IP.

transmit *vb.* To send information over a communications line or a circuit. Computer transmissions can take place in the following ways:

- asynchronous (variable timing) or synchronous (exact timing)
- serial (essentially, bit by bit) or parallel (byte by byte; a group of bits at once)
- duplex or full-duplex (simultaneous two-way communication), half-duplex (two-way communication in one direction at a time), or simplex (one-way communication only)
- burst (intermittent transmission of blocks of information)

Transmit Data *n.* *See* TXD.

transmitter *n.* Any circuit or electronic device designed to send electrically encoded data to another location.

transparent *adj.* **1.** In computer use, of, pertaining to, or characteristic of a device, function, or part of a program that works so smoothly and easily that it is invisible to the user. **2.** In communications, of, pertaining to, or characteristic of a mode of transmission in which data can contain any characters, including device-control characters, without the possibility of misinterpretation by the receiving station. For example, the receiving station will not end a transparent transmission until it receives a character in the data that indicates end of transmission (and thus will not end communications prematurely). **3.** In computer graphics, of, pertaining to, or characteristic of the lack of color in a particular region of an image so that the background color of the display shows through.

transponder *n.* A transceiver in a communications satellite that receives a signal from an earth station and retransmits it on a different frequency to one or more other earth stations.

#
A
B
C
D
E
F
G
H
I
J
K
L
M
N
O
P
Q
R
S
T
U
V
W
X
Y
Z

transportable computer *n.* *See* portable computer.

transport layer *n.* The fourth of the seven layers in the ISO/OSI model for standardizing computer-to-computer communications. The transport layer is one level above the network layer and is responsible for both quality of service and accurate delivery of information. Among the tasks performed on this layer are error detection and correction. *See also* ISO/OSI model.

transpose *vb.* To reverse, as in reversing the order of the letters in a misspelled word (*hte* for *the*) or reversing two wires in a circuit.

transputer *n.* Short for **trans**istor com**puter.** A complete computer on a single chip, including RAM and a floating-point unit (a circuit that performs mathematical calculations), designed as a building block for parallel computing systems.

trapdoor *n.* *See* back door.

tree *n.* A data structure containing zero or more nodes linked together in a hierarchical fashion. If there are any nodes, one node is the root; each node except the root is the child of only one other node; and each node has zero or more nodes as children. *See also* child (definition 2), leaf, node (definition 3), parent/child (definition 2), root.

tree network *n.* A topology for a LAN in which one machine is connected to one or more other machines, each of which is connected to one or more others, and so on, so that the structure formed by the network resembles that of a tree. *See also* bus network, distributed network, LAN, ring network, star network, token ring network, topology.

tree search *n.* A search procedure performed on a tree data structure. At each step of the search, a tree search is able to determine, by the value in a particular node, which branches of the tree to eliminate, without searching those branches themselves. *See also* branch (definition 1), tree structure.

tree structure *n.* Any structure that has the essential organizational properties of a tree. *See also* tree.

trichromatic *adj.* Of, pertaining to, or characteristic of a system that uses three colors (red, green, and blue in computer graphics) to create all other colors. *See also* color model.

trigger *n.* In a database, an action that causes a procedure to be carried out automatically when a user attempts to modify data. A trigger can instruct the database system to take a specific action depending on the change attempted. Incorrect, unwanted, or unauthorized changes can thereby be prevented, helping to maintain the integrity of the database.

triple-pass scanner *n.* A color scanner that performs one scanning pass on an image for each of the three primary colors of light (red, green, and blue). *See also* color scanner.

tristimulus values *n.* In color graphics, the varying amounts of three colors, such as red, blue, and green, that are combined to produce another color. *See also* color, color model.

Trojan horse *n.* A destructive program that is disguised as a game, a utility, or an application. When it is run, a Trojan horse does something harmful to the computer system while appearing to do something useful. *See also* CERT, virus, worm.
troll *vb.* To post a message in a newsgroup or other online discussion hoping that someone else will consider the message so outrageous that it demands a heated reply. A classic example of trolling is an article in favor of torturing cats posted in a pet lovers' newsgroup. *See also* YHBT.
troubleshoot *vb.* To isolate the source of a problem in a program, computer system, or network and remedy it. The term often refers especially to dealing with hardware malfunctions. *See also* debug.
trouble ticket *n.* A report of a problem with a device or system that is tracked through the workflow process. Electronic trouble tickets are featured by many workflow and help-desk applications. *See also* help desk (definition 2), workflow application.
true color *n. See* 24-bit color.
TrueType *n.* An outline font technology introduced by Apple Computer in 1991 and by Microsoft in 1992 as a means of including high-grade fonts within the Macintosh and Windows operating systems. TrueType is a WYSIWYG font technology, which means that the printed output of TrueType fonts is identical to what appears on the screen. *See also* bitmapped font, outline font, PostScript.
truncate *vb.* To cut off the beginning or end of a series of characters or numbers; specifically, to eliminate one or more of the least significant (typically rightmost) digits.
trunk *n.* In communications, a channel connecting two switching stations. A trunk usually carries a large number of calls at the same time.
truth table *n.* A table showing the value of a Boolean expression for each of the possible combinations of variable values in the expression. *See also* AND, Boolean operator, exclusive OR, NOT, OR.
TSR *n.* Acronym for **t**erminate-and-**s**tay-**r**esident. A program that remains loaded in memory even when it is not running, so that it can be quickly invoked for a specific task performed while another program is operating. Typically, these programs are used with operating systems that are not multitasking, such as MS-DOS. *See also* hot key[1].
TTFN *n.* Acronym for **T**a **t**a **f**or **n**ow. An expression sometimes used in Internet discussion groups or chat sessions to signal a participant's temporary departure from the group.
TTL *n. See* Time to Live.
tuple *n.* In a database table (relation), a set of related values, one for each attribute (column). A tuple is stored as a row in a relational database management system. It is analogous to a record in a nonrelational file. *See also* relation.

#
A
B
C
D
E
F
G
H
I
J
K
L
M
N
O
P
Q
R
S
T
U
V
W
X
Y
Z

turnaround time *n.* **1.** The elapsed time between submission and completion of a job. **2.** In communications, the time required to reverse the direction of transmission in half-duplex communications mode. *See also* half-duplex transmission.
turnkey system *n.* A finished system, complete with all necessary hardware and documentation and with software installed and ready to be used.
turnpike effect *n.* The communications equivalent of gridlock; a reference to bottlenecks caused by heavy traffic over a communications system or network.
turtle *n.* A small on-screen shape, usually a triangle or a turtle shape, that acts as a drawing tool in graphics. A turtle is a friendly, easily manipulated tool designed for children learning to use computers. It takes its name from a mechanical, dome-shaped "turtle," developed for the Logo language, that moved about the floor in response to Logo commands, raising and lowering a pen to draw lines.
turtle graphics *n.* A simple graphics environment in which a turtle is manipulated by simple commands. Some versions display the turtle and its track on screen; others use electromechanical turtles that write on paper.
tutorial *n.* A teaching aid designed to help people learn to use a product or procedure. In computer applications, a tutorial might be presented in a manual or as an interactive disk-based series of lessons provided with the program package.
TWAIN *n.* Acronym for **t**echnology **w**ithout **a**n **i**nteresting **n**ame. The de facto standard interface between software applications and image-capturing devices such as scanners. Nearly all scanners contain a TWAIN driver, but only TWAIN-compatible software can use the technology. *See also* scanner.
tweak *vb.* To make final small changes to improve hardware or software performance; to fine-tune a nearly complete product.
tween *vb.* In a graphics program, to calculate intermediary shapes during the metamorphosis of one shape into another.
twinaxial *adj.* Having two coaxial cables contained in a single insulated jacket. *See also* coaxial cable.
twisted-pair cable *n.* A cable made of two separately insulated strands of wire twisted together. It is used to reduce signal interference introduced by a strong radio source such as a nearby cable. One of the wires in the pair carries the sensitive signal, and the other wire is grounded.
two-dimensional *adj.* Existing in reference to two measures, such as height and width—for example, a two-dimensional model drawn with reference to an *x*-axis and a *y*-axis.
two-dimensional model *n.* A computer simulation of a physical object in which length and width are real attributes but depth is not; a model with *x*- and *y*-axes. *Compare* three-dimensional model.
two-tier client/server *n.* A client/server architecture in which software systems are structured into two tiers, or layers: the user interface/business logic layer and the database layer. *See also* client/server architecture. *Compare* three-tier client/server.

TXD *n.* Short for Transmit **(tx) D**ata. A line used to carry transmitted data from one device to another, as from computer to modem. *Compare* RXD.

.txt *n.* A file extension that identifies ASCII text files. In most cases, a document with a .txt extension does not include any formatting commands, so it is readable in any text editor or word processing program. *See also* ASCII.

Tymnet *n.* A public data network available in over 100 countries, with links to some online services and Internet service providers.

type¹ *n.* **1.** In programming, the nature of a variable—for example, integer, real number, or text character. Data types in programs are declared by the programmer and determine the range of values a variable can take as well as the operations that can be performed on it. *See also* data type. **2.** In printing, the characters that make up printed text; the design of a set of characters (typeface); or, more loosely, the complete set of characters in a given size and style (font). *See also* font, typeface.

type² *vb.* To enter information by means of the keyboard.

type-ahead buffer *n.* *See* keyboard buffer.

type-ahead capability *n.* The ability of a computer program to gather incoming keystrokes in a temporary memory reservoir (buffer) before displaying them on the screen. This ensures that keystrokes are not lost if they are typed faster than the program can display them.

typeface *n.* A named design of a set of printed characters, such as Helvetica Bold Oblique, that has a particular stroke weight (thickness of line, such as bold or light) and a specified style (obliqueness, or degree of slant, such as roman or italic). A typeface is not the same as a font, which is a specific size of a specific typeface, such as 12-point Helvetica Bold Oblique. Nor is a typeface the same as a typeface family, which is a group of related typefaces, such as the Helvetica family including Helvetica, Helvetica Bold, Helvetica Oblique, and Helvetica Bold Oblique. *See also* font.

typematic *adj.* The keyboard feature that repeats a keystroke when a key is held down longer than usual. *Also called* auto-key, auto-repeat. *See also* repeat key.

typeover mode *n.* *See* overwrite mode.

type size *n.* The size of printed characters, usually measured in points. *See also* font, point¹ (definition 1).

type style *n.* **1.** The obliqueness, or degree of slant, of a typeface. **2.** Loosely, the overall design of a typeface or a typeface family. **3.** One of the variant forms of a type character, including roman, bold, italic, and bold italic.

U

UA *n. See* user agent.

UART *n.* Acronym for **u**niversal **a**synchronous **r**eceiver-**t**ransmitter. A module, usually composed of a single integrated circuit, that contains both the receiving and transmitting circuits required for asynchronous serial communications. A UART is the most common type of circuit used in personal computer modems. *Compare* USRT.

ubiquitous computing *n.* A term coined by Mark Wieser at the Xerox PARC Computer Science Lab to describe a computing environment so pervasive in daily life that it is invisible to the user. Household appliances such as VCRs and microwave ovens are contemporary low-level examples of ubiquitous computing. Ubiquitous computing is considered to be the third stage in the evolution of computing technology, after the mainframe and the personal computer. *Acronym:* UC. *Also called* calm technology.

UC *n. See* ubiquitous computing.

UDP *n.* Acronym for **U**ser **D**atagram **P**rotocol. The connectionless protocol within TCP/IP that corresponds to the transport layer in the ISO/OSI model. UDP converts data messages generated by an application into packets to be sent via IP but does not verify that messages have been delivered correctly. Because UDP is more efficient than TCP, it is used for various purposes, including SNMP; the reliability depends on the application that generates the message. *See also* communications protocol, ISO/OSI model, packet (definition 2), SNMP, TCP/IP. *Compare* IP, TCP.

UDT *n.* Acronym for **U**niform **D**ata **T**ransfer. The service used in the OLE extensions to Windows that allows two applications to exchange data without either program knowing the internal structure of the other.

UI *n. See* user interface.

ultralight computer *n. See* portable computer.

UMA *n.* Acronym for **u**pper **m**emory **a**rea. The portion of DOS memory between the first 640 KB and 1 MB. It is used primarily for the ROM BIOS and control hardware such as the video adapter and I/O ports. *Compare* conventional memory, high memory area.

unbuffered *adj.* Of, pertaining to, or characteristic of something that does not store data characters in memory but instead processes them as they are received. *See also* buffer[2].

unbundled *adj.* Not included as part of a complete hardware/software package; the term particularly applies to a product that was previously bundled, as opposed to one that has always been sold separately.

UNC *n. See* Uniform Naming Convention.

uncompress *vb.* To restore the content of a compressed file to its original form. *Also called* decompress. *Compare* compress.

undelete[1] *n.* The act of restoring deleted information. An undelete is comparable to (and usually included as part of) an Undo command—although an undo reverses any previous act, whereas an undelete reverses only a deletion. Undeleting generally refers only to excised text or deleted files. *See also* undo. *Compare* delete.

undelete[2] *vb.* **1.** To restore deleted information, ordinarily the last item deleted. **2.** In file storage, to restore a file's storage information so that a deleted file becomes available for access again. *Also called* unerase. *See also* file recovery.

undeliverable *adj.* Not able to be delivered to an intended recipient. If an e-mail message is undeliverable, it is returned to the sender with information added by the mail server explaining the problem; for example, the e-mail address may be incorrect, or the recipient's mailbox may be full.

underline *vb.* To format a selection of text so that the text is printed with a line slightly below it.

Undernet *n.* An international network of IRC servers, created as an alternative to the larger and more chaotic main IRC network. *See also* IRC.

underscore *n.* An underline character often used to emphasize a letter or a word; on nongraphics displays, generally used to indicate italic characters.

undo *vb.* To reverse the last action—for example, to undo a deletion, thus restoring deleted text to a document. *See also* undelete.

undock *vb.* **1.** To detach a laptop or other portable computer from a docking station. **2.** To move a toolbar from the edge of a window so that the toolbar becomes its own free-floating window.

unerase *vb. See* undelete[2].

Unicode *n.* A 16-bit character encoding standard. By using 2 bytes to represent each character, Unicode enables almost all the written languages of the world to be represented using a single character set. (By contrast, 8-bit ASCII is not capable of representing all the combinations of letters and diacritical marks that are used just with the Roman alphabet.) *Compare* ASCII.

Uniform Data Transfer *n. See* UDT.

Uniform Naming Convention *n.* The system of naming files among computers on a network so that a file on a given computer will have the same pathname when accessed from any of the other computers on the network. For example, if the directory *c:\path1\path2\...pathn* on computer *servern* is shared under the name *pathdirs,* a user on another computer would open *\\servern\pathdirs\filename.ext* to access the file *c:\path1\path2\...pathn \filename.ext* on *servern*. *Acronym:* UNC. *See also* URL, virtual path.

Uniform Resource Citation *n.* A description of an object on the World Wide Web, consisting of pairs of attributes and their values, such as the Uniform Resource Identifiers (URLs) of associated resources, author names, publisher names, dates, and prices. *Acronym:* URC.

Uniform Resource Identifier *n.* A character string used to identify a resource (such as a file) from anywhere on the Internet by type and location. The category of URIs includes URNs and URLs. *Acronym:* URI. *See also* relative URL, Uniform Resource Name, URL.

Uniform Resource Locator *n.* *See* URL.

Uniform Resource Name *n.* A scheme for uniquely identifying resources that may be available on the Internet by name, without regard to where they are located. The specifications for the format of URNs are still under development. URNs include all URIs having the schemes urn:, fpi:, and path:—that is, those that are not URLs. *Acronym:* URN. *See also* Uniform Resource Identifier, URL.

uninstall *vb.* To remove software completely from a system, including the elimination of files and components residing in system locations such as the Registry in Windows 95. Some applications have built-in uninstall utilities, and in other cases a separate uninstall program can be used. *Also called* deinstall.

uninterruptible power supply *n.* *See* UPS.

union *n.* **1.** *See* OR. **2.** In database management, a relational operator. Given two relations (tables), A and B, that are union-compatible (contain the same number of fields, with corresponding fields containing the same types of values), A UNION B builds a new relation containing those tuples (records) that appear either in A or in B or in both.

universal asynchronous receiver-transmitter *n.* *See* UART.

universal serial bus *n.* *See* USB.

universal synchronous receiver-transmitter *n.* *See* USRT.

Universal Time Coordinate *n.* For all practical purposes, the same as Greenwich Mean Time, which is used for the synchronization of computers on the Internet. *Acronym:* UTC. *Also called* coordinated universal time format.

UNIX *n.* A multi-user, multitasking operating system originally developed by Ken Thompson and Dennis Ritchie at AT&T Bell Laboratories for use on minicomputers. UNIX is considered a powerful operating system that, because it is written in the C language, is more portable—that is, less machine-specific—than other operating systems. UNIX is available in several related forms, including AIX (a version of UNIX adapted by IBM to run on RISC-based workstations), A/UX (a graphical version for the Apple Macintosh), and Mach (a rewritten but essentially UNIX-compatible operating system for the NeXT computer).

UNIX-to-UNIX Copy *n.* *See* UUCP.

unknown host *n.* A response to a request for a connection to a server indicating that the network is unable to find the specified address. *See also* server (definition 1).

unknown recipients *n.* A response to an e-mail message indicating that the mail server is unable to identify one or more of the destination addresses.

unload *vb.* **1.** To remove a storage medium, such as a tape or disk, from its drive. **2.** To remove software from system memory. *See also* memory.

unmoderated *adj.* Of, pertaining to, or characteristic of a newsgroup or mailing list in which all articles or messages received by the server are automatically available or distributed to all subscribers. *Compare* moderated discussion.
unmount *vb.* To remove a disk or tape from active use. *Compare* mount.
unpack *vb.* To restore packed data to its original format. *Compare* pack.
unpopulated board *n.* A circuit board whose sockets are empty. *Compare* fully populated board.
unread *adj.* **1.** Of, pertaining to, or being an article in a newsgroup that a user has not yet received. Newsreader client programs distinguish between read and unread articles for each user and download only unread articles from the server. **2.** Of, pertaining to, or being an e-mail message that a user has received but has not yet opened in an e-mail program.
unrecoverable error *n.* A fatal error—one from which a program is unable to recover without the use of external recovery techniques. *Compare* recoverable error.
unshielded cable *n.* Cable that is not surrounded with a metal shield. If the wires in an unshielded cable are not at least twisted around each other in pairs, the signals they carry have no protection from interference by external electromagnetic fields. Consequently, unshielded cable should be used only over very short distances. *Compare* coaxial cable, ribbon cable, twisted-pair cable, UTP.
unshielded twisted pair *n. See* UTP.
unsubscribe *vb.* **1.** In a newsreader client program, to remove a newsgroup from the list of newsgroups to which one subscribes. *See also* newsgroup. **2.** To remove a recipient from a mailing list. *See also* mailing list.
untar[1] *n.* A utility, available for systems in addition to UNIX, for separating the individual files out of an archive assembled using the UNIX tar utility. *Compare* tar[1].
untar[2] *vb.* To separate the individual files out of an archive assembled with the UNIX tar utility. *Compare* tar[2].
unzip *vb.* To uncompress an archive file that has been compressed. *See also* compress.
up *adj.* Functioning and available for use; used in describing computers, printers, communications lines on networks, and other such hardware.
update[1] *n.* A new release of an existing software product. A software update usually adds relatively minor new features to a product or corrects errors (bugs) found after the program was released. Updates are generally indicated by small changes in software version numbers, such as 4.0b from 4.0. *See also* version number. *Compare* release[1].
update[2] *vb.* To change a system or a data file to make it more current.
upgrade[1] *n.* The new or enhanced version of a product.
upgrade[2] *vb.* To change to a newer, usually more powerful or sophisticated version.
uplink *n.* The transmission link from an earth station to a communications satellite.

A B C D E F G H I J K L M N O P Q R S T U V W X Y Z

upload[1] *n.* **1.** In communications, the process of transferring a copy of a file from a local computer to a remote computer by means of a modem or network. **2.** The copy of the file that is being or has been transferred.
upload[2] *vb.* To transfer a copy of a file from a local computer to a remote computer. *Compare* download.
uppercase *adj.* Of, pertaining to, or characterized by capital letters. *Compare* lowercase.
upper memory area *n. See* UMA.
UPS *n.* Acronym for **u**ninterruptible **p**ower **s**upply. A device, connected between a computer and a power source (usually an outlet receptacle), that ensures that electrical flow to the computer is not interrupted because of a blackout and, in most cases, protects the computer against potentially damaging events such as power surges. All UPS units are equipped with a battery and a loss-of-power sensor; if the sensor detects a loss of power, it switches over to the battery so that the user has time to save his or her work and shut off the computer.
upstream *adv.* or *adj.* The term used to describe data traffic moving from an individual computer to a remote network. With certain communications technologies, such as ADSL, cable modems, and high-speed 56-Kbps modems, data flows more slowly upstream than downstream. For example, a 56-Kbps modem can deliver data at a 56-Kbps maximum downstream only; upstream, it delivers data at either 28.8 or 33.6 Kbps. *Compare* downstream.
uptime *n.* The amount or percentage of time a computer system or associated hardware is functioning and available for use. *Compare* downtime.
upward-compatible *adj.* Of, pertaining to, or characteristic of a computer product, especially software, designed to perform adequately with other products that are expected to become widely used in the foreseeable future.
urban legend *n.* A widely distributed story that remains in circulation in spite of being untrue. Many urban legends have been floating around the Internet and other online services for years, including the request for cards for the sick boy in England (he's long since recovered and grown up) and the cookie or cake recipe that cost $250 (it's a myth). *See also* Good Times virus.
URC *n. See* Uniform Resource Citation.
URI *n. See* Uniform Resource Identifier.
URL *n.* Acronym for **U**niform **R**esource **L**ocator. An address for a resource on the Internet. URLs are used by Web browsers to locate Internet resources. A URL specifies the protocol to be used in accessing the resource (such as http: for a Web page or ftp: for an FTP site), the name of the server on which the resource resides (such as //www.whitehouse.gov), and, optionally, the path to a resource (such as an HTML document or a file on that server). *See also* FTP[1] (definition 1), HTML, HTTP, path (definition 2), server (definition 2), virtual path, Web browser.
URN *n. See* Uniform Resource Name.

usable *adj.* Of, pertaining to, or characteristic of the ease and adaptability with which a product can be applied to the performance of the work for which it is designed. A high degree of usability implies ease of learning, flexibility, freedom from bugs, and good design that does not involve unnecessarily complicated procedures.

USB *n.* Acronym for **u**niversal **s**erial **b**us. A serial bus with a bandwidth of 1.5 Mbps for connecting peripherals to a microcomputer. USB can connect up to 127 peripherals, such as external CD-ROM drives, printers, modems, mice, and keyboards, to the system through a single, general-purpose port by daisy-chaining the peripherals together. USB supports hot plugging and multiple data streams. Developed by Intel, USB competes with DEC's ACCESS.bus for lower-speed applications. *See also* bus, daisy chain, hot plugging, input/output port, peripheral. *Compare* ACCESS.bus.

Usenet or **UseNet** or **USENET** *n.* A worldwide network of UNIX systems that has a decentralized administration and is used as a bulletin board system by special-interest discussion groups. Usenet, which is considered part of the Internet (although Usenet predates it), is composed of thousands of newsgroups, each devoted to a particular topic. Users can post messages and read messages from others in these newsgroups in a manner similar to users on dial-in BBSs. Usenet was originally implemented using UUCP software and telephone connections; that method remains important, although more modern methods, such as NNTP and network connections, are now more commonly used. *See also* BBS (definition 1), newsgroup, newsreader, NNTP, UUCP.

Usenet User List *n.* A list maintained by MIT that contains the name and e-mail address of everyone who has posted to Usenet. *See also* Usenet.

user account *n.* On a secure or multi-user computer system, an established means for an individual to access the system and its resources. Usually created by the system's administrator, a user account consists of information about the user, such as password, rights, and permissions. *See also* group[1], logon, user profile.

user agent *n.* In the terminology established by the ISO/OSI model for LANs, a program that helps a client connect with a server. *Acronym:* UA. *See also* agent (definition 3), ISO/OSI model, LAN.

User Datagram Protocol *n.* *See* UDP.

user-defined function key *n.* *See* keyboard enhancer, programmable function key.

user-friendly *adj.* Easy to learn and easy to use.

user group *n.* A group of people drawn together by interest in the same computer system or software. User groups, some of which are large and influential organizations, provide support for newcomers and a forum where members can exchange ideas and information.

user interface *n.* The portion of a program with which a user interacts. Types include command-line interfaces, menu-driven interfaces, and graphical user interfaces. *Acronym:* UI.

#
A
B
C
D
E
F
G
H
I
J
K
L
M
N
O
P
Q
R
S
T
U
V
W
X
Y
Z

username *n.* The name by which a user is identified to a computer system or network. During the logon process, the user must enter the username and the correct password. If the system or network is connected to the Internet, the username generally corresponds to the leftmost part of the user's e-mail address. *See also* e-mail address, logon.

user name *n.* The name by which a person is known and addressed on a communications network. *See also* alias (definition 2).

user profile *n.* A computer-based record maintained about an authorized user of a multi-user computer system. A user profile is needed for security and other reasons; it can contain such information as the person's access restrictions, mailbox location, type of terminal, and so on. *See also* user account.

USnail *n.* **1.** Slang for the U.S. Postal Service. USnail, a term used on the Internet, is a reference to how slow the postal service is in comparison to e-mail. **2.** Mail delivered by the U.S. Postal Service. *See also* snail mail.

/usr *n.* A directory in a computer system that contains subdirectories owned or maintained by individual users of the system. These subdirectories can contain files and additional subdirectories. Typically, /usr directories are used in UNIX systems and can be found on many FTP sites. *See also* FTP site.

USRT *n.* Acronym for **u**niversal **s**ynchronous **r**eceiver-**t**ransmitter. A module, usually composed of a single integrated circuit, that contains both the receiving and transmitting circuits required for synchronous serial communications. *Compare* UART.

UTC *n. See* Universal Time Coordinate.

utility *n.* A program designed to perform a particular function. The term usually refers to software that solves narrowly focused problems or those related to computer system management. *See also* application.

utility program *n.* A program designed to perform maintenance work on the system or on system components (for example, a storage backup program, disk and file recovery program, or resource editor).

UTP *n.* Acronym for **u**nshielded **t**wisted **p**air. A cable containing one or more twisted pairs of wires without additional shielding. UTP is more flexible and takes up less space than shielded twisted-pair cable but has less bandwidth. *See also* twisted-pair cable. *Compare* STP.

.uu *n.* The file extension for a binary file that has been translated into ASCII format using uuencode. *Also called* .uud. *See also* ASCII, binary file, uuencode[1]. *Compare* .uue.

UUCP *n.* Acronym for **UNIX**-to-**UNIX** **Cop**y. A set of software programs that facilitate transmission of information between UNIX systems using serial data connections, primarily the public switched telephone network. *See also* uupc.

.uud *n. See* .uu.

uudecode[1] *n.* A UNIX program that converts a uuencoded file back to its original binary format. This program (along with uuencode) allows binary data, such as images or executable code, to be disseminated through e-mail or newsgroups. *Compare* uuencode[1].

uudecode[2] *vb.* To transform a uuencoded file back into its binary original using the uudecode program. *Compare* uuencode[2].

.uue *n.* The file extension for a file that has been decoded from ASCII format back into binary format using uudecode. *See also* ASCII, binary file, uudecode[1]. *Compare* .uu.

uuencode[1] *n.* A UNIX program that converts a binary file, in which all 8 bits of every byte are significant, to printable 7-bit ASCII characters without loss of information. This program (along with uudecode) allows binary data, such as images or executable code, to be disseminated through e-mail or newsgroups. A file thus encoded is one-third again as long as the original. *Compare* uudecode[1].

uuencode[2] *vb.* To transform a binary file into printable 7-bit ASCII text using the uuencode program. *Compare* uudecode[2].

uupc *n.* The version of UUCP for IBM PCs and compatibles running DOS, Windows, or OS/2. This version is a collection of programs for copying files to, logging on to, and running programs on remote networked computers. *See also* UUCP.

V

V.120 *n.* An ITU standard that governs serial communications over ISDN lines. Data is encapsulated according to a specific protocol, and more than one connection may be multiplexed on a communications channel. *See also* communications channel, communications protocol, ISDN, multiplexing.
V.27ter *n.* The CCITT (now ITU-T) recommendation that specifies the modulation scheme used in Group 3 facsimile for image transfer at 2,400 and 4,800 bps. *See also* CCITT V series, fax.
V.29 *n.* The CCITT (now ITU-T) recommendation that specifies the modulation scheme used in Group 3 facsimile for image transfer at 9,600 bps over point-to-point leased circuits. *See also* CCITT V series, fax.
V.32terbo *n.* A modem protocol developed by AT&T for 19,200-bps modems, with fallback to the speeds supported by the CCITT V.32 standard. This protocol is proprietary to AT&T and was not adopted by CCITT or ITU-T. In the CCITT V series, V.34 takes the place of V.32terbo. *See also* CCITT V series.
V.54 *n.* The CCITT (now ITU-T) recommendation that specifies the operation of loop test devices in modems. *See also* CCITT V series.
V.56bis *n.* The ITU-T recommendation that defines a network transmission model for evaluating modem performance over two-wire voice-grade connections.
V86 mode *n.* *See* virtual real mode.
VAB *n.* *See* voice answer back.
value *n.* **1.** A quantity assigned to an element such as a variable, symbol, or label. **2.** *See* tone (definition 1).
value-added network *n.* A communications network that offers additional services, such as message routing, resource management, and conversion facilities, for computers communicating at different speeds or using different protocols. *Acronym:* VAN.
value-added reseller *n.* A company that buys hardware and software and then resells it to the public with certain added services, such as user support. *Acronym:* VAR.
value list *n.* A list of values used by an application, such as a database, as a search string or as values for a filtered query. *See also* filter (definition 1), query (definition 1), search string.
VAN *n.* *See* value-added network.
vaporware *n.* Software that has been announced but not released to customers. The term implies sarcastically that the product exists only in the minds of the marketing department. *Compare* freeware, shareware.

VAR *n.* *See* value-added reseller.

variable *n.* In programming, a named storage location capable of containing data that can be modified during program execution. *See also* data structure, data type.

VBA *n.* *See* Visual Basic for Applications.

VBScript *n.* *See* Visual Basic, Scripting Edition.

VCR-style mechanism *n.* **1.** A user interface for playing movie files that has controls similar to those on a videocassette recorder (VCR). **2.** A type of motorized docking mechanism in which a laptop or notebook computer is physically locked into place by the docking station. This type of mechanism provides an electrically consistent, secure bus connection. *See also* docking mechanism, docking station, laptop, portable computer.

VDD *n.* Acronym for **v**irtual **d**isplay **d**evice driver. *See* virtual device driver.

VDSL *n.* *See* very-high-rate digital subscriber line.

VDT *n.* Acronym for **v**ideo **d**isplay **t**erminal. A terminal that includes a CRT and keyboard. *See also* CRT.

VDU *n.* Acronym for **v**ideo **d**isplay **u**nit. *See* monitor.

vector *n.* In computer graphics, a line drawn in a certain direction from a starting point to an endpoint, both of whose locations are identified by the computer using *x-y*-coordinates on a grid. Vectors are used in the output of some graphics programs instead of groups of dots (on paper) or pixels (on screen). *See also* vector graphics.

vector display *n.* A CRT that allows the electron beam to be arbitrarily deflected, based on *x-y*-coordinate signals. For example, to draw a line on a vector display, the video adapter sends signals to move the electron beam over the path of the line; there is no background composed of scan lines, so the line drawn on the screen is not constructed of pixels. *See also* CRT. *Compare* raster display.

vector font *n.* A font in which the characters are drawn using arrangements of line segments rather than arrangements of bits. *See also* font. *Compare* bitmapped font.

vector graphics *n.* Images generated from mathematical descriptions that determine the position, length, and direction in which lines are drawn. Objects are created as collections of lines rather than as patterns of individual dots or pixels. *Compare* raster graphics.

verify *vb.* To confirm either that a result is correct or that a procedure or sequence of operations has been performed.

Veronica *n.* Acronym for **ve**ry **e**asy **r**odent-**o**riented **N**etwide **i**ndex to **c**omputerized **a**rchives. An Internet service developed at the University of Nevada that searches for Gopher archives by keywords. Users can enter Boolean operators, such as AND, OR, or XOR, to help narrow or expand their search. If any matching archives are found, they are listed on a new Gopher menu. *See also* Boolean operator, Gopher. *Compare* Archie, Jughead.

version *n.* A particular issue or release of a hardware product or software title.

A B C D E F G H I J K L M N O P Q R S T U V W X Y Z

version number *n.* A number assigned by a software developer to identify a program at a particular stage, before and after public release. Successive public releases of a program are assigned increasingly higher numbers. Version numbers usually include decimal fractions. Major changes are generally marked by a change in the whole number, whereas for minor changes only the number after the decimal point increases.

vertical application *n.* A specialized application designed to meet the unique needs of a particular business or industry—for example, an application to keep track of billing, tips, and inventory in a restaurant.

vertical bandwidth *n.* The rate at which a display screen is refreshed entirely, expressed in hertz. The vertical bandwidth of display systems ranges from 45 Hz to over 100 Hz. *Also called* vertical scan rate, vertical sync, V-sync.

vertical scan rate *n. See* vertical bandwidth.

vertical scrolling *n.* Movement up or down in a displayed document. *See also* scroll, scroll bar.

vertical sync *n. See* vertical bandwidth.

vertical sync signal *n.* The part of a video signal to a raster display that denotes the end of the last scan line at the bottom of the display.

very-high-rate digital subscriber line *n.* The high-speed version of the xDSL communication technologies, all of which operate over existing phone lines. VDSL can deliver up to 52 Mbps downstream, but it is effective only within about 4,500 to 5,000 feet of the central exchange. The data delivery rate is, in fact, related to the distance the signal must travel. To attain a rate of 52 Mbps, for example, the subscriber must be within 1,000 feet of the exchange office. At a distance of 5,000 feet, the data rate drops to about 13 Mbps. *Acronym:* VDSL. *See also* central office, downstream, xDSL.

very-low-frequency electromagnetic radiation *n. See* VLF radiation.

VESA[1] *adj.* Having VL bus expansion slots. *Also called* VLB. *See also* expansion slot, VL bus. *Compare* VESA/EISA, VESA/ISA.

VESA[2] *n.* Acronym for **V**ideo **E**lectronics **S**tandards **A**ssociation. An organization of hardware manufacturers and vendors dedicated to drafting and improving standards for video and multimedia devices.

VESA/EISA *adj.* Having both EISA and VL bus expansion slots. *See also* EISA, expansion slot, VESA[2], VL bus. *Compare* VESA[1], VESA/ISA.

VESA/ISA *adj.* Having both ISA and VL bus expansion slots. *See also* expansion slot, ISA, VESA[2], VL bus. *Compare* VESA[1], VESA/EISA.

VESA local bus *n. See* VL bus.

V.everything *n.* A marketing term used by some modem manufacturers to describe modems that comply with both the CCITT V.34 standard and the various proprietary protocols that were used before the standard was adopted, such as V.Fast Class. A V.everything modem should be compatible with any other modem that operates at the same speed. *See also* CCITT V series, V.Fast Class.

V.Fast Class *n.* A de facto modulation standard for modems implemented by Rockwell International prior to approval of the V.34 protocol, which is the standard. Although both V.Fast Class and V.34 are capable of 28.8-Kbps transmission, V.Fast Class modems cannot communicate with V.34 modems without an upgrade. *Acronym:* V.FC. *See also* CCITT V series.

V.FC *n. See* V.Fast Class.

VGA *n.* Acronym for **V**ideo **G**raphics **A**rray. A video adapter that duplicates all the video modes of the Enhanced Graphics Adapter and adds several more. For example, it offers display resolutions of up to 640×480 pixels and can display up to 256 different colors at a time. *See also* video adapter.

video *adj.* Of or pertaining to the visual component of a television signal. In relation to computers, the term refers to the rendering of text and graphic images on displays. *Compare* audio.

video accelerator *n. See* graphics engine (definition 1).

video adapter *n.* The electronic components that generate the video signal sent through a cable to a video display. The video adapter is usually located on the computer's main system board or on an expansion board, but it is sometimes built into the terminal. *Also called* video adapter board, video board, video card, video controller, video display adapter.

video adapter board *n. See* video adapter.

video board *n. See* video adapter.

video capture board *n. See* video capture device.

video capture card *n. See* video capture device.

video capture device *n.* An expansion board that converts analog video signals to digital form and stores them in a computer's hard disk or other mass storage device. Some video capture devices are also capable of converting digital video to analog video for use in a VCR. *Also called* video capture board, video capture card. *See also* expansion board.

video card *n. See* video adapter.

video clip *n.* A file that contains a short video item, usually an excerpt from a longer recording.

video compression *n.* Reduction of the size of files containing video images stored in digital form. Without compression, 24-bit color video at 640×480 pixels would occupy almost one megabyte per frame, or over a gigabyte per minute. Video compression can, however, be lossy without affecting the perceived quality of the image. *See also* lossy compression, Motion JPEG, MPEG.

video conferencing *n.* Teleconferencing in which video images are transmitted among the various geographically separated participants in a meeting. Today, video conferencing uses compressed digital images transmitted over wide area networks or the Internet. A 56K communications channel supports freeze-frame video; with a 1.544-Mbps (T1) channel, full-motion video can be used. *See also* 56K, desktop conferencing, freeze-frame video, full-motion video, T1, teleconferencing. *Compare* data conferencing.

video controller *n. See* video adapter.

video digitizer *n.* A tool used in computer graphics to convert analog video signals into a digital format. This tool can consist of software, hardware, or both. Most often the signal is converted into a digital video format such as MPEG. A frame grabber, which is a type of video digitizer, offers the alternative of capturing only one frame of video at a time and converting it into an image file format such as JPEG. *See also* digitize. *Compare* digital camera.

videodisc *n.* An optical disc used to store video images and associated audio information. *See also* CD-ROM.

video display *n.* Any device capable of displaying, but not printing, text or graphics output from a computer.

video display adapter *n.* *See* video adapter.

video display board *n.* A video adapter implementation using an expansion board rather than the computer's main system board. *See also* video adapter.

video display card *n.* *See* video display board.

video display terminal *n.* *See* VDT.

video display tube *n.* *See* CRT.

video display unit *n.* *See* monitor.

video DRAM *n.* *See* video RAM.

video driver *n.* Software that provides the interface between the video adapter hardware and other programs, including the operating system. The user can access the video driver during the setup process to specify the resolution and color-bit depth of images on the monitor. *See also* driver, monitor, video adapter.

video editor *n.* A device or program that is used to modify the contents of a video file.

Video Electronics Standards Association *n.* *See* VESA[2].

video game *n.* *See* computer game.

Video Graphics Array *n.* *See* VGA.

video graphics board *n.* A video adapter that generates video signals for displaying graphical images on a video screen.

video look-up table *n.* *See* color look-up table.

video mode *n.* The manner in which a computer's video adapter and monitor display on-screen images. The most common modes are text (character) mode and graphics mode. In text mode, characters include letters, numbers, and some symbols, none of which are "drawn" on screen dot by dot. In contrast, graphics mode produces all screen images, whether text or art, as patterns of pixels (dots) that are drawn one pixel at a time.

video port *n.* A cable connector on a computer for output of video signals to a monitor.

video RAM *n.* A special type of dynamic RAM (DRAM) used in high-speed video applications. The video circuitry can access the video RAM serially (bit by bit), which is more appropriate for transferring pixels to the screen than is the parallel access provided by conventional DRAM. *Acronym:* VRAM. *See also* dynamic RAM.

video server *n.* A server designed to deliver digital video-on-demand and other broadband interactive services to the public over a wide area network.

video signal *n.* The signal sent from a video adapter or other video source to a raster display. *See also* RGB monitor.
video terminal *n.* *See* terminal.
view[1] *n.* **1.** The display of data or an image from a given perspective or location. **2.** In relational database management systems, a logical table created by specifying one or more relational operations on one or more tables. *See also* relational database.
view[2] *vb.* To cause an application to display information on a computer screen.
viewer *n.* An application that displays or otherwise outputs a file in the same way as the application that created the file. An example of a viewer is a program that displays the images stored in GIF files or JPEG files. *See also* GIF, JPEG.
viewport *n.* In computer graphics, a view of a document or image. A viewport is similar to the view in a window, but usually only part of the document or graphical image is visible. *Compare* window.
virgule *n.* The forward slash (/) character. *See also* /, //. *Compare* backslash.
virtual *adj.* Of or pertaining to a device, service, or sensory input that is perceived to be what it is not in actuality, usually as more "real" or concrete than it actually is.
virtual 8086 mode *n.* *See* virtual real mode.
virtual 86 mode *n.* *See* virtual real mode.
virtual address *n.* In a virtual memory system, the address that the application uses to reference memory. The memory management unit translates this address into a physical address before the memory is actually read or written to. *See also* virtual memory.
virtual circuit *n.* A communications link that appears to be a direct connection between sender and receiver, although physically the link can be routed through a more circuitous path.
virtual community *n.* *See* online community.
virtual desktop *n.* A desktop enhancement tool that provides access to the desktop when it is covered by open windows or that expands the size of the working desktop. *See also* desktop.
virtual device *n.* A device that can be referenced but that does not physically exist. Virtual-memory addressing, for example, uses magnetic disk storage to simulate memory larger than that physically available.
virtual device driver *n.* Software in Windows 95 that manages a hardware or software system resource. If a resource retains information from one access to the next that affects the way it behaves when accessed, a virtual device driver must exist for it. Virtual device drivers are described using three-letter abbreviations beginning with V and ending with D; the middle letter indicates the type of device, such as D for a display, P for a printer, T for a timer, and *x* when the type of device is not under discussion. *Acronym:* V*x*D. *See also* device driver.
virtual disk *n.* *See* RAM disk.

#
A
B
C
D
E
F
G
H
I
J
K
L
M
N
O
P
Q
R
S
T
U
V
W
X
Y
Z

virtual display device driver *n. See* virtual device driver.

virtual image *n.* An image that is stored in computer memory but that is too large to be shown in its entirety on the screen. Scrolling and panning are used to bring unseen portions of the image into view. *See also* virtual screen.

virtual LAN *n.* Short for **virtual l**ocal **a**rea **n**etwork. A LAN consisting of groups of hosts that are on physically different segments but that communicate as though they were on the same wire. *See also* LAN.

virtual machine *n.* Software that mimics the performance of a hardware device, such as a program that allows applications written for an Intel processor to be run on a Motorola chip. *Acronym:* VM.

virtual memory *n.* Memory that appears to an application to be larger and more uniform than it is. Virtual memory may be partially simulated by secondary storage such as a hard disk. Applications access memory through virtual addresses, which are translated (mapped) by special hardware and software onto physical addresses. *Acronym:* VM. *Also called* disk memory. *See also* paging.

virtual monitor *n.* An enhanced monitor viewing system for visually impaired users that uses a virtual-reality headset to move enlarged text across the screen in a direction opposite to head motion. *See also* virtual reality.

virtual name space *n.* The set of all hierarchical sequences of names that can be used by an application to locate objects. One such sequence of names defines a path through the virtual name space, regardless of whether the hierarchy of names reflects the actual arrangement of objects around the system. For example, the virtual name space of a Web server consists of all possible URLs on the network on which it runs. *See also* URL.

virtual network *n.* A part of a network that appears to a user to be a network of its own. For example, an ISP can set up multiple domains on a single HTTP server so that each one can be addressed with its company's registered domain name. *See also* domain name, HTTP server (definition 1), ISP.

virtual path *n.* A sequence of names that is used to locate a file and that has the same form as a pathname in the file system but is not necessarily the actual sequence of directory names under which the file is located. The part of a URL that follows the server name is a virtual path. For example, if the directory c:\bar\sinister\forces\distance on a server named miles is shared on the local area network at foo.com under the name \\miles\baz and contains the file elena.html, that file may be returned by a Web request for http://miles.foo.com/baz/elena.html.

virtual peripheral *n.* A peripheral that can be referenced but that does not physically exist. For example, an application might treat a serial port through which data is being transmitted as a printer, but the device receiving the data might be another computer instead.

virtual printer *n.* A feature in many operating systems that allows printer output to be saved to a file until a printer becomes available.

virtual printer device driver *n. See* virtual device driver.

#
A
B
C
D
E
F
G
H
I
J
K
L
M
N
O
P
Q
R
S
T
U
V
W
X
Y
Z

virtual private network *n.* A set of nodes on a public network such as the Internet that communicate among themselves using encryption technology so that their messages are as safe from being intercepted and understood by unauthorized users as if the nodes were connected by private lines. *Acronym:* VPN.
virtual reality *n.* A simulated 3-D environment that a user can experience and manipulate as if it were physical. The user sees the environment on display screens, possibly mounted in a special pair of goggles. Special input devices, such as gloves or suits fitted with motion sensors, detect the user's actions. *Acronym:* VR.
Virtual Reality Modeling Language *n. See* VRML.
virtual real mode *n.* A feature of the Intel 80386 and higher microprocessors that allows them to emulate several 8086 (real-mode) environments at the same time. The microprocessor provides a set of virtual registers and virtual memory space to each virtual 8086 environment. A program running in a virtual 8086 environment is completely protected from other virtual 8086 environments in the system and behaves as if it had control of the entire system. *Also called* V86 mode, virtual 8086 mode, virtual 86 mode. *See also* real mode.
virtual root *n.* The root directory that a user sees when connected to an Internet server, such as an HTTP or FTP server. The virtual root is actually a pointer to the physical root directory, which may be in a different location, such as on another server. The advantages of using a virtual root include being able to create a simple URL for the Internet site and to move the root directory without affecting the URL. *Also called* v-root. *See also* root directory, server (definition 2), URL.
virtual route *n. See* virtual circuit.
virtual screen *n.* An image area that extends beyond the dimensions of the physical screen on the monitor, allowing manipulation of large documents or of multiple documents that lie partially outside the normal screen view. *See also* monitor.
virtual server *n.* A virtual machine that resides on an HTTP server but has the appearance to the user of being a separate HTTP server. Several virtual servers can reside on one HTTP server, each capable of running its own programs and each with access to input and peripheral devices. Each virtual server has its own domain name and IP address and appears to the user as an individual Web site. Some ISPs use virtual servers for clients who want to use their own domain names. *See also* domain name, HTTP server, IP address.
virtual storefront *n.* A company's point of presence on the Web, providing opportunities for online sales. *Also called* electronic storefront.
virtual terminal *n. See* terminal emulation.
virtual timer device driver *n. See* virtual device driver.
virtual world *n.* **1.** A 3-D modeled environment, often created in VRML, where a user can interact with the viewer to change variables. *See also* viewer, VRML. **2.** An electronic environment that has no basis in the physical world.

A B C D E F G H I J K L M N O P Q R S T U V W X Y Z

Multi-user dungeons, talkers, and chat rooms are often considered virtual worlds. *See also* chat[1] (definition 1), MUD, talker.

virus *n.* An intrusive program that infects computer files by inserting copies of itself in those files. The copies are usually executed when the file is loaded into memory, allowing them to infect still other files, and so on. Viruses often have damaging side effects—sometimes intentional, sometimes not—such as destroying a computer's hard disk or taking up memory space that could otherwise be used by programs. *See also* Good Times virus, Trojan horse, worm.

virus signature *n.* A portion of unique computer code contained in a virus. Antivirus programs search for known virus signatures to identify infected programs and files. *See also* virus.

visible page *n.* In computer graphics, the image being displayed on the screen. Screen images are written into display memory in sections called pages, each of which contains one screen display.

Visual Basic *n.* A high-level, visual-programming version of Basic. Visual Basic was developed by Microsoft for building Windows-based applications. *See also* Basic, Visual Basic for Applications, Visual Basic, Scripting Edition, visual programming.

Visual Basic for Applications *n.* A version of Visual Basic that is used to program many Windows 95–based applications and is included with several Microsoft applications. *Acronym:* VBA. *See also* Visual Basic.

Visual Basic Script *n.* *See* Visual Basic, Scripting Edition.

Visual Basic, Scripting Edition *n.* A subset of the Visual Basic for Applications programming language, optimized for Web-related programming. As with JavaScript, code for Visual Basic, Scripting Edition, is embedded in HTML documents. *Also called* VBScript, Visual Basic Script. *See also* Visual Basic for Applications.

visual interface *n.* *See* graphical user interface.

visualization *n.* A feature of an application that displays data in the form of a video image. For example, some databases can interpret and show data in the form of a two- or three-dimensional model.

visual programming *n.* A method of programming using a programming environment or language in which basic program components can be selected through menu choices, buttons, icons, and other predetermined methods.

VLAN *n.* *See* virtual LAN.

VLB[1] *adj.* *See* VESA[1].

VLB[2] *n.* *See* VL bus.

VL bus *n.* Short for **V**ESA **l**ocal **bus**. A type of local bus architecture introduced by the Video Electronics Standards Association. The VL bus specification allows up to three VL bus slots to be built into a PC motherboard and allows bus mastering (wherein "intelligent" adapter cards can do some processing independently of the CPU). A VL bus slot consists of a standard connector plus an additional 16-bit Micro Channel Architecture connector and must be built into the motherboard by the manufacturer. Standard connectors cannot simply be converted to VL bus slots. A non–VL bus adapter card can be used in a VL bus slot, but it cannot use the local bus and so performs as it normally would in a non–VL bus slot. *Also called* VL local bus. *See also* local bus, PCI local bus.

VLF radiation *n.* Short for **v**ery-**l**ow-**f**requency **radiation**. Electromagnetic radiation at frequencies in the range of approximately 300 Hz to 30,000 Hz (30 kHz). Computer monitors emit this type of radiation. A voluntary standard, MPR II, regulates the amount of VLF radiation a monitor can emit. *See also* MPR II.

VL local bus *n. See* VL bus.

voice answer back *n.* The use of sound-recorded messages by a computer in responding to commands or queries. *Acronym:* VAB.

voice-capable modem *n.* A modem that can support voice messaging applications along with its data-handling functions.

voice-grade channel *n.* A communications channel, such as a telephone line, with an audio bandwidth of 300 to 3,000 Hz, suitable for carrying speech. A voice-grade channel can also be used for transmitting facsimile, analog, and digital information at rates up to 33 Kbps.

voice input *n.* Spoken instructions that a computer translates into executable commands using voice recognition technology or that are embedded in documents with the aid of a microphone. *See also* voice recognition.

voice mail *n.* A system that records and stores telephone messages in a computer's memory. Unlike a simple answering machine, a voice mail system has separate mailboxes for multiple users, each of whom can copy, store, or redistribute messages.

voice messaging *n.* A system that sends and receives messages in the form of sound recordings.

voice modem *n.* A modem with a switch that allows the user to change between telephony and data transmission modes. Such a device might contain a built-in loudspeaker and microphone for voice communication, but more often it uses the computer's sound card. *See also* modem, sound card, telephony.

voice navigation *n.* The use of spoken commands to control a Web browser. Voice navigation is a feature of some plug-in applications that embellish Web browsers, allowing the user to navigate the Web by means of voice commands. *See also* Web browser.

voice-net *n.* A term used on the Internet to refer to the telephone system, often preceding the user's telephone number in an e-mail signature.

voice output *n. See* speech synthesis.

voice recognition *n.* The ability of a computer to recognize the spoken word for the purpose of receiving commands and data input from the speaker. Systems have been developed that can recognize limited vocabularies as spoken by specific individuals, but dealing with a variety of speech patterns and accents, as well as with the various ways in which a request or statement can be made, is more difficult, although advances are being made in

A B C D E F G H I J K L M N O P Q R S T U V W X Y Z

this area. *Also called* speech recognition. *See also* artificial intelligence, dictation software, neural network.

voice synthesis *n. See* speech synthesis.

volatile memory *n.* **1.** Memory, such as RAM, that loses its data when the power is shut off. *Compare* nonvolatile memory. **2.** Memory used by a program that can change independently of the program, such as memory shared by another program or by an interrupt service routine.

volume *n.* **1.** A disk or tape that stores computer data. Sometimes, large hard disks are divided into several volumes, each of which is treated as a separate disk. **2.** The loudness of an audio signal.

volume label *n.* A name for a disk or tape. MS-DOS systems, which seldom use disk names except in directory listings, use the term volume label. Apple Macintosh systems, which often refer to disks by name, use the term volume name. *Compare* volume serial number.

volume name *n. See* volume label.

volume reference number *n. See* volume serial number.

volume serial number *n.* The optional identifying volume number of a disk or tape. MS-DOS systems use the term volume serial number. Apple Macintosh systems use the term volume reference number. A volume serial number is not the same as a volume label or volume name. *Compare* volume label.

VON *n.* Acronym for **v**oice **o**n the **n**et. A broad category of hardware and software technology for real-time voice and video transmission over the Internet.

VPD *n.* Acronym for **v**irtual **p**rinter **d**evice driver. *See* virtual device driver.

VPN *n. See* virtual private network.

VR *n. See* virtual reality.

VRAM *n. See* video RAM.

VRML *n.* Acronym for **V**irtual **R**eality **M**odeling **L**anguage. A scene description language for creating 3-D interactive Web graphics similar to those found in some video games, allowing the user to "move around" within a graphic image and interact with objects. VRML was created by Mark Pesce and Tony Parisi in 1994. VRML files can be created in a text editor, although CAD packages, modeling and animation packages, and VRML authoring software are the tools preferred by most VRML authors. VRML files reside on an HTTP server; links to these files can be embedded in HTML documents, or users can access the VRML files directly. To view VRML Web pages, users need a VRML-enabled browser, such as WebSpace from Silicon Graphics, or a VRML plug-in for Internet Explorer or Netscape Navigator. *See also* 3-D graphic, HTML document, HTTP server (definition 1).

v-root *n. See* virtual root.

V series *n. See* CCITT V series.

V-sync *n. See* vertical bandwidth.

VTD *n.* Acronym for **v**irtual **t**imer **d**evice driver. *See* virtual device driver.

VxD *n. See* virtual device driver.

W

w³ *n. See* World Wide Web.
W3 *n. See* World Wide Web.
WAIS *n.* Acronym for **W**ide **A**rea **I**nformation **S**erver. A UNIX-based document search and retrieval system on the Internet that can be used to search over 400 WAIS libraries, such as Project Gutenberg, for indexed files that match a series of keywords. WAIS can also be used on an individual Web site as a search engine. Users need a WAIS client to use a WAIS server. *See also* Project Gutenberg, search engine.
WAIS database *n. See* WAIS.
waisindex *n.* **1.** A UNIX utility for building an index to text files for access using WAIS query software. **2.** A URL for accessing WAIS. The URL takes the form wais://*hostport*/*database* [?*search*].
WAIS server or **waisserver** *n. See* WAIS.
wait state *n.* A processing cycle of the microprocessor during which it only waits for data from an input/output device or from memory. Although a single wait state is not perceptible to humans, the cumulative effect of wait states is to slow system performance.
wallet PC *n.* A pocket-size portable computer designed to function like a wallet, carrying "virtual" versions of one's identification, money, credit cards, and other essentials, as well as a mobile information source and communications tool. The wallet PC is still under development.
wallpaper *n.* In a graphical user interface, a pattern or picture in the screen background that can be chosen by the user. *See also* graphical user interface.
WAN *n. See* wide area network.
wand *n.* Any pen-shaped device used for data entry, such as a graphics tablet's stylus or the scanning instrument used with many bar code readers. *See also* optical scanner, scan head. *Compare* stylus.
wanderer *n.* A person who frequently uses the World Wide Web. Many such people make indexes of what they find.
warm boot *n.* The restarting of a running computer without first turning off the power. *Also called* soft boot, warm start.
warm start *n. See* warm boot.
.wav *n.* The file extension that identifies sound files stored in waveform (WAV) audio format. *See also* WAV.
WAV *n.* A file format in which Windows stores sounds as waveforms. Such files have the extension .wav. Depending on various factors, one minute of sound can occupy as little as 644 KB or as much as 27 MB of storage. *See also* waveform.

waveform *n.* The manner in which a wave's amplitude changes over time.

WBEM *n.* Acronym for **W**eb-**B**ased **E**nterprise **M**anagement. A protocol that links a Web browser directly to a device or application that monitors a network. *See also* communications protocol.

web *n.* A set of interlinked documents in a hypertext system. The user enters the web through a home page. *See also* World Wide Web.

Web *n. See* World Wide Web.

Web address *n. See* URL.

Web-Based Enterprise Management *n. See* WBEM.

Web browser *n.* A client application that enables a user to view HTML documents on the World Wide Web, another network, or the user's computer; to follow the hyperlinks among them; and to transfer files. Text-based Web browsers can serve users with shell accounts but show only the text elements of an HTML document. Most Web browsers, however, require a connection that can handle IP packets but will also display the graphics in the document, play audio and video files, and execute small programs, such as Java applets or ActiveX controls, that can be embedded in HTML documents. Some Web browsers require helper applications or plug-ins to accomplish these tasks. In addition, most current Web browsers permit users to send and receive e-mail and to read and respond to newsgroups. *Also called* browser. *See also* ActiveX controls, helper application, hyperlink, Java applet, Mosaic, plug-in.

webcasting *n.* A popular term for broadcasting information via the World Wide Web, using push and pull technologies to move selected information from a server to a client. An emergent technology in 1997, webcasting was developed to provide users with customized content—for example, sports, news, stocks, and weather—that can be updated regularly and automatically. Webcasting allows users to specify the type of content they want to see, and it gives content providers a means of delivering such information directly to the user's desktop. *See also* pull, push. *Compare* surf.

Web development *n.* The design and coding of World Wide Web pages.

Web directory *n.* A list of Web sites, giving the URL and a description of each site. *See also* URL.

Web index *n.* A Web site intended to enable a user to locate other resources on the Web. The Web index may include a search facility or may merely contain individual hyperlinks to the resources indexed.

Webmaster or **webmaster** *n.* A person responsible for creating and maintaining a Web site. A Webmaster is often responsible for responding to e-mail, ensuring that the site is operating properly, creating and updating Web pages, and maintaining the overall structure and design of the site. *Also called* Webmistress, Webweaver.

Webmistress or **webmistress** *n. See* Webmaster.

Web page *n.* A document on the World Wide Web. A Web page consists of an HTML file, with associated files for graphics and scripts, in a particular directory on a particular machine (and thus identifiable by a URL). Usually a Web page contains links to other Web pages. *See also* URL.

Web phone *n. See* Internet telephone.

Web server *n. See* HTTP server.

Web site *n.* A group of related HTML documents and associated files, scripts, and databases that is served up by an HTTP server on the World Wide Web. The HTML documents in a Web site generally cover one or more related topics and are interconnected through hyperlinks. Most Web sites have a home page as their starting point, which frequently functions as a table of contents for the site. Many large organizations, such as corporations, will have one or more HTTP servers dedicated to a single Web site. However, an HTTP server can also serve several small Web sites, such as those owned by individuals. Users need a Web browser and an Internet connection to access a Web site. *See also* home page, HTML, HTTP server (definition 1), Web browser.

Web terminal *n.* A system containing a CPU, RAM, a high-speed modem or other means of connecting to the Internet, and powerful video graphics, but no hard disk; intended to be used solely as a client to the World Wide Web rather than as a general-purpose computer. *Also called* network computer.

Webweaver or **webweaver** *n. See* Webmaster.

webzine *n.* An electronic publication distributed primarily through the World Wide Web, rather than as an ink-on-paper magazine. *See also* ezine.

welcome page *n. See* home page.

wetware *n.* Slang for living beings and their brains, as part of the environment that also includes hardware and software.

"what-if" evaluation *n.* A kind of spreadsheet evaluation in which certain values in a spreadsheet are changed in order to reveal the effects of those changes. For example, a spreadsheet user can use "what-if" evaluation to try different mortgage rates and terms to see the effect on monthly payments and on total interest paid over the life of a loan.

What You See Before You Get It *adj. See* WYSBYGI.

What You See Is What You Get *adj. See* WYSIWYG.

whiteboard *n.* Software allowing multiple users across a network to work together on a document that is simultaneously displayed on all the users' screens, as though they were all gathered around a physical whiteboard.

white pages *n. See* DIB (definition 2).

whois *n.* **1.** An Internet service, provided by some domains, that enables a user to find e-mail addresses and other information for users listed in a database at that domain. **2.** A UNIX command to access the whois service. **3.** A command that displays a list of all users logged on to a Novell network.

whois client *n.* A program (such as the UNIX whois command) that enables a user to access databases of usernames, e-mail addresses, and other information. *See also* whois.

whois server *n.* Software that provides the usernames and e-mail addresses from a database (often listing people who have accounts at an

Internet domain) to users who request the information using whois clients. *See also* whois.

Wide Area Information Server *n. See* WAIS.

wide area network *n.* A communications network that connects geographically separated areas. *Acronym:* WAN.

wideband transmission *n. See* broadband network.

widow *n.* A last line of a paragraph, shorter than a full line, appearing at the top of a page. A widow is considered visually undesirable on the printed page. *Compare* orphan.

wildcard character *n.* A keyboard character that can be used to represent one or many characters. The asterisk (*), for example, typically represents one or more characters, and the question mark (?) typically represents a single character. Wildcard characters are often used in operating systems as a means of specifying more than one file by name.

window *n.* In applications and graphical interfaces, a portion of the screen that can contain its own document or message. In window-based programs, the screen can be divided into several windows, each of which has its own boundaries and can contain a different document (or another view into the same document).

windowing environment *n.* An operating system or shell that presents the user with specially delineated areas of the screen called windows. Windowing environments typically allow windows to be resized and moved around on the display. The Macintosh Finder, Windows, and the OS/2 Presentation Manager are all examples of windowing environments. *See also* graphical user interface, window.

window random access memory *n. See* WRAM.

Windows *n.* An operating system introduced by Microsoft Corporation in 1983. Windows is a multitasking graphical user interface environment that runs on both MS-DOS–based computers (Windows and Windows for Workgroups) and as a self-contained operating system (Windows 95, Windows 98, and Windows NT). Windows provides a standard interface based on drop-down menus, windowed regions on the screen, and a pointing device such as a mouse.

Windows-based application *n.* A software application designed for use with the Windows environment.

Windows-based accelerator *n.* A type of SVGA video adapter designed specifically to run Windows and Windows-based applications more quickly than a standard SVGA video adapter, by using special routines built into the adapter's read-only memory. These routines relieve the operating system of some of the video-related duties it must perform on a nonaccelerated system. *Also called* Windows-based accelerator card. *See also* SVGA.

Windows CE *n.* A scaled-down version of the Windows platform designed for use with handheld PCs. Windows CE includes scaled-down versions of several Microsoft applications, such as Excel, Word, and an e-mail client. *See also* handheld PC.

Windows for Workgroups *n.* A version of Windows designed to run on an Ethernet-based LAN without the need for separate LAN software. *See also* LAN, Windows.

Windows Metafile Format *n.* A graphics file format used by Windows to store vector graphics in order to exchange graphics information between applications and to store information between sessions. *Acronym:* WMF. *See also* vector graphics.

Windows NT *n.* An operating system developed by Microsoft Corporation, sometimes referred to simply as NT. The high-end member of a family of operating systems from Microsoft, it is a completely self-contained OS with a built-in graphical user interface. Windows NT is a 32-bit, preemptive multitasking operating system that features networking, symmetric multiprocessing, multithreading, and security. This portable operating system can run on a variety of hardware platforms including those based on the Intel 80386, i486, and Pentium microprocessors and MIPS microprocessors; it can also run on multiprocessor computers. Windows NT supports up to 4 gigabytes of virtual memory and can run MS-DOS, POSIX (loosely, a portable operating system interface based on UNIX), and OS/2 (character-mode) applications. *See also* MS-DOS, operating system, OS/2, Windows.

Windows Open System Architecture *n. See* WOSA.

win.ini *n.* In Windows 3.*x* and MS-DOS, the initialization file used to pass the program configuration information necessary to run the Windows operating environment. The win.ini file has been supplanted by the Registry database in Windows 95 and in Windows NT. *See also* configuration file, ini file, Registry.

WINS *n.* Acronym for **W**indows **I**nternet **N**aming **S**ervice. A Windows NT Server method for associating a computer's host name with its address. *Also called* INS, Internet Naming Service. *Compare* DNS (definition 2).

Wintel *adj.* Of, pertaining to, or characteristic of a computer that uses the Windows operating system and an Intel CPU. *See also* Windows.

wired *adj.* **1.** Of, pertaining to, or characteristic of an electronic circuit or hardware grouping in which the configuration is determined by the physical interconnection of the components (as opposed to being programmable in software or alterable by a switch). *See also* hardwired (definition 1). **2.** Knowledgeable about Internet resources, systems, and culture. **3.** Having access to the Internet.

wire-frame model *n.* In computer graphics applications such as CAD programs, a representation of a three-dimensional object using separate lines that resemble strands of wire joined to create a model. *Compare* solid model, surface modeling.

wireless *adj.* Of, pertaining to, or characteristic of communications that take place without the use of interconnecting wires or cables, such as by radio, microwave, or infrared.

wireless LAN *n.* A local area network that sends and receives data via radio, infrared optical signaling, or some other technology that does not require a

#
A
B
C
D
E
F
G
H
I
J
K
L
M
N
O
P
Q
R
S
T
U
V
W
X
Y
Z

physical connection between individual nodes and the hub. Wireless LANs are often used in office or factory settings where a user must carry a portable computer from place to place.

wire-pin printer *n. See* dot-matrix printer.

wizard *n.* **1.** Someone who is adept at making computers perform their "magic." A wizard is an outstanding and creative programmer or a power user. *Compare* guru. **2.** A participant in a multi-user dungeon who has permission to control the domain, even to delete other players' characters. *See also* MUD. **3.** An interactive help utility within an application that guides the user through each step of a particular task, such as starting a word processing document in the correct format for a business letter.

wizzywig *n. See* WYSIWYG.

.wmf *n.* A file extension that identifies a vector image encoded as a Windows metafile.

WMF *n. See* Windows Metafile Format.

word *n.* The native unit of storage on a particular machine. A word is the largest amount of data that can be handled by the microprocessor in one operation and is also, as a rule, the width of the main data bus. Word sizes of 16 bits and 32 bits are the most common. *Compare* byte.

word processing *n.* The act of entering and editing text with a word processor. *Acronym:* WP.

word processor *n.* A program for creating and manipulating text-based documents. A word processor is the electronic equivalent of paper, pen, typewriter, eraser, and, most likely, dictionary and thesaurus. Depending on the program and the equipment, word processors can display documents either in text mode (using highlighting, underlining, or color to represent italics, boldface, and other formatting) or in graphics mode (in which formatting and, sometimes, a variety of fonts appear on the screen as they will on the printed page). All word processors offer at least limited facilities for document formatting, such as font changes, page layout, paragraph indention, and the like. Some can also check spelling, find synonyms, incorporate graphics created with another program, align mathematical formulas, create and print form letters, perform calculations, display documents in multiple windows, and enable users to record macros that simplify difficult or repetitive operations. *Compare* editor, line editor.

wordwrap or **word wrap** *n.* The ability of a word processing program or a text-editing program to break lines of text automatically so that they stay within the page margins or window boundaries of a document, without the user having to break the lines with carriage returns (as on a typewriter). *See also* hard return, soft return.

workaround *n.* A tactic for accomplishing a task, despite a bug or other inadequacy in software or hardware, without actually fixing the underlying problem. *See also* kludge.

workbook *n.* In a spreadsheet program, a file containing a number of related worksheets. *See also* worksheet.

workflow application *n.* A set of programs that aid in the tracking and management of all the activities in a project from start to finish.
workgroup *n.* A group of users working on a common project and sharing computer files, often over a LAN. *See also* groupware.
workgroup computing *n.* A method of working electronically in which various individuals on the same project share resources and access to files using a network arrangement, such as a LAN, enabling them to coordinate their separate tasks. This is accomplished through using software designed for workgroup computing. *See also* groupware.
worksheet *n.* In a spreadsheet program, a page organized into rows and columns appearing on screen and used for constructing a single table.
workstation *n.* **1.** A combination of input, output, and computing hardware that can be used for work by an individual. **2.** A powerful stand-alone computer of the sort used in CAD and other applications requiring a high-end, usually expensive, machine with considerable calculating or graphics capability. **3.** A microcomputer or terminal connected to a network.
World Wide Web or **World-Wide Web** *n.* The total set of interlinked hypertext documents residing on HTTP servers all around the world. Documents on the World Wide Web, called pages or Web pages, are written in HTML, identified by URLs that specify the particular machine and pathname by which a file can be accessed, and transmitted from node to node to the end user under HTTP. Codes embedded in an HTML document associate particular words and images in the document with URLs so that a user can access another file, perhaps halfway around the world, with a keypress or a mouse click. These files may contain text, graphics, movie files, and sounds as well as Java applets, ActiveX controls, or other small embedded programs that execute when the user activates them by clicking on a link. A user visiting a Web page also may be able to download files from an FTP site and send messages to other users via e-mail by using links on the Web page. The World Wide Web was developed by Timothy Berners-Lee in 1989 for the European Laboratory for Particle Physics (CERN). *Acronym:* WWW. *Also called* w^3, W3, Web. *See also* ActiveX controls, HTML, HTTP, HTTP server (definition 2), Java applet, URL.
worm *n.* A program that propagates itself across computers, usually by creating copies of itself in each computer's memory. A worm might duplicate itself in one computer so often that it causes the computer to crash. Sometimes written in separate segments, a worm is introduced surreptitiously into a host system either as a prank or with the intent of damaging or destroying information. *See also* bacterium, Trojan horse, virus.
WORM *n.* Acronym for **w**rite **o**nce, **r**ead **m**any. A type of optical disc that can be read and reread but cannot be altered after it has been recorded. WORMs are high-capacity storage devices. Because they cannot be erased and rerecorded, they are suited to storing archives and other large bodies of unchanging information. *See also* compact disc.

WOSA *n.* Acronym for **W**indows **O**pen **S**ystem **A**rchitecture. A set of application programming interfaces from Microsoft intended to enable Windows-based applications from different vendors to communicate with each other, such as over a network.

.wp *n.* A file extension used to identify files formatted for the WordPerfect word processor.

WP *n. See* word processing.

WRAM *n.* Acronym for **w**indow **r**andom **a**ccess **m**emory. A type of RAM used in video adapters. Like video RAM, WRAM allows the screen to be repainted while a graphical image is being written, but WRAM is faster. *Compare* video RAM.

wrap around *vb.* To continue movement, as with the cursor or a search operation, to the beginning or to a new starting point rather than stopping when the end of a series is reached. For example, a program starting a search-and-replace operation in the middle of a document might be instructed to wrap around to the beginning rather than stop when it reaches the end of the document.

.wri *n.* The file format that identifies document files in the Microsoft Write format.

wrist support *n.* A device placed in front of a computer keyboard to support the wrists in an ergonomically neutral position, thereby safeguarding against repetitive strain injuries such as carpal tunnel syndrome. *Also called* wrist rest. *See also* carpal tunnel syndrome, repetitive strain injury.

write[1] *n.* A transfer of information to a storage device, such as a disk, or to an output device, such as the monitor or printer. For example, a disk write means that information is transferred from memory to storage on disk. *See also* output[1]. *Compare* read[1].

write[2] *vb.* To transfer information either to a storage device, such as a disk, or to an output device, such as the monitor or a printer. Writing is the means by which a computer provides the results of processing. A computer can also be said to write to the screen when it displays information on the monitor. *See also* output[2]. *Compare* read[2].

write access *n.* A privilege on a computer system that allows a user to save, change, or delete stored data. Write access is usually set by the system administrator for a networked or server system and by the owner of the computer for a stand-alone machine. *See also* access privileges.

write error *n.* An error encountered while a computer is in the process of transferring information from memory to storage or to another output device. *Compare* read error.

write mode *n.* In computer operation, the state in which a program can write (record) information in a file. In write mode, the program is permitted to make changes to existing information. *Compare* read-only.

write protect *vb.* To prevent the writing (recording) of information, usually on a disk. Either a floppy disk or an individual file on a floppy or a hard disk can be write protected (though not necessarily infallibly). *See also* write-protect notch.

write-protect notch *n.* A small opening in the jacket of a floppy disk that can be used to make the disk unwritable. On a 5.25-inch floppy disk, the write-protect notch is a rectangular hole on the edge of the disk jacket; when this notch is covered, a computer can read from the disk but cannot record new information on it. On a 3.5-inch microfloppy disk that is enclosed in a plastic shell, the write-protect notch is an opening in a corner; when the sliding tab in this opening is moved to uncover a small hole, the disk is protected and cannot be written to. *Also called* write-protect tab. *See also* write^2.

write-protect tab *n. See* write-protect notch.

.wrl *n.* The file extension required for saving all Virtual Reality Modeling Language (VRML) documents. *See also* VRML.

WWW *n. See* World Wide Web.

WYSBYGI *adj.* Acronym for **W**hat **Y**ou **S**ee **B**efore **Y**ou **G**et **I**t. Providing a preview of the effects of the changes the user has selected before the changes are finally applied. For example, a dialog box in a word processing program might display a sample of a chosen font before the font is actually changed in the document. The user can cancel changes after previewing them, and the document will be unaffected. *See also* WYSIWYG.

WYSIWYG *adj.* Acronym for **W**hat **Y**ou **S**ee **I**s **W**hat **Y**ou **G**et. Allowing a user to view a document as it will appear in the final product and to directly edit the text, graphics, or other elements within that view. A WYSIWYG language is often easier to use than a markup language, which provides no immediate visual feedback regarding the changes being made. This term is commonly pronounced “wizzywig.” *Compare* markup language.

X

x86 *n.* Any computer based on an 8086, 80286, 80386, 80486, or Pentium microprocessor.

***x*-axis** *n.* The horizontal reference line on a grid, chart, or graph that has horizontal and vertical dimensions.

Xbase *n.* A generic name for database languages based on dBASE, a copyrighted product of Ashton-Tate Corporation. The term was originally coined to avoid litigation with Ashton-Tate. Xbase languages have since developed characteristics of their own and are now only partly compatible with the dBASE family of languages.

XCMD *n.* Short for e**x**ternal **com**man**d.** An external code resource used in HyperCard, a hypermedia program developed for the Macintosh. *See also* HyperCard, XFCN.

xDSL *n.* An umbrella term for all the digital subscriber line technologies, which use a variety of modulation schemes to pack data onto copper wires. The *x* is a placeholder for the first or first two letters of a member technology, which might be ADSL, HDSL, IDSL, RADSL, or SDSL. *See also* digital subscriber line, modulation.

xerography *n. See* electrophotography.

XFCN *n.* Short for e**x**ternal **func**tio**n**. An external code resource that returns a value after it has completed execution. XFCNs are used in HyperCard, a hypermedia program developed for the Macintosh. *See also* HyperCard, XCMD.

XGA *n. See* eXtended Graphics Array.

XML *n.* Acronym for e**X**tensible **M**arkup **L**anguage. A condensed form of SGML that lets Web developers and designers create customized tags, offering greater flexibility in organizing and presenting information than is possible with the older HTML document coding system. *See also* SGML.

Xmodem *n.* A file transfer protocol used in asynchronous communications that transfers information in blocks of 128 bytes.

Xmodem 1K *n.* A version of the Xmodem file transfer protocol designed for larger, longer-distance file transfers. Xmodem 1K transmits information in 1-kilobyte (1,024-byte) blocks and uses a more reliable form of error checking. *See also* Xmodem.

Xmodem-CRC *n.* An enhanced version of the Xmodem file transfer protocol that incorporates a 2-byte cyclical redundancy check to detect transmission errors. *See also* CRC.

XMS *n. See* extended memory specification.

XMT *n.* Short for transmit. A signal used in serial communications.

XON/XOFF *n.* An asynchronous communications protocol in which the receiving device or computer uses special characters to control the flow of data from the transmitting device or computer. When the receiving computer cannot continue to receive data, it transmits an XOFF control character that tells the sender to stop transmitting; when transmission can resume, the computer signals the sender with an XON character. *Also called* software handshake. *See also* handshake.

XOR *n.* *See* exclusive OR.

X-Y display *n.* *See* vector display.

***x-y* matrix** *n.* An arrangement of rows and columns with a horizontal (*x*) axis and a vertical (*y*) axis.

***x-y* plotter** *n.* *See* plotter.

***x-y-z* coordinate system** *n.* A three-dimensional system of coordinates that includes a third (*z*) axis running perpendicular to the horizontal (*x*) and vertical (*y*) axes. The *x-y-z* coordinate system is used in computer graphics for creating models with length, breadth, and depth.

Y

Y2K *n*. *See* Year 2000 problem.
***y*-axis** *n*. The vertical reference line on a grid, chart, or graph that has horizontal and vertical dimensions.
Year 2000 problem *n*. A potential problem for computer programs when the year 2000 is reached, in that a variety of logic checks within programs may suddenly fail if they rely on two-digit year indicators. In the past, before RAM became much cheaper, one way to conserve memory was to indicate years with only two digits ("63" for 1963, for example), and this method of handling dates has remained at the core of much software. For example, suppose a computer checks the validity of report dates by confirming that a report's date sequentially follows the date for a report the previous year. Such a check will fail when the report for year "00" follows year "99." Other possible faults include unanticipated shortening of index numbers, stock numbers, and the like, when the digits for the year occur first and are accidentally read as leading zeros and so deleted. For example, the stock number 00123 could be shortened to 123. Such problems may not be evident until programs start failing after 12:00 A.M., January 1, 2000. It is practically impossible to test all extant software for this problem, but, as a precaution, critical software can be tested by changing the date and time set in the computer to the year 2000.
Yellow Pages *n*. **1.** The former name of a UNIX utility, provided by SunSoft (Sun Microsystems system software), that maintains a central database of names and locations of the resources on a network. The Yellow Pages enable processes on any node to locate resources by name. This utility is now known formally as NIS (Network Information Service). **2.** InterNIC Registration Services' database of domain names and their IP addresses. *See also* domain name, IP address. **3.** Any of several Internet business directory services. Some are print publications, some are strictly electronic, and some are both.
YHBT *n*. Acronym for **y**ou **h**ave **b**een **t**rolled. An expression used in e-mail and newsgroups to indicate that the receiver has taken a deliberately set bait. *See also* troll.
YHL *n*. Acronym for **y**ou **h**ave **l**ost. An expression used in e-mail and newsgroups, often following YHBT. *See also* YHBT.
Ymodem *n*. A variation of the Xmodem file transfer protocol that includes the following enhancements: the ability to transfer information in 1-kilobyte (1,024-byte) blocks, the ability to send multiple files (batch file transmission), cyclical redundancy checking, and the ability to abort transfer by transmitting two CAN (cancel) characters in a row. *See also* CRC, Xmodem.

Z

zap *vb.* **1.** To erase permanently. For example, to zap a file means to remove it without hope of retrieval. **2.** To damage a device, usually by discharging static electricity through it.

z-axis *n.* The third axis in a three-dimensional coordinate system, used in computer graphics to represent depth. *See also* *x-y-z* coordinate system.

zero suppression *n.* The elimination of leading (nonsignificant) zeros in a number. For example, zero suppression would truncate 000123.456 to 123.456.

z-fold paper *n.* *See* continuous-form paper.

.zip *n.* A file extension that identifies a compressed archive file encoded in ZIP format. *See also* compressed file.

Zip drive *n.* A disk drive developed by Iomega that uses 3.5-inch removable disks (Zip disks) capable of storing 100 MB of data. *See also* disk drive.

Zmodem *n.* An enhancement of the Xmodem file transfer protocol that handles larger data transfers with less error. Zmodem includes a feature called checkpoint restart, which resumes transmission at the point of interruption, rather than at the beginning, if the communications link is broken during data transfer. *See also* Xmodem.

zone *n.* On a local area network, a subgroup of users within a larger group of interconnected networks.

.zoo *n.* The file extension that identifies compressed archive files created with the zoo file compression utility.

zoom *vb.* To enlarge a selected portion of a graphical image or document to fill a window or the screen. Zooming is a feature of many programs, including drawing, word processing, and spreadsheet programs, that allows the user to select a small part of the screen, zoom it, and make changes to the enlarged portion at a finer level of detail. *See also* window.

zoom box *n.* A control in the upper right corner of the frame of a window on the Macintosh screen. When the user clicks on the zoom box, the window toggles between the maximum size and the size the user has set for it by dragging. *See also* window.

The manuscript for this book was prepared and submitted to Microsoft Press in electronic form. Text files were originally prepared using Microsoft Word 97. Pages were composed in Adobe PageMaker 6.5 for Windows 95, with text in Garamond and display type in Garamond Bold. Composed pages were delivered to the printer as electronic prepress files.

Microsoft Press

Cover Designer
Patrick Lanfear

Interior Graphic Designers
Kim Eggleston
Jim Kramer

Frog Mountain Productions

Production
Jean Trenary

Proofreading
Deborah Long

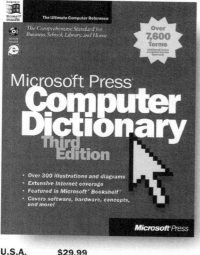